Drama and

A. B. Walkley

Alpha Editions

This edition published in 2019

ISBN : 9789353977443

Design and Setting By
Alpha Editions
email - alphaedis@gmail.com

DRAMA AND LIFE

BY

A. B. WALKLEY

METHUEN & CO.
36 ESSEX STREET W.C.
LONDON

NOTE

THESE papers are reprinted, with alterations, from *The Times*, except the first and second, which are from *The Edinburgh Review*. To the respective proprietors, who have courteously permitted republication, I tender my grateful thanks.

A. B. W.

CONTENTS

DRAMA AND LIFE

MODERN ENGLISH AND FRENCH DRAMA

WHAT do we mean precisely by "modern" and "ancient"? Each term implies the other, and Messrs. Taper and Tadpole are not the only phrase-mongers who have found it impossible to keep them apart. It was Mr. Taper, according to the author of *Coningsby*, who suggested to Mr. Tadpole the electioneering cry of "Our Young Queen and our Old Institutions."

"The eyes of Tadpole sparkled as if they had met a gnomic sentence of Periander or Thales; then, turning to Taper, he said:

"'What do you think of "ancient" instead of "old"?'

"'You cannot have "Our Modern Queen and our Ancient Institutions,"' said Mr. Taper."

Ingenious writers sometimes amuse themselves by explaining how many things that pass for ancient are of all things most modern; how the Darwinian hypothesis may be discovered lurking in the speculations of some forgotten Greek philosopher, and how the *Pickwick Papers* may be discerned, by those who have eyes to see, in the *Odyssey*. Thus Matthew Arnold exhibited the modernity of the chattering Sicilian women in a Theocritean idyll. M. Jules Lemaître

I

points out how Euripides, in *Ion*, "méprise Scribe vingt-quatre siècles d'avance, ce qui est prodigieux" —as prodigious it assuredly is—and how—(he is speaking of Herondas) "certains dialogues de la *Vie Parisienne*, du *Journal* ou de *L'Echo de Paris* vous donnent une idée fort exacte de ce que furent les *mimes* grecs." And what chiefly interests Mr. Herbert Paul in the *Poetics* of Aristotle is the fact that they are "intensely modern."

This is to darken counsel, as well as to fly in the face of Molière's common-sense observation that "les anciens sont les anciens et nous sommes les gens d'aujourd'hui."

It may be thought that, whatever the general vagueness about "ancient" and "modern," there can be no difficulty in assigning them a precise meaning when applied to drama. There is the "ancient" drama of the Greeks and Romans, the drama about which the Examiners were expected to interrogate the Heathen Passee, with his

> "notes on the rise of the Drama,
> A question invariably set;"

and there is the "modern" drama which came into being towards the end of the sixteenth century. It should not, however, be difficult to show that this line of cleavage between ancient and modern drama is misplaced.

Where then is the true line of cleavage to be found? In order to answer that question an obvious course is to examine a few typical plays, selected from successive theatrical periods, and to seek the causes which differentiate them from the drama of to-day, or rank them with it, as the case may be. By common consent, the most "modern" of all Shakespeare's plays is the tragedy of *Hamlet*. Its hero exhibits what the nineteenth century was fond of calling "la maladie du siècle," as something pre-eminently its own. His case is, in Shelley's phrase, "a pure anticipated cognition" of the late lamented Henri Frédéric Amiel. Hazlitt discerned a Hamlet in all modern men. Musset wrote a *Lorenzaccio* so rife with Hamletism that Mme. Sarah Bernhardt, after appearing as the protagonist of that play, was in the nature of things bound to undertake the Prince of Denmark. One peculiarly " modern " novelist, Tourgenev, cannot choose but write a " Hamlet russe," while another, M. Paul Bourget, reproduces the whole story in *André Cornélis*. Then there is the veteran author of *John Gabriel Borkman*, who gives us a Hamlet, as it were, reversed, a Hamlet who makes " il gran rifiuto," and blithely refuses to take up the burden of the old generation under which the Shakespearian Hamlet was crushed. Nevertheless, it has to be asked, does *Hamlet* show the distinguishing marks of the drama as we understand it to-day? Does every scene contribute to the advancement of the story? Do every action and word take their due place in the composition of a character? Nothing of the kind. With the *data* of the play, its business, according to modern ideas, is to exhibit the progress of the conflict between Hamlet's temperament and his duty, between his irresolution and his revenge " mission." But this business is persistently neglected. Any irrelevance serves to set Hamlet off at a tangent. While he is waiting on the platform at Elsinore for the Ghost, someone drops an observation about the King keeping " wassail," whereupon he moralises upon the general passion for strong drink. Meanwhile the play marks time. When the players arrive, Hamlet puts aside his revenge project in order to deliver a lecture upon histrionics. If he meditates on suicide, he must bring in a reference to the law's delay and the insolence of office — matters which have nothing to do with his case. In the church-yard he must "draw" the gravedigger. It is in complete forgetfulness of his "mission" that he accepts the challenge to a bout of fence with Laertes. His mind, on this side of it, is like Squire Brooke's, "a jelly that runs easily into any mould." The obvious truth is that Shakespeare, having, as Walter Bagehot said, the "experiencing temperament," must needs endow Hamlet with that temperament too. He expressed himself in Hamlet in disregard of dramatic propriety. The story might get on as best it could; what he was intent upon was exhausting the possi-bilities of the moment—"enjoying the moment for the moment's sake," as Pater might have said. The same disregard of dramatic propriety runs through the other characters. Polonius, a fool at one moment, is a sage at another, so that Coleridge was driven to contend that he is not a comic character. Laertes cannot take leave of his sister without generalisations about princes' love and maidens' modesty, so that, only half in jest, a former Examiner of Plays described him as an instance of heredity.[1] Gertrude, rushing in with the shocking news of Ophelia's death, pauses to deliver a set piece of poetic description—

"There is a willow grows aslant a brook,"

---

[1] Mr. Bodham Donne. See *More Letters of Edward FitzGerald*, p. 131: "Had any one quoted to me Laertes' parting advice to his sister, I should have sworn it was Polonius." Donne thinks that Shakespeare may have intended pedantry in the blood."

with eighteen lines to follow—during which Laertes has to stand aside and bottle up his emotion. It comes to this, that, any topic once started, Shakespeare proceeds to expatiate upon it at large, and he is comparatively indifferent as to which character shall be his mouthpiece or to the progress of the dramatic action. Clearly *Hamlet* bears the marks of something essentially different from a " modern " play.

To draw attention to these points of technical method is not, of course, to call in question for a moment the virtues of *Hamlet* as a poetic tragedy, its "noble excess" as the *fine fleur* of Renaissance romanticism, its triumphant fulfilment of the test laid down by Goethe for all work really classic—namely, that it shall be "energetic, fresh, and well-liking." Such aspects of the matter are beyond discussion. But Shakespeare was no more free than any other man from the material limitations of the theatre in which his plays were produced ; and it is in those material conditions that the explanation of his craftsmanship is to be found. Yet how seldom is that explanation sought in this the only proper quarter ! We have seen S. T. Coleridge and Bodham Donne, two men of letters, explaining Polonius, one solemnly, the other only half jocularly, by purely literary and logical means. To this day our Shakespearian commentators, in the seclusion of their studies, pursue this false method—the bookman's method — of exegesis. If they would only come out of their studies and look at the stage — at some picture or model of the Elizabethan playhouse — they would save themselves the discovery of many mares' nests. There was not long ago a project for the erection of an Elizabethan playhouse in *facsimile*, as a Shakespeare memorial, in one of the new London thoroughfares. I can perceive one, and only one, good reason for this otherwise fanciful scheme ; it would provide an object-lesson for the bookmen. Meanwhile one may refer them back to their Aristotle. The author of the *Poetics*—whom nothing could escape—saw the distinction between what I have called the bookman's point of view in regard to drama and that which will be taken in the present inquiry. " Whether tragedy is to be judged in itself, or in relation also to the stage (πρὸς τὰ θέατρα) "—that, he said, is ἄλλος λόγος, another question.[1] Here, however, it happens to be not another question, but *the* question. The bookmen have been used to consider drama exclusively "in itself." It is high time to consider drama πρὸς τὰ θέατρα, in its relation to the material conditions of the stage.

This aspect of the matter, so strangely neglected, is quite simple. That has happened in the theatre which has happened in every congregation gathered round the same centre of interest. Whether it be John Wesley preaching to the miners on a Cornish hillside, or a socialist haranguing the loafers in Hyde Park, or an acrobat tumbling for pence in a by-street, he chooses his "pitch" and the crowd forms a ring. The earliest theatres, then, were naturally circular, with the stage in the centre. Naturally, too, the stage was bound to gravitate towards the circumference, in order that the performers might reach their platform and retire from it without traversing the crowd. It is superfluous to describe the minor modifications of this arrangement in the Elizabethan playhouse—everybody knows them—but it is not superfluous to point out the effects of this arrangement

[1] *Poetics*, ch. iv.

on the Elizabethan play. With actors on a raised platform, devoid of scenery and surrounded by the spectators on three sides, there could be no such thing as illusion, in the modern sense of the term, no attempt at a plastic reproduction of actual life. An Elizabethan actor was not, like his modern successor, a figure set in perspective in a framed picture whose conversation with his fellows is overheard by the audience. He stood forth among the crowd, hardly separated from them, and addressed them as an orator would address them. The Elizabethan drama, then, was of necessity a rhetorical drama. Each successive passage of dialogue was not so much the link between what preceded and followed it as a new "topic," which the speakers between them were expected to exhaust. The scene in itself, the scene of the moment, was everything; the logical *nexus* of the scenes nothing or next to nothing. Internal evidence of this has been adduced from *Hamlet*. A curious piece of external evidence is forthcoming from a Frenchman who visited London shortly after the Restoration, one Samuel Sorbière, whose *Relation* of his visit was published in 1667. This, to be sure, was after Shakespeare's time; but the point is immaterial, for the position of the platform stage in the playhouse was still what it had been in Shakespeare's time. Sorbière was struck by the indifference of the English audience to logical *nexus* of scenes in their drama, and gives the explanation furnished to him: " Il ne leur importe que ce soit un pot-pourri, parce qu'ils n'en regardent, *disent-ils*, qu'une partie après l'autre, sans se soucier du total." Sorbière's English friends here put him on the right track, and our bookmen should lose no time in adding

the *Relation* to their libraries. "Ne regarder qu'une
partie après l'autre sans se soucier du total:" that
was the inevitable frame of mind in the spectator of
a platform-drama.

It is a simple fact, little suspected by the bookmen,
or indeed by the common-sense students of our stage,
that its history up to a period so recent as to be within
the memory of people now living is the history of the
platform-drama.   As time went on, the dimensions of
this platform gradually shrank, like the shagreen skin
in Balzac's story.   A notable passage in Colley Cibber
throws light on this process.   As a rule, the lives of
the players may be said to belong to the least
important branch of entomology; but an exception
must be made in favour of Cibber's *Apology*, which is
always interesting and sometimes, as in the ensuing
extract, of great documentary value.   Cibber is
comparing Drury Lane, as altered by Rich, with the
structure of the old theatre :—

"It must be observ'd, then, that the Area or Platform
of the old Stage projected about four Foot forwarder,
in a Semi-oval Figure, parallel to the Benches of the
Pit; and that the former lower Doors of Entrance for
the Actors were brought down between the two
foremost (and then only) Pilasters; in the place of
which Doors now the two Stage-Boxes are fixt.   That
where the Doors of Entrance now are, there formerly
stood two additional Side-Wings, in front to a full set
of Scenes, which had then almost a double Effect in
their Loftiness and Magnificence.

"By their original Form, the usual Station of the
Actors, in almost every scene, was advanc'd at least
ten Foot nearer to the Audience than they now can

be; because, not only from the Stage's being shorten'd in front, but likewise from the additional Interposition of those Stage-Boxes, the Actors (in respect to the Spectators that fill them) are kept so much more backward from the main Audience than they us'd to be: But when the Actors were in Possession of that forwarder Space to advance upon, the Voice was then more in the Centre of the House, so that the most distant Ear had scarce the Least Doubt or Difficulty in hearing what fell from the weakest Utterance: All Objects were thus drawn nearer to the sense; every painted Scene was stronger; every grand Scene and Dance were extended; every rich and fine-coloured Habit had a more lively Lustre: Nor was the minutest Motion of a Feature (properly changing with the Passion or Humour it suited) ever lost, as they frequently must be in the Obscurity of too great a Distance."

Here is a striking confirmation of the view already set forth that the rhetorical drama was what the mathematicians would call a " function " of the platform-stage. The histrionic elements which Cibber singles out for mention are elements of rhetoric—the " voice," the " utterance." Cibber talks of the actors as we should now talk of orators—just as Plato had talked of them when proposing that καλλίφωνοι ὑποκριταί, "the actors with their beautiful voices," should be banished from his ideal State. The stage was still essentially a platform, projecting among the audience, though already showing a tendency to withdraw towards the curtain. Spectators still lined the sides of the stage as in Elizabethan times, no longer seated upon it, however, but placed in " stage-boxes." A full century passed and we find Jane Austen, in 1813 (" September 15,

½ past 8 "—"documentary" evidence is not always so precise)—writing from London to her sister Cassandra: "I talked to Henry at the play last night. We were in a private box—Mr. Spencer's—which made it much more pleasant. *The box is directly on the stage.* One is infinitely less fatigued than in the common way."[1] Well into the last century, then, the boxes which Cibber had seen placed at the side of the stage were still in their old position. The stage remained even then, to all intents and purposes, a platform-stage.

These facts account for the form not only of the Restoration but of the Georgian drama. The Restoration plots were beneath contempt. Who can remember Congreve's? From the modern point of view his *dénouements* are childish; some sudden "discovery," some hasty production of "a certain parchment," brings down the curtain to a general song and dance. "What," says Witwoud at the close of *The Way of the World*, "are you all got together, like players at the end of the last act?" The players are, in fact, always got together, and the final direction is "Exeunt Omnes." Congreve, to be sure, made some pretence to concern for the logical *nexus* of his plot. In his Epistle Dedicatory to *The Double Dealer*, he asserts that "the mechanical part of it is regular. I made the plot as strong as I could because it was single, and I made it single because I would avoid confusion, and was resolved to preserve the three unities of the drama." But in practice Congreve's notion of orthodoxy was rather like that put into the mouth of one of his personages—"Orthodox is Greek for claret." Who cares about what is going to happen next in *The Way of the World*? Each scene of raillery between

[1] *Letters of Jane Austen*, ed. Lord Brabourne (1884), vol. ii. p. 147.

Millamant and Mirabell is self-contained.   In the
feigned madness of Valentine in *Love for Love*, there
is a riot of rhetoric.   " Mad scenes " were a constant
feature of the platform-drama, because they gave
the freest opportunity for bombastic, or discursive,
or lyrical declamation.   Valentine repeats some of
Hamlet's very phrases.   " Sir," said Johnson of
Garrick and *Irene*, " the fellow wants me to make
Mahomet run mad, that he may have an opportunity
of tossing his hands and kicking his heels."   Tilburina
went mad in white satin.   The stage vogue of lunacy
in those days is only to be matched by the vogue of
hysteria—the hysteria of the *Saphos* and the *Zazas*—
in our own.   The contrast is worth passing notice, as
showing how the change from the platform to the
modern picture-stage has affected the field of histrionic
representation, even in the matter of physical ailments.
As to Congreve's practice, it accorded, whatever he
may have said, with the theory of Vanbrugh, which
was the true theory of the platform-stage.   " I cou'd
say a great deal against the too exact observance of
what's called the Rules of the Stage, and the crowding
of a Comedy with a great deal of Intricate Plot.   I
believe I cou'd show, that the chief entertainment, as
well as the Moral, lies much more in the Characters
and the Dialogue, than in the Business and the
Event." [1]   And why?   The justification had already
been anticipated by Sorbière : " Il ne leur importe que
ce soit un pot-pourri, parce qu'ils n'en regardent
qu'une partie après l'autre, sans se soucier du total."

We have seen that Congreve by no means practised
what he preached.   The fact is, in his theories of drama

[1] From Vanbrugh's reply to Jeremy Collier in *A Short Vindication*,
1698.

he was curiously ahead of his age. " In any part of a play," he says, " if there is expressed any knowledge of an audience, it is insufferable."[1] That would be true of our modern illusion-stage; it was not true of the platform-stage. In the rhetorical drama the actor, under the pretext of conversing with his fellows, was in reality talking *at* his audience. The original players of the *The School for Scandal*, as Elia pointed out in a famous essay, surpassed their successors precisely because they recognised this. The " teasings " of Sir Peter (while King acted it) were evidently as much played off at you as they were meant to concern anybody on the stage. The original players gave the true spirit of the play because they treated it frankly as a piece of rhetoric. Kemble is singled out by Lamb on this very account. " His exact declamatory manner " (in Charles Surface) " as he managed it, only served to convey the points of his dialogue with more precision; it seemed to head the shafts, to carry them deeper. Not one of his sparkling sentences was lost." This was over a hundred years ago. To-day every so-called " revival " of *The School for Scandal* is an absolute counter-sense. What was written as a platform-play is presented as a picture-play.

But the platform-play diéd hard. It even survived the platform. It was kept alive by a succession of declamatory actors steeped in the traditions of the platform-stage, from Kemble and Siddons to Macready and Phelps. An amusing side-light is thrown on those traditions by the descriptions of amateur theatricals so frequent in the women novelists of the " palmy days "—Miss Burney, Miss Ferrier, and Jane Austen. Lionel (in *Camilla*) " returned to ask who would come

---

[1] Dedication to *The Double Dealer*.

forth to spout with him." "Spouting" was the proper
business of the platform-stage. An amateur actor (in
Patronage) is condemned because "he would regularly
turn his back upon the audience"—an absurdity on a
platform-stage, a perfectly legitimate effect on our
modern illusion-stage. M. Antoine, when he played
La Mort du Duc d'Enghien in London a few years ago,
turned his back upon the audience throughout a long
scene. Perhaps the best indirect evidence that a play
was naturally assumed to be a piece of rhetoric, and that
acting was identical with spouting, is supplied by Miss
Austen. When the private theatricals at Mansfield
Park were afoot, Tom Bertram asserted of his father that

"for anything of the acting, spouting, reciting kind, I
think he has always a decided taste. I am sure he
encouraged it in us as boys. How many a time have
we mourned over the dead body of Julius Cæsar, and
to be'd, and not *to be'd*, in this very room, for his amusement! And I am sure, *my name was Norval*, every
evening of my life through our Christmas holidays."

All that Mr. Yates, another of the amateurs,
demanded from a part, we are told, was "good ranting
ground," and his great objection to one character was
that "there was not a tolerable speech in the whole."
This remark, curiously enough, gets repeated almost
word for word by the old-fashioned tragedian in Mr.
Pinero's *Trelawny of the Wells*, who objects to a new
piece that "there isn't a speech—not what you call
a real speech—in it."

Gradually the platform-drama sank into the inanimate
or semi-animate condition of a "survival." The sham
Elizabethanisms which passed for tragedy were beginning to pall. Thomas Lovell Beddoes called the

drama of his time "a haunted ruin," and advocated the policy of "a clean slate." "Say what you will," he wrote, "I am convinced the man who is to awaken the drama must be a bold trampling fellow—no reviver even, however good. These re-animations are vampire cold. . . . With the greatest reverence for all the antiquities of the drama, I still think we had better beget than revive." The works of Talfourd and Sheridan Knowles—nay, even *Money* and *The Lady of Lyons*—were rhetorical plays, and are now, indeed, "vampire cold." One of the latest efforts to keep the old art alive was *The Patrician's Daughter* of Westland Marston (1842), which aimed at establishing "the principle of characters talking poetically in plain dress" —a principle which resulted in the description of a marriage settlement by a family solicitor as

> "the accustomed deed
> Determining the rights and property
> Of such as stand affianced."

When some years later one of the last of the rhetorical actors quitted the stage, Tennyson addressed a sonnet to "Macready, moral, grave, sublime," and in the last epithet hit off the ideal of platform tragedy. Rhetorical comedy had its "sublimities" too. In Dion Boucicault's *London Assurance* (1841) Grace Harkaway talks as no young lady ever talked in 1841, or, we may be sure, in any other year, but as players were expected to talk in the platform period of drama :—

"I love to watch the first tear that glistens in the opening eye of morning, the silent song that flowers breathe, the thrilling choir of the woodland minstrels, to which the modest brook trickles applause; these, swelling out the sweetest chord of sweet creation's matins, seem to pour some soft and merry tale into the daylight's ear, as if the waking world had dreamed a happy thing, and now smiled o'er the telling of it."

Then there is Lady Gay Spanker's description of the hunt and its emotions :—

" Time then appears as young as love, and plumes as swift a wing. Then I love the world, myself, and every living thing—a jocund soul cries out for very glee, as it would wish that creation had but one mouth that I might kiss it."

These, and such as these, were the " real speeches " to which Mr. Pinero's broken-down actor referred.

Surely here is ample evidence that down to the very middle of the last century the modern English drama, the drama as we know it to-day, had not come into being. From the reign of Queen Elizabeth right into the reign of Queen Victoria there had been a continuous tradition of a stage technique which is not ours. It was a technique, as has been seen, conditioned by the material arrangements of the playhouse, and chiefly by the situation of the stage with respect to the audience. The history of the gradual modification of that technique is the history of the gradual withdrawal of the stage from the pit to the curtain line. Here, then, is another of the many cases in which art has been shaped less by its own inherent needs than by external causes, economic and social. For it was the pressure of population that step by step forced the stage back into its present place—changed it from a platform into the lower plane of a framed picture. While the number of London theatres was strictly limited by privilege, the number of people desiring to frequent them steadily increased. Rich, as we have seen, in Cibber's time, tried to meet the increasing demand by contracting Drury Lane stage in order to expand the pit. But this measure was insufficient, and every time Drury Lane was burnt down it rose from its ashes more vast than before, until the younger Colman declared that a semaphore was needed to signal the actions of the players to the occupants of the topmost gallery. The result was twofold : the shrinking of the stage made it as absurd to retain the old rhetorical methods of the platform drama as the enlargement of the house itself made it impossible to abandon them. In such conditions no new drama could be born. That was not possible until the privilege of the " patent houses " was abolished, and theatres could be built of reasonable size and in sufficient numbers to satisfy the popular demand. The necessary change was effected by the Theatres Regulation Act of 1843, which established free trade in drama. In addition to freedom, the change meant specialisation. A patent house had been justly called by Charles Matthews " a huge theatrical omnibus." When Macready took over Covent Garden in 1837, he had to provide a company for tragedy, another for comedy, a third for opera, to say nothing of a staff of pantomimists. Now every manager was free to form a repertory suited to his house and the talents of his players. The stage was in the picture-frame, rhetoric an anachronism, and the natural action and talk of actual life a possibility. From this moment the birth of the modern drama in England was only a question of time.

In what way and to what extent the drama is a " function " of the stage on which it is played should now be clear. The transformation of the old drama of rhetoric into the modern drama of illusion is the artistic outcome of a mechanical transformation—the transformation of the platform-stage into the picture-stage. This process of evolution is, of course, not peculiar to England. Throughout Western Europe it has been the same story—the platform superseded by the picture, theatrical monopoly superseded by free trade, rhetoric superseded by illusion. The only foreign theatre, however, with which we need concern ourselves is the French, for that is the only foreign theatre which has exercised a continuous and vital influence upon our own. It is a noteworthy fact that, whatever other differences there may have been between the French and English stages, there has been next to no difference in the particulars which we have been considering. It is sufficient to say that down to 1759 spectators lined both sides of the Parisian stage, being actually seated upon it, and that, placed in boxes, they continued to line it until the eighteenth century had come to a close. A well-known drawing by Moreau le Jeune, illustrating the crowning of Voltaire's bust at the Théâtre Français in 1778, shows these side-boxes and shows, too, how far the stage projected as a platform into the auditorium. When, then, did the picture-stage make its appearance in France ? A casual entry in the *Journal des Goncourt*, curiously enough, supplies the answer :—

"*Dimanche*, 31 *Mars*, 1861.—Déjeuner chez Flaubert avec Sari et Laugier, et conversation toute spéciale sur le théâtre. . . . Ce n'est que depuis ce siècle que les acteurs cherchent en leurs silhouettes l'effet *tableau* : ainsi Paulin Ménier montrera au public des effets de dos pris aux dessins de Gavarni; ainsi Rouvière

2

apportera à la scéne les poses tordues et les épilepsies
de mains, des lithographies du *Faust* de Delacroix."

It is piquant to find a French actor deliberately
essaying those very "effets de dos" for which, as we
saw, the amateur in Miss Ferrier's *Patronage* was
ridiculed.   With the "effet *tableau*" the modern
French drama has arrived.

It arrived a little in advance of our own, and it
is not very difficult to see why.   For one reason,
theatrical "privilege"—we have already seen the
relation between that and the rhetorical drama—
was abolished earlier on the other side of the
Channel than on this.   Article I. of a decree of the
National Assembly, dated November 19, 1791, runs
as follows:—"Tout citoyen pourra élever un théâtre
public, et y faire représenter des pièces de tous les
genres." It is true that monopoly was restored by
an imperial decree of 1807, and that France had to
wait for the definitive establishment of free trade in
drama until 1864.   But the point is that, decrees or
no decrees, for full fifty years before theatres began
to multiply in London they were numerous in Paris,
and their number steadily increased.[1] A much more
important reason, however, for French priority in
modern drama is to be found not in the history of
French institutions, but in the mental constitution
of the French race.   It is a race with a peculiar
turn for logic; and even when the drama of both
countries was acted upon a platform-stage this
peculiarity of the French gave a symmetry of

---

[1] Eleven in 1791, eighteen in 1829, twenty-one in 1833. See, on the
whole question, Pougin, *Dictionnaire du Théâtre*, 1885, art. "Liberté des
Théâtres."

structure and a progressiveness of development to
their drama which were not to be detected in ours.
In ours we have seen the platform-stage producing
two effects—discursive rhetoric and a certain discon-
tinuity of action. It was this second effect which
struck the attention of our French visitor Sorbière,
in that an English play seemed to him a *pot-pourri*.
Our playgoers, as they admitted to him, considered
only each facet of the play as it came into view,
without regard to the play as a whole. But the
French, with their logical instinct, did care for the
play as a whole, and were concerned not merely
for each scene as it passed, but for its relation to
the other scenes, for the *growth*, that is to say, of the
action. Here was the difference between the French
platform-drama and ours. Theirs was quite as
rhetorical; indeed, it was far more rhetorical.
From Racine to Voltaire, from Voltaire to Campistron,
there was a maximum of tirades, " confidences,"
monologues, " forensic " dialogues—all the artifices
of rhetoric—to a minimum of action. Another racial
characteristic, no doubt, contributed to this excess of
rhetoric : I mean the French turn for didactic moralising. French tragedy might or might not be a poem ;
it was always a sermon. Thus Sterne, while
professing to think French tragedies " absolutely
fine," significantly added, " and whenever I have a
more brilliant affair upon my hands than common, as
they suit a preacher quite as well as a hero, I generally
make my sermon out of 'em; and for the text,
Cappadocia, Pontus and Asia, Phrygia and Pamphylia,
is as good as any one in the Bible." This persistent
didacticism of French drama found its *reductio ad
absurdum* in both the theory and the practice of

Diderot. " It is always," said he, " virtue and virtuous
people that a man ought to have in view when he
writes. Oh, what good would men gain if all the arts
of imitation proposed one common object, and were
one day to unite with the laws in making us love
virtue and hate vice!" In Diderot's *Père de Famille*
a father addresses his child in this strain: " Marriage,
my daughter, is a vocation imposed by Heaven. . . .
If marriage exposes us to cruel pain, it is also the
source of the sweetest pleasures. . . . O sacred bond,
if I think of thee, my whole soul is warmed and
elevated." Mr. John Morley's comment on this
passage is much to the point. If the drama is to be
a great moral teacher, " it will not be by imitating the
methods of that colossal type of histrionic failure, the
church pulpit." [1] It may be added that the moralising
strain in French drama is to be found a full century
after Diderot in the *raisonneurs* of the younger Dumas.
But the important fact is that with all this excess of
moralising rhetoric over action, the French turn for logic
had its way. Such action as there was tended steadily
to an ordained end, never zigzagging or marking time
or deviating into mere irrelevance, as was, for the most
part, the case with our English platform-drama. Logical,
well ordered, as French drama was by comparison
with our own, it was not logical enough for the French
critics. The aim of their playwrights is all the more
unmistakable from the frequency with which they
deplored failure to attain it. We have heard Diderot as
a dramatist, but listen to him as a critic of drama :—

" En général il y a plus de pièces bien dialoguées,
que de pièces bien conduites. Le génie qui dispose

[1] *Diderot*, vol. i. p. 327 (1886).

les incidents paraît plus rare que celui qui trouve les vrais discours. Combien de belles scènes dans Molière ! On compte ses dénouemens heureux. On serait tenté de croire qu'un drame devrait être l'ouvrage de deux hommes de génie, l'un qui arrangeât et l'autre qui fît parler." [1]

Here is Diderot virtually passing the very criticism on Molière that I have passed on Congreve. In both the dialogue surpasses the "conduct of the fable." How many " belles scènes " in both ! How few " dénouemens heureux " ! And by this time the cause of the resemblance between the two national dramas, in so far as resemblance there was, ought to be manifest enough ; it was the common factor in each, the platform-stage, always favourable to rhetoric and unfavourable to the strict ordering of plot. But there is this great difference between the two cases, that the French spirit, its turn for logic, almost from the first reacted against the influence of the platform-stage, whereas the English did not. Nothing could be more significant on this head than a remark of Voltaire's in his commentary on Horace. " Tout doit être action dans la tragédie," he says ; " chaque scène doit servir à nouer et à dénouer l'intrigue, chaque discours doit être préparation ou obstacle." Voltaire failed to observe his own precepts ; but he has here stated in the clearest terms what is nothing else than the ideal of modern drama.

For that ideal, whatever else it may cover, includes simplicity and strict economy of plot, and in these respects the French have always been ahead of us. Go back as far as " that memorable day, in the first

[1] Diderot, *De la poésie dramatique.*

summer of the late war, when our navy engaged the Dutch "[1] (June 3, 1665), and you will find the English and the French ideals compared by Dryden. It was one of the objects of his *Essay*, as all readers know, to contrast the two national theatres and to make the best case he could for the English. Lisideus, the advocate for France, observes that "another thing in which the French differ from us is that they do not embarrass or cumber themselves with too much plot; they only represent so much of a story as will constitute one whole and great action sufficient for a play; we, who undertake more, do but multiply adventures, which, not being produced from one another, as effects from causes, but barely following, constitute many actions in the drama, and consequently make it many plays." To which Dryden, in the character of Neander, answers by decrying the "barrenness" of the French plots and praising the "variety and copiousness" of the English. But the point is that he never attempts to dispute Lisideus's main fact: "The French carry on one design, which is pushed forward by all the actors, every scene in the play constituting and moving towards it."

It was because the French did this, even in the period of the platform-stage, that, so soon as that stage had given place to the picture-stage, they were the first to create what is legitimately entitled to be called modern drama. Literary historians, each docilely repeating the commonplaces of his predecessors, were for long accustomed to trace the modern French drama back to the great Romantic movement of the thirties. The best opinion of to-day is dead against that attribution. What is there in the contemporary French theatre that can be shown to owe its origin

[1] *Essay of Dramatic Poesy*: opening paragraph.

to Romanticism ? People talk of a "romantic" revival,
but these are the people who cannot see any further
than Cyrano's nose. M. Rostand's plays are "romantic"
in a sense—because the word "romance" can be used
in almost any sense, the sense of anti-classicism or of
anti-realism or of mere troubadourism—and out of these
senses one or more can be found to fit M. Rostand. But
Cyrano de Bergerac and *L'Aiglon* and *La Princesse
Lointaine* are not romantic in the sense of 1830. Must
we come to the conclusion that the Romantic movement
was merely an episode in the history of the French
stage ? We can hardly recognise Victor Hugo's plays
as modern drama; they belong to the old drama of
rhetoric. Every one of them is based upon an
antithesis—a king at odds with a bandit, a queen
enamoured of a lackey, a court fool turned tragic protagonist—and antithesis is a figure of rhetoric. Rhetoric,
the monologue of Charles Quint before the tomb
of Charlemagne. Rhetoric, the "scène des portraits."
Rhetoric, the address of Ruy Blas to the ministers.
That grotesque document the preface to *Cromwell*,
so far as it had any intelligible meaning whatever,
meant a rhetorical dramaturgy. The author of *Hernani*
was not the first of the modern dramatists; he was
the last of the rhetoricians. So much was written
about the excitement over the "première" of *Hernani*,
to say nothing of Gautier's red waistcoat, that at last
the public was fooled into believing that there must
be something in it. The legend grew up, and "epoch-
marking" became the cant word about it. But an
ounce of fact is worth a pound of legend. And
the fact is that the first of the moderns was the
author of *Antony*, a play which substituted for the
Romantic formula a brand-new formula of its own.

Here at last was a tale in plain (indeed, in bad) prose about the actual life of the day as Dumas saw it. Dumas, to be sure, saw life neither steadily nor whole. But what he saw, or thought he saw, he took bodily into the theatre. For he was a born dramatist. *Antony* is all rapidity and fire, all action and passion. It is easy to laugh at the Byronic, Wertherian, Satanic hero. But Antony was a true type of his time, brother to Stendhal's Julien Sorel, and to the exorbitant adventurers of Balzac—the men of a generation burning with the Napoleonic fever driven inwards. This type of ferocious egoist had a long stage posterity down to the " homme fort " of Feuillet and the " strugfor-lifeur " of Alphonse Daudet. Countless, too, are the descendants in French drama of Adèle d'Hervéy, at once heroine and adulterous woman. But Dumas did something more important than fix types of modern stage-character. He hit in *Antony* upon the great modern dramatic theme, the conflict of passion and the social world, of the individual and opinions—the very stuff out of which his son's plays were afterwards to be made. While Dumas *père* supplied the motive power of the new drama, Scribe perfected its mechanism. It is the present fashion to speak contemptuously of Scribe, as a mere manufacturer, turning out machine-made plays by the gross. But that is because we are wise after the event. Scribe triumphantly vindicated in practice a position of Aristotle's, which has been violently but by no means intelligently assailed—the position that while you can have drama without character you cannot have drama without plot.[1] No doubt Aristotle overestimated the importance of plot. I suspect that he did so deliberately, in the belief that in neglect of

[1] *Poetics*, ch. iv.

plot lay the special pitfall for the "bas-relief" drama
of his time. Be that as it may, it would be untrue to
say to-day, as Aristotle said, that plot was the end of
drama; but it is, assuredly, the beginning. Scribe
made too much of it, made everything of it. Nevertheless, he fulfilled a purpose useful for the moment.
A new craftsmanship was wanted for the picture-stage,
the old craftsmanship of the platform-stage being as
useless as a sedan-chair on a railway. Scribe supplied
what was wanted, just when it was wanted. If he
was only a craftsman, he could at least make instruments which others were to put to real use; and that
is what Scribe actually did for Augier and the younger
Dumas. He gave them the neat framework of the
" well-made piece," and within that framework they did
what he could not do, they worked out ideas of their own.

What ideas were these? Of what kind were they?
What relation had they to reality, to the practical
conduct of life? To answer these questions is to
indicate the fundamental difference between modern
French and English drama. The ideas of Augier
and Dumas *fils* were ideas about society, its economic
structure, its hierarchy of castes, its pressure on the
individual; and they were ideas about private ethics,
the relations of men and women, fathers and children,
the disparity between the Civil Code and the moral
law. In other words, these men made the French
drama, in Matthew Arnold's phrase about poetry, a
"criticism of life." That has been the vital, the prime
characteristic of the French stage for half a century
and more—its rule—whereas with our modern English
drama it has been the exception. Only in quite
recent years have one or two English plays attempted
anything like a "criticism of life," and even in the rare

instances wherein these plays have been accepted by the public, they have been accepted against the grain. The English attitude in this matter is well illustrated in a brief passage of irony from the *Critic* :—

" *Mrs. Dangle.* Well, if they had kept to that [*i.e.* " serious " comedy from the French], I should not have been such an enemy to the stage ; there was some edification to be got from those pieces, Mr. Sneer !

" *Sneer.* I am quite of your opinion, Mrs. Dangle : the theatre, in proper hands, might certainly be made the school of morality ; but now, I am sorry to say it, people seem to go there principally for their entertainment !

" *Mrs. Dangle.* It would have been more to the credit of the managers to have kept it in the other line.

" *Sneer.* Undoubtedly, madam ; and hereafter perhaps to have it recorded that, in the midst of a luxurious and dissipated age, they preserved two houses in the capital, where the conversation was always moral at least, if not entertaining ! "

What Sheridan said wittily enough over a hundred years ago the majority of English playgoers are tiresomely repeating to-day. We go to the theatre, they say, for " entertainment " ; we want to leave the world behind us, to escape from the pressure of reality ; we do not go there for a criticism of life. There is a double fallacy underlying this popular statement of the case. " Entertainment," in the fullest sense of the term, is, of course, the aim of all drama, from the *Prometheus Bound* or *Lear* down to *Box and Cox* or *Charley's Aunt*. Further, to treat reality as a spectacle is in the very act to relieve it of its pressure. Art, however faithfully it may follow the lineaments of life, is not life itself ; it is life which has undergone a κάθαρσις, life purged of the will-to-live. What the popular statement merely means is that the typical English playgoer does not find entertainment where the typical French playgoer does, in a criticism of life. And in that sense the statement is undeniable. If the English playgoer stopped there, if he were content with the admission that he found moral questions in drama a bore, whatever we might think of his intelligence, we could not contest his right to choose his own pleasures. But he goes further. He considers it "immoral" to raise moral questions on the stage. This habit he acquired, it would seem, from the moment that Dumas *fils* began to raise those moral questions. *La Dame aux Camélias* was produced in 1852. At the Theatrical Fund dinner of 1853 a speaker, after admitting that the English owed much to the French stage (it was, indeed, living upon French adaptations), went on to say: "But we should limit our obligations to the French, in order to keep our own drama pure; and, in availing ourselves of their art, we should be careful to avoid their immorality." Unfortunately, his very next sentence gave the case away. "We cannot be insensible to the changes that are taking place around us in our theatres. Covent Garden is given up to the seductions of a foreign opera, and the legitimacy of Old Drury is displayed by the antipodean feat of a gentleman who walks on the ceiling with his head downwards."[1] Such was the result of "availing ourselves of French art," in so far as it was mere amusement, and of "limiting our obligations" so as to keep out anything like a criticism of life. The French playgoer was being introduced to the master-

[1] *Dramatic Register* for 1853.

pieces of Augier and Dumas *fils*, while the English
playgoer was gazing at a gentleman walking upside
down.   Fortunately, we have done something since
towards mending our ways.   The contrast between
the two stages has long ceased to be as tragi-comic
as it was in 1853.   But it is still sufficiently humili-
ating.   It is no exaggeration to say that while in
the intervening half-century every social and ethical
question of importance has found its way into the
French theatre, from the English theatre all, or nearly
all, such questions have been rigorously excluded.

There is no need to recite the long catalogue of plays,
sufficiently well known and more than sufficiently discussed, by which Augier and Dumas *fils*, in their several
ways, converted the French drama into an active social
force.   It is impossible to dissociate these twain, because
they worked to the same end ; but there is a marked
difference in their work.   Augier was much less of a
preacher than Dumas, and much more of a *bourgeois* ;
but, though he had the "burgess mind," we must be
cautious about disparaging a mind which has given
the world *Le Gendre de M. Poirier*.   He took that
"respectable," comfortable, tolerant view of men and
things which one finds so complacently adopted in the
novels of Anthony Trollope.   He disliked the "idle
rich," the haughty aristocrat, the Bohemian journalist,
the "Daughters of Joy"—and everything else which
the *bourgeois* disliked.   His plays have aged now, as
Trollope's novels have aged, but, like those, they can
still be read with pleasure.   Notably, he was a good-
humoured man ; whereas Dumas, like the medical
gentleman in *Pickwick* when he forbade his patient
crumpets, was "werry fierce."   It is the foible of
earnest reformers, and Dumas believed in his mission,

and the mission of the stage, if ever man did. He ascribed to himself priestly functions. In his preface to *Le Fils Naturel* (dated 1868, though the piece was begun in 1853, the year of the topsy-turvy gentleman at Drury Lane—*annus mirabilis !*) he actually put the theatre alongside the Catholic Church :—

"The Church is wrong to attack us, for we are both marching willy-nilly towards the same end, since we start from the same principle: the representation of the Idea by man. Under penalty of death or degradation we can only proceed, like her, by propagating the highest morality. Like her we address assemblies of men, and you cannot speak long and effectively to the multitude save in the name of the higher interests."

The drama, he went on, was doomed "unless we hasten to press it into the service of the great social reforms and the great hopes of humanity." "Inaugurons donc, he cried, "le théâtre *utile*." To the theorists of art for art's sake, to say nothing of mere playhouse loafers, these may seem wild and whirling words; but to question the sincere conviction, the true vocation, of the writer is impossible. His conception of his priestly duties certainly brought him into queer company. Fallen—or falling—women became his especial care. There is an elderly rake in one of Mr. Pinero's plays who confesses he could never approach women "in the missionary spirit." Dumas *fils* could do nothing else. Everyone knows how modern art has turned to account what a learned professor of the University of Finland calls the "veiled polyandry and polygamy which lie at the bottom of modern society."[1] Dumas *fils* may be considered to have exhausted all the variations and

[1] *The Origins of Art*, by Yrjo Hirn, p. 240.

combinations afforded by this subject. Sometimes he had the offenders taken out and shot, at other times he brought in a verdict of " Not guilty, but don't do it again." Then he attacked the Code, pleading the right to prove affiliation, the right of divorce, and the identical responsibility of both parties in cases of seduction and adultery. He did it all "in the missionary spirit," and yet the missionary never got the better of the dramatist. For, with all his ideas and moral aims, he had his father's dramatic instinct and adhered to the Scribe *technique.* He took care that his plays should always fulfil the ultimate end of every play, the end of "entertainment," so that, while appealing to Mrs. Dangle, he would also have conciliated Mr. Sneer.

And yet there was a great difference between the earlier and the later Dumas, the Dumas of *La Dame aux Camélias* and the Dumas of *Francillon.* The one play was written as M. Sarcey[1] said, *à la diable,* dashed off by a young fellow in the twenties who was making theatrical "copy" out of his own experience. The other was formed upon a deliberately conceived plan, to demonstrate in action a proposition about the *lex talionis* in conjugal relations. The fact is, between the two, his first piece and his last, Dumas had invented the thesis-play.

What is a thesis? In general, of course, any kind of proposition; in drama, a proposition about life and conduct. And a thesis about life and conduct necessarily implies a moral precept. " Honesty is the best policy " is a thesis; the implied precept is " Be honest." There is a general thesis at the back of every drama which makes any appeal to the intellect. Take two examples from the platform-stage. The general thesis of

---

[1] *Quarante Ans de Théâtre,* p. 191.

Shakespeare's Chronicle plays is that the king is very human, but still your king; their implied precept is " Honour the king and behave like a true-born Englishman." The general thesis of Molière's comedies is the Horatian one that nature, though you expel it with a fork, will yet recur; their implied precept is " Follow Nature, avoid affectation, and don't be a ' crank.'" But the thesis-play proper, invented by Dumas as his contribution to the picture-stage, deals with a particular proposition, and is constructed from first to last to demonstrate that proposition. It is a play, as people say, with a purpose. This is a peculiarly French product. Even the French farce-writers, the mere amusers, cannot resist a thesis. Labiche, for instance, abounds in theses. His *Voyage de M. Perrichon*—to take his most characteristic work —is framed with geometrical symmetry round the Rochefoucauldian thesis that we like the people we have benefited more than the people from whom we have received benefits. But the conscious, deliberate thesis-playwright was Dumas *fils*.

The later history of the thesis-play is rather curious. When Dumas died in 1895 it had already fallen into disfavour. The public had accepted his theses because of his dramatic verve inherited from his father, and because he could " tell a story" as neatly as Scribe, or as the second and greater Scribe, Sardou. If he had made the theatre an active social force, it was because of his sæv' indignation, the " fire in his belly," not because of his ratiocination. A thesis, after all, holds good only for the particular case. Gustave Flaubert hits upon this objection in one of his letters to George Sand :—" Put what genius you like into a fable, taken as an example, some other fable can be

adduced to the contrary, for *dénouements* are not conclusions. From a particular case you cannot proceed
to a general induction, and those who try to do so
are flying in the face of modern science, which insists
upon the accumulation of innumerable facts before
establishing a law." The real truth is that a dramatic
thesis proves nothing, for the simple reason that you
cannot prove a case by manufacturing the evidence.
These were, and are, the objections to the thesis judged
by the "practical reason." But if we look for the
immediate causes of its temporary eclipse, we shall
find them in an artistic movement. Before the end of
the eighties, a new generation of French playgoers
had had time to grow up since the war, and, like all
new generations, it demanded a new art. For a time
it seemed as though the new art had been found in
naturalism. That was, of course, originally a novel-
istic movement, and Flaubert and Zola and Daudet all
failed in the theatre, where novelists generally do fail.
A dramatist, however, was not long wanting for the
movement. This was Henri Becque, who in *Les
Corbeaux* (1880) and *La Parisienne* (1885) established
a formula for naturalism in the theatre. The ingenious plot of Scribe and Dumas and Sardou was
abandoned. No "exposition," no "*dénouement*," no
"sympathetic personage"; only what M. Jean Jullien,
the theorist of the school, called "slices of life." [1] The
new school found a home in the Théâtre Libre,
founded in 1887 by M. André Antoine, who also
instituted a new school of "naturalistic" acting for the
interpretation of the new plays. After a brief career
of audacities, too often merely scandalous, naturalism
fell by its own excesses, but not without impressing an

[1] *Le Théâtre Vivant* (1892), p. 2.

indelible mark on the stage. It left the French drama more simple in construction than it found it, more accurately observant, and, it must be added, a little more insidiously erotic. Though sexual passion had been the chosen subject of Dumas, he had always painted it in the blackest colours; it is the perpetual theme of men like Donnay and Lavedan and Porto-Riche, whose moral purpose in the exposure of its seamy side is by no means so apparent. It must be remembered that the French theatre has always been, like St. Augustine in his youth, " in love with love," from Racine to Marivaux, from Musset to Meilhac. The present men are only carrying on an historic tradition, though one may think that tradition better served by the old idealism than by the new realism.

Be that as it may, the amorists hold only a secondary position in the French drama of to-day. The primacy belongs to Paul Hervieu and Eugène Brieux. The one has been called a second Dumas, the other a second Augier; and not without reason, for they have revived the vogue of the thesis-play. But they are more austere men than their prototypes, without a tincture—they would consider it a taint—of Scribism. With them the thesis is presented in all its simplicity, naked and not ashamed. Nothing, for example, could be simpler than the thesis of M. Hervieu's *La Course du Flambeau*, a play which has been presented to Londoners by Madame Réjane. It is the familiar figure which Lucretius took from the Greek torch-race:—

> "Et quasi cursores vitaï lampada tradunt."

Each generation has to sacrifice the last to itself and then itself to the next; thus is the torch of life carried on. You have a widowed mother renouncing her chance

3

of second marriage because her daughter is not yet
married and settled; later, becoming a forger to save
her son-in-law from ruin; ultimately confronted by a
choice between the death of her daughter and that of
her mother, the consumptive daughter needing a high
altitude in the Engadine which is fatal to the grand-
mother's heart-disease. " Pour sauver ma fille j'ai tué
ma mère," cries the heroine, or rather the middle term
of the "rule of three" sum, as the curtain descends.
Q.E.D.   Everything in the play is conditioned not by
the probabilities and proportions of life, but by the
mathematical requirements of the thesis, and the conse-
quence is that you cannot believe a word of it.   Again,
nothing could be simpler than the thesis of *Les Trois
Filles de M. Dupont,* by M. Brieux, which is that women,
whether they elect to be dependent on men in either
regular or irregular relations, or to be independent
of men, are all equally badly off.   To prove this, one
of the daughters marries, another goes on the streets,
and the third withers in single-wretchedness.   Ultimately they compare notes, and each admits herself to
be as dissatisfied as either of the other two.   Indeed,
the play might almost be rewritten as a mediæval
morality, and called *Everywoman : or Dame Goodwife,
Dame Lechery, and Dame Maidenhood.*   Here, again,
the thesis, not life, dictates the form of the play, which
is not a play but a triangle; and once more you cannot
believe a word of it.   We leave the French, then, with
their turn for logic more in evidence than ever.   We
have seen how it gave them a formula for modern
drama, a vehicle for a true criticism of life.   Now we
see the formula piercing through the drama, and life
subordinated to the criticism.   The French stage is
suffering from intellectual hypertrophy.   Where is the

remedy to be found? Assuredly not, as some enthusiasts deceive themselves into believing, in the rhymed
fantasies of M. Rostand. Practical conduct, life as we
know it, is the staple commodity of French drama.
This does not exclude great poetry, for a great poet
will always have a " message " for his day. M. Rostand
only offers it a copy of verses. An inspired schoolboy,
like our own Landor, he can turn anything into metre
—gasconnades, a duel, pâtisserie, a protuberant nose,
the Old Guard, a battlefield, Napoleon's cocked hat,
what you will. He was with difficulty dissuaded from
addressing the French Academy in verse. *Il ne
manquait que ça!* No, the French drama is not to
be saved by prosody. One prefers to regard Rostandism
as a passing mirage, if, indeed, it be not a mirage already
dispelled. If a French Ibsen . . . but a French Ibsen
is a contradiction in terms. And, in any case, it is no
business of ours to prescribe.

Were we English to offer the French that impertin-
ence, nothing but their traditional politeness could save
us from the obvious retort about the mote and the
beam. The English stage of to-day is in little danger
of intellectual hypertrophy; in mid-nineteenth century
—the point at which we left it—it was in no danger
at all. It was an absent-minded drama. It whistled
as it went, for want of thought. And it went in another
sense, it went into the *Ewigkeit.* Where is that drama
now? The French drama of that date still lines our
shelves—volume after volume of Augier and Dumas
and even of Labiche. These French playwrights still
permit themselves to be read and not seldom to be
played. But who can read the *Théâtre Complet* of
Bulwer Lytton or the " acting editions " of Boucicault
or Tom Taylor or Charles Reade or John Oxenford?

It is impossible even to think of the early Victorian
theatre without a yawn, so "unidea'd" was it, so
ephemeral, so paltry and jejune. One shrinks from
dwelling on this tedious theme. Our concern here is
not with the imitators, the adapters, the mere purveyors,
but with the elect few who have done something new—
no matter whether good or bad, so long as it is new
to drama—the *Fortschrittsmänner* as the Germans call
them, the men who give a new lead in art. The first
of these men, in the history of the modern English
theatre, was T. W. Robertson. In the Robertsonian
drama—which includes not merely the author of *Caste*
and *Society* and *School*, but minor and coarser Robertsons
like H. J. Byron and James Albery—is to be found
the first intelligent employment in England of the
picture-stage. A plausible representation of actual life
and manners and speech, with all rhetoric and rhetorical
conventions abolished, with no aim but the aim of
illusion, was for the first time presented to an English
playhouse audience. The world of the sixties is now
so remote from us—are not the humours of its remote-
ness the very point of Mr. Pinero's *Trelawny of the
Wells?*—that it is odd to think of Robertson as a
realist; nevertheless, a realist he was in his day. I am
not referring to the "real door-handles" of *Society* or
the "real snow" of *Ours*, or the other novelties of
accurate *mise-en-scène* of which the history is written in
the annals of the old Prince of Wales's Theatre under
the *régime* of the Bancrofts. These mechanical details
were bound in time to be invented for the new requirements of the picture-stage, though that consideration
does not detract from the credit of the actual inventors.
Still less am I referring to the structure of the
Robertsonian drama, the "motivation" of its plot. It

is here, of course, that realism can best justify itself—
in the action and the springs of action—so that the
impression produced on the spectator's mind may be
the exact opposite of Judge Brack's, the impression
that "these are the very things people do." Robertson
was no realist in this sense. His plots are always
feeble, often merely silly, and the motives of his
character have little in common with those of live
people. Nevertheless Robertson was a true realist in
aim, and more often than not he did succeed in trans-
ferring to the stage certain types of character, the
current ideals and ambient atmosphere of so much of
the outside world as he had the opportunity of studying.
That was a limited opportunity, no doubt ; Robertson's
was a cockney and a middle-class world ; but then so
much of England in the sixties was cockney and
middle-class. This was the new, the "forward," element in Robertson's plays that ranks him among our
Fortschrittsmänner ; he did, however imperfectly, bring
the stage into some sort of relation to life. As with
all new developments, the method was a method of
exaggeration. Hawtrey and Eccles and Polly and
Sam Gerridge are caricatures, but the basis of observed
fact underlies them all. Hawtrey is a caricature which
might have been signed "John Leech," as Eccles or
Sam Gerridge might have been signed "Charles
Keene." Robertson, then, accomplished something.
The Robertsonian drama counts. It gave a lead, and
a fairly good one, for the picture-stage. But, English
in its many good qualities, it was English also in its
chief defect ; it was "unidea'd." Happily no quotation
in proof of this statement is called for—happily, because
Robertsonian prose is absolutely unreadable. *School*
and *Ours* and *Caste* have been revived in quite recent

years, so that the present generation of playgoers has
had ample opportunity of acquaintance with some
typical Robertsonian plays. They show that, while
Robertson observed his time and responded to its
pressure, he had no critical ideas about it. By ideas
one does not, of course, mean the puerile commonplaces
of the copybook.

In harping upon this question of ideas, their presence
or their absence, I do not forget that I am presenting
only one aspect—important as that aspect may be—
of a many-sided matter. The future historian of the
English stage—unhappily the epithet " future," which
has long since become stale in this connection, is still
obligatory—the future historian of the English stage
will have to describe many phases of it which are here
left out of account. My less ambitious endeavour is to
contrast the modern French and English theatres, and
that contrast turns upon the inequality in their stock
of ideas: abundance, even to excess, on the one hand,
on the other a lamentable penury. To such an inquiry
the theatrical record for many years after Robertson's
death is scarcely relevant. Those years witnessed the
rise of Henry Irving, the return of London society, at
his call, to a theatre from which it had long held aloof,
the gradual perfection of the art of *mise-en-scène*, and
many other important things. But none of these
important things had aught to do with the theatre of
ideas. That suited neither Sir Henry Irving's interesting qualities as a romantic actor nor his still more
conspicuous ability as a manager, a generalissimo of
stage forces. Sir Henry, to be sure, added Tennyson
to our list of acted poets, but only, I fancy, with the
result of bringing the world in general to the mind of
Tennyson's candid friend " Old Fitz," who " wished

A. T. had not tried the stage." [1]   And, of course, there were those gorgeous Shakespearian revivals which it is a duty to remember, as well as those pseudo-poetic plays of W. G. Wills which it is a pleasure to forget. Of the Shakespearian revivals there is one thing to be said germane to the present purpose.   They represented an effort to pour old wine into new bottles : to accommodate the platform-drama to the picture-stage. Charles Kean had made a similar attempt in the fifties, which failed, because the new conditions were imperfectly understood, and because public opinion had not yet escaped from the bondage of the old rhetorical ideal.   In the eighties this ideal had vanished, and though a few veterans grumbled, the Lyceum experiment did achieve a certain success.   It was Walter Bagehot who said that, though Eton boys might not learn much Latin or Greek, they left school with the firm impression that there *were* such languages.   So the Lyceum public, all agape at the "solid sets" and the rich costumes, carried away a conviction that there had indeed been a Shakespeare.   As to the difference between the old and the new styles one cannot do better than give the unconscious evidence of FitzGerald and his cronies, who had seen both.   They found the scenery of the Lyceum *Much Ado* "too good," while "Irving was without any humour, Miss Terry with simply animal spirits." [2]   On the other hand, of Macready's Macbeth FitzGerald remembered the actor's "Amen stu-u-u-u-ck in his throat." [3]   In other words, overelaboration of scenery was the besetting sin of the picture-stage, as that of the platform-stage had been

---

[1] *More Letters of Edward FitzGerald*, p. 273.
[2] *Letters of Edward FitzGerald to Fanny Kemble*, p. 255.
[3] *Ibid*. p. 45.

over-emphasis of delivery or "ranting." The truth is, Sir Henry Irving stood apart. By sheer force of individuality he impressed himself on the time; he rendered signal service to the playhouse by making it once more a social institution, and to the actor's calling by making it, perhaps for the first time, an entirely respectable profession; but in the development of modern drama, as I am considering it, he took no share.

This complete, if "splendid," isolation of the Lyceum in the later eighties reminds one of those enthusiastic Parisian anglers who, so the story runs, continued to fish for gudgeon under the Pont-Neuf while the Revolution was raging overhead. The Seine might run with blood, a stray body might be hurled over the parapet, incendiary fires might "incarnadine" the sky, but still they placidly fished on. Not otherwise was the "ancien régime" of the theatrical world solemnly keeping up its consecrated ritual inside the Lyceum walls, while the world outside resounded with the din of two new factions, the Ibsenites and the Anti-Ibsenites. Translated by Mr. William Archer, explained and pierced to his "substantificque moëlle" by Mr. Bernard Shaw,[1] played by a little band of enthusiasts and even by Mr. Beerbohm Tree, the Norwegian dramatist for a brief moment frighted the isle from its propriety. Conservative playgoers mistook for a new Reign of Terror what proved to be little more than a storm in a teacup. "Ibsenism" soon passed away without establishing itself in this country as a vital force. Nevertheless it left its mark upon our drama. Without the Ibsen episode we could hardly have had the serious plays of Mr. Pinero, of Mr. Henry Arthur Jones, or of

[1] *The Quintessence of Ibsenism*, 1891.

Mr. Sydney Grundy. Without the Ibsen episode the world would certainly have been the poorer by the brilliant dramatic vagaries of Mr. Bernard Shaw. In the eighties Mr. Pinero, who had learnt the technical tricks of the stage as an apprentice to the actor's calling, was known as the author of a series of farces brimful of "modernity" and bubbling over with wit. Then came the Ibsen movement, which gave Mr. Pinero "furiously to think." The result of his furious thinking was *The Profligate* (1889), followed by a group of plays beginning with *The Second Mrs. Tanqueray* in 1890, and ending with *Iris* (1901), which represent the high-water mark of our modern English drama. They are our closest approximation to the theatre of ideas, to a criticism of life through the medium of drama. One is constrained to say approximation, for the impression left on the mind by the whole group of plays is that Mr. Pinero, in the expressive Americanism, never quite "gets there." Perhaps exception should be made in favour of *Iris*, which does not shirk the logical conclusion from its premises; but *Iris* is a character-study rather than a play, a picture of woman's weakness and self-indulgence coarsening to vice and ending in degradation worse than death. The other plays of the group, also studies in feminine perversity, but studies which show the collision of wills, and are therefore strict drama, do not offer a valid criticism of life because they shirk a real *dénouement*. The suicide of Paula Tanqueray is an arbitrary termination, not a conclusion; the "white-washing" of Agnes Ebbsmith and of the frail woman in *The Benefit of the Doubt* is logically an absurdity as well as a concession to English cant. The truth, apparently, is that Mr. Pinero has lacked the courage

to defy his audience, as Dumas *fils* defied it and as
Ibsen defied it.   He has tried to run with the hare
and hunt with the hounds; to be the "disinterested"
artist and yet to please the "compact majority."   This
means a lack of single-minded purpose; we do not
get ideas, but half-ideas, or adumbrations of ideas.
The spectator is always asking himself: What does
Mr. Pinero really think?   That is not only a natural
but an inevitable question about all serious drama,
which, however "objective" it may be in comparison
with other arts, should still be a projection, a revelation
of the dramatist.   In all art the really interesting
thing is the "état d'âme," the temperament, the
outlook upon life of the artist behind it.   What is
Mr. Pinero's "état d'âme"?   What, in the colloquial
phrase, is he driving at?   Probably he would reply
that he is driving at simple realism; that he gives us
studies from life, as accurate as he can make them.
That, however, is not to give us the drama of ideas, a
criticism of life.

One is in much the same state of dubiety about Mr.
Henry Arthur Jones.   His language, especially in his
prefaces, papers, and manifestoes, is that of an earnest
man, almost a Hot-gospeller; but what is he earnest
about?   At first while vowing he would ne'er consent
he consented to become an Ibsenite.   He talked of
Ibsen's "drains" or "cesspools" or whatever the
elegant figure was; but he nevertheless wrote "confession" dramas under the inspiration of *The Pillars
of Society*.   At another moment he was inventing
Ouidaesque dukes or Corellian barmaids.   Then he
turned to France and produced *The Case of Rebellious
Susan*, which is a vulgarised *Francillon*.   Two later
plays, *The Liars* and *Mrs. Dane's Defence*, are tolerable

achievements from the mere "story-telling" point of view; but what is their moral? In the one case, that an elopement is a mistake because you will be cut by your friends and "the world," whereas it is better to be taken out to supper by a brute of a husband; in the other, that an unprotected female, trying to conceal a doubtful "past," must expect to be bullied and hounded out of Society by a shrewd lawyer, and serve her right! The Ibsenite *malgré lui* has now become fugleman of the compact majority! Upon errors like *The Lackey's Carnival* and *The Princess's Nose*, with their coarseness of feeling and their provinciality of thought, it is better not to dwell. But what a chaotic output! How is Mr. Jones's criticism of life to be disengaged from this tangle of themes and modes, schools and styles, violent affirmations and flat contradictions? He flouts Mrs. Grundy in *Lady Susan*[1] and brings her in as "dea ex machinâ" for *The Liars*. He was an idealist in *The Crusaders*, and a sentimentalist in *The Dancing Girl* and a cynic in *The Tempter*, and Mr. Worldly Wiseman in *Mrs. Dane* and goodness knows what in *The Princess's Nose*. Is it permissible to suppose that a hodge-podge like this was ever inspired by any constant ideal, directed towards any definite end? Your serious French dramatist knows his own mind and takes care that we shall know it too. The purpose of Dumas *fils* we have seen emphatically declared in the preface to *Le Fils Naturel*, and Dumas kept his word. M. Hervieu says his purpose is to plead the cause of the oppressed; M. Brieux regards himself as the "commis voyageur de l'intellectualité." We all know, then, what these men are driving at.

---

[1] Of *malice prepense* it would seem; see the preface to the printed play.

But what Mr. Jones or Mr. Pinero is driving at remains an inscrutable mystery.

It is a refreshment to glance for a moment at a man with real ideas and a definite purpose which he is at no pains to conceal—Mr. Bernard Shaw. No one need ask what Mr. Shaw's "message" is; he is always ramming it down our throats. For his general philosophy you have this: "The tragedy and comedy of life lie in the consequences, sometimes terrible, sometimes ludicrous, of our persistént attempts to found our institutions on the ideals suggested to our imagination, by our half-satisfied passions, instead of on a genuinely scientific natural history." [1] There it is, as circumstantial, and almost as long-winded, as a power of attorney. Mr. Shaw's plays are so many attacks upon what he considers our false ideals, and so many attempts to illustrate what he calls a scientific natural history. The only drawback is that "with such a being as man, in such a world as the present," Mr. Shaw's plays do not count as plays at all. They offer such a criticism of life as the average man cannot even begin to understand. Mr. Shaw assumes a world of unimpeded intellect; he addresses himself to the pure reason; his characters do not love or hate, laugh or cry, they merely argue it out. It is the Euclidean drama—or would be, if Euclid had set himself to prove that two sides of a triangle are *not* greater than the third, and that it is a vulgar error to suppose a point to be without parts or magnitude. It is better not to enter, however, into so dangerously controversial a subject as the value of Mr. Shaw's criticism of life; nor is there any need, seeing that he fails to express it in terms of drama. The essential law of the theatre is

[1] Preface to *Unpleasant Plays* (1898).

thought *through emotion.* No character exhibits real emotion (though occasionally there is a show of " temper ") in those fascinating exercises in dialectic which Mr. Shaw miscalls plays. This fatal defect long condemned him to remain a dramatist of the study or, at best, the dramatist of a coterie. If any one of our playwrights who appeal to the public at large had only a tithe of Mr. Shaw's independence and originality of thought, to say nothing of his vivacity and wit, the reproach that the modern English drama is " unidea'd " would be heard no more.

It is, of course, irrelevant to this inquiry to consider the case of Mr. Stephen Phillips. One has been examining the modern French drama and the English on a specific point, appraising their relative contributions to a criticism of life, contrasting the ample stock of ideas in the one with the intellectual poverty of the other. The drama of beauty and mystery and passion enshrined in verse—and some of Mr. Phillips's work takes high rank in that dramatic region—stands outside the present comparison. How far the vogue of Mr. Phillips has been a vogue of pure poetry, what, on the other hand, has been the amount of its debt to two enterprising actor-managers of the moment—Mr. Alexander and Mr. Tree—may some day be an interesting question. But here it is what Aristotle would call ἄλλος λόγος.

July 1902.

SOME FRENCH AND ENGLISH PLAYS

I F it be true that every nation has the drama which
it deserves, we English can scarcely plume ourselves on our present merits.   Our old theatrical hands
are not idly so called, for theirs is handiwork rather
than head-work.   If there are one or two younger men
of promise, they are still in the stage in which promise
makes a better display than performance.   We have
no Experimental Theatre, no laboratory for the cultivation of dramatic germs ; and we have no Repertory
Theatre, no museum for the permanent exhibition of
classic specimens.   One or both of these institutions
may in time be provided by such organisations as the
Stage Society and the Irish National Theatre ; but
that is mere conjecture.   There is a small minority of the
playgoing public which shows symptoms of discontent.
Its artistic conscience, if not deeply stirred, is at any
rate gently pricked.   It signs manifestoes, writes to
the newspapers, and in other futile ways gives vent to
its suspicions that something ought to be done.   But
what precisely ought to be done nobody knows.
Meanwhile, the music-halls, along with the theatres
which are music-halls in everything but name and an
atmosphere of tobacco-smoke, have it all their own way.
The vast majority of the public takes its theatrical
amusement, as it takes its newspaper information, in
snippets.   It is a public without patience, without the
capacity for sustained attention, and, like Lady Teazle

when she married Sir Peter, it has no taste. To speak of the drama as an art to such a public as this is to talk a language which it does not understand, and has no inclination to learn. *Vox clamantis in deserto.*

If we turn to Paris—and in the discussion of any theatrical question it is as obligatory to turn to Paris as for a Mahomedan to turn towards Mecca—we find a not altogether unlike posture of affairs. There, also, the *café-concert* triumphs over the playhouse. There, also, the theatre of ideas has to maintain an incessant fight for life. But it continues to keep its flag flying. The Français has its *habitués* as well as its subvention ; Antoine and Lugné Poe have their subscribers as well as their intelligent audacity. And the merely frivolous theatres, whatever we may think of their ethics, maintain a level of workmanship which, compared with that of our " musical comedies," may almost be called intellectual. It is true that the entertainments offered by the Athénée and the Nouveautés, the Capucines and the Grand Guignol — the favourite resorts of " mundane " pleasure-seekers — are more often than not quite heartless and conscienceless ; but it is also true that they are anything but silly. Paris has not been Theatropolis all these years for nothing. Its playhouses are for the most part more stuffy than ours, more uncomfortable, far less pleasant houses than ours to gossip or to lounge or to slumber in ; for French audiences concern themselves far less than ours about these subsidiary matters. What they do concern themselves about is the play. By tradition and temperament the Parisian is a playgoer, and, from practice, an expert playgoer. Herein he differs from an Englishman of the same class. No doubt, in all our modern democracies the average citizen is largely dependent on fiction for his means of realising the stratum of society in which he lives, and, still more, those strata in which he does not live. But while it is a typical English habit to seek this fiction in print and nowhere else, it is a typical French habit to seek it on the other side of the footlights.

To this constant and urgent theatrical demand in France corresponds an unfailing and abundant supply. Playwrights are as numerous in that country as beggars in Spain or Grand Army veterans in the United States. One summer the *Figaro* invited some two or three score playwrights to say how they were spending their holidays, and it appeared that they were all busy over several plays apiece for next season, plays in verse and in prose, plays of ideas and plays of mere amusement —all the items of Polonius's lengthy catalogue. The plays of ideas were, of course, a small minority, as they always must be. But plays of ideas have an importance out of all proportion to their number. It is by virtue of these plays that the theatre becomes a vital part of the national organism. It is well to call them plays of ideas not only because that is what they are, but because one may thereby hope to satisfy M. Paul Hervieu, who protests against the common label of "thesis - play" as intended to imply something essentially tiresome.

"From every piece" (says M. Hervieu)[1] "that is not a piece of sheer farcical foolishness, you may disengage a signification which you may, if you like, call a 'thesis.' *Le Voyage de M. Perrichon,* by Labiche, contains and demonstrates from beginning to end the 'thesis' that men prefer those whom they have

[1] *L'Année Psychologique,* tome x. Conversation with M. A. Binet.

benefited to their benefactors. The very titles of many plays announce a 'thesis,' if you will have the word—Vacquerie's *Souvent homme varie;* Pailleron's *L'Age Ingrat* and *Le Monde où l'on s'ennuie;* Musset's *On ne badine pas avec l'amour* and *Il ne faut jurer de rien.* The point at which a play of senti-mental demonstration or social bearing begins to be called a 'thesis play' has always seemed to me as arbitrarily fixed as that where the Boulevard des Capucines becomes the Boulevard des Italiens."

This is obvious enough; so obvious, indeed, that some time ago I happened to make the same remark, and to choose the very same illustration from Labiche.[1] Nevertheless, the use of "thesis-play" as a term of reproach is not without a certain justification. When M. Hervieu speaks of "disengaging" a signification, or thesis, he is really begging the question at issue. The objection to so many of these plays is that the thesis, instead of being something implied and latent in the piece, something which you may, if you will, disengage, is thrust under your nose, meets you at every turn, interrupts and in the end destroys your sense of illusion. It is the primary business of a play to persuade you that what you are witnessing has happened, or might happen. And this business is only executed to perfection when the resultant impression is one of inevitability, the feeling that the thing could not have happened otherwise. But let the dramatist for one moment excite the suspicion that this or that incident is there merely because his thesis requires it to be there, and the game is up.

The truth is that plays of ideas must, first of all, be

[1] See preceding article.

4

plays of emotion. " Primum vivere, deinde philosophari."
The "idea" is excellent, as giving a meaning and
unity to the play, but if it be allowed to obtrude itself
so as to impair the sense of reality the flow of emotion
is immediately arrested. Emotion, not logic, is the
stuff of drama. A play that stirs our emotions may be
absolutely " unidea'd." That is a case of emotion for
emotion's sake—the typical case of melodrama. The
play really great is the play which first stirs our
emotions profoundly and then gives a meaning and
direction to our feelings by the unity and truth of some
underlying idea. Such a play, if I am not mistaken,
is M. Hervieu's work *Le Dédale*. It is a play with a
guiding idea—one of those ideas about sexual relationship which would have delighted Dumas *fils*—but it is
also a play which sounds emotional deeps quite beyond
the reach of Dumas. It aches and throbs with passion,
but is chastened by a certain austerity, the vague
dread of calamity to come. Its high seriousness, the
dignity of its style, its torrential force, its inexorable
catastrophe constitute it a real tragedy.

Its governing idea, right or wrong, is simple enough :
that a woman who abandons the father of her child
under the law of man does so at her peril because she
is infringing a higher law of Nature. Marianne has
divorced her vicious husband Max. With a child of
tender years to bring up, and still in the heyday of her
youth, she has every inducement to marry again ; and
in Guillaume she finds a second husband with all the
virtues which her first husband lacked. But her second
marriage is not brought about without grave difficulty.
Her mother, a fervent Catholic, who cannot contemplate
the marriage of a divorced person without horror, is
dead against the project. That is the veto of Religion.

There is also the veto of Social Opinion. Marianne's cousin Paulette tells her that a woman cannot afford to run the risk of being seen in a drawing-room between her first and her second husband; a thing "good society will never stand." And yet, replies Marianne, you are not ashamed to be seen in a drawing-room between your husband and another man who is secretly your lover. Oh, rejoins Paulette, the secrecy makes all the difference! This is scarcely the sort of argument to convince a woman like Marianne, the soul of frankness and loyalty. She is also a woman of clear head and strong will. All objections duly weighed, she decides that she ought to marry again; and she does.

But she has reckoned without the veto of Nature. There comes a time when Max and she are again in presence. The purport of his visit is to ask for more frequent access to their little son, and this request Marianne cannot refuse. The matter, however, does not end there. Marianne is unsettled by the sight of her first husband, who is a changed man, repentant, subdued, haggard with grief at the thought of the happiness that he has wickedly thrown away. He has no hope of recapturing the woman; nor she any fear of falling again under his sway. But the mere juxtaposition of two people whose relations, however distant now, have been of all human relations the closest, is not without its silent effect. Nothing is openly said, or even definitely realised, by either party; but the subconscious influence of sex is at work. Time, complete separation, new interests, might avert all danger. But again there is juxtaposition, and of the closest kind. The boy falls ill, and the father obtains permission to aid the mother in watching over the sick-bed.   At the moment when the child is declared to be out of danger and the father comes to take his leave, the smouldering ashes of past affection burst into flame.   The woman's nerves are unstrung; she has been worn out by vigils shared with the man who once had been to her what no other man ever can be.   " L'homme qui m'a rendue mère," she cries, "je ne peux pas l'arracher de mes entrailles."   And so, almost automatically and unconsciously, they fall into each other's arms.   It is a physical accident.

The catastrophe swiftly follows.   In her hysterical anguish over the horrible trick that fate has played her, Marianne could not keep the truth to herself, even if she would.   She feels that she can never again be Guillaume's wife; nor will she disgrace herself by living in open sin with Max.   What is to be the way out of this *dédale*, this " maze "?   Clearly there is no way out so long as all three parties remain alive.   The only question is, which of the three will the dramatist kill off.   Marianne?   Assuredly not; there would be too savage a cynicism in leaving the two husbands flying at one another's throats over the corpse of the wife. But if Marianne is not to die, then there are tremendous objections against sparing the lives of either of the men.   Kill Max, and you leave Marianne alone with Guillaume, whom she does not love and whose wife she has sworn never to be again.   Kill Guillaume, and you rebuild the happiness of Max and Marianne over the grave of the one just man.   Irresistible logic, then, condemns both men to death; and accordingly they pull one another over a precipice.   Ignorant of what has happened, the woman passes across the scene, answering the call of her child.   In the child you see the only hope for her future life.

It will be observed that in *Le Dédale*, as in all
his plays, M. Hervieu's method is that of the logician.
And, like the Living Skeleton, he is "proud of the
title." Replying to M. Binet's questions[1] as to his
mental processes in play-writing, he says: "The indispensable quality, as it seems to me, is logic . . . to
be quite sure where you are going . . . to see that
your conclusion follows from your premises." And he
gives an illustration from *Le Dédale*. The child of
Paulette, Marianne's frivolous cousin, is stricken by
the same malady as Marianne's.

"I was two days hesitating whether Paulette's child
ought to die or to survive. The child dead, the
mother in black . . . an ugly black dress . . . it
will be painful, disagreeable . . . the child alive, she
will appear in a pink hat. . . . But, the child dead,
there was the means of regenerating Paulette's
character. Also a winding up of the subsidiary intrigue, the principal intrigue having to be continued
without Paulette. . . . Logic triumphed over the fear
of risking the success of the play by sombreness."

But what distinguishes this play of M. Hervieu's from
the others is that its logic is never obtrusive; closely
reasoned out though it is, step by step, its strongest
appeal is always an appeal to the emotions. In the
scenes between mother and daughter the case of religious
convictions *versus* common sense is argued out for all
it is worth; but what is chiefly brought home to us is
the anguish of a breach between mother and daughter,
both good women. Paulette's child dies from logical
necessity, as we have just seen; but what concerns the
spectator of the play is the agony of Paulette's grief.

[1] *L'Année Psychologique*, tome x.

Though Marianne falls into Max's arms to illustrate
M. Hervieu's thesis, what affects us is the swift inevitability with which the "circuit" of passion between
the two is "completed." And when Max and Guillaume
go over the precipice, while we know that it is the process of reasoning by "exhaustion" which dictates their
fate, we are none the less shaken by the horror of it,
none the less thrilled by the little piping treble of the
child's call to its mother at the next moment. Best
of all, the play has the true tragic dignity. Its whole
fabric is reared upon a physiological fact—or assumption ; its chief scene turns upon a *surprise des sens*; it
might easily have been coarse, ignoble, even repulsive. It
might have been, but never is ; so tactfully has the subject
been handled, with restraint so perfect, with so fastidious a taste. Beyond cavil *Le Dédale* confers upon M.
Hervieu the primacy of the contemporary French stage.

If M. Hervieu is a dramatic artist, working in the
region of ideas, M. Brieux is an ideologue, for whom
dramatic art is only an instrument of propagandism.
Indignation, on very old authority, "makes verses";
with M. Brieux it also makes plays. He desires to
awaken the collective conscience ; his plays are fierce
exposures of social abuses, injustices, impostures. In
L'Évasion he denounced the tyranny of medical
pseudo-science, in *Les Trois Filles de M. Dupont* he
handled the "woman question," in *Blanchette* he
exhibited the evils of educating people beyond their
station, and in *Les Bienfaiteurs* his moral was "O
Charity, what crimes are committed in thy name!"
One of his latest plays, *Maternité*, deals with the
population question. It is, as everybody knows, a
burning question in France, where the birth-rate is, or
until the other day was, steadily decreasing. A senator,

M. Piot, has founded a League for the encouragement
of large families. Thereupon it occurs to M. Brieux
to play the part of devil's advocate by marshalling the
various cases in which births are not a blessing but a
curse—as, *e.g.*, when they are illegitimate or when
there are no means to maintain the offspring. As
generally happens with M. Brieux, his play is a series
of variations on a single theme; his personages are
not so much human beings as the helpless puppets of
his *idée fixe*; his plot is a mere revolving platform
designed to bring each aspect of the one subject in
turn under the eye of the spectator. The Sub-
Prefect Brignac zealously distributes the Ministerial
circular on the duty of all good citizens to repopulate
the country. He admires its style, and reads it aloud
to the Mayor and the Commandant of the Garrison
and Mme. Brignac. Madame does not share her
husband's enthusiasm; perpetual child-bearing has
brought her to the condition of a slave. There is
another sense, as the Sub-Prefect soon finds, in which
maternity, like charity, begins at home. His wife's
young sister Annette has a shameful confession to
make. She has been betrayed and abandoned.
Appeal to her seducer's family—promptly made by
Mme. Brignac—is fruitless, for Annette is *sans dot*.
Then the Sub-Prefect forgets all his fine phrases about
maternity and turns Annette out of doors. There
are establishments, says he, for such cases as hers
where no questions are asked and no names divulged.
In such an establishment Annette dies from an illegal
operation, and the play concludes in an Assize Court
where the *sage-femme* is brought to trial, together
with some of her customers—unlike poor Annette,
married, but too poor to rear children. The judge

bullies everybody, the counsel hurl insults at one another, Mme. Brignac, called as a witness for the prosecution, goes into hysterics, and the curtain comes down on a scene of ignominy and confusion. Nearly all the matters which M. Brieux here discusses with emphatic frankness would in England rank among the *tacenda*. They are matters for the legislator and the physician, and M. Brieux's play affords no evidence that they gain anything by being treated in the theatre. *Maternité* shocks our feelings without contributing any solution of the difficulties attending the question at issue. It merely leaves the spectator in a mood of what Dr. Johnson called "inspissated gloom." Art that merely depresses—Aristotle long ago laid down a canon about that—is bad art. And *Maternité* is not even good propagandism.

It is a relief, if only a slight relief, to turn to another play of ideas, *L'Oasis*, by M. Jean Jullien. This curious work preaches the religion of humanity in a vein of optimistic idealism and with a deluge of rhetoric. Its Eastern atmosphere revives one of the classic literary traditions of the eighteenth century, a tradition that assigned to Persians and to Chinese virtuous sentiments calculated to put our Western civilisation to shame. Somewhere in the desert the children of Islam have sought refuge from the European invader. The chief, Mohamed ben Moktar, having captured a Catholic nun, marries her by force (the incident was less revolting as presented at the Œuvre Theatre than might have been feared), and carries her off to an oasis, where he proposes to live for climate and the affections and the "higher life." It is to be a humanitarian oasis, where everybody is to be as happy as the day is long, uttering sententious platitudes like the people in *Rasselas*. But this Utopian community, oasis and all, is captured by the " Europeans "—dressed in the uniform of the French colonial army—who burn and slay in the interests of " civilisation." European civilisation is made to look the poor thing that M. Jullien evidently thinks it when Mohamed's wife, the ex-nun, declines to return to Christianity and vows that she never, never will desert Mr. Micawber — I should say, Mohamed ben Moktar. Ultimately Mohamed and his wife are allowed to retire to another oasis, where they found a second Utopian community, and this time are left in peace. There is some effective satire on European methods of " civilising " what it considers " inferior " races, but the play is drowned in verbiage and cloyed with a rather namby-pamby sentimentalism, and the total impression is of something slightly absurd. Such ideas as it deals in might fitly have been expressed in a *conte moral*, just as the ideas of M. Brieux's play might fitly have been expressed in a medico-legal treatise. It is significant of the paramount importance of the theatre in France that it tends to become a Universal Provider and to impress all ideas, all questions, into its service, even those unsuited to its purpose.

It is the national system of conscription transferred to the world of art. Every Frenchman must serve in the army, and every French author must be enlisted for the theatre. Another " pressed man " is M. Anatole France. It is a great pity. M. France's genius and method are everything but theatrical. It is not in his way to construct a " story," in the novelist's sense, far less a play-plot. He deals not in action, but in contemplation. His gentle irony, his

air of perpetual negation, his subdivisions of the
infinitely little in thought and feeling, his Shandean
humour, the fastidious charm of his style, and everything that is his—what have they to do with the
hard, emphatic, garish art of the theatre? And yet he
has been induced in an evil hour to bring his other
self, M. Bergeret, before the footlights. It is the
M. Bergeret of *Le Mannequin d'Osier*, the M. Bergeret
of the conjugal misadventure, the M. Bergeret who
was so distressingly interrupted in the composition of
his *Virgilius Nauticus* by the plaints of the servant
girl Euphémie. Of course the inevitable happens.
What the play succeeds in rendering is just that part
of the book which is devoid of significance and passes
almost unobserved by the reader—the mere external
incidents, incidents of no account apart from the comments for which they are the pretext. What the play
does not and cannot render is the quintessence of
Bergeret, the strange blend in him of ordinary human
weaknesses and what he would call philosophic
"ataraxy." Take the "adventure" of the faithless
Mme. Bergeret and M. Roux. In the book the brut-
ality of the incident only serves as a foil to Bergeret's
queer reception of it—the obsession of a physical
picture amid the details of notes on etymology, the
anguish of a deceived husband tempered by the reflection that M. Roux is a good Latinist. On the stage,
while the brutal element is necessarily softened into
something comparatively decent and at the same time
commonplace, not so much as a hint can be given of
M. Bergeret's quaint mental state. And all the proportions, all the "values," as the painters would say,
are spoiled. In the book Mme. Bergeret is merely
dull and mean and small; raised to theatre-pitch she

acquires all the dignity of a " protagonist." Bergeret himself, a will-less person in the book, has to have a will and to take action, since will and action are indispensable to a stage-character. Further, the story has to be padded out with stupid stuff about the " engagement " of one of Bergeret's daughters, while our ecclesiastical friends of the book, the Abbé Guitret and the Abbé Lantaigne, are reduced to the ranks of " supers." And so M. France has been butchered, or rather has immolated himself, in order that M. Guitry of the Renaissance may show how cleverly he can " make up " as M. Bergeret ! To all good Anatolians the affair must have been deplorable. Probably there would have been no such affair to deplore had it not been for M. Guitry's earlier success in his adaptation of M. France's pathetic little story *Crainquebille*. But that was, in more senses than one, another story. The misfortunes of the old costermonger have no kinship with the psychological subtleties, the complicated *vie intérieure*, of a Bergeret ; on the stage a sequence of simple scenes, just as in the book a bare recital of a few external facts, serves to bring out the full pathos of them. Moreover, old Crainquebille is not a great classic type like Bergeret, of whom multitudes of readers have formed their own cherished image and are sure to resent another image thrust upon them by this or that actor. There is something indecent in the spectacle of a stage-player pretending to be Mr. Pickwick or Mr. Pecksniff, Major Dobbin or Captain Costigan, Mr. Elton or Mr. Collins ; one feels that a gross liberty has been taken with one's most intimate friend. M. Bergeret belongs to that sacrosanct body.

There is, however, just one feature in this stage version of *Le Mannequin d'Osier* which relates its

intention, if not its actual accomplishment, to a vener-
able tradition of the French Theatre. Its main interest
is an interest of character. It is primarily an answer
to the question, not What happened in the Bergeret
household? but What sort of a man is Bergeret? No
doubt there is a sense in which Aristotle's assertion
that plot is more important than character must
always remain true. But it is only true in a very
limited sense of the comedy of character, a dramatic
genre virtually unknown to Aristotle (who, for that
matter, made his assertion about tragedy); and it
counts for next to nothing in the comedy of "static"
character. Such a comedy is *Les Affaires sont les
Affaires*, by M. Octave Mirabeau. By a "static"
character I mean one that is a fixed quantity in the
play; essentially the same force in magnitude and
direction from the rise to the fall of the curtain. It
does not move; it is we who are taken all round it,
so that we may see its various facets. It is not
moulded by the successive incidents of the play, but
only disclosed by them; *sibi constat.* This "static"
treatment is familiar enough in universal drama, from
Plautus to Ben Jonson; but it has perhaps been
practised most continuously and successfully in France
ever since Molière drew his "miser" and his "vale-
tudinarian." M. Mirabeau's "static" character, Isidore
Lechat, is the born virtuoso in the art of money-
making, the ferocious egoist who lives for the main
chance, who is in the cant phrase a "Napoleon of
finance." And, like Napoleon, he is non-moral, a
natural force, like gravity or heat. Just as this is one
of the most familiar types in the actual world, so it is
one of the stock figures of novel and drama. In *John
Gabriel Borkman* Ibsen gave the type a touch of the

grandiose by a quasi-poetic treatment. M. Mirabeau, too, sees that in any great force, even a force that makes for evil, there is an aspect of grandeur. A colossal egoist is, at any rate, colossal. The colossal egoist Lechat compels admiration by his devout self-worship, his expansive geniality, his sheer delight in the exercise of his own ruthless force. He is odiously vulgar, thick-skinned, and conscienceless, but almost captivating by virtue of his buoyancy, indomitable courage, and gigantic strength. He is a Nietzschean who has never heard the name of Nietzsche. For three out of four acts M. Mirabeau exhibits this character exclusively by the "static" method, "sampling" it as it were at all points, showing you the millionaire—for of course Lechat is a millionaire—as host, as parent, as bargainer, and so forth. Then comes a final act of tragic catastrophe, when the millionaire, in the supreme moment of his triumph, is stricken down by the sudden death of his son, the only creature, next to himself, that he loves in the world. For sheer brute vitality this character of Lechat is one of the most notable achievements of the contemporary French stage.

It was magnificently acted at the Théâtre Français by M. de Féraudy, who, not long afterwards, again distinguished himself by his performance of a very different part in M. Marcel Prévost's comedy, *La Plus Faible*. What a contrast to Isidore Lechat this Louis Gourd, grotesquely ugly, painfully timid, hopelessly inarticulate, craving for a woman's love but without any of the showy qualities by which a woman's love is too often won ! There comes a moment when he confronts a rival endowed with those showy qualities, and proves himself the better man of the two—Dobbin, say, asserting himself for once and making George

Osborne look small—and that is the moment in which
M. de Féraudy almost persuades you that M. Marcel
Prévost has written a play of sterling worth.   But one
good moment does not make a play, and in fact
M. Prévost's comedy is only a conventional exercise in
story-telling over which there is no profit in lingering.
It deals with a subject sufficiently time-worn—the
struggle between passion which seeks to be free and
the prejudices, interests, and ordinances of the social
and family environment.   Incidentally the point is
urged that an irregular union, however " distinguished,"
however deliberately entered upon by two advanced
" intellectuals " as a protest against orthodox marriage,
is in the long run a less convenient and on the whole
less rational arrangement than the institution against
which it is a protest.   These, to be sure, are " ideas "
—there are ideas, as M. Hervieu has pointed out,
underlying every play—but *La Plus Faible*, for all
that, is not entitled to rank as a play of ideas.   Its
ideas are merely a pretext for its story, and as the
story, in one form or another, has often been told
before, and as it is not very strikingly told now, one
need say no more about it.

Paris is seldom without a " success of scandal," and
a specimen of this disagreeable class is *Le Retour de
Jérusalem*, by M. Maurice Donnay.   Much excellent
work stands to M. Donnay's credit in the past—
artistically excellent work, be it understood, for the
ethical quality of such plays as *Amants* and *La
Douloureuse* is quite another matter—but this Anti-
Semitic exploit of his cannot but have disappointed
and   disconcerted   his   more   judicious .admirers.
Exploitation, perhaps, would be a fitter word, did the
English language permit its use ; for M. Donnay has

deliberately chosen to make capital out of a racial prejudice and to flatter the baser instincts of the Boulevard mob. Stripped of its Anti-Semitism, *Le Retour de Jérusalem* would offer little that is distinguishable from the orthodox elements of an elopement drama. A. (with a placid wife, whom he despises) "bolts" with B. (wedded to a man whom she detests). Then the new couple find in time that they too are unsuited for each other, and they part, with hearty expressions of mutual dis-esteem. This is one of the patterns which every theatrical emporium always keeps in stock, and, accordingly, to give it a specious air of novelty M. Donnay tacks on to this old framework an assortment of the caricatures by which an outwitted, outpaced, and outbidden society seeks to take its revenge on the modern Jew. He makes A. a French aristocrat and B. a Jewish "intellectual" (" une sale Juive " is the less complimentary description of A.'s wife Suzanne), who is seen gradually disenchanting and finally revolting A. by exhibiting the supposed characteristics of her race. She exhibits them in the garish colours of her costumes, in her "practical" instincts, and, worst of all, in the composition of her *salon*. Here we meet with the "pushful" Jew, and the cosmopolitan Jew (a gross caricature of Dr. Max Nordau), and the Jew who reviles the army, and the Jew who wants to know what on earth people mean by "patrie." A., after defining "patrie" in a tirade which sends every Chauvinist amongst the audience into an apoplexy of delight, turns B.'s Jewish friends out of the house, and the *ménage* comes to an abrupt end. Then A. would like to be reconciled to his wife Suzanne, but she, too, has had enough of him, and so everybody lives unhappy ever afterwards. I said that

the formula of the play was a stale one, but perhaps
an exception has to be made in favour of the conclusion which concludes nothing. For there we have a
distinct departure from the old, or Dumasian, practice,
which would certainly have brought down the curtain
upon a pistol-shot or some other violent catastrophe
—such a catastrophe, for instance, as terminates
Antoinette Sabrier, by M. Romain Coolus. Here,
again, you have a dissatisfied wife who seeks " consolation " in an elopement; or would seek it, were not the
plan frustrated at the critical moment by the ruin of
the lady's husband. To run away from a bankrupt
husband is apparently a breach of the theatrical point
of honour. Unfortunately things have gone too far to
be successfully concealed, and the husband, under the
shock of the truth, blows out his brains. The treatment
of this play, however, is neither so *banal* nor so brutal as
its plot. M. Coolus writes with sobriety and distinction,
and the capital scene of the play, in which an unforeseen
but entirely natural accident makes all things only too
plain to the husband, reveals the true " fingering of the
dramatist." Once more, in *L'Adversaire*, by MM.
Alfred Capus and Emmanuel Arène, the Parisian
playgoer has been offered his favourite " thrill," the
detection of a wife's infidelity by the pertinacious
questionings of a husband, and, as in M. Donnay's
case, there is to be noted a revolt against the
Dumasian *dénouement*. A Dumasian husband would
have fought the lover; but this one has the sense to
see that a duel would prove nothing and settle
nothing. He sees also that his wife, despite her
infidelity, still loves him, as he still loves her. Shall,
then, bygones be bygones? No, for though you may
forgive, you cannot by effort of the will forget. The

only sensible course is for the husband and wife to
remain apart. No doubt that is the true ending,
viewed in the cold light of reason; but Joe Gargery
would say that it "do not overstimulate" the spectator
in search of an evening's amusement. It is only right
to add that M. Capus is as a rule the most joyous of
playwrights. Londoners have had the opportunity of
seeing three of his most characteristic performances,
La Veine, *Les Deux Écoles*, and *La Bourse ou La Vie*,
plays with a morality which may be charitably called
"easy" and a sense of the *joie de vivre* which may
not uncharitably be called exorbitant. I confess to
preferring M. Capus the madcap "amuser" of these
plays to M. Capus the austere moralist of *L'Adversaire*.
For his fun, if not very straitlaced, is always good-
humoured; his great success—he is the most popular
playwright in France at the present day—may be
taken to mark the complete and final rout of that
morbid product of a few years ago, the deliberately
and callously offensive play, the *genre rosse*.

It will have been seen that the French theatre, on
the whole, is still able to show a continuous and an
abundant supply of plays really alive. What a
painful contrast confronts us in the English theatre—
anæmia, sluggish circulation, a general condition of
depressed vitality! Our stage is languishing for lack
of fresh blood and fresh air. We have a handful of
accomplished playwrights with commonplace ideas or
no ideas at all, and we have one or two men with
ideas, but only an imperfect mastery of dramatic
resources. The unidea'd experts seem to have grown
of late a little tired, and have communicated part of
their fatigue to their audiences, while the comparatively
unskilled men of ideas either enjoy public fame by a

5

very precarious tenure or have altogether to dispense
with it. There are, to be sure, some adroit purveyors
of light "digestive" entertainments—plays which have
their interest from the point of view of box-office
receipts, but which it would be absurd to reckon as
substantial assets in any other than a commercial
estimate of our theatrical possessions. This is a
meagre display. We are occasionally reminded that,
bad as things are to-day, they were worse only a few
years ago, in the period, say, immediately preceding
that lively time when Mr. Pinero dazzled the town
with *The Second Mrs. Tanqueray*, and Mr. Jones
announced what he was pleased to call "The Rena-
scence" of the English Drama. That is true, but not
exactly consoling. For it comes to this, that the
brisk movement of the nineties has left us in a condition
only a degree less stagnant than that of the eighties.
Our stage needs a current of fresh ideas, a spirit of
eager and audacious experimentation; even a little
reckless iconoclasm would do no harm.

For its fresh ideas it is at present almost entirely
dependent on two men, Mr. Barrie and Mr. Bernard
Shaw. Not that Mr. Barrie is an ideologue. He has
no foible for intellectual gymnastic. Such philosophy
as he has to offer is by no means profound. His
ideas and his philosophy are only interesting because they are his; because they go with his other
qualities, his fancy and whim and tenderness, to make
up a character of rare charm. For we must not be
duped by the cant about the "impersonality" of drama.
Like any other art, drama is in the last analysis a
revelation of the artist, and Barrie's plays charm us
because we are aware of a lovable nature at the back
of them. His most felicitous thing, so far, is *The*

Admirable Crichton, a Voltairean *conte philosophique*, told, however, with a simple kindliness of tone which suggests anyone in the world rather than Voltaire. It showed how a very slight modification of the material conditions of life will at once upset all the "values" of the social hierarchy and turn the *personnel* of a fashionable West-End mansion topsy-turvy. Transferred from Mayfair to a desert island, the butler becomes King and the Earl a slave. In "natural" conditions it is only "natural" capacity that tells. So overwhelming is its advantage that the butler-King is in danger of developing into a despot; but the arrival of a rescue party from a man-of war at once restores the artificial standards of "civilisation," and

". . . . tout rentre ici dans l'ordre accoutumé."

Back again in Mayfair, the born ruler of men becomes once more the butler, quite content with the prospect of retirement to a snug little public-house in the Harrow Road. The logical circle is complete. Notable as the dialogue was for its rippling flow of good-humoured gaiety, the play disclosed something more notable still in its use of that pantomime which, at the right moment, is far more significant than speech. It is just there that the true dramatic instinct reveals itself, in the practical application of the principle that what is shown counts on the stage for much more than what is said. For evidence of Mr. Barrie's dramatic instinct one need only mention two scenes of pantomime: that wherein the party who have revolted from Crichton's leadership slink back silent and subdued, drawn by the sheer force of hunger to the stew he is preparing, and that of the sudden arrest of the dance at the booming of the ship's gun. In each of these scenes not a word was uttered; it was the action that "spoke volumes." A slighter effort of Mr. Barrie's, *Quality Street*, had the delicate fragrance of Jane Austen, whose period it recalled. Even slighter was *Little Mary*, a prank rather than a play, flimsy in texture, with something of the facile cleverness of an improvisation, but redeemed by the humour of its episodic scenes and by a character of exquisite pathos —one of those tender little maidens with a gift for "mothering" whom Mr. Barrie has more than once portrayed.

What is the quintessence of Mr. Barrie's charm? Kindliness, perhaps; a pervading, but never cloying, sweetness of nature. With this supreme quality goes an unfailing freshness of observation. For Mr. Barrie is a close and patient observer. Thus he is perpetually annexing new corners of life for stage use, tapping new sources of theatrical supply. This faculty of minute and accurate observation is as rare as it is valuable. It is, so far as one can tell, almost entirely lacking in Mr. Bernard Shaw, and there perhaps is the ultimate reason why this original thinker and brilliant writer stops just a little short of complete success in his stage work. One has to put it conjecturally, for Mr. Shaw's case is a little puzzling. You recognise, with the joy of a collector in a new curio, the unique personality revealed in his plays. They delight most of us, with reservations, when acted, and without reservation when read. You revel in their waywardness, their unexpectedness, their audacious self-confidence, not to say self-worship. They wake up a somnolent world and set it furiously thinking. It is possible to hold that he not seldom talks nonsense and at the same time to have a sneaking affection for his nonsense as more

diverting and stimulating than other men's sense. But
I am dealing here with the art of drama and the
effective forces of the stage, and the fact is not to be
ignored that, with all one's delight over Mr. Shaw's
plays, there remains in the mind a vague sense of balked
expectation, a feeling that there is a screw loose
somewhere.

In the familiar phrase, the plays do not exactly
"come off." Is the real secret of this what I have
suggested—Mr. Shaw's lack of observation ? Close
observers of human nature are so because they love it,
because they are keenly interested in what men and
women are like. The facts of life fascinate them as
facts—"theirs not to reason why." Evidently that is
not Mr. Shaw's nature. He takes little, if any, pleasure
in the mere contemplation of the *comédie humaine* and
the registration of its minute peculiarities. His pleasure
only begins with the reasoning why. He recalls a
certain brilliant talker, described by R. L. Stevenson,
who was perpetually interrupting his interlocutor with
"Wait a moment, I should have a theory for that."
The only difference is that Mr. Shaw never needs this
moment's grace ; his theory arrives with the fact, and
sometimes precedes it. The ordinary everyday surface
of the universe is to him only a spring-board from
which he jumps into the space of ratiocination—his own
peculiar space, a space of four dimensions. This is not
the frame of mind for seeing facts clearly and reporting
them faithfully. Whatever other qualities a dramatist
may require, he must have something in him of the
painter, must desire to reproduce what he sees, just as
it is, merely because it is a pleasure to him to see it as
it is. But Mr. Shaw is never in love with the thing as
it is ; he is in love with his own thoughts about it.

How, for that matter, can he love the thing when his
thoughts have a perpetual tendency to tell him that it
is a wrong thing?   Most of the facts of human nature
seem to Mr. Shaw to be egregious blunders.   Our
ideals are wrong, our conduct is irrational, we "found
our institutions on the ideals suggested to our imagination by our half-satisfied passions," instead of on a
genuinely scientific natural history.   The right theory
of life and conduct, which its author is fond of calling
Shawism or the "Shavian philosophy," is revealed to
us in Mr. Shaw's plays.   Apparently this philosophy,
though it is not without its obligations to Schopenhauer
and Ibsen and Nietzsche, is mainly of Mr. Shaw's own
invention.   But one need not discuss it here, for it does
not affect the question of Mr. Shaw's dramaturgic
quality.   Before one can consider its philosophic
content, a play must give the illusion of life, and
to put it most favourably, in Mr. Shaw's plays that
illusion is intermittent.   If, for example, you take
Candida, one of the best of Mr. Shaw's plays, written
a few years ago, but only recently performed in
London, you get the illusion of life from some of the
characters and some parts of the action, but not from
all the characters or from the action as a whole.   The
young wife of a hard-working East End clergyman finds
that her husband's religious activity and zeal for good
works do not help her to live her own life.   (Every
young wife who has seen Nora in *A Doll's House*
must now live her own life.)   A boyish poet woos her,
offers her the large and liberal life of romance, all
rhapsody and colour—a love, in short, that shall be
richer than her present mere sentimentalisation of conjugal duty.   In the end Candida decides in favour of
the prosaic life, and remains with her husband.   She

arrives at this conclusion by a strict process of ratiocination, summoning parson and poet to her presence, weighing their respective claims upon her affections, and finally opting for the parson, not because he is her husband, but because he needs her most.   Of these three characters, Candida is real—the sensible, helpful " managing " woman that everybody knows—and so is the parson ; but the poet seems a mere patchwork from biographies of Shelley, a walking symbol of the poetic temperament.   The glaring unreality, however, of the play is its *dénouement*, with its preposterous assumption that such a choice as Candida's is to be made by reason instead of by feeling. In real life the sole question (our conventional morality as to the obligation of marriage vows being *ex hypothesi* ruled out) would be, Which of the two men does the woman love?   Passion, not ratiocination, would decide it.   But Mr. Shaw seems wholly incapable of representing passion.   He thinks the world and the stage make too much of it already ; he reproves it severely in more than one of his prefaces.   In that case, he ought to avoid dramatic situations which are essentially situations of passion ; to drain them of their passion and then fill them with the workings of the pure intellect deprives them of all resemblance to life. The fact is, a writer who represents men and women carrying on their lives by the light of reason is offering us a world as fantastic as anything imagined by Swift or M. Jules Verne or Mr. H. G. Wells.   A " scientific natural history " that leaves out of account our subconscious states, our animal appetites, the unchastened will-to-live, all the blind forces of which human action is the resultant, strikes one as a fearful kind of wild-fowl.   Of the existence and potency

of these brute natural forces Mr. Shaw must of course
be as well aware as anyone else; only they do not
happen to fit in with his dramatic method. He has
tried to represent one of them in his *Man and Superman*, and has signally failed. This work is Mr.
Shaw's response to a casual suggestion that he should
write a Don Juan drama. Nowadays, says Mr. Shaw,
the relations of Don Juan and his victims are reversed.
It is woman who pursues, man who is her prey.
Nature, working out her own ends, has contrived (it is
the familiar theory of Schopenhauer) that man, with all
his boasted superiority, shall be the helpless fly caught
in the web of the spider—woman. And lo! in illustrating this theory Mr. Shaw gives us a heroine who has
not a particle of womanly attraction. It is true that
her weak victim is constantly declaring himself subjugated, constantly crying out in affright that he is
caught in the toils; but we feel all the time that he
only does so because Mr. Shaw's thesis requires it. To
give dramatie existence and force to the typical woman
of Mr. Shaw's case you must be able to paint passion,
the obscurer instincts and emotions of sex, and that is
just what Mr. Shaw always fails to do. Of course, the
play is full of good things—Mr. Shaw could not be
dull if he tried—though its very best thing, an ironic
dialogue in Hades presenting a new analysis of Old
Nick, can hardly be said to belong to the play, but to
be tacked on to it from outside.

When all is said, however, it remains true that for
sheer energy and fineness of brain, as well as for
pioneering quality—the spirit which attacks fresh
problems and carries the drama into unexplored regions
—we have no one on the English stage comparable
to Mr. Shaw. Our drama needs pioneers even more

than expert dramatists. And it is for that reason that we all ought to welcome such experiments as Mrs. Alfred Lyttelton's *Warp and Woof*, which was doubtless weak from the point of view of technical skill, but which did attempt to deal with an actual question of social economics. How far Mrs. Lyttelton's picture *à la* Brieux of overworked sempstresses, rapacious and bullying employers, hoodwinked factory inspectors, and selfish lady customers was justified by the facts, is a debatable point. The play may not have been a first-rate example of its species, but it is something to have a play of this species written at all. The smallest contribution to our existing stock of dramatic themes should be thankfully received.

Meanwhile the great theme of drama is still the duel of sex. Our dramatists cannot keep their hands off that, though they know well enough, in face of average English feeling on the subject, the risk they run of burning their fingers. It is not only that many people object to the way in which the drama discusses questions of " free " love, seduction, adultery, and divorce ; they would like the drama, if that were possible, to ignore such subjects altogether. There is the Puritan strain in us to be reckoned with. There are still numerous classes of Englishmen for whom the theatre is a place of perdition. Writing in his diary on his twenty-third birthday Mr. Gladstone classed the theatre with the racecourse as sinful; he subsequently changed his opinion, but the entry is significant, representing as it does the extreme view held by many of Mr. Gladstone's countrymen to-day. Even among playgoers there is often to be found a prejudice against the treatment of sexual questions in the theatre. They are held to be too serious for consideration in a place which, whatever else it may be, is essentially a place of amusement. It would be only natural if this disposition in the public were to intimidate our dramatists, were to tempt them to tamper with their artistic conscience by Bowdlerizing life instead of unflinchingly representing things as they are.

We all know that this is what occurs when the more frivolous French pieces are adapted into English: lovers become lawful husbands, and guilty intrigues are softened into foolish flirtations; in brief, to put it figuratively, trousers are fitted to the legs of the piano. Such plays are mere merchandise and must be accommodated to their market. But with plays having serious pretensions to art the case is very different. No doubt their atmosphere or their incidents may legitimately be modified to suit the public taste or even an individual caprice. We now know that Victor Hugo's *Marion de Lorme* was originally a mere piece of historical description, and only became a thesis-play, demonstrating the possible regeneration of a courtesan, by reason of a change of *dénouement*, demanded by an actress two years after the completion of the play in its first form. M. Hervieu's *L'Énigme*, played in London as *Cæsar's Wife*, was originally intended to maintain the doubt as to the identity of the guilty woman up to the fall of the curtain; the author was induced to resolve the doubt by representations that the public would be irritated by being left in the dark. In deference to the popular demand for happy endings, Mr. Pinero radically altered the conclusion of *The Profligate*. But what it is certainly not legitimate for a serious dramatist to accommodate to any demand save his own is his moral attitude, the lesson and "message" of his play. For his artistic integrity is involved in that; it is his criticism of life, part and parcel of the man himself. The proper name for compromise in this quarter is hypocrisy.

Now it would be quite unjustifiable to suggest that Mr. Pinero descends to any such compromise as this. I do not, of course, know the workings of his mind, and have no ground for supposing that his plays do not represent his genuine convictions. One is bound to credit him with absolute sincerity. Unhappily, this means that one is also bound to credit him with a certain Philistinism of thought, a certain complacency of agreement with conventional British ideals. One is bound to credit him, for instance, with a real belief in the "whitewashing" process under clerical supervision with which he concludes the adventures of Agnes Ebbsmith and of the woman in *The Benefit of the Doubt*. One is bound to credit him with the assumption that the best way of demonstrating the virtue of humdrum domesticity and the viciousness of romantic amours is to write a play like *Letty*. A shop-girl hesitates between two courses: lawful marriage with an intolerable rowdy of her own social rank and "guilty splendour" with a fine gentleman who loves her. The odious vulgarity of the would-be husband nearly drives her into the arms of the would-be seducer, and she is only saved by an accident. In the end she chooses neither of these men, but a commonplace little photographer, with whom she settles down in smug suburban respectability, while the aristocratic Don Juan is condemned to die of consumption. It is, to be sure, a conclusion of unexceptionable morality, but was it worth while writing such a play for that particular thesis? It is

the thesis, you may say, of *Madame Bovary*, and
with Emma Bovary it was not virtue but vice that
triumphed; yet Flaubert contrived to be far more
"moral" with his tragic catastrophe than Mr. Pinero
with his lawfully begotten baby in the photographer's
parlour.   You are sure that Mr. Pinero feels convinced
of the propriety of Letty's choice; but it is unfortunate
that he contrives so to present it as to leave you
with a dominant impression of its tame and slightly
ludicrous commonplace.   You admire his dramaturgic
skill.   The scene of the "bounder's" supper party, the
scene of the frustrated seduction, were little master-
pieces.   But even on the technical side you are not
wholly satisfied.   Mr. Pinero writes badly, for he
makes his characters "talk like a book."   That is to
say, he does not seem to grasp the difference between
language intended to be read and language intended to
be spoken.   In the printed page all language has to be
raised to a higher pitch than natural talk, for it has to
do without the life and colour imparted to it by the
human voice and personality.   But on the stage the
human voice and personality are restored to it, so that
"book" language in a play at once offends the ear; it
is pitched too high.   This fault seems to have grown
on Mr. Pinero; both Letty and her Don Juan indulge
in a remarkably pompous lingo.

As for Mr. Jones, he has once more been playing
round the precincts of the Divorce Court.   But, as
usual, he manages to keep his characters out of the
box.   In *Joseph Entangled*, as in several other plays
of his, we have the couple who *almost* elope, the home
which is *almost* broken up, so that morality is technically safeguarded.   Only technically, however, for we
have the same fun as though it had been infringed,

the joy of the illicit, the winks and nods and allusions. Joseph is entangled, through a piece of sheer stupidity, with a married lady; and all their friends believe it to be an "entanglement" in the baser sense of the word. The innocent pair cannot convince the world of their innocence. Nobody believes in the lady's virtue, least of all her own husband. Ultimately her character is cleared by the ancient device of eaves-dropping behind a curtain. It was on the whole an amusing comedy, of the same class as *The Liars*, if an inferior specimen of that class: cynical, worldly, leaving a slightly bitter taste in the mouth—but amusing. If we cannot have the theatre of ideas, we must put up with the theatre of amusement. Fortunate Parisians, who have both!

October 1904.

THE MODERNITY OF THE *POETICS*

I T is long since the learned world abandoned the
habit of darkening counsel by citations from the
"master of them that know." When L'Intimé in
Les Plaideurs appealed to the authority of Aristotle
in a case of fowl-stealing he was answered by
Dandin :—

> "Avocat, il s'agit d'un chapon
> Et non point d'Aristote et de sa 'Politique,'"

and that reply is nowadays held conclusive of the
matter. Yet there are some few people who think
that the reaction, as is usual with reactions, has gone
too far ; and to these at any rate it will be a pleasure
to find a writer so vigorous and (in the best sense) so
mundane as Mr. Herbert Paul saying a good word
for Aristotle. Mr. Paul, discoursing of *Art and
Eccentricity*,[1] declares that in many questions of modern
criticism "il s'agit" still of Aristotle—not, indeed, of
his *Politics* (though there are many neat "tips" even
about literary criticism in that discursive work), but of
his *Poetics*. It is with the proposition concerning the
function of the poet—"not to tell us what actually
happened, but what might happen, and what is possible
according to likelihood and necessity"—that Mr. Paul
chiefly deals, and he has some excellent remarks to
make about the difference between scientific and

[1] *Men and Letters* (1903).

artistic truth, verity in life and verisimilitude in fiction. It is true that Aristotle, after being smothered in compliments, is in the end used as stick to beat a dog with—Ibsen and Zola and the *Barrack Room Ballads* and *Mrs. Warren's Profession* and *Sir Richard Calmady* and the Lord Chancellor and every other object of Mr. Paul's dislike which happens to come handy. For he has his prejudices, and sometimes they lead him a pretty dance—as, for example, when he criticises Ibsen's *Ghosts*. " In *Ghosts*, if I remember rightly, a mother makes her son drunk on the stage. That mothers have made their sons drunk cannot, I suppose, be denied. Everything not physically impossible must have happened before now in this most miscellaneous of all possible worlds. But the object of art is not to represent what has happened. It is to represent what may happen in accordance with the law of likelihood or necessity." Admirably put—only the unfortunate thing is that Mr. Paul's memory has deceived him, so that it really is a case for answering that " il s'agit d'un chapon " and not of Aristotle and his τὰ δυνατὰ κατὰ τὸ εἰκὸς ἤ τὸ ἀναγκαῖον. For Mrs. Alving in Ibsen's play does not made Oswald drunk. Indeed, it is difficult to see how a bottle of champagne between three could make any of the party drunk— especially as the drinking even of that "modest quencher" is cut short by an outbreak of fire. Let Mr. Paul stick to Aristotle by all means; but he would do better to leave Ibsen alone.

Nor is this the only case in which he is more successful in expounding an Aristotelian proposition than in applying it. Adverting to Lamb's defence of the Reformation dramatists against Macaulay " on the ground that the life of the stage was a totally different

thing from the life of the world," he says that Lamb
was right, because "a play is not a series of interviews "
—*i.e.* not a record of what has actually happened, but
a picture of what might happen according to likelihood and necessity.   But that, surely, was precisely
Macaulay's point.   He never contended that *The Way
of the World* or *The Country Wife* was a transcript of
actual fact, but that they were both pictures of fact
only too possible and "inevitable" in the eyes of the
man in the pit.   It was because they fulfilled the
Aristotelian law that they were morally dangerous.
Lamb's defence was tantamount to saying that they
broke the Aristotelian law by being semi-fantastic.
Common sense, I think, is still on the side of Macaulay
in that little controversy.   Again, Mr. Paul dislikes
realism in fiction, and says: "The whole of the
realistic school flies in the face of Aristotle's maxim.
It is enough for them that a thing has happened.
Mean, ugly, disgusting, or rare, it becomes thereupon
a legitimate element in fiction."   This is an amazing
account of what is meant by realism in art.   What
realist can Mr. Paul name who has based the introduction of some abnormal event into fiction on the
ground that it was taken from actual life?   The
novelist who will come most readily to most people's
minds for his trick of "lifting" odd events and
characters from life into fiction is the novelist who
described death by spontaneous combustion, the
Dustman's millions and Boythorn's eccentricities; and
Dickens was the very opposite of a realist.   One had
thought that realism meant a stricter observation of
life, the vindication of natural law in the artistic
world, care that the villain who has swallowed arsenic
shall not forthwith die (as he generally does in the

popular melodramas) with every symptom of strychnine-poisoning—in short an exceptional solicitude for that very εἰκὸς and that very ἀναγκαῖον of Aristotle which Mr. Paul flings at the realists' heads.   The poor belaboured realists may be tempted to say that Mr. Paul, quoting their own pet passage of Aristotle against them, is almost as hard to bear as the devil quoting Scripture to his purpose.

Mr. Paul is better at political gibes.   Remarking with justice on the obscurity of Aristotle's statement that what is probable but impossible should by the poet be preferred to what is possible but will not be believed, he makes a sly hit.   " The latter class," he says, " is intelligible enough.   It is possible for the Archbishop of Canterbury to forge a cheque in payment of his debts at cards, or for the Lord Chancellor to treat all his friends unkindly when he has patronage to distribute, and yet nobody would treat these incidents as credible if they were incorporated in a work of fiction.   But how can what is impossible be probable ? " Well, one very good " shot " at an answer to this question was made a hundred years ago by that comfortable parson and delightful letter-writer the Rev. Thomas Twining, whose notes to the *Poetics* (impious though it be to say it) strike me as sometimes better worth reading than the text itself.   " Such a being as Caliban, for example," says Twining, " is impossible.   Yet Shakespeare has made the character appear probable, not certainly to reason, but to imagination.   Is not the Lovelace of Richardson, in this view, more out of nature, more improbable than the Caliban of Shakespeare ?   The latter is at least consistent.   I can imagine such a monster as Caliban ; I never could imagine such a man as Lovelace."   In

6

other words Aristotle is justifying romance. The artist
in fiction is entitled to his own standpoint—which he
may fix at whatever degree of distance from actual life
he chooses. But having once chosen his plane he
must keep in that plane, and must observe the law of
probability whether he be working in the plane of
" impossibility " or of reality. Aristotle's expression,
by the way—ἀδύνατα εἰκότα—is not exactly as Mr.
Paul puts it, but " probable impossibilities." This
would apply, for instance, to most of the fun of Mr.
Gilbert's Savoy *libretti*. It was impossible for the
Duke oi Plaza-Toro in *The Gondoliers* to run himself
as a syndicate, but the idea is in the Aristotelian sense
probable, or, as we should now say, plausible. So it is
with Swift's Liliputians and Brobdingnagians, or the
people in *Erewhon*, or those in the astronomical
romances of Mr. H. G. Wells. If once their initial
impossibility is waived they act " probably " according
to the law of their assumed being. They are
ἀδύνατα εἰκότα. And Aristotle's point is that they
are preferable in fiction to the δυνατὰ ἀπίθανα,
the incredible possibilities—*e.g.* Mr. Hall Caine's
Romans or the Englishwomen of Miss Marie
Corelli.

Nothing is easier than to give, in this way, modern
applications of Aristotelian laws. At the same time,
when Mr. Paul says that the *Poetics* are " intensely
modern," he is, one cannot help thinking, the victim of
a fallacy. What is meant by saying that an ancient
author is " modern " ? Surely, that the whirligig of
time has brought in his revenges, that the author's turn
has come round again, through some quality of his
mind or temper which makes him peculiarly at home
in our own day. Thus Montaigne may fairly be

called "modern" in this age of "introspection" and Bashkirtseffism. In the same way some of the little intimate passages in Euripides seem strangely "modern" in this age of "naturalistic" literature. But in no such sense can the word "modern" be applied to Aristotle. It is true that many of his critical propositions are as valid and fresh to-day as they ever were, but they are not more valid to-day than they were in the days of Elizabeth or than they were in the days of Le Roi Soleil. They have never ceased to be valid, because they are inherent in the nature of things; it is a case of the eternal verities, not the case of Sir Roger de Coverley's coat which had been in and out of the fashion forty times. Euclid is true to-day, but he is not accurately to be described as "intensely modern." And as a matter of fact what strikes the modern reader of the *Poetics* is not their modernity, as a whole, but their antiquity. Much of the work, and that the part by which perhaps Aristotle set most store, is as dead as Poor Fred in the epitaph. If the exaggerated importance which Aristotle ascribed to plot is not quite dead, it is assuredly moribund, while his rules about the choice of heroes and of catastrophes are so obsolete as to be almost unintelligible to the modern reader. Why must the hero of a tragedy be neither very good nor very bad? Why must his fate be determined by error and not by wickedness? Why ought the culminating fatality of a tragedy to be the work of ignorance and its true nature to be only discovered afterwards? The answers to these questions, of course, are known so soon as the reader has become aware of the "moralistic" trend in Greek criticism, of the difficulty which even the "master of them that know" had in completely differentiating art from

actual life.   It is this vein running through the *Poetics*
that reduces it so often to a merely "documentary"
value.   Part of the work, then, must be called dead;
you may call the rest of it immortal if you will, but it
is an abuse of language to call it modern.

PROCESSES OF THOUGHT IN PLAYMAKING

IN reviewing the *Life of George Eliot* at the time of publication, Mr. John Morley recalled a discussion in which the novelist took part one day at the Priory in 1877. She spoke of the different methods of imaginative art, saying that she began with moods, thoughts, passions, and then invented the story for their sake, and fitted it to them; whereas Shakespeare picked up a story that struck him, and then proceeded to work in the moods, thoughts, passions as they came to him in the course of meditation on the story. "We hardly need the result," says Mr. Morley, "to convince us that Shakespeare chose the better part." This comment begs a vexed and still obscure question. Shakespeare no doubt chose the better part—for Shakespeare. But it is conceivable also that George Eliot chose the better part for George Eliot. In any case, is it quite correct to say that an author "chooses" his method of invention? Are the first beginnings of imaginative conception directed by the will? Are they, indeed, conscious at all? Do they not rather emerge unbidden from the vague limbo of subconsciousness? Shakespeare picked up a story that struck him; yes, but why did that story strike him at that moment? Because it fell in with some precedent train of thought, harmonised with some pre-existing mood. Even if we accept the theory of "choice," there may be another explanation for Shakespeare's plan of "picking up" a story. For all we know to the contrary, he may have had a theme for a play in his head and then ransacked the story-books for a narrative to illustrate the theme. For instance, he may quite possibly have been turning over in his mind the dramatic possibilities of a crime perpetrated by a weak man at the instigation of a wife of sterner mould. Then he happens to turn up Holinshed, and says, "Why, here is the very thing I wanted for my play!" Nothing, I fancy, is more difficult than to trace with certainty the genesis of a work of art.

To-day we know what elusive things mental processes are. But two thousand years ago, when a scientific psychology was neither born nor thought of, people were more cocksure; and accordingly you find a very eminent philosopher and critic, whom *Punch* has described as the author of a clever brochure on Dramatic Principles, laying down the law even more positively than Mr. Morley as to what is "the better part" in imaginative composition. For Aristotle was not content with declaring plot to be the principal element of tragedy; he went on to assume that it must be the first in order of invention. In fact, he made this assumption the basis of a series of recipes, set forth in the cut-and-dried manner of a cookery-book. You might either take your story ready-made or construct it for yourself; but in any case you should first sketch its general outline, and then fill in your episodes and amplify in detail. Your plot must be of this or that kind. Your episodes must be so and so. Then followed some items of purely technical instruction. You should *visualise* your action—that is to say, get a mental picture of what we should now call the *mise-en-scène*, so as to avoid material absurdities or impossibilities. Further, you should, while composing, use gestures appropriate to your several characters. This would help you to feel what they ought to be feeling. And so on, and so on. These precepts would not have satisfied Mr. Crummles. For they were tantamount to saying that young Nickleby ought not to write a play round a real pump. If real pumps and the like were the only things round which it is possible to write plays, there would be no occasion for qualms about this passage in the *Poetics*. But plays may also be written round an idea, a " humour," a character ; and very good plays have been so written. Which was conceived first, the plot of *L'Avare* or the character of the protagonist ? Which were conceived first, the characters of Mirabell and Millamant and Lady Wishfort or the story (which is no story) of *The Way of the World* ? I have taken two instances almost at random ; and a moment of reflection over them will suffice to show that Aristotle's generalisation is far too sweeping, and that, while Shakespeare may have been right in his method, George Eliot need not have been wrong in hers.

But there is one class of plays, a peculiarly modern class, about which it is possible to affirm with certainty that the plot does not come first in order of invention—the plays designed to illustrate some idea in the region of morals or society, plays designated specifically " of ideas." It is interesting to see how these plays—so much in dispute just now, so eagerly demanded by some playgoers, so energetically rejected by others—first emerge into the authors' consciousness and gradually take shape there. The worst of it is that the authors themselves can seldom be trusted to tell the truth of the matter. Either they have not the skill—very few people have—to analyse their own mental processes, or they give a fancy sketch in answer to

the misdirected questions of some "interviewer" intent
merely upon a piece of picturesque reporting.   A
really systematic investigation of the subject is rare.
You may, however, find this rare thing in an article
contributed by M. Binet, Director of the Laboratory of
Psychology at the Sorbonne, to Volume X. of *L'Année
Psychologique.*   The article is a detailed study, the outcome of seven conversations, or rather cross-examina-
tions, of two hours each, of the way in which M. Paul
Hervieu thinks out his plays.   M. Hervieu has shown
himself the most able of all French dramatists in the
presentation of general ideas.   He calls himself, in the
course of one of these conversations with M. Binet,
"an organiser of conflicts of ideas, feelings, and
passions."   A writer of thesis (or, in our cant English
phrase, problem) plays he declines to be called.   For,
says he, all plays, save madcap farce, have a signification which it is permissible to call a "thesis," and the
point at which a play of sentimental demonstration or
of social bearings begins to be called a thesis-play has
always seemed to him "as arbitrarily fixed as the
point at which the Boulevard des Capucines becomes the
Boulevard des Italiens."   He admits that all his personages have a common habit of arguing it out (somebody
else has described them as people who are always
standing out for their rights), but he points out that
they all perform actions as well.   Still, he is pre-eminently a logician, and it is interesting to examine the
way in which a mind of that type works for the stage.
The first thing one notices is the comparative neglect
of Aristotle's advice about visualising your play.
Evidently M. Hervieu begins by thinking of ideas, not
of people or of places.   He starts from an abstraction.
He has the same disdain for the mere stage-carpentering

instinct as Dumas *fils*, whose intellectual successor he
is. He sees in imagination only "the big things, the
characteristic attitudes, such as the act of kneeling, or
that of bursting into tears." It is as a writer, he says,
that he approaches the theatre, seeing in it at the outset only "*du papier à noircir*." Of many, perhaps of
most, dramatists the contrary would have to be said.
They approach the theatre, not as writers, but virtually
as actors; they act within themselves the characters
they are inventing. Presumably this was the process
which Aristotle had in view when he advised the
playwright to reproduce the gestures of his characters.
M. Hervieu, it seems, uses no gesture to assist him in
composition save the one of clenching the fists, with
stiffened arms—characteristically enough, a gesture
signifying a general idea, the idea of force. M. Binet
makes an acute remark on the style of dramatists who,
like M. Hervieu, have nothing of the virtual actor in
them. They write, necessarily, without allowing for intonation, so that their phrase, having to be self-sufficient,
to do without this musical aid, is more expressive and
substantial than the phrase of the "actor" authors; on
the other hand, it has the drawback of disdaining the
verbal simplicity of passion. M. Binet has there
touched both the strength and the weakness of M.
Hervieu's style. His phrasing is always compact,
nervous, weighty; but it does, perhaps, occasionally
smell of the lamp.

M. Binet elicits some particulars as to the prime
origin of one or two of M. Hervieu's plays and the
process of their invention which bear upon the general
question. Thus, originally, *La Loi de l'Homme* was
to be a vindication of women's rights, with a woman of
the people, a Louise Michel, for protagonist. When

the piece was accepted for the Théâtre Français, the
social scale of the characters had to be raised, and the
"feminist" questions had to be narrowed down to the
social inferiorities of the married woman. Here, then,
was a case of plot being adapted to ideas, not ideas to
plot. Another play, *La Course du Flambeau*, shows a
plot deliberately constructed round an idea—the idea
that each generation sacrifices itself to its successor—
just as *Le Dédale* has a plot deliberately built round
the idea that a woman, divorced or not, remarried or
not, always feels herself to belong to the man through
whom she first became a mother. On the other hand,
l'Énigme did not originate in any preoccupation over a
moral problem ; there was no deliberate resolution to
treat this or that subject. It was written in the thick
of the Dreyfus scandal, and reflected a mental obsession.
Is this person guilty or not guilty ? That question had
laid hold of M. Hervieu's mind—and the piece is a
"projection" of that mood. In not a single one, then,
of these important plays do you find that process of
beginning with the story, which Mr. Morley calls
choosing the better part. The process is George Eliot's
process. The conclusion seems to be that, despite
Aristotle, despite Mr. Morley, there is no orthodox
method of play invention. It all depends on the kind
of play—and the kind of playwright.

LAWS OF CHANGE

PURISTS may make a wry face over a new name in a Drury Lane programme—"melo-farce"— but students of the drama will be more concerned with the fact that a new name, good or bad, had to be invented. It is by no means an isolated circumstance. Our playbills have for some time shown a tendency to burst the old bonds of nomenclature. One dramatist labels his plays "pleasant" and "unpleasant"; another selects the novel epithet "uncomfortable." The truth is, that the old descriptions of "tragedy," "comedy," and "farce" have long since been found unsuitable; plays have run from one category into the other, or have proved, in the existing conditions of language, wholly nondescript. Criticism—always leaning to the conservative side—has girded at the dramatists, as though they were to blame. Even to-day critics will be found objecting that "the author has called his play a comedy, whereas it is obviously a farce," or that "this so-called tragedy is nothing but a melodrama." Such objections are really uncritical; or, at any rate, they are directed to the wrong address, ignoring as they do the patent fact that the growth of names never keeps pace with the growth of things. It is this disparity which accounts for the barbarous neologisms or downright misnomers which disfigure our theatrical programmes. "The ancients are the ancients," said Molière, "and we are the people of to-day." Polonius's elaborate list of dramatic categories, once exhaustive, is now useless. The terminology of ancient drama will not accurately fit the drama of to-day, and yet there is none other handy; and our more cautious dramatists acknowledge, without meeting, the difficulty when they seek refuge in the vaguely general term " play."

Leaving philologists to squabble about the names, one may, perhaps, more profitably try to discover what one of Ibsen's characters would call "the law of change " in the things themselves. Dangerous though it may be, as a rule, to import the language of one art into the. discussion of another, there can be little harm in finding a vital distinction between the "colour " and the "form " of a play. By the "colour " I mean the particular quality of the appeal which the play makes to the spectator's emotions. A play is grave or gay, realistic or fantastic, "pleasant " or "unpleasant," "comfortable " or "uncomfortable "—that is to say, it aims at exciting a particular quality of mood in us; it solicits our laughter or our tears, addresses itself to our sense of recognition or our sense of wonder, soothes us into acquiescence or stimulates us into opposition. In other words, out of the infinity of moods which make up human life it selects a certain set, and this set I call its colour. The various sets—the various "colour-schemes "—constitute the several categories of drama. If they are simple schemes—to pursue the figure, let us call them monochromatic — they give the old orthodox categories, tragedy, comedy, melodrama, farce. With the complex schemes — polychromatic schemes, we must call them—we get the modern "mixed " sorts of drama, from the "farcical comedy " of a few years ago down to this "melo-farce " of the present day.   Note that it is the colour, not the form, which marks off the category.   The same structural arrangement is common to all classes of play. Whether it be a tragedy or a farce, you must have exposition, " crisis " and " catastrophe."

Why do I insist upon this distinction between colour and form in drama?   For this reason; that the two elements have, if I am not mistaken, widely different " laws of change."   Speaking generally, you may say that, in dramatic colour, the monochromatic tends to disappear in favour of the polychromatic. Pure tragedy, " high " comedy, unadulterated farce are virtually obsolete.   The fact is certain; the explanation is hazardous, and I can only make a shot at it.   Pure tragedy, the exclusive appeal to pity and terror, presupposes a certain intellectual *naïveté*, or even downright ignorance.   Our modern aim is to understand the causes of calamities and to provide against them, not to attribute them to an inscrutable will before which we are to bow down. When once the world has grown out of a belief in " fate " and " oracles " it has grown out of a perfect relish for the *Œdipus Tyrannus*.   Of course, we may make a deliberate effort to throw ourselves back into the old frame of mind; we may still enjoy a *Paolo and Francesca*, but only artificially, as an act of dilettantism.   As to " high " comedy, many attempts have been made to account for its disappearance. Hazlitt thought he had found the reason in the drabness of our modern civilisation; the requisite contrasts of social sets and individuals have been worn away.   Mr. George Meredith went nearer the mark when he found the enemies of high comedy in the sentimentalists; such comedy was essentially

cruel. *Le Monde où l'on s'ennuie* is often cited as a
late species of "high" comedy, but it is largely
sentimental; and even that has had no successor.
For purely sentimental comedy it may be that there
is yet a chance—*Cousin Kate* was an excellent specimen
of the class—but sentimental comedy is a "mixed"
genre, it does not belong to the monochromatic types
which I am here considering. Sheer farce has gone,
or is rapidly going, because it outrages our modern
sense of the realities of life. Whenever a farce is
produced, note with what relief the audience fastens
upon any passing episode of comedy; a total divorce
from life is felt to be intolerable. The polychromatic
drama, then, "holds the field." But here, again, there
is a law of change, a law within a law. The balance
of colours is upset. We are now disposed to laugh
just where our forefathers pulled their longest face.
Richard III. has become a sort of Punchinello, and Sir
Henry Irving played him with a rich vein of humour.
Or from quarters wherein our forefathers found only
"inspissated gloom" we seek to find light and a
touch of the *joie de vivre*. Compare the record
of Betterton's or Garrick's Hamlet with our experience
of the part as played by Mr. Forbes Robertson. Or
else, we find, contrariwise, a grave dignity in what
only struck our forefathers as boisterously comic;
examples, Shylock and Sir Peter Teazle, Tartuffe and
George Dandin. Change is the playgoer's nature;
changed ideas of the ludicrous and the pathetic, and
to some extent a mere love of change for its own sake
—"the swing of the pendulum"—have brought about
a complete revolution in the dramatic colour-scheme.

A very different "law of change," I think, will be
found in dramatic form. While in colour we have

moved from the simple to the complex, not to say chaotic, in form we are tending to revert to severe ＇ simplicity. Your Elizabethan play was encyclopædic, your Restoration comedy was disorderly and shapeless. Where they revelled in a variety of impression, we demand a strict unity. Even the three classic unities may be found satisfied in many a modern play. More often we get our unity in the logical development of a single idea, as in the French *pièces-à-thèse* or in such a play as *The Admirable Crichton*, or else in the reduction of the drama to its critical moment, as in Ibsen's social plays, or again, in the successive exhibition of the several facets of a single character, according to the latest formula illustrated by such pieces as *L'Indiscret* and *Les Affaires sont les Affaires* and, less rigorously, by Mr. Pinero's *Iris*. On the one hand, then, we have an entire rearrangement of the dramatic palette; on the other, a strict attention to dramatic form. It is a piquant combination which promises interesting developments in the near future.

But what about the distant future? Suppose we consider the theatrical prospect of 2270 A.D. In *Sur La Pierre Blanche*, M. Anatole France gives a fancy picture of the world at that date, when Europe will have converted itself into one vast Socialist Federation. The theatre, he conjectures, will then have become almost exclusively musical. "An exact knowledge of reality" and "a life without violence" will have made the human race almost indifferent to drama and tragedy, while the unification of classes and sex-equality will have deprived comedy of nearly all its subject-matter. Thus M. France arrives (though by another route) at Walter Pater's conclusion, that "all art aspires towards a condition of music." I do not know whether Mr. H. G. Wells's scientific forecasts of the future have ever dealt with the theatre. If not, one may venture to suggest the subject to him. Meanwhile let us look at M. France's conjectures. Fanciful though they may seem in a world where licensed playhouses are almost as numerous as taverns and pictorial postcard shops, I believe there is a good deal to be said for them.

We may, to begin with, reckon confidently on the disappearance of tragedy. Tragedy was the art of primitive man, reflecting his ferocity, his preoccupation with physical suffering (gouged eyes, flayed skins, mutilated limbs, " Luke's iron crown and Damiens' bed of steel "), his exaggerated interest in death, his terror of the unknown and the unseen. It is true that Aristotle invented the delightful apology of tragedy as a cathartic; but we think Rousseau was nearer the mark when he said people liked it as a means of seeing others suffer without suffering themselves. We do not easily endure tragedy to-day. It survives only in a few classic examples, and even in these the tragic sting has to be taken out. Sir Henry Irving, as I have said, had to drop all the fee-faw-fum business of Richard Crookback, and to present him as a humorist. Mr. Forbes Robertson has been the most acceptible Hamlet of our time, because he insisted on the sunny side of the man, and generally gave Elsinore a thorough " airing." Evidently, tragedy will be the first of the dramatic categories to go by the board. Comedy will follow — at any rate, the comedy of manners and the comedy of intrigue, every form of comedy which assumes social differences. I fancy there is still a long innings before the comedy of character, because this kind depends upon individual

differences, and the Socialist Confederation of 2270
A.D. will scarcely have abolished those. Besides, the
craving of the actors for "character parts" is to all
appearances quite ineradicable. Then drama, drama
proper, according to M. France, will vanish with the
popularisation of an "exact knowledge of reality."
Who can doubt it? Drama postulates the conflict
of individual wills, sudden crises, arbitrary wants.
But "drum and trumpet" history is an anachronism,
the "great man theory" obsolete, and we read history
as a record of gradual economic changes, the resultant
of social forces—that is to say, we read it panoramic-
ally, not dramatically. "Streams of tendency" are
too big for the playhouse. Statistical tables, curves
of imports and exports, the rate of wages, and
the price of the quartern loaf, are too dull for it.
If we had all read Arthur Young and Taine, we
should be unable to sit out the average French
Revolution play—all guillotines, tumbrils, and Sea-
Green Incorruptibles — with patience. Then the
psychology of the stage is too summary. Think
of what the novel can do in this direction — Mr.
Henry James's *Golden Bowl*, for instance. Only the
merest fraction of the reality in that book could be
conveyed through the medium of the theatre.

I will risk a conjecture on my own account about
this spread of "an exact knowledge of reality." It
will abolish the theatre by making *acting* impossible.
We shall reject acting as by its very nature absurd.
For it is in the very nature of acting to present effects
divorced from causes. A young man apes an old one
by painted wrinkles, a grey wig, and an artificial squeak
in his voice. A Londoner who has just dined at his
Club, and come down to the theatre in a hansom,

7

proceeds to harangue the Roman mob over Cæsar's corpse or to fight in full armour with Richmond on Bosworth Field. These imitations of reality pass muster with us, because of our ignorance. But an "exact knowledge of reality" would reveal to us a thousand little touches of age which the young actor has missed, and must miss, because he is not really aged. It would convince us that such a "cause" as a Londoner of to-day, with his individuality and environment and life, cannot by any possibility produce such an "effect" as a Mark Antony or a Richard. Nietzsche has drawn attention to this impossibility in his own blunt fashion. "It is the blissful illusion of actors," says he, "that the historical persons represented by them really have felt as they do during their performance; but in this they are greatly mistaken. Their power of imitation and divination, which they are desirous of representing as a clear-sighted faculty, only penetrates far enough to explain gestures, accents, and looks— in short, the exterior; that is, they grasp the phantom soul of a great hero, statesman, warrior, of an ambitious, jealous, desperate person : they come pretty near the soul, but fail to arrive at the spirit." This "pretty near," which satisfies us to-day in our ignorance, will by and by repel us in our completer knowledge. It is the little rift within the lute. In fact, to the eye of omniscience (the eye we are attributing to 2270 A.D.) there will be no such thing as successful imitation, because nothing ever really duplicates another thing in the universe. Everything stands alone, a point to which myriads of different forces, acting through all conceivable time, have at that moment converged. But in another aspect everything in the universe is in causal relationship with everything else; so that, as a sage has observed, "If we knew one thing thoroughly, we should know everything." Thus, with an exact knowledge of reality made universal, the subtlest conceivable acting would be but a flagrant imposture. Even as it is, though none of us has the exact knowledge, there lurks in our subconsciousness enough feeling for the essential truth and harmony of things to give us discomfort in the presence of so-called " Protean " acting, the twisting of one personality into the form of another by a *tour de force*. It is significant that we hear less and less of the old complaint that such and such an actor "always plays himself." In reality, it is the best thing he can do. ˅ He offends less, in that way, against the inexorable laws of nature. He gives us a greater proportion of effects undivorced from causes, he is less out of harmony with the essential truth of things. Consequently, he is the one actor who will outlive the rest—until his fatal hour comes, *circa* 2270 A.D.

THE ART OF ACTING

IT is unfortunate, but not surprising, that actors can seldom be got to let us into the secrets of their art. It is not surprising, because acting, which is the art of impersonating other people, is the very opposite of introspective analysis, which is the art of first knowing and then scientifically measuring your own inmost self. The most illuminating things about acting have been said by mere literary critics like Diderot (*Paradoxe sur le Comédien*), who never acted, or like G. H. Lewes (*Actors and Acting*), who did once try to act and succeeded in being perhaps the very worst Shylock ever seen. In a popular magazine, an actor, Mr. Tree, has been discoursing on " How to Act." His remarks are desultory rather than systematic—system, perhaps, ought not to be required from a text that, for all one knows, may have been primarily designed as a suitable margin for photographs—but they are in any case remarks worth examining.

What, according to Mr. Tree, is the proper equipment for an actor? First of all, and this seems matter of course, he must have the impulse to act, the mimetic temperament. Mr. Tree does not analyse this temperament, and there was no need, for we all know it, and indeed all, at some moment or other of our lives, if only for that moment, share it. It belongs, however, peculiarly and especially, to the man whose bent is towards thinking of himself as being looked at and listened to by his fellows. The born actor is the very opposite of the recluse, the sufferer from agora-phobia. The very idea of him involves the idea of spectators and listeners; like the orator and the dandy, he is of those who, in Buffon's phrase, "parlent au corps par le corps." You cannot imagine Crusoe acting on his island. It was not until Friday appeared, and fell to conveying his feelings in dumb-show, that acting began. Evidently, again, the histrionic temper-ament must be one peculiarly susceptible to external appearances. An actor must be impressed by the outward and visible signs of things rather than by the things themselves. Here, perhaps, is a reason why acting comes more naturally to women than to men. Is education, as generally understood, good for the actor? Mr. Tree thinks not. For education, as generally understood, means a thorough knowledge of a few subjects; whereas what the actor requires is a little of everything, a little music, a little French, German, and Italian. "The little knowledge which is supposed to be dangerous in most walks of life is the *desideratum* of the stage artist." Education, as generally understood, also tends to the repression of emotion, while the actor lives and moves and has his being in its expression. Further, education, as generally understood, involves continuous and hard reading, but the actor, according to Mr. Tree, can easily have too much reading. It is, he thinks, destructive of the imaginative faculty. This, you remember, was the opinion of Lord Foppington, who preferred the natural sprouts of his own brain to the forced products of other men's. Anyhow, it is pretty clear that Mr. Tree is here preaching to the converted. A man

with a turn for reading is by nature a "solitary,"
which, as we have just seen, the born actor is not.
No more, for that matter, is the born playgoer. Your
typical playgoer is not a cloistered student. He
belongs *ex hypothesi* to the class which is "fond of
company"; he would not, even if he could, imitate
Macaulay by reading Plato with his feet on the
fender; he must have bustle, the sense of human
kinship brought home to him by sitting elbow to
elbow with his neighbour; he desires to see and be
seen. (Parenthetically, I may suggest that this is
why dramatic criticism finds its real public of readers
among neither players nor playgoers, but the people
who, in Pascal's phrase, "sit still in their parlours.")
Further, Mr. Tree does not regard a University education as advantageous to the actor; it represses originality and is ill-calculated to open up the artistic mind.
This is rather a backhander for the Benson company and many ornaments of the O.U.D.S. now
decorating the London stage. Finally, while insisting
on the value of technical training (is there not an
Academy of Dramatic Art somewhere in Gower
Street?), Mr. Tree counsels the actor to follow his
temperament and to rely upon it.

This question of temperament is interesting enough
to warrant closer examination. Every stage character
consists of two parts, one determinate (call it a),
indicated by the text, the stage directions, and *nothing
else*, the other (x), vague and varying, representing
the rest of the character, as it is behind the scenes
and was before the curtain went up. The reader of
the play forms a mental image of x by deductions
from a, and so gets his conception of the whole
character $a + x$. I may say, in passing, that the

vice of academic criticism of Shakespeare in this country, as in Germany, is to discuss $a + x$ as an actual person, forgetting or ignoring that a is the only part of the character for which we have the poet's warranty, and that x is merely our own surmise. But that is "another story." The point here is that, while we all have to give a value to x, we none of us give the same value, since no two imaginations coincide. That is why the student of Shakespeare is always disconcerted when first he sees a favourite play either illustrated in a picture or performed on the stage. This, he says, is all very well, but it is not *my* Romeo or *my* Cordelia. Now the actor's business with a is comparatively simple. He has to speak the words and do the things set down for him. It is with x that his real difficulties begin; for in place of our vague, floating notion of the character as a whole he has to offer us his own real person and temperament. Here the *acting* side of him is in the long run far less important than what the man naturally *is*. For it is, of course, flagrantly untrue, though often· spoken of as true, that an actor can divest himself of his own personality and put on the personality of someone else. Just as an author is always really identical with his work ("for, after all," as Walter Bagehot said, "we know that authors don't keep tame steam-engines to write their books"), so the actor's histrionic is always part and parcel of his real, everyday self. You may so paint wrinkles on your brow, so modulate your voice and order your bearing as to pass, behind the footlights, for a mad old King of Britain, but the fact remains that you are Mr. Brown, a taxpayer of to-day, with an address in the London Postal Directory, and a pretty taste in claret and cigars. This fact will for ever prevent you from absolutely realising x. It may even do so in some obvious physical way ("His weak, white, genteel hands, and the shape of his stomach," said Tolstoy, on his visit to *Siegfried*, "betrayed the actor "). But, even though your disguise be perfect, the fact that the soul within you is not the soul of Lear—or rather, not the soul of Shakespeare as projected in Lear—but the soul of Mr. Brown must for ever mark off a measurable distance between x and your impersonation. The measure of that distance is, inversely, the measure of your success in the part. On the other hand, your reality (the Mr. Brown in you), while it prevents you from fully and satisfactorily representing x— that is to say, coinciding with the spectator's mental image of your part—will give you the great advantage over that vague, pale image of definiteness and substance. What is lost in harmony and perfect propriety of conception is gained in precision and intensity of effect—provided always that your personality is not absolutely at variance with the spectators' conception. You are able to offer him a real man for an imaginary one.

What is the upshot of all this? That your skill as an actor, necessary as it is to get through the plain business of a and to give the spectator that measure of illusion without which play-acting becomes mere meaningless nonsense, is of small account as compared with your real self, your personality, your temperament, call it what you will. Are you what young ladies call a "nice" man? Are you "sympathetic," winning people by the mere manner of you as you enter the stage? Are you "magnetic," endowed with the peculiar property of impressing your fellow-creatures

by mere glance and voice and presence? It is by
such tests as these that ultimately as an actor you
must stand or fall. Salvini, Duse, Bartet, Irving—
take any illustrious stage-names you please, and the
secret of their greatness will be found not in consummate skill—one takes that item for granted—but
in the mystery of temperament.

Mr. Tree's remarks on "How to Act" have a
reverse side. They virtually admit that the actor
is not as other men, and cannot be. Many actors are
peculiarly, and I venture to think rather absurdly,
sensitive on this point. They even go so far as to
contend that the actor's profession does not stamp him.
If that were so he would be the one solitary exception
to the general rule that the dyer's hand is subdued to
what it works in. I have never heard that those
useful domestics whose duties involve constant genu-
flexion object to being warned against "housemaid's
knee," or that "clergyman's sore throat" is a tabooed
topic in country parsonages; but it has often been
made known that you must never talk of "the histrionic
temperament," still less of *cabotinage*. And yet here is
Mr. Tree telling us that the good actor is condemned
to be a smatterer, to read as little as possible, and to
be excluded from a University training. In other
words, the peculiar qualifications for life inside the
playhouse are what are generally held to be disqualifica-
tions for life outside it.

THE DYNASTS AND THE PUPPETS

M R. THOMAS HARDY'S closet - play *The Dynasts*, like Mr. Charles Surface's conduct, has given several worthy readers cause for much uneasiness. A drama of the Napoleonic wars, " in three parts, nineteen acts, and one hundred and thirty scenes," is, indeed, a fearful sort of wild-fowl. Were Mr. Hardy a contemporary of Théophile Gautier and Augustus Mackeat and Philothée O'Neddy, one might surmise that his whim was to *épater le bourgeois*. In any case the burgess has an uncomfortable sense of disorientation. He is uncertain what to make of *The Dynasts*; he is only certain that it is not what he expected. Where is he to place this so-called "drama"? Clearly, it will not go on the same shelf with either *Macbeth* or *Charley's Aunt*. Apparently, Mr. Hardy himself shares the belief of his critics that he has produced something " new and strange." That is a mistake. The author of *The Dynasts* has not invented a new dramatic or *quasi*-dramatic species. But he has certainly developed it, and given it promotion, an improved *status*. Before any attempt to make this good, however, there is something to be said about one or two general questions which Mr. Hardy raises in his preface.

There is, first, the general question of plays which are not intended to be played, but only to be read, plays " for mental performance," as Mr. Hardy puts it.

To those who urge that an unplayable play is a contradiction in terms he replies that "the question seems to be an unimportant matter of terminology." Compositions cast in the dramatic shape, he says, were without doubt originally written for the stage only; "but in the course of time such a shape would reveal itself to be an eminently readable one." Would it? Has it? Surely not. But even if it be conceded that some plays happen to be readable, does that prove that plays ought to be written in order to be read? By no means. Some plays may be read, just as, *faute de mieux*, shoe-leather may be used as an article of diet instead of as a protection for the feet. But, to adapt a familiar line from an Oxford Prize Poem,

> It *may* be eaten, but it is not good.

No, with all respect to Mr. Hardy, the question is much more than an unimportant matter of terminology. It is a question of the relation of means to ends. Just as a play may be readable, so an opera score may be playable in a pianoforte arrangement. Mr. Hardy would call it an opera wherein everything that the piano cannot render is left for mental performance. Most people call it an abuse of the opera, which is intended for the stage, and an abuse of the piano, which is intended for pianoforte music. Surely it is a commonplace that every art-form is conditioned by its medium? The shape, the structure, the points of inflection, the perspective of a play are all determined by the mechanical necessities of the theatre and the fact that it is something to be seen and heard by a spectator. A book, which is something to be read, has no such restrictions; it has others, but not these. If you impose upon a book the form of a play—a form,

that is to say, designed to meet exigencies which in its
case do not exist—you are misapplying or wasting the
means at your disposal; you are running a sack-race;
you are playing fives, like Cavanagh in Hazlitt's essay,
with your clenched fist.   At the best, you have
achieved a *tour de force*.   Let me take an example
from Mr. Hardy's old profession.   It is an elementary
principle in architecture that structure is conditioned
by material.   Stone demands one kind of building,
iron another, wood a third.   Suppose an architect were
laboriously to construct an iron bridge under the
limitations proper to a stone bridge, would Mr. Hardy
applaud the feat?   No, he would say it was bad
architecture.   So one may say when it is attempted
to build a book according to the methods of a play,
or a play according to the methods of a book.   Lessing has something very much to the point (*Hamburg Dramaturgy*, 5th February, 1768): "It is not
enough that a work produces an effect on us"—*e.g.*
that a play is readable—"its effect must also be that
which properly belongs to it. . . . What is the use of
building a theatre, dressing up men and women, putting
their memories to the torture, crowding the whole town
into a hall, if any work when represented is only to
produce some of the effects which might have been
produced by a story read in the chimney-corner?"   So
one may ask, What is the use of enjoying all the
means open to the story-teller if he is to sacrifice most
of those means to the vain hope of rivalling the playwright, who has quite other means?

Nor will it do to rely, as Mr. Hardy does, upon the
imagination of the reader, or "mental" spectator.   "The
spectator, in thought, becomes a performer whenever
called upon, and cheerfully makes himself the utility

man of the gaps." Unfortunately, the "gaps" in a closet-play, being just those parts of a play which cannot be expressed in dialogue, are its vital parts. The great passions are mute. The culminating point of a play is not a speech, but an action, or a picture of which the effect resides in the mere juxtaposition of certain personages. It is at these moments that the closet-playwright suspends—is bound to suspend—work, while the "mental" spectator comes in and takes up the burden. Asking so much of him, Mr. Hardy is rather unkind to call him merely a utility man. The fact that the whole burden of producing "mental drama" is shifted from the author to the reader at the most important moment of the story seems to me a crushing condemnation of the *genre*. Mr. Hardy is quite right in calling it a "mental performance"; but it is the reader who has to bear the brunt of the performing. And so I fully agree with Mr. Hardy when he goes on to say: "Whether mental performance alone may not eventually be the fate of all drama, other than that of contemporary or frivolous life, is a kindred question not without interest." It has, indeed, a fearful interest for those of us who, like the Shah, prefer to have our dancing done for us. As a matter of fact, the spectacular resources of the romantic stage were never so abundant as they are at present; the art of giving an environment of illusion to the archaic, the mystic, the poetic was never before brought to so high a pitch.

There remains the specific question as to the suitability of *The Dynasts* for stage representation. Obviously it is not possible for the ordinary theatre. It "thinks in continents" and deals in whole fleets and armies, Houses of Commons, vast cathedral congrega-

tions, and thronged streets.   That is to say, it is on too
vast a scale for the ordinary stage.   Further, its scheme
includes a " chorus " of spirits, for whom there could be
no appropriate place on any stage.   Are we, then, with
Mr. Hardy, to relegate the play to the region—the No
Man's Land—of " mental performance " ?   Well, one
may suggest that this is not after all inevitable.   Mr.
Hardy himself, it is plain, has hankerings after
actual performance, something " taking the shape of a
monotonic delivery of speeches, with dreamy conventional gestures, something in the manner traditionally
maintained by the old Christmas mummers, the curiously hypnotising impressiveness of whose automatic
style—that of persons who spoke by no will of their
own—will be remembered by all who ever experienced
it.   Gauzes or screens to blur outlines might still
further shut off the actual."   Here Mr. Hardy is
" getting warm," as the children say ; he has come very
near to guessing the way in which his panoramic drama
might be performed.   For performed his play could be,
I feel convinced ; because it really is dramatically
conceived.   I mean that Mr. Hardy—it is the test of
the dramatist—always sees things solid.   Venables said
of Carlyle (Sir M. Grant Duff's *Diary*, March, 1881):
" He had a stereoscopic imagination ; he put everything
before you in a solid shape."   That quality, which is a
luxury in an historian, is a necessity in a dramatist.
You find it in the author of *The Dynasts*; he has a
stereoscopic imagination.   In other words, he allows
himself no passages of analysis, reverie, mere description,
or other expedients of the novelist which are non-
transferable to space of three dimensions.   But, as I
have said, no ordinary theatre has the space for a
panoramic play.   What, then, is the solution ?   To

anyone who has glanced at the play, with a desire to
see it represented, the answer "leaps at the eyes."
Speaking of the human protagonists, one of the Spirits
describes them as "mere marionettes," and again we
read :—

> "Forgetting the Prime Mover of the gear
> As puppet-watchers him who pulls the strings."

Indeed, that idea is at the very core of Mr. Hardy's
drama, the idea that these Napoleons and Pitts and
Nelsons are puppets, blind parts of the Immanent Will.
And now you cannot help seeing how this play should
be represented; it should be a puppet-show—or rather
(for the perspective of vast crowds is best managed that
way) a series of shadow pictures. It would be an
adaptation of the puppet-show to philosophic drama.
That, as I began by saying, is not an entirely new
dramatic species. Some years ago, at the Chat Noir,
this very "Epopée" of the Napoleonic wars was
presented in a series of "Ombres Chinoises" designed
by M. Caran d'Ache. M. Jules Lemaître speaks
enthusiastically of the profound impression created by
these little silhouettes, the sense of multitude, of destiny
actuating the movements of armies, which is precisely
the impression to be created by *The Dynasts*.

Mr. Hardy's philosophic thesis is that the Nietzschean
"overmen" of a century ago were puppets. Why not,
then, actually *show* them as puppets? By that means,
and by that means alone, the actual mechanism of the
performance would be a perpetual symbol and reminder
of the philosophy impressing the whole work. Such a
chance for securing complete harmony between the
medium of expression and the meaning to be expressed
is rare indeed. In his preface Mr. Hardy alludes to
Æschylus. His mention of that mighty dramatist

serves as a reminder that certain plays of M. Maeterlinck have been described as " de l'Eschyle pour *pupazzi malades.*" Withdrawing the epithet " malades," which is inapplicable to Mr. Hardy's robust characters, one may describe *The Dynasts* as " Æschylus for puppets." And to say that is really to pay Mr. Hardy a magnificent compliment.

Like Partridge, many of us " love a puppet-show of all the pastimes upon earth." Happy Partridge ! For it was in his time (according to the puppet-showman) that " the present age was not improved in anything so much as in their puppet-shows ; which, by throwing out Punch and his wife Joan and such idle trumpery, were at last brought to be a rational entertainment." Since that day (whether by the reintroduction of Punch and Judy I know not) the puppet-shows have declined, and the judicious would catch with delight at the chance offered by *The Dynasts* of bringing them " to a rational entertainment " once again. Of course, for your puppet-show " new model," your puppet-show of high philosophic reach, such a showman as Fielding's honest ignoramus would not suffice. That worthy's philosophy, it will be remembered, did not extend beyond a tolerance of all religions, save that of the Presbyterians, " because they were enemies to puppet-shows," and our new showman would have to be a poet (say Mr. Hardy) rolling out his blank verse as he manipulated the wires. Here and there in *The Dynasts* he would have some practical trouble. For example, in Act VI., scene 5, which describes the meeting of Napoleon and Francis after Austerlitz, the stage direction is " They formally embrace." Anyone who has ever seen an embrace of marionettes will know that it is an exceedingly difficult operation. They fall generally with a jerk into each other's arms. One trembles to think how they would manage a "formal" embrace between august Sovereigns. But there is one thing even more difficult than embracing on the puppet-stage, and that is the delivery of a letter. On the regular stage this is considered the meanest kind of employment. People cannot render higher testimony to the self-sacrifice of this or that veteran at the Théâtre Français than to say that he will consent to "come on with a letter." Now on the marionette stage this is the greatest exploit of all—the transfer of a letter from one person to another. The ineffectual quiverings, sudden darts, agonised wobblings, desperate shots, and clutches at nothing which take place before the transfer is effected! So, when you read in Act VI., scene 6, of Mr. Hardy's play, the stage direction "Presents a despatch to Pitt," you feel that for the puppets the critical moment has arrived. With careful study, however, these difficulties could be got over. The fact is we want a new *Poetics*—puppet-show *Poetics* ("de l'Aristote pour *pupazzi*").

Mr. Hardy boldly champions the cause of unplayable plays. To the question why, if you are writing a narrative to be read, forgo all the privileges of narrative art and hamper yourself by the restrictions proper to a spectacle, Mr. Hardy answers, in effect, that is the artist's affair, he has a right to his caprice, and "the artistic spirit is at bottom a spirit of caprice." Well, caprices must be judged by their fruits; and criticism would fail in its duty if it did not point out that this particular "caprice" of aiming by the medium of one art at the pleasure proper to another, a very popular caprice at the present day, is as noxious as it is popular. It has covered, for example, the Academy walls with "anecdote" pictures, pictures which aim at a literary

8

pleasure and not at the pleasure to be got out of paint.
It has filled the circulating libraries with novels of
" description," which aim at a " pictorial" pleasure
instead of the pleasure of literature. It has filled our
playhouses with " adapted " novels, which aim at the
pleasure of the novel instead of the pleasure of the
play. It has filled our concert-halls with " tone poems "
and " programme music," aiming at the pleasure of
thought instead of at the pleasure of sound. In short,
this artistic " caprice " is one of the direst artistic plagues
of the time. Says Mr. Hardy, the artists are there to
indulge this or any other " caprice." Yes, and the
critics are there to pounce on them, and to distinguish
between good caprices and bad. But there need be
no talk about " caprice " over *The Dynasts*. Mr. Hardy
believes himself to have capriciously written an unplayable play. I have ventured to suggest that he has written
a real play without knowing it, and that the means of
actual representation lie ready to his hand. But he
will not have it, he resents the aspersion of having done
something quite regular, and wishes to be regarded as
having indulged in a " caprice." This is rather like
Lydia Languish, who doated on the contraband
" Beverley " but rejected the honourable addresses of
Jack Absolute.

CURIOSITY AND HORROR IN THE THEATRE

TWO questions of more than ephemeral interest are suggested by the present playbill of Wyndham's Theatre (March 1902). The main interest of *Cæsar's Wife* is an interest of curiosity; the sole interest of *Heard at the Telephone* is an interest of horror. What are we to think of these two theatrical interests? To crowds of playgoers they are both very real interests. One must take leave, however, to advance the opinion that the interest of curiosity has a very humble place in the region of art, while the interest of horror has no place in that region at all.

And, first, as to curiosity. That is the distinguishing mark of the child in civilised, and of the adult in savage, communities. The state of mind which is always wondering what is going to happen next, rather than forming judgments upon what has happened, is a naïve state. In primitive periods it accounts for the importance of oracles, prophets, and soothsayers. It still makes kitchen-maids the ready victims of "fortune-tellers" and the eager readers of *Zadkiel's Almanac*. In a higher stratum of intelligence it means the popularity of the "detective novel"; curiosity here becoming a mere amusement, a form of dilettantism, so that men of really gigantic intellect, but of a intellect which is dormant on the artistic side —Darwin and Bismarck are illustrations of the type— are accustomed to take delight in the stories of

Gaboriau, du Boisgobey, and Conan Doyle. To the average mind a "mystery" is always more fascinating than the co-ordination and analysis of ascertained facts. That is why someone or other will always be discovering Bacon "ciphers"; such things appeal to the average man more intimately than the pleasure of reading either Bacon's or Shakespeare's works for what they are. The same feeling, the preference of the mysterious, the unaccountable, to the rational, scientifically explicable, moved the numerous supporters of the Tichborne claimant. So, the interest still taken in the authorship of Junius's letters is an interest wholly unconcerned with the literary or political importance of their contents. The clever "boom" of *An English-woman's Love Letters* is another case in point. To return to drama, the aim of the great artist is not to surprise the spectator with an unforeseen, but to gratify him with an "inevitable," action. It is not to provoke his curiosity about what is going to happen so much as to excite in him a keen desire that a certain thing shall happen, and then to satisfy that desire to the full. To the Greek dramatists the interest of curiosity was virtually unknown ; or, if they knew it, they despised the use of it. *Œdipus Tyrannus* is perhaps an exception, though even in that play the spectator's feeling is not so much curiosity about what is going to happen as sympathetic anguish for the victim of a fate which the spectator knows, but the victim does not know, to be impending. The state of feeling is very like that excited by Maeterlinck's poignant little play of *Intérieur*, wherein the spectator sees a drowned body being brought home. The shadows of the as yet happy family are seen on the window-blind, and the interest is not in what will happen behind that blind when the body is brought in—we all know the commotion, the horror, the grief that will ensue—but in the contrast between the present happiness of the household and the thought of the sudden end to that happiness which is impending. So indifferent were the Greek dramatists to the interest of curiosity that they did not scruple to announce their plot in advance. Euripides used prologues for this very purpose. Lessing, commenting on the practice in his *Hamburg Dramaturgy*, maintains that " the dramatic interest is all the stronger and keener the longer and the more certainly we have been allowed to foresee everything," and he adds, " so far am I from holding that the end ought to be hidden from the spectator that I don't think the enterprise would be a task beyond my strength were I to undertake a play of which the end should be announced in advance, from the very first scene." Lessing was something of a fanatic where the Greeks were concerned, but he had the root of the matter in him. And the fact remains, that the question put in *Cæsar's Wife*—which of two possible women is guilty of an adulterous intrigue?—is a trivial question compared with the questions which the playwright treats as of minor importance—why the guilty woman came to be guilty, and what will be the consequences of her guilt?

As to the theatrical use of sheer horror, there is always a tendency to it. In the first place, the spectacle of helpless physical suffering has a secret attraction for the primeval brute—the *gorille féroce* as Taine calls it—which slumbers in all of us. A poor dog run over in a London street will attract a fascinated crowd, gathered not to assist but to gloat. Burke said that a theatre where a tragedy was a-playing

would at once be deserted by an audience who learnt
that a real execution was going on outside. But in
default of the real bloodshed, the audience will content
itself with the sham. Dandin, the judge in Racine's
comedy of *Les Plaideurs*, offers to amuse Isabelle by
the spectacle of a little torturing. "Eh! Monsieur,"
exclaims Isabelle—"Eh! Monsieur, peut-on voir souffrir
des malheureux?" and Dandin, in his reply, speaks
for a large proportion of the human race: "Bon! cela
fait toujours passer une heure ou deux."

Hence the popularity of the torture scene in *La
Tosca*. Besides, there is a law in æsthetics, which
corresponds to the physiological law that a steady level
of sensation can only be maintained by increasing
doses of stimulant. Tastes jaded by the merely terrible
crave for the horrible. And so we have such exhibitions as that of *Heard at the Telephone*, wherein a man,
conversing with his wife at a great distance by this
instrument, is driven raving mad by hearing thieves
breaking into the house and murdering her. He can
do nothing; it is as though the murder were being
committed in his presence, while he is gagged and
bound. Now such incidents do not belong to
dramatic art, because that art deals with the collision
of human wills, whereas in this incident we have merely
the spectacle of human powerlessness. They humiliate
our common human dignity. A man overwhelmed by
an avalanche is no more than a fly or a gnat. Con-
ceive some man revered among men, a Socrates or a
John Wesley or a George Washington, fallen among
cannibals, tortured before our eyes, then cooked and
eaten—You turn with a faugh! even from the mental
picture. So there are things in the massacre of
Cawnpur which no one to this day dares to think of.

There are some calamities so dreadful, so irreconcilable
with a rational universe, that we can only writhe over
the thought of them with an agonised cry of Why?
Why? Why?   The dramatist who uses such themes
as these (and the telephone story is one of them) is
travelling outside the region of art.   They belong to the
region of what Aristotle called ἀτύχημα, sheer accident,
misadventure, the irrational element of life.   The sensation excited by the picture of them is too violent
to be an æsthetic sensation, we are oppressed and
shocked by it, whereas the aim of all art, even of tragic
art, is to exhilarate and relieve.   For the same reason
no skill is demanded for such exhibitions.   There is
skill in the first scene of *Heard at the Telephone*,
wherein we see the family of women left unprotected
in the lonely house, and fear gradually mastering them
as a sense grows upon them of something uncanny,
some hidden presence in the place.   It is the same
effect which has been attained, on a higher plane of
workmanship, in Maeterlinck's *L'Intruse.*   But in the
actual telephone scene there is no skill.   The idea
suffices of itself.   The pit receives the scene with
" thunders of applause " ?   Yes, and the fact suggests
a train of by no means agreeable reflections.   Evidently
the primeval man lurking within us is more potent than
some of us had thought; evidently the lust for strong
emotion is a far more considerable force than respect
for art; evidently we still have our Dandins, with their
" Bon! cela fait toujours passer une heure ou deux."
Once more the commonplace is brought home to us,
that our civilisation is only skin-deep.

EURIPIDES

HIPPOLYTUS

(LYRIC THEATRE, *June* 1904)

IN the "penny gaff" of a little village on the Norman littoral I once heard a comic singer extolling celibacy. He praised it, if I remember rightly, because it was cheap. The idiotic refrain of his song still lingers in my ear :——

> " J'ai choisi, donc, le célibat
> Le céli—céli—célibat."

That is the case of Hyppolytus in this tragedy of Euripides. He has chosen celibacy, not, to be sure, because it is cheap, but because it is pure. He declares himself—

> "stainless quite. No woman's flesh
> Hath e'er this body touched. Of all such deed
> Naught wot I, save what things a man may read
> In pictures or hear spoke ; nor am I fain,
> Being virgin-souled, to read or hear again."

Further, he is a woman-hater. He objects to the place and function of woman in the scheme of creation—

> "O God, why hast Thou made this gleaming snare,
> Woman, to dog us on the happy earth ?"

Anticipating Benedick's reflection that the earth must be peopled, he suggests that it would have been

a better arrangement if we could buy " new child-souls "
of the gods with hard cash, just as Sir Thomas Browne
wished that human beings could have been " grown "
like trees. To the modern playgoer this virgin-souled
misogynist is distinctly amusing. Of course, I use
the word amusing in its wider and nobler sense—the
sense in which it was used by D. G. Rossetti when he
said that poetry, whatever else it is, must be amusing.
Pope, in one of his letters, speaks of the " amusing
power of poetry." A celibate hero, then, is amusing
to us moderns. Our contemporary stage will not
have him at any price. Thouvenin, in *Denise*, pleaded
for him, but in vain.

This is the real question about the *Hippolytus*, as
presented in Mr. Gilbert Murray's rhymed verse translation : What is its amusing power for us to-day ?
One was occasionally bored by the Chorus. The
Chorus has some exquisitely beautiful things to say, or
rather to sing, but one heard them only imperfectly.
There were moments when the Chorus seemed to be
crying " Matches," falteringly, and then to add, *sotto
voce*, " We hope to goodness nobody hears us." All
the rest was immensely amusing. The chief source of
pleasure was the " modernity" of the whole affair.
First of all, the modernity of Euripides. It is, of
course, a commonplace to remark that Euripides is
conspicuously modern. The text-books and commentaries all hammer away at that. And M. Jules Lemaître
has turned some of Euripides' dialogue into the contemporary slang of the boulevard and the *barrière*.
But there are certain features of the performance at
the Lyric Theatre which are modern over and above
the inherent modernity of the work, modern in spite
of Euripides, modern just because of the difference

between B.C. 429 and A.D. 1904. Let me try to distinguish between these two aspects of the matter.

And, first of all, as to the supernatural " machinery." Ostensibly, it is the anger of the goddess Aphrodite with a too exclusive devotee of the goddess Artemis which causes all. the mischief in the story. But Mr. Murray tells you, and you believe him, that the two goddesses are not real goddesses. They are not real goddesses any more than the snakes in the "mongoose" story were real snakes. They are, in fact, forces of nature. What could be more modern ? Phædra's passion is a disease, and Hippolytus's virginity of soul a morbid condition of the blood. Does not M. Pierre Janet, on the staff of the Salpétrière, tell us that love is only a neurosis? Phædra is a neuropath. The false accusation she brings, upon her suicide, is a familiar mark of hystero-epilepsy. The root-idea of the play, then, is startlingly modern. Phædra is a modern *détraquée*, even in her pleasures. Look at the things which she singles out as her own peculiar private gratifications—

> "And many are delights beneath the sun !
> Long hours of converse ; and to sit alone
> Musing—a deadly happiness !—and shame."

She snatches a fearful joy from happiness that is "deadly," and has even been able to hug her shame. And Hyppolytus—yes, the virgin-souled Hyppolytus— has (like a public school) his modern side. He makes a remark about woman (to the intense annoyance of his simple *vieux jeu* father) which sounds for all the world like a quotation from Schopenhauer—

> "Through every woman's nature one blind strand
> Of passion winds, that men scarce understand."

Most of all is he modern in the supreme and fastidious
"elegance" of his *amours*.   For, while reviling women,
mere flesh-and-blood women, he is all the time in love
with a goddess.   There is no mistake about it.   He
calls Artemis his "mistress loved," he gloats (with
reverence) over her "golden hair."   His love has the
distinguishing mark of all love—joy in monopoly—

> "For, sole of living men, this grace is mine,
>   To dwell with thee."

What is more, Artemis (discreetly) returns his love—
and tells her love, when there can be no harm in it—

> ". . . him I loved best of mortality."

This little Platonic romance is deliciously modern.   It
is the Troubadour and the Princess Far-away; Ruy
Blas and Doña Maria; Count Fersen and Marie
Antoinette.   For two pins I would call the "virgin-
souled" Hippolytus the most subtly and perversely
sensual of amorists.   He reminds one of an eighteenth-
century Venetian *raffiné* secretly intriguing with a nun.
As to the Nurse, she is palpably, grossly, truculently
modern.   In her Euripides out-Shakespeares Shakespeare and out-Merediths Meredith.   The Greeks "of
the best period" called her "immoral," but that was
because the Greeks of the best period had not risen
to the idea of "unmorality."   To be "unmoral" is to
be inexpugnably modern.   Listen to the woman's
contempt for respectable *bourgeois* "gigmanity":—

> "A straight and perfect life is not for man ;
>   Nay, in a shut house, let him, if be can,
>   'Mid sheltered rooms, make all lines true."

But "overmen" (and "overwomen") ought to "love on

and dare." This is your right Nietzschean doctrine of
" Live dangerously."

The inventory of modern articles in the Euripidean
stock is not yet exhausted. The idea of the binding
oath, which prevents Hippolytus from telling all he
knows and the Chorus from telling all they know,
and so " dishing " the whole tragedy, may seem at
first sight what schoolboys call a " stumper." But
we have plenty of plays to-day which turn upon
expedients quite as artificial as this, plays which would
fall to pieces if somebody would only open his mouth.
And Euripides' use of the sanctity of an oath is not
a whit more forced than is Scott's in the trial of
Effie Deans. It is, to be sure, on the technical side
that our search for modern features in a Greek tragedy
is most likely to be baffled. Nevertheless, the suicide
of Phædra on the other side of a closed door is also
a modern effect. There is nothing, says Victor Hugo,
so thrilling as a tragedy on the other side of a closed
door. And remember Maeterlinck's *Mort de Tintagiles*.
Mr. Murray himself remarks (in speaking of Theseus'
allusion to his wife's " fit of the old cold anguish ") that
" it is characteristic of Euripides to throw these sudden
lights back on the history of his characters." A very
modern trick of technique, this; as readers of Ibsen
know.

These are some of the modern things in Euripides.
He is not responsible for certain other modern things
to be found in the performance at the Lyric. The
grouping of the Chorus about the steps of the Temple
suggests an Academy picture of the eighties—or whenever " Sir Frederick " was P.R.A. It is quite certain
that a picture of this sort was not presented in the
Theatre of Dionysus; equally certain that no modern

"producer" of a Greek tragedy can avoid "thinking in pictures." He has no choice; the relative positions of players and audience demand it. As pictures go, you may like best the final one, when the crowd stand petrified, with arms stiff and palms turned outwards, at the descent of the goddess Artemis. Where the modernity of the presentation comes out, perhaps, most curiously is in the *listening*. When an actor had to spout one of his long speeches, what did the listener do B.C. 429? I doubt if he took any part in the stage-picture at all. If he did, he would be wearing an expressionless mask, and would simply stand at ease. To-day, he has to stand to attention, to be all ears, all facial play; has, in fact, to listen for all he is worth. Our actors are trained to be good listeners; but then they never have to listen to speeches for ten minutes by the clock. At the Lyric they have to apply their modern methods to an ancient *coupe* of dialogue—and the effect is a little odd.

This is not the actors' fault. Some of them do wonderfully well. The Phædra of Miss Edyth Olive is by no means unworthy to compare with the Phèdre of Mme. Bernhardt. It has classic dignity and breadth, and at the same time the romantic "thrill." It will be long before some of us forget the figure of this young actress facing the Chorus to deliver the long speech—

> "O women, dwellers in this portal-seat
> Of Pelops'land . . ."

or the music of her utterance. Mr. Ben Webster's Hippolytus, Mr. Brydone's Theseus, and Mr. Granville Barker's Messenger are all careful, intelligent performances, and the rival goddesses, Miss Florence Bourne and Mrs. Gwendolen Bishop, are goddesses who take care to be distinctly heard. As the Nurse Mrs. A. B. Tapping was a little too " monumental." One missed the meaning glance, the wheedling tongue, the " gusto " (as Hazlitt would have said) of the character.

But the amusing power of this great Greek tragedy done into worthy English and competently played is tremendous. That is the thing that matters. It may well be that I have exaggerated the " modernity " of Euripides—a critic is always tempted to " make out a case "—but I certainly have not overstated the quantity of my pleasure.

ELECTRA

(COURT THEATRE, *January* 1906)

NO doubt it has occurred to most of us, when at school, to wish that we had been born Greeks "of the best period." It would have saved us much toil, and stripes not a few. The mere linguistic advantage would have been enormous. We should have known all about verbs in $\mu\iota$ from our cradles, and aorists would have come as naturally to us as our second teeth. But there would have been a still more magnificent "score" for us. We should not have missed a single "thrill" in assisting at the performance of a Greek tragedy. Its story would have been familiar to us from the nursery, and we should no more think of doubting its truth than we now think of scoffing at the Sermon on the Mount. It would have filled us with religious awe, shaken us with genuine terror, moved us to floods of tears, gratified our taste for dexterous forensic debate, indulged our craving for a glimpse of supernatural beings—and it would have combined these joys with music and dancing, the refreshing breezes of the open air in the most delightful of climates, and the spectacle of all the big-wigs of the city in their best clothes. Further, all this pleasure would have come to us in the guise of a social duty; we should at once have been "having a good time" and "doing the proper thing." Happy, happy Greeks to the best period!

How different our fate to-day! In a stuffy theatre, not in the least like the original, we look on at something which we never even begin to believe in, and though we derive a considerable amount of pleasure from the process, it is a very chequered pleasure. We are wearied by the long speeches. We are worried by the chorus. Too many of the characters are like the bore whom Disraeli met at Gibraltar; they are for ever expounding the obvious. What most annoys us is that the things in the story which we are dying to see are the very things which—it would almost seem maliciously—are kept out of sight; the magic-lantern is always extinguished just when the most exciting slide is due. It is true that someone is then obligingly sent on to tell us that *he* has seen the slide, and that it really *was* exciting; whereat, of course, we are more annoyed than ever, learning that we have just missed what this fellow has had the luck to fall in for.

Of course there are reasons for all the things that disconcert and puzzle us. We were taught those reasons at school, and, even if (as sometimes happens) we have since forgotten them, text-books are cheap. We know all about the historical spirit, all about the Chorus conventions and the Messenger conventions, all about the god out of a machine, all about everything. But the question is not what we *know* of Greek tragedy, but what exact amount and kind of pleasure we get out of its performance (in a translation, under necessarily changed conditions of performance) at the present moment. Onr knowledge, of course, does make a difference. It saves us from that utter bewilderment which would assuredly beset the absolutely unsophisticated, uninstructed spectator of a Greek tragedy at the present time. It even adds slightly to our pleasure; it adds the sense of satisfaction which the mind experiences in perceiving the under-lying reasonableness of things superficially *bizarre*. But that is an intellectual pleasure—the same kind of pleasure we enjoy in solving a proposition of Euclid. It is not a theatrical pleasure. And that brings me to the point. What is the precise amount of theatrical pleasure—pleasure proper to the art of drama—which we derive from Mr. Gilbert Murray's rhymed transla-tion of Euripides' *Electra*, as presented at the Court Theatre?

Well, you begin by being pleased with the peasant, Electra's husband. A right Tolstoyan peasant this. He is too delicate, knows his place too well, to be anything but a "spiritual" husband to a lady so high-born. It is what the French call (M. Lemaître has written a play on the theme) a *mariage blanc*. He is a true gentleman, too; hospitable as some old mountain "solitary" in Wordsworth, and not ashamed of his poor fare, knowing that "gentle" men "will take good cheer or ill With even kindness." And then you find pleasure in Electra for her natural housekeeping vexation when her "man" invites "visitors" on a banyan-day. Here, indeed, we recognise the touch of "our Euripides the human." Even more pleasurable than the humanity of Euripides is his subtle observation, his quite modern psychology, of the female sex. He presents Electra as soured, exasperated by the starva-tion of the natural affections of woman (the seamy side of the *mariage blanc*). He presents Clytemnestra as having something to say for herself; no mere *traîtresse* of melodrama, but a complex person who might have read *Man and Superman*. You are pleased, again, with the old retainer. He reminds one of Shakespeare's

9

Adam. (If I lug in these modern comparisons it is with a purpose. They show that we have one pleasure denied to the Greek of the best period, the pleasure of letting the mind wander through the ages, the pleasure of recognising the innumerable points of contact between the " classic " and the " romantic.") Also you have pleasure in detecting the artifices of Euripides the playwright—as, for instance, in the matter of Orestes' identity. Common sense suggests the question at the outset: Why does not Orestes say who he is at once and have done with it? The answer, of course, is that Euripides wanted his old Adam, wanted speeches from Electra that could never have got themselves spoken had she known at once that the stranger was her brother, wanted his " recognition " scene. Euripides, you see, was not only " human," he was *malin*. No doubt the recognition scene now pleases us less for its own sake than for its suggestion of its vast theatrical progeny—all those "strawberry marks" that have identified "long-lost brothers" since the year 4 1 3 B.C.

But perhaps this is "seeking noon at fourteen o'clock." After all, the main pleasure you get from this *Electra* is the pleasure mankind has always got: the sense of beauty, dignity, sympathy for human suffering not ignobly borne, and the " connoisseur " pleasure in choice workmanship, rhythm, *la ligne*. Mr. Murray's verse is of the choicest, and though I incur the ridicule cast on our old friend " the pedant in Hierocles " who sampled a house by a brick, I cannot resist quoting this single specimen :—

> " The grim
> Troy spoils gleam round her throne, and by each hand
> Queens of the East, my father's prisoners, stand,

> A cloud of Orient robes and tangling gold.
> And there upon the floor the blood, the old
> Black blood, yet crawls and cankers, like a rot
> In the stone."

And, in the catalogue of pleasures, let me not forget the pleasure of witnessing some really good acting, especially good on the spindle side. Miss Edith Wynne-Matthison, who as Electra bears the burden of the performance on her shoulders, makes an extremely impressive figure of the heroine, impressive in varied moods, now stately and statuesque, now mere womanly, and again a passionate semi-hysterical *révoltée*. The brief appearance of Clytemnestra is long enough for Miss Edyth Olive to present a real character, a "disquieting" temperament; one understands the fascination of Aegisthus. Is not Mr. Harcourt Williams a rather forcible-feeble Orestes? The question, after all, may be a compliment; for it may be that forcible-feebleness is the true "note" of the Euripidean Orestes. Mr. J. H. Barnes is capital as old Adam. As to the Chorus, no doubt the ladies do their best; it is not their fault that they cannot present, either in evolution, intonation, or significance, a genuine Greek chorus.

SHAKESPEARE

THE TWO GENTLEMEN OF VERONA

(COURT THEATRE, *April* 1904)

THERE is a subtle fascination for many of us in the more faulty work of a great artist. For one thing, it brings him, just for a moment, into line with us; we feel that he is human after all and no mere monster of perfection. We like to note the prentice hand in *Waverley*, and do not altogether dislike the symptoms of decrepitude in *Count Robert of Paris*. There is something repellent in absolute flawlessness, and we should hate the man who discovered the lost arm of the Venus in the Louvre. Nor does that feeling fully explain the fascination of the imperfect. A crude sketch often tells you more about the artist than a finished picture. And in literature there are half-failures which give you more intimate revelations of life than whole successes; *L'Éducation Sentimentale* provokes sharper thrills than *Madame Bovary*. What a comfort that Shakespeare had his weaker, that is to say, his earlier, moments! "Every schoolboy knows" the faults of *The Two Gentlemen of Verona*, and one is quite content to leave them to the schoolboys.

I had never seen the play (it has only been played in London once or twice in my time) until it was

revived at the Court Theatre the other night. I went
with no little misgiving, and came away under so
strong a charm that I almost told the cabman "To
Mantua —by sea!" Was it Shakespeare that one had
been enjoying or something from the *Théâtre Impossible*
of Alfred de Musset? Who were these twain under
the lady's balcony—Proteus and Thurio, or Cyrano de
Bergerac and his "cadet de Gascogne"? And all this
casuistry of love, was it not Marivaux—turned into
archaic English? No, evidently it was Shakespeare.
A leaflet, distributed with the playbill, was sufficient
evidence of that . . . Dr. Brandes . . . Schlegel . . .
John Kemble . . . Meres's *Palladis Tamia* . . . the
usual thing. I do not reproach the compiler; he did
his work thoroughly. But one cannot abide a wheel,
however well made, when it is used to break a butterfly.
One does not want the mood created by a Shakesperian
love-comedy to be disturbed by horrid matter-of-fact
comments. In such a mood references to Shakespeare's borrowings from George de Montemayor are
as tiresomely irrelevant as the latest Stock Exchange
quotations. It is a mood of sheer hedonism. We are
intent upon our pleasure, romantic, languid, voluptuous
pleasure. The nights are warm in Mantua, and the
ladies, though virtuous, unashamedly amorous. A
rope-ladder, as Valentine knows, is an article that no
gentleman's wardrobe should be without. We feel our
moral standard pleasantly giving way. We can even
sympathise with Proteus. He loves Julia, and no
wonder, for she is as sleek and as soft and as full of
mischief as a Persian kitten. The next moment, Julia
being out of the way, he transfers his heart to Silvia.
Why not? What could any gentleman, with eyes in
his head, say to Silvia if not what Disraeli said to the

Duchess who was inquisitive about Cabinet secrets—
"You darling!" I observe that some writers have
taken the fickle Proteus quite seriously. His conduct
pains them. "Et moi qui vous croyais homme du
monde!" they seem to say—as the chemist's assistant
in Labiche's farce said to the man who gave him a
black eye. Proteus is "no gentleman." Thus do we
confound the *Pays de Tendre* with the Metropolitan
Cab Radius. It is true that Shakespeare makes
Proteus ashamed of himself in the end—just five bare
lines of repentance. But that is "only his"—Shakespeare's—"fun." For my part, I feel sure that he had
"been there." Proteus is his hint of a Don Juan
"caught young"—or a Cherubino grown up. The
thought gives an agreeable Mozartian blend to our
pleasures. Then comes a touch of Schubert with
"Who is Silvia?" I liked Mr. Holthoir's modest,
breathless singing of this song better than many
concert "renderings" I have heard. And he makes so
handsome a Sir Thurio that you half wonder how
Silvia could find it in her heart to reject him for either
of the Veronese gentlemen. But I am forgetting
that the play is not *A Gentleman of Mantua*. Sir
Eglamour, too, is a very pretty fellow. An inconsol-
able widower? Fudge. All the rest (save the
bandits) live "for climate and the affections." And
one sits in the Court Theatre, sympathising and
approving. Decidedly, this play does not make for
austerity. But even the austere Pascal wrote a treatise
on "Les Passions de l'Amour," and sages like Michelet
and Renan—when quite elderly men, as old as the
Duke of Milan or Antonio, father to Proteus—laboriously analysed these passions. Why, even this same
Duke of Milan poses (falsely, but plausibly enough to

deceive Valentine) as what they call on the Boulevards a *vieux marcheur*—

> "There is a lady in Verona here
> Whom I affect, but she is nice and coy
> And nought esteems my aged eloquence ;
> Now therefore would I have thee to my tutor."

Whereupon Valentine gives him "tips." Is there not, by the way, just a tinge of "decadence" in this spectacle of a youngster instructing the greybeard whom he would make his father-in-law in the tricks of abduction and the use of "ladders, quaintly made of cords"? But I do not wonder that Valentine was caught by the deception. Nothing is so flattering to a young man as to be consulted by his senior as an authority on lady-killing. These little touches in *The Two Gentlemen* ought to tell the intelligent spectator more about the secrets of Shakespeare's own life than whole volumes of facts about second-best bed-steads.

And the two ladies, Julia and Silvia, reveal to us, if we will but keep our eyes open, a good deal about the damsels of (Shakespeare's) Stratford. Their complete absorption in love, as the only thing in the world a woman ought to concern herself with, is as naïve as in Boccaccio's—or Brantôme's—women. And you observe that these women are played by our actresses to-day with perfect naturalness, without any sense of a changed point of view either on their part or the spectator's ; whereas the men obviously "date." You draw your own conclusions—and, if you are wise, will keep them to yourself. The lessee of the Court Theatre has done an excellent thing in reviving this delicious comedy of love. He might, by the way, head his playbill with an appropriate remark of Dryden's (*Essay of Dramatic Poesy*): "Love is the most frequent of all the passions, and, being the private concernment of every person, is soothed by viewing its own image in a public entertainment."

MUCH ADO

(HIS MAJESTY'S THEATRE, *January* 1905)

I T is complained by a few people who ought to know better, and by many more who may be charitably assumed to know nothing, that Mr. Tree takes unpardonable liberties with Shakespeare, embroiders the text with new business, over-elaborates the scenic background, and has his own way of interpreting the stage-directions. Tiresome as it is to be forced to expound the obvious, one must remind these good people that the Shakespearian text—even assuming that we possess the true text, which pretty clearly we do not—hardly ranks as a holy sacrament. The brutal fact is that Shakespeare was a man, and a man who, working three centuries ago, could but make the best of the tools then at his command. We of to-day go to the theatre with precisely the same object as the playgoers of Shakespeare's time —to be interested and amused. We go, that is to say, for our pleasure, and, in the theatre (which is not a library or a lecture-hall) we care not a jot for Shakespeare except in so far as he subserves our pleasure. I am aware that there are certain enthusiasts—for instance, the Elizabethan Stage Society— who attempt (it can never be a wholly successful attempt) to revive Shakespeare intact, and as originally played. These efforts have their place in an educa-

tional curriculum, but none in the catalogue of pleasures.
Reconstitute the Elizabethan stage as you may, you
cannot restore the Elizabethan frame of mind.   Even
supposing that our stage had remained unaltered in
its mechanical conditions for three centuries, even
supposing that an Edwardian audience had virtually
the same mental equipment as an Elizabethan audience,
a *fixed* Shakespearian tradition would still be out of
the question.   As an artist, Shakespeare was primarily
a pleasure-monger, and therefore to strike us as his old
self he must constantly be putting on a new self.   As
Mr. Balfour has pithily expressed it in his *Foundations
of Belief*, a "steady level of æsthetic sensation can only
be maintained by increasing doses of æsthetic stimulant."
We talk, it is true, of the "immortal" classics; but
the principle of life in a classic is this very principle
of perpetual change.   Sainte-Beuve in a famous essay
defined a classic as "energique, frais et dispos."   And
how does it remain "fresh"?   By its property of self-
renewal, the property of responding in different ages to
different demands for pleasure.

Mr. Tree, then, is not only justified in giving us a
fresh treatment of Shakespeare; he simply cannot help
himself, if he would keep Shakespeare alive; and the
text-worshippers, the strait sect which would turn
Elizabethan stage-directions into phylacteries, are in
reality the people who can only think of Shakespeare
as dead.   Their absurd attitude is at the acme of
absurdity when adopted over such a play as *Much
Ado About Nothing*, which *as* a play is as bad as
bad can be.   It is just the play which Aristotle
might have had, by anticipation, in mind when he
dwelt on the supreme importance of plot.   Everybody knows the weaknesses of *Much Ado*.   It has

the initial weakness—shared with many another of Shakespeare's plays—of a dramatised novel. In the church scene Claudio is cheerfully degraded into a blackguard for the sake of a *coup de théâtre*. The cock-and-bull story of Hero's death is invented, and Claudio is turned into a weak ass, for the sake of another *coup de théâtre* in the final scene. What, then, is it that, despite its crying faults, makes *Much Ado* so delightful? It is, to begin with, its strong and pulsing vitality—the expression of Shakespeare's experiencing and enjoying faculty—the intense animal, semi-savage vitality of Benedick and Beatrice, the " May of youth and bloom of lustihood " in Claudio, the enduring vitality of Leonato and Antonio leaping out into flame in their old age, the minx-like vitality of Margaret and Ursula, the roystering and bacchanalian vitality of Borachio, the sturdy bovine vitality of Dogberry. And then it is its *panache*, its careless non-moral Renaissance romance. And, again, it is its Hugoesque touch of the luridly-fiendish in Don John set against the shifting polychromatic revel of masque and dance. Here is the "virtue" of the play, the set of elements by which it lives ; and all the questions we need ask ourselves about the present revival are concerned with these elements. Does it make the best of them ? Are they helped or are they hindered by Mr. Tree's innovations?

I believe that any jury of "average sensual men " will unhesitatingly find for Mr. Tree on both counts. The acting is brimming over with that vitality which, as I have said, is the prime characteristic of the play. Mr. Tree "keeps the pot a-bilin'" as merrily as Mr. Pickwick when hustled down the slide by Sam Weller. There are parts, it may be, in which his temperament would be more comfortably at home; his Benedick is, however, a very careful and on the whole successful "composition." If, as has been objected, he has his own way with stage directions, I can see no harm in it. He climbs a tree in the scene in the arbour instead of hiding behind the usual shrubbery, he jots down "The God of Love, that sits above" on his tablets instead of singing the song—and why should he not? There is tremendous vitality in Mr. Calvert's Dogberry —an altogether admirable piece of work. But this Dogberry harangues the watch from a window, instead of from the causeway. Heavens, what sacrilege! Vitality, again, is the mark of the scene in Leonato's garden, which in Mr. Tree's version becomes the capital scene of the play—the vitality of nature as well as of men and women. Moonlight dwindles to darkness, darkness greys into dawn, dawn glows into broad sunshine; a strepitous carnival is stilled to dead silence, which gives way to the song of birds and cheerful morning sounds—always there is movement, always a sense of life. But the stage-directions give no warrant for all this. Bless us and save us! Nor do they authorise Beatrice in leaving the church for the cloisters before bidding Benedick "Kill Claudio!" Accordingly the question has been gravely asked whether secular incidents may or may not take place without impropriety in an Italian church. And why, I ask in my turn, does all sense of humour desert so many excellent people when they go to see Shakespeare acted? And—good gracious!—I had almost forgotten the oranges. There are oranges at His Majesty's, real oranges, one of which is stolen by a page under Leonato's very nose—and Mr. Tree has no textual warrant for either his oranges or his thieving page, and someone or other hints, not darkly, that he is no better than a contriver of pantomime. What would Shakespeare have said to a commentator of this calibre? I think I can guess. " Via, goodman Dull ! "

HAMLET

(ADELPHI THEATRE, *April* 1905)

THE time has long gone by for the extravagance of rapture over a new Hamlet. Our perfervid forefathers went crazy over a Betterton and almost corybantic over a Garrick. Those were the days of the "sublime"; when ghosts were ghosts, smelling of real sulphur that could be appreciated by the nostrils of the Footmen's Gallery, not transient embarrassed phantoms explained away by a Psychical Research Society; when a play was the more enjoyed the more it digressed into what Mr. Pinero's broken-down tragedian calls "real speeches"; when "pity" and "terror" were genuine, not to say fashionable, emotions, instead of being far-fetched quotations from Aristotle. In those days, then, a new Hamlet was as important as a new comet, or a new religion, or a new House of Commons. We take our new Hamlets more coolly now, after the fashion of the turkey-hen, celebrated in immortal verse by Marjorie Fleming, who

> ". . . was more than usual calm
> And did not give a single dam."

For we have grown a little weary, like Hamlet himself, of words, words, words—words that we know by heart long before the speaker utters them—words that have acquired the hollow reverberation of an ecclesiastical

ritual—and, further, we have had in our time to
associate Hamlet with personalities so numerous and
so diverse that we begin, like the American young
lady after a ball-supper, to "guess we're pretty well
crowded." If it is a duty to remember the curious
and characteristic Hamlet of Sir Henry Irving, it is a
pleasure to forget the daringly *décolleté* Hamlet of the
late Mr. Wilson Barrett. There was M. Mounet Sully's
Hamlet, as mad as a hatter, who reminded one of Dr.
Johnson's saying that if *he* had played Hamlet, he
"would have frightened the ghost." Some of us
declared Mr. Forbes Robertson's Hamlet to be the
very man, until Mme. Sarah Bernhardt persuaded us
that hers was the very woman. Others, again, have
shed tears over the Werther-Hamlet of Mr. Beerbohm
Tree. Then there was the athletic Hamlet of Mr.
Benson, who carried off the corpse of Polonius on his
shoulders. The only Hamlet we have not had the
advantage of seeing in this country is the "steel-cage"
Hamlet, not long ago a great favourite in the United
States with audiences who were able to throw missiles
at him, safe behind his bars, without interrupting the
performance. It may be perverse, but I confess I
should like to add him to my collection.

Meanwhile, we have a new Hamlet in Mr. H. B.
Irving, who—despite our feelings of repletion in the
matter of Hamlet—is entitled to our sympathetic
attention for two excellent *a priori* reasons, not to
mention the others. In the first place he has the
honour to be the son of his father. Nothing gives the
sense of theatrical continuity like the handing on of a
classic part from one player to another of the same
name and blood. Actors in such case become the
Lucretian torch-bearers : *vitaï lampada tradunt.* Con-

noisseurs in heredity will no doubt detect all sorts of
resemblances between the Hamlets of Irving *père* and
fils.   We are given, however, to understand that the
son has not actually seen his father in the part; and I
have certainly no intention of comparing the two.   For
(and this is the second of our two reasons for according
the new Hamlet a hearty welcome) Mr. Irving has the
honour to be himself.   He has established an independent reputation; to the knowledge of all playgoers he
has a temperament and a talent of his own.   The
temperament is perhaps a little hard, a temperament of
more force than grace; the talent dry (in the champagne
sense) rather than rich.   There are supple players, with
personalities like Squire Brooke's mind, which was "a
jelly that ran easily into any mould."   Mr. Irving is
not one of these.   His individuality is sharp-edged.
If he takes up a part, be sure he will leave his mark
upon it.   For the rest, he appears to be a " cerebral,"
as the French say, rather than a " passionate " actor;
better, perhaps, at thinking out a part than at feeling
it; better, certainly, at portraying thought than
feeling.

Well, that estimate, it may be said, is of good
promise for Hamlet, who is of all tragic protagonists
the most thoughtful, who is sicklied o'er with the pale
cast of thought, who tells us that nothing is good or
bad, but thinking makes it so, whose whole story is
that of action paralysed by excess of thought—and
who at the same time demands more careful, studious,
consecutive thinking-out from the actor than any other
character in drama.   You are, then, in no way surprised
to find Mr. Irving's a pre-eminently intellectual Hamlet.
I am not sure that this quality does not attain to what
the language of the conventicle calls " intellectual pride."

The student of Wittenberg almost tends at times to become the don. One notes this feature, a certain air of didacticism, in the several passages displaying Hamlet the virtuoso. There is a touch of something like professorial authority in this Hamlet's instruction to the First Player. One thinks less of the Prince of Denmark, a cultivated amateur (with a freedom in criticising " professionals " pardonable in a Royal personage), than of a stage-veteran teaching a novice at the School of Dramatic Art. Hamlet's little lesson to Rosencrantz and Guildenstern on the recorders has a faint flavour of a " demonstration." It would not be altogether out of place on a fashionable Friday night in Albemarle Street. And this Hamlet " lectures " his mother in more senses than one; not merely upbraids her, but has a manifest relish (like any type-character of Mr. Bernard Shaw's) in explaining her to herself. Of course, these elements are all in the play; my point is that they are the elements upon which Mr. Irving's temperament naturally fastens, so that they are brought into somewhat undue prominence. One is a little too conscious of the " cerebral " actor in the full vigour and enjoyment of cerebration. In minor details of " business " whatever thought can do has by Mr. Irving been done. He has thought of shivering all forlorn after the interview with the ghost until Horatio takes off his cloak and wraps it about his friend, who says, affectionately, " Let us go—together." He has thought of sitting by the fire, gazing into the embers, to say " To be or not to be." He has thought of innumerable pauses, breaks, hesitations, to give the hackneyed passages a proper *impromptu* air. He has very carefully thought out the scene of parting with Ophelia— thought out the various fine shades of distinction

10

between genuine hysteria and melting tenderness (when he supposes they are alone), as well as between feigned madness and unfeigned indignation (when he discovers they are being spied upon). If I speak of melting tenderness I must not be understood to imply that Mr. Irving makes the usual concession in this scene to the sentimentalists. He is, on the whole, fully as harsh to Ophelia as, apparently, Shakespeare meant Hamlet to be.

That brings me to another feature of this Hamlet. I have said that Mr. Irving's temperament is a little hard. Hamlet, too, has, as we all know, his hard side. He says he is cruel only to be kind, but that is rather a self-indulgent statement of the case. He behaved brutally to Polonius during the old man's life, and callously when he put an end to that life. He was, as I have just been saying, terribly harsh to Ophelia. His contempt for Rosencrantz and Guildenstern, justifiable enough, was an unnecessarily savage contempt. This hard side of Hamlet comes into especial prominence under Mr. Irving's treatment. He positively bullies Gertrude. He snarls and snaps at the two unhappy youths sent to spy upon him, and at one moment actually slaps Rosencrantz's face. Mr. Irving's humour, too, tends to become sardonic, slightly Mephistophelean. This is Hamlet in part, but only in part. For after all the epithet that finally rings in our ear for Hamlet is "sweet." He is the "sweet Prince," affable, in a few breathing spaces even sunny in mood, and in the long run of a gentle, persuasive charm. It is here that you may like Mr. Irving's Hamlet least. It is an authoritative (not to say a domineering) Hamlet, rather than a Hamlet of winning charm. I have read somewhere or other that he has tried to profit by a recent exposition we have had of Hamlet's character from the pen of Professor Bradley, who is for an heroic, as against a "sentimental," Prince. Well, I submit that, while an actor may show us Hamlet as "strong" within certain limits, he must at the same time strive to make the strength bring forth sweetness. *Ex forti dulcedo* should be his motto, and a little more *dulcedo* would certainly do Mr. Irving's Hamlet no harm. He impresses, and that is much; but you wish he would be at a little more pains to seduce. When, however, all is said, one must recognise in this Hamlet a sterling performance. It absorbs the attention, fires the imagination, and satisfies the reason. In the technical qualities of elocution, deportment, presence, and "business" it is a little masterpiece. There are cries from the heart in it which tempt me to reconsider my first judgment that Mr. Irving is not by temperament a "passionate" actor. And in the death scene, if in no other, it does compass the effect I have been speaking of—the effect of captivating charm. On the whole, then, let it stand as a fine achievement, one of the best Hamlets this generation has seen.

PROFESSOR BRADLEY'S *HAMLET*

IT is often assumed that wrong-headed methods of criticism, like poets, are born, not made. It so happens, however, that of one of these methods it is possible to trace the first rough construction. In 1777 a forgotten Shakespearian commentator, one Maurice Morgann—forgotten, at any rate, until he was exhumed and reprinted in a volume on Eighteenth Century Shakespearian Literature by Mr. Nicol Smith—published what would then have been called an elegant and ingenious *Essay on the Dramatic Character of Sir John Falstaff,* wherein the curious may read this passage: " If the characters of Shakespeare are thus whole, and as it were original, while those of almost all other writers are mere imitation, *it may be fit to consider them rather as Historic than Dramatic beings*; and, when occasion requires, to account for their conduct from the whole of character, from general principles, from latent motives, and from policies not avowed." Here in the words italicised may be noted the first appearance of a heresy that by and by, with the great " Romantic " critics, became something very like an orthodox creed. The strange habit was acquired of considering the personages of Shakespeare's plays as " historic," not " dramatic " beings, as actual flesh-and-blood people instead of fictitious inventions. Thus was the distinction ignored between nature and art, realities and appearances. In part, no doubt, the vogue of this method is to be explained by the circumstances of the "Romantic" epoch. It was the moment of extravagant Shakespeare worship, and a theory of criticism which assigned to Shakespeare the powers of the Divine Creator came exceedingly handy. But we live in different times—times, to be sure, still devoted to the worship of Shakespeare, but with a rationalised substituted for a mystic cult—and one would have thought it almost superfluous to point out the fallacy of a critical method which works on the assumption that a dramatist's characters are real people.

The plain trnth, of course, is that "historic" and "dramatic" beings, to use Morgann's nomenclature, are the resultants of wholly different sets of forces. A real person is the resultant of his will, hereditary circumstances, environment, and millions of causes entirely beyond his control. A dramatist's personage is a mere projection of one man's mind, limited by his powers of observation and imagination, something vague that has been held in solution in the dramatist's consciousness until it is "precipitated" in the form of words written upon paper. It is, as the mathematicians say, a mere "function" of the dramatist, and can utter nothing, think nothing, be nothing outside the range of the dramatist's own nature and mental vision. Now the confusion between the "historic" and the "dramatic" personage is natural enough. The whole art of fiction, particularly the art of drama, with its flesh-and-blood materials, is based upon the possibility of producing this confusion in the reader's or spectator's mind. The confusion gives pleasure, for we seem, by yielding to it, to be witnessing a veritable act of creation and to be enlarging, enriching, vividly colouring our experience of life. But deliberately to import this confusion into

criticism is quite another matter.   For it is the object
of criticism not to flatter the fancy, but to understand,
to trace results to true causes, to see the thing as it
really is.   If we want to understand the subject of
bread we must consider such matters as wheat and
flour, mills and ovens; it will not help us in the least,
but mislead us, to pretend that bread grows ready-
baked in the front garden.   And so if we want to
understand the play of *Hamlet* we shall not do so by
assuming that it is a piece of real life, lived by people
who have independent lives outside it.   We can only
hope to understand it by starting with the simple
commonplace truth that it is a work of art contrived
by a certain man at a certain time under certain influences and with certain objects.   I should apologise for
expatiating on the obvious were it not that the old
fallacy, the old confusion between reality and art, is
still to be met with among our foremost Shakespearian
critics.   The reason, no doubt, is that, as Morgann put
it, Shakespeare is so much greater than the other men
that he seems to be different in kind, and not merely
in degree—whereas, of course, he is not different in
kind, and it is hopelessly uncritical to assume that he
works under different conditions from those of other
playwrights merely because he does so much better
than they do.   Yet that assumption constantly vitiates
the best work of our Shakespearian commentators.
There was Coleridge, for instance, who, unable to
reconcile Polonius's foolishness with his sage advice to
Laertes when starting for Paris—which would have
been irreconcilable had Polonius been a real man—was
driven to declare that Polonius was *not* a comic
character.   Similarly, to account for the inopportune
"wassail" speech of Hamlet when waiting for the

Ghost—inopportune, had Hamlet been a real man—
Coleridge declares it an attempt on Hamlet's part " to
smother the impatience of the moment in abstract
reasoning"! Into such absurdities, such deviations
from the path of true research, did a wrong theory
of criticism lead one of our acutest intellects!

Now I have seen it stated, and I quite agree,
that Coleridge has had no such worthy successor as
Professor Bradley, author of *Shakespearian Tragedy.*
Certainly this is a notable book, always sane and accurate,
sometimes profound, a credit to our academic scholarship. It is the last book wherein one would expect
to find so unsound a critical method as that which
Morgann first indicated and the " Romantic" critics so
zealously adopted. Nevertheless the method is there,
not overt, but unconscious ; there is nearly always the
underlying assumption that Hamlet is to be argued
about and explained as a real person. Take a few
instances. Mr. Bradley combats the view that Hamlet
planned the play-scene in the hope that the King
would betray his guilt to the Court, by showing, from
the text, that his object was to convince himself by the
King's agitation that the Ghost had spoken the truth.
Then, " It may be well to add that, although Hamlet's
own account of his reason for arranging the play-scene
may be questioned, it is impossible to suppose that, if
his real design had been to provoke an open confession
of guilt, he would have been unconscious of this design."
Excellently reasoned—about a real person—but what
if Shakespeare was merely fascinated by the dramatic
effectiveness of a play within a play, and meant to have
that effective scene ? Then Hamlet's motives become
mere afterthoughts, mere *ficelles*. The assumption that
Hamlet is a real person involves search for the reasons

of the play-scene in Hamlet's character; whereas it is
in Shakespeare's dramatic needs of the moment and
keen eye for the theatrically effective that the true
cause of that play-scene is, I submit, to be found.
Again you read that, "Though he (Hamlet) has been
disappointed of the throne, everyone shows him respect,
and he is the favourite of the people, who are not given
to worship philosophers. . . . If he was fond of acting,
an æsthetic pursuit, he was equally fond of fencing, an
athletic one." Excellent, once more—of a real person.
But does it not occur to Professor Bradley that these
things are thus merely because Shakespeare wanted (1)
a "sympathetic" hero; (2) an amateur of acting (or
what would have become of the play-scene?); and (3)
a fencer—for the *dénouement*? Further on you read,
"Doubtless in happier days he was a close and constant
observer of men and manners," and "All his life he
had believed in her (Gertrude), we may be sure, as
such a son would"—remarks that show Mr. Bradley
as unconsciously wandering into speculations about
Hamlet as a real person, existing off the stage, and
independently of Shakespeare's play. This kind of
speculation even pursues him into the discussion of
Hamlet's madness: "His adoption of the pretence of
madness may well have been due in part to fear of the
reality." Might one suggest to Mr. Bradley that
Shakespeare, fond, like all the Elizabethan dramatists, of
madness as a dramatic *motif*, meant to have "mad
scenes" for Hamlet at any cost; that as he also wanted
him for sane actions and speeches, the madness had to
be feigned; and that, nevertheless, when the madness
motif was being treated on the stage, Shakespeare (as
was the custom of his theatre) treated it "for all it was
worth," careless of the boundaries between feigning and

reality? I will give only one more instance, a really delicious specimen, of Mr. Bradley's unconscious application of Morgann's method. He is puzzled by the insensibility of the Court after the play-scene. " Everyone," he says, " sees in the play-scene a gross and menacing insult to the King. Yet no one shows any sign of perceiving in it also an accusation of murder. Surely that is strange. Are we, perhaps, meant to understand that they do perceive this, but out of subservience choose to ignore the fact?" Evidently the Professor is serious; evidently he cannot be intentionally parodying the famous explanation of Lord Burleigh's nod. His delightful *naïveté* is merely the result of his considering the Court in *Hamlet* as a real Court, and not a stage-crowd put there to manœuvre in a striking theatrical situation.

Let me not be thought to undervalue the really important part of Mr. Bradley's book, his scrupulously careful examination of the text and his skill in bringing all " into a concatenation accordingly" by means of the text. But to understand Shakespeare you have to supplement examination of the text by consideration of other matters, and it is here that I hold the Professor to be at fault. What is outside the text? He says (by implication) a set of real lives, which have to be divined and reasoned about as we might reason about Napoleon or our second cousins or any other actual person. I say, Shakespeare's dramatic needs of the moment, artistic peculiarities, and available theatrical materials. He would ascribe Hamlet's characteristics of intellectual curiosity, discursiveness, dilettantism to some precedent *état d'âme* in Hamlet himself. I would ascribe them to the fact that Shakespeare himself had these characteristics, and sought expression for them on the stage without a perpetual solicitude for consistency or intelligibility of character in his mouthpiece. A father is addressing his son starting on a journey. Shakespeare sees the "good things" appropriate to that situation in general, and at once puts them in the mouth of Polonius, though it suits him afterwards to make Polonius a "tedious old fool." The condition of the stage—a platform-stage, a stage of rhetoric, not a stage of illusion, a stage of "turns," rather than of what the old French critics used to call the *liaison des scènes* —permitted this process, which would be altogether out of place on our modern "picture-stage." The fact is, the technique of Elizabethan drama was somewhat in the condition of our contemporary "programme music." Londoners had Richard Strauss conducting his *Symphonia Domestica* at the Queen's Hall the other day. You heard the themes of the father, the mother, and the child. By these the composer gave musical expression to certain moods that were in him, and, as each theme came up, you took it for the pleasure of the moment. So it was with Shakespeare and his audience over *Hamlet*. The theme of the moment was " A Father's Advice to his Son " or " The Art of Acting " or " Meditations on Suicide," and all the dramatic resources of that theme were duly "exploited " on the spot. But the method which Mr. Bradley has inherited from Morgann through Coleridge would lead him to ignore themes in favour of some supposed biographical facts. He would search Dr. Strauss's score for evidence that the baby's eyes were blue or brown. He would say that " The father, we may be sure, sowed his wild oats before marriage," just as he speculates on what Hamlet was like before the curtain goes up.

And yet I do not doubt that he has the root of the

matter in him. Speaking of Hamlet's humour he says: "The truth probably is that it was the kind of humour most natural to Shakespeare himself, and that here, as in some other traits of the poet's greatest creation, we come into close contact with Shakespeare the man." *Brigadier, vous avez raison!* But why, with this clue, the real key to the whole play, does Mr. Bradley persist in discussing Hamlet and his fellows as real, independent existences? Why does he not perceive that Shakespeare " the man " is speaking again and again in the person of Hamlet, whose busy, curious, hedonistic, characteristically Renaissance temperament is the outcome of the dramatist's need for self-expression and of nothing else? What could be more absurd, on any view of Hamlet as a real person, than his sudden recovery from the agonising farewell scene with Ophelia to the calm virtuosity of the instruction to the players? What more baffling than Hamlet's perpetual breaking off from melancholy about his revenge "mission" to indulge in art, in connoisseurship, in an eager cultivation of the *joie de vivre*? Yet take these things for what, as I hold, they are, moods of self-expression, themes in the "programme music," and all difficulty vanishes. To explain Hamlet, or any other stage character, by assuming him to be a real person, and speculating about that part of his life which, on the same hypothesis, exists though we do not see it, is to offer an exact parellel in criticism to the exploit in histrionics of the actor who thought the right way of playing Othello was to black himself all over.

MEASURE FOR MEASURE

(ADELPHI THEATRE, *March* 1906)

THOUGH *Measure for Measure* does not happen to be one of my favourite *livres de chevet*, I would far rather read it than see it played. For in reading one can skip most of the "story part" and all the "comic business" in order to dwell at leisure on the "sentiments" with their fine rhetorical moralising on the great commonplaces of life and death, mercy and justice, passion and chastity. In the theatre, of course, no such process of selection is possible. There the childishness of the plot is thrust under our noses, and the absolutely idiotic behaviour of the Duke is, so to speak, rubbed into us. There the jack-pudding nonsense of Pompey and the appalling tiresomeness of Elbow and the wishy-washy japes of Lucio must be doggedly endured. There, too, one cannot help seeing what a "thin" piece of work is the character of Angelo and what a mere *ficelle* is Mariana. Thus the resultant impression from the acted play is by no means one of unmixed pleasure. We have seen a number of people, very few of whom we can entirely believe in and none of whom we can entirely like. We cannot like a Duke who deserts his post just to see how a substitute will behave in his place—for the reason he himself puts forward about a stricter administration of justice is, of course, too hollow to deceive an infant. We cannot

entirely like so feeble a hero as Claudio. It is not that
we necessarily dislike him for clinging to life even at
the price of his sister's shame. That is quite human.
It is that he has not the courage of that position. We
think that he ought to have made out a far better case
for a brother's life *versus* a sister's chastity than he
actually does. He never pushes his point; he seems
a mere drifter. Nor can we entirely like Isabella
herself. We feel that she exaggerates the importance
of chastity, and we think of more amiable women,
essentially as virtuous as she—a Saint Mary of Egypt,
a Monna Vanna—who took a saner view. It may be
said that to feel like that is to quarrel with the whole
motif of the play, and that one must concede to
Shakespeare the right to adopt the moral view of his
time. Of course; but then we do not take the historic
standpoint in the theatre, we are subject to the sympathies
and antipathies of the moment, and one undoubtedly
feels a certain antipathy, along with one's admiration, for
this " thing ensky'd and sainted." When Isabella finally
pairs off with the Duke, hugging and kissing a man in
regard to whom she has previously shown not the
slightest symptom of affection, we feel a positive disgust.
As to Angelo one might have liked him better, villain
as he is, if he had shown a little genuine passion. But
though he calls himself a sensualist, he does not offer,
so far as I can see, the true characteristics. He is
merely coldly and deliberately vicious. Finally, we
cannot entirely like Mariana, who lends herself to an
unworthy trick in order to secure Angelo for her husband.
We do not like these people, and we do not like many
of the sentiments which govern their actions. They
had what are to us very odd views about marriage, for
instance. Marriage made everything right; absence of

"marriage lines" made everything wrong. They had odd views about what the gentleman in *The Mikado* calls "fitting the punishment to the crime." And they had odd views about fun, attaching a value to kicks and thwackings as elements of the humorous which we now consider excessive. Nor can we nowadays share their inordinate zest for Malapropisms. Once more, all these views, of course, have their historical explanation. Everybody, knows why Shakespeare held them, and could have held no others. But, once more, in the theatre one is not accounting for the play, or indulging in any mere intellectual exercise; one is seeking the pleasure of the moment, and there are many moments in *Measure for Measure* which are anything but pleasurable.

On the other hand, the one or two great scenes do, of course, profit immensely by stage-representation. There is the great scene wherein Isabella turns with rage and loathing upon Angelo. There is the still greater scene of Isabella's dismay and total *bouleverse-ment* when she finds that her brother clings more to his own life than to his sister's honour. These are two splendid opportunities for the actress who plays Isabella. Does Miss Lily Brayton make the most of them? Well, she makes a great deal of them. She has among her resources beauty, sincerity, "petitionary grace"; she has, too, the art of distinct, sonorous elocution. What she lacks is power. When she reaches what musicians would call the *fff* passages she shows signs of strain, her voice becomes monotonous, she has a tendency to "scold." But hers is a very difficult task. I cannot think at this moment of any ideal Isabella. Miss Brayton's limitations are obvious enough; within them her intelligence and skill and charm are no less conspicuous. The Claudio of Mr. Harcourt Williams is quite a pretty fellow, a butterfly fluttering helplessly within gloomy prison walls; and I have no objection, for that is quite a tenable view to take of the Claudio of Shakespeare. Mr. Oscar Asche's Angelo is a fine sombre, not to say fuliginous, performance; so far as we can believe in the character at all we can put our faith in Mr. Asche's rendering of it. On the whole a creditable affair, this revival of *Measure for Measure*, and it is by no means through any shortcomings of the players that the dominant impression left on the mind is not altogether one of delight.

HENRY IRVING

IN *DANTE*

(DRURY LANE, *January* 1903)

JUST as Mr. Crummles was not a Prussian, so it may be confidently asserted that the average Drury Lane playgoer is not a Dantist. No doubt he is vaguely aware that a long time ago an Italian named Dante Alighieri wrote a poem called *La Divina Commedia*; but he is probably more familiar with Doré's illustrations to this poem than with its text, or even a translation of its text. The famous fresco profile of Dante he cannot fail to have seen. For the rest, modern playwrights have brought him acquainted with the story of Paolo and Francesca da Rimini. Evidently, then, he is not a Dantist. It is necessary to insist upon this point, for the simple reason that the *Dante* which Sir Henry Irving has produced at Drury Lane has been produced, naturally, for the Drury Lane playgoer. It is directly addressed to him; it takes into account his little fraction of knowledge and his very big fraction of ignorance; if the average Drury Lane playgoer believes in it, likes it, and is impressed by it, why, then it has achieved its object.

It is necessary to insist upon this point, because for Dantists, for people who know and love their *Divina Commedia*, the Drury Lane *Dante* will not do at all.

When they are asked, as they are, to swallow the story of an amour—an adulterous amour—between Dante and Pia dei Tolomei, they will at once remark that, where much is uncertain, one thing is quite certain, and that is that Dante had not even a bowing acquaintance with this lady. And for the evidence they will say: see Canto v. of the *Purgatorio*. Further, they will point out that the house of the Malatesta was not at Florence; that the love-story of Bernardino, brother of Francesca da Rimini, and Gemma, daughter of Dante by Pia dei Tolomei, is all nonsense; that it was not Cardinal Colonna who reigned in Avignon; that the several "circles" in the Inferno and Purgatory scenes of the third act are all mixed up, like Sancho Panza's cabbages and baskets; and so forth and so forth. They will say all this, and more. Probably they will invent an additional "circle" in Hell, for the especial benefit of MM. Sardou and Moreau, who have laid sacrilegious hands upon one of the greatest poems in the literature of the world. They say? What do they say? Let them say. *Dante* at Drury Lane is not for them.

The people for whom this *Dante* is intended are, first and foremost, the playgoers—there are legions of them—who have fallen under the spell of Sir Henry Irving's magic personality. Whatever he chooses to play is, they feel, good enough for them. So long as he figures in the foreground of the scene, giving them the postures and the diction and the picturesque presence which they know, they are quite content. Then, again, there are the people to whom drama always appeals on the spectacular side, if on no other; these will get the meat which their soul loveth at Drury Lane. There remain the people—men and brethren, even these, as weak as flesh, if not weaker

11

(like the celebrated wooden leg)—who cling to the old-fashioned prejudice that a play should be a play; that it should have a strong, continuous, and cumulative dramatic interest. These people will leave Drury Lane not quite so contented as the others. It will be said that the inherent difficulties of the subject made the complete gratification of these people impossible; that neither Sardou nor anybody else could weave episodes from the life of Dante and his great poem into drama pure and simple—drama "in its quiddity," *dramatic* drama. And the answer is, surely, plain enough. Sardou was not bound to choose this particular subject. Having chosen it, he had two courses open to him. (1) Either he should have handled the poet's life (or so much as anyone knows of it) and the poet's text (or so much as he understood of it) faithfully and reverently. The result would have been a set of scenic illustrations to the Divine Comedy *plus* a little (derivative) literature. But to have done that Sardou would have had to be more of a man of letters than he is or ever has been. Or (2) he should have let life and text go, and have invented a brand-new drama of his own. The result might very well have been an excellent play, called (for want of any better name) *Dante.* As a matter of fact, Sardou has tried to blend both methods. He has strung little Dantean episodes, more or less authentic, on a cock-and-bull story of his own invention. The result is a ramshackle, confusing, rather irritating "machine." While the Dantists will be exasperated, the average playgoer in search of a play will be more than half disappointed. But there is always the scenery, the stupendous mechanical "effects," the triumphs of stage-management. And there is always Sir Henry Irving.

As for Sir Henry, it is, of course, obvious that if ever man was born to *look* Dante to the life, he is that man. The moment he emerges from the porch of the church at Pisa you recognise the fresco profile. And he wanders through the play—for really he is only a wanderer, a bystander, a perambulating commentator —with just the right air and accent of ascetic severity and melancholy "aloofness." He seems not to be of common clay—for that matter Sir Henry Irving (even if he be playing Jingle or Macaire) never does. And yet Sardou would have us believe him to be of the commonest clay; he is the lover of Pia dei Tolomei, a married lady, and the father of her child Gemma. No sooner have we learned this than we are interrupted by a hollow groan from a tower-window on the left, at which a gaunt form appears, crying for bread. It is, of course, Count Ugolino. When Dante, horror-stricken, pleads for the starving man's release, the terrible Archbishop Ruggieri throws the keys of the tower into the river. Dante, enraged, dashes down the Archbishop's crozier, and is forthwith excommunicated. But he does not quit the scene until he has replied with what may be called a counter-curse.

Act I. opens with a glow of colour and sunshine— the springtide fête at Florence. A young painter is at his easel; who could it be but Giotto? A cloaked figure crosses the stage scowling; it is Malatesta, who has moved house from Rimini to Florence. And that fair-haired girl? Gemma, Dante's daughter, " grown up." And that cowled monk? Dante himself, the exile returned, in disguise. After an affecting interview between father and daughter (in which Sir Henry reaches an unusual pitch of simple tenderness) a woman's shriek is heard from Malatesta's house. The

scene rapidly changes to the interior, and we see
Malatesta wiping his bloody sword, and the dead
bodies of the lovers half-hidden behind a curtain.   In
the confusion, Pia's husband, Nello della Pietra, carries
off Gemma, pursued by Dante; and the spectator's
mind begins to get as confused as the turmoil of the
scene.

In Act II. we see the actress (Miss Lena Ashwell),
who was Gemma a moment ago, turned to Pia once
more.   Confusion worse confounded !   As Pia she dies
in the foul air of the marshes, and immediately
reappears as Gemma in the convent of San Pietro.
Comic business (rather ignoble) of quarrelling nuns ;
a touch of Boccaccio rather than of Dante, but a
vulgarised Boccaccio.   Enter Dante and Bernardino,
leading a rescue party.   Dante, hiding with Gemma
behind the arras, nearly suffers the fate of Polonius.
The sword of one of the soldiery, probing the arras,
has pierced his side, and he is left for dead on the
floor.

But in Act III. he is alive again, mourning over the
tomb of Beatrice in the Campo Santo at Florence.
His old love appears to him in a vision, and bids him,
if he would find Gemma (who has again, it seems, been
carried off), visit the Nether World, and ascertain the
girl's whereabouts from the spirit of her mother, Pia.
So said, so done.   Virgil—practically a *persona muta*
—promptly appears, and conducts Dante to the Door
of Hell, past the Fiery Graves (interview with Ruggieri),
through the Circle of Ice (interview with Ugolino and
Nello della Pietra), on towards the bridge of Rocks
(interview with Pia), and finally to the Valley of
Asphodels.   These various interviews result in the
simple piece of information that Gemma has fled with

Bernardino to Avignon. Needless to say that all the Infernal and Purgatorial "circles" are triumphs of scenic weirdness.

Finally (Act IV.) Dante arrives at Avignon, where the man who ought to be a Pope, but is (in deference, it is said, to certain susceptibilities) only a Cardinal Legate, has just condemned Gemma and Bernardino to the stake. But Dante tells him that his own hour has come—and tells him so in one of the finest declamations of the play. At the stroke of six down falls the Cardinal Legate a dead man. Bernardino and Gemma are saved.

Was this rather puerile story of the hairbreadth escapes of Gemma and Bernardino (with Dante to the rescue) worth inventing? Could not some real poet have contrived a worthier scenic arrangement of the Dante legend which might still have exhibited Sir Henry Irving on every side of his remarkable personality? I think that a quite possible achievement.

WESTMINSTER ABBEY

(FRIDAY, *October* 20, 1905)

TO-DAY the dust that was Henry Irving is enshrined at Westminster. Henceforth he is a name, a tradition, a legend. Like all who, in Buffon's phrase, *parlent au corps par le corps*, the stage-player, if our eyes cannot see him nor our ears hear him, is as nothing. We may dispute among ourselves over his exact rank, and ransack our dictionaries for names to call him by; but just what the actor was, just what he did for us who saw and heard him, we cannot create again by words. What remains of Betterton? A few pages of Steele and Colley Cibber. What of Edmund Kean? An essay or two of Hazlitt. But these are mere printed signs; not the warm, pulsing, radiating forces that were Betterton and Kean. To read of dead actors, when all is said, is to learn nothing more than that our forefathers were pleased; it is not to share their pleasure. It will be——it is already——thus with Henry Irving. Catalogues of plays and characters, dates of this and that occurrence, reams of comment—what have all these to do with the thrills of pleasure we have had from the actual presence of the living man? This, the eternal commonplace of all acting, is peculiarly true of such acting as Henry Irving's. The player of ductile, fluid temperament, who sinks himself in his part, who is a born mime—as Diderot said of Garrick, *naturellement singe*—is never so utter a loss as the player whose virtue is his own peculiar personality. The finest thing—not seldom the only fine thing—in any stage-character of Irving's was Irving himself. And so it is an effort to recall the details of his playing—how he emphasised this, with what gesture or "business" he illustrated that—but what the man was in his totality, as he stood there before us, can still be felt in every fibre of our being.

And that, no doubt, is why, as one lets one's mind range over recollections of the man during the past quarter of a century, one finds oneself thinking most naturally, and most affectionately, not of any particular one of his stage-impersonations, but of his look and manner and speech at the moment he used to come before the curtain to return thanks to the cheering audience. The dignity and grace and sweetness of it! The last time I saw him, and was ever to see him, only a few months ago at Drury Lane, there had been such a night of enthusiasm as I should think must be rare in the annals of the theatre. Even the actor seemed caught by the emotion of the public, for his voice faltered a little as, in his customary formula, he professed himself their obliged, respectful, loving servant. An unforgettable scene.

That was Irving's secret, a personal domination. He never charmed by mere beauty or amazed by mere skill; one was simply fascinated, subjugated by the man himself. The influence of personality, despite the investigations of Psychical Researchers, still remains a mystery. We call it, by analogy, "magnetism"; but how it really operates we cannot explain. If, however, we cannot explain it we may say of it what Johnson said of something else: "We *know* what it is, Sir,

and there's an end on't." We know that some men
have it, while others have it not. The great teachers
—a Socrates, a Dr. Arnold, a Jowett—were great
because of it, not because of what they taught. In
art, and that the very highest, it is often absent. The
poet, the painter, the musician may dispense with it;
their works, to be sure, are emanations of themselves,
but not the emanation that we mean by personal
magnetism. It is permissible to conjecture that
Shakespeare was without it, or else we may be sure we
should have heard more about him from his con-
temporaries. But to the histrionic artist it is indispensable. In Irving this gift of personal domination
was so great as occasionally to swamp the play.
Whatever part he impersonated was bound to become
the very centre and core of the whole. His Iago would
overtop another man's Othello; his Malvolio became
the protagonist of *Twelfth Night*, his Jingle the hero of
Pickwick; his Mathias in *The Bells*, compared, say,
with the more orthodox Mathias of M. Coquelin, was
as a mountain to a molehill. There was a native
grandeur in the man, so that even his very villains, his
Macaires, and the other parts he adopted from the
repertory of Frederick Lemaître, became gorgeous,
flamboyant, *quasi*-regal in their villainy. When, after
his early struggles, he "found himself," it was always
to find himself in a part of personal domination—a
Charles I., a Richelieu, a Wolsey, a Becket. He
instinctively turned to playing leaders of men because
he was a leader of men. As a manager he had a
Napoleonic faculty for organisation and command; as
a *metteur-en-scène* he could not help doing everything
"in the grand style." He was not content until he
had enlisted the first archæologists and painters and

musicians of the day in the service of the theatre. All he did was done with a certain magnificence.

The followers of his professsion do well to honour him to-day, for it was he who vindicated the dignity of that profession, insisting upon the actor's right to respect off the stage as well as on it—*in republica* (the quotation was once used about Irving himself by Lord Coleridge) *tanquam in scena.* Macready had been ashamed of his calling. Irving was proud of it, and felt a stain on its honour "like a wound." It is true that he did more for his fellow-players than for the play-wrights of his day. But how could it be otherwise? How could this strange and picturesque figure, this hidalgo, this living " old master," descend, without a touch of incongruity, to our modern "coat-and-waistcoat" pieces of everyday realism? No, his appointed place was in the world of romance, the world of Renaissance palaces, Illyrian shores, groves of cedar and cypress in Messina, Rosamond's maze, the battlements of Elsinore. But one must not stray at this moment into criticism, or reservations of any sort. To-day there is only one sad word to say—Farewell to our obliged, respectful loving servant.

A. W. PINERO

IRIS

(GARRICK THEATRE, *September* 1901)

THERE is a sense—not strictly accurate, but permissible, perhaps, by " extension "—in which Mr. Pinero's *Iris*, together with *Mrs. Tanqueray* and *Mrs. Ebbsmith* and *The Benefit of the Doubt*, may be said to form a tetralogy. These four plays are bound together, not by any continuity of story, but by identity of theme. Each portrays an erring woman and her fate. The woman's fate is, of course, the *dénouement* of the play; and it has always seemed hitherto that in his *dénouements* was to be found Mr. Pinero's weak point. They were apt to be arbitrary or to shirk logical results. Paula Tanqueray committed suicide, and sudden death is a cheap plot-solution; not so cheap, however, as the "whitewashing" of Agnes Ebbsmith and Theophila Fraser by the aid, spiritual or social, of the Anglican Church. In *Iris* Mr. Pinero, for the first time, does not shrink from a real *dénouement*. And it must have cost him much to nerve himself to it. For the *dénouement* of *Iris* overwhelms the spectator with horror. There is hardly room for pity. Indeed, there are no tears throughout the piece, save the *lacrymæ rerum*. Further, although the *dénouement* is felt to be exactly right, the spectator

170

does not foresee it. At no step in the play does one
foresee the next step, and yet, so soon as anything has
happened, one feels that it must have happened and
just in that way. This means, of course, what everybody knew already, that Mr. Pinero has at least one
quality of the born dramatist, the art of stimulating
curiosity, of stimulating it to a degree wherein it
becomes almost gnawing anxiety, and then of satisfy-
ing it to the full.

One more point of comparison with the three other
plays of what I have very loosely called Mr. Pinero's
tetralogy. They have each dealt with women of
strongly marked characters, women whose wills were
active forces. Paula was headstrong and perverse,
Agnes steadily determined, Theophila rash. And this
choice was all to Mr. Pinero's advantage, because will
is the very stuff out of which drama is made. But
here, in *Iris*, he has set himself a far harder task.
For Iris Bellamy is will-less, or, what comes to the
same thing, has a constantly divided will. At the crisis
of her fortunes she has to choose, as she puts it herself,
between recklessness and self-denial. But she has
neither the courage for the one nor the firmness for the
other ; her character is too weak. And in the penalty
she pays for her weakness lies the tragedy of the play.
She knows her own weakness of will, this rich young
widow, and also her love of luxury. So, too, presumably did her late husband when he left a will
forbidding her to remarry on pain of losing her fortune.
We hear of that will at the rise of the curtain, and are
consequently not surprised to find ourselves at once
confronted with two suitors for her hand, Mr. Laurence
Trenwith and Mr. Frederick Maldonado. Mr. Trenwith
has youth, all the graces, and no money. He could

only offer his bride a log-hut in British Columbia. Mr. Maldonado is a burly, aggressive Jew; but he is also a millionaire. Of course, Iris loves Trenwith; but she cannot face poverty, and, to save herself from her lover, hastily accepts Maldonado. Hardly has she told Trenwith of this step when she begins to repent, and whispers to him to come back to the house that night after the others have left. When he returns she finds she has not the strength to part with him, gives him a note for Maldonado breaking off her engagement, and falls into his arms. This first act has been most adroitly conducted. By a novel device of dropping the curtain for a few seconds at a time, so as to divide the evening into three " episodes," it has shown us Iris's nature, her embarrassing situation between the two men, and the characters of those men — Trenwith's simple, sincere, rather docile; Maldonado's fierce, violent, almost volcanic. It is evident from the first that there is going to be trouble with Maldonado.

In the second and third acts we are at Cadenabbia, where Iris and Trenwith are living "for climate and the affections," to a mandoline accompaniment. But already there is a little rift within the mandoline. Trenwith has his livelihood to earn; he cannot live on Iris's money; he is resolved to depart for British Columbia, and begs Iris to come out there and be married to him, poverty notwithstanding. She cannot consent to beggar herself; and yet in a few moments, and in a wholly unlooked-for way, beggared she is. The newspapers, just arrived from England, tell her that her solicitor and trustee has gambled away the whole of her fortune. At this juncture the spectator instinctively looks round for Maldonado—who promptly appears. At first Iris takes her misfortune bravely;

it seems to brace her up. Though she declines to go
out straightway with Trenwith to British Columbia, for
fear she should be a burden to him, she promises to
wait patiently for him until he can see his way to
keeping a wife, say in two or three years, when he is
to return to claim her. The lovers part, after a harrow-
ing scene——a scene of astonishing truth in every detail,
a scene which shows that Mr. Pinero draws from life
and not from the stage—and Maldonado, who has
become effusively cordial, sees Trenwith on his journey.
Then the "episodic curtain" is again employed, and
we are shown Maldonado's return to the villa to wish
Iris good-bye. She is going away to live on the
wretched £150 a year which has been saved from the
wreck of her fortune; and when Maldonado offers
her a cheque-book, saying he has opened a small
account in her name upon which he trusts she will
draw in an emergency, she has the courage to refuse.
He leaves the book behind him, however, and in a few
moments, to do an act of kindness to a young girl, Iris
finds herself automatically drawing a cheque. And,
as the curtain descends on the third act, she quietly
drops the cheque-book into her travelling bag.

When the curtain again rises, two years have elapsed,
and we are at a gorgeous flat in Mayfair, where Iris is
"discovered" richly dressed, but pale and haggard,
with a grey forelock like Signora Duse's. (And, by
the way, what a part for Signora Duse!) A man
enters, and the spectator knows very well who that
man will be—Maldonado, of course, now a brutal
tyrant. His plot has succeeded, and, taking advantage
of the woman's poverty and weakness—a painful story,
told in a confession, too long for narration here—he has
had his revenge. Even now, however, he would marry

the woman, who, dazed, terrified, a sullen slave, says
she will " think it over." But the inevitable happens.
Trenwith, who knows nothing (or only that Iris's letters
have unaccountably ceased), returns to claim his bride.
The savage irony of this situation is too terrible for
tears, and it is in something akin to torture that you
follow the scene in which the wretched woman tells
her old lover the truth. Stunned by the blow, he can
only mutter, " I am sorry, I am sorry." She begs him
to return to her; was not her first fault committed
through love of him? But he only mutters, " I am
sorry, I am sorry," as he staggers from the room.
Then swiftly comes the woman's fate. Maldonado,
in hiding, has overheard everything, and knows that he
was not Iris's first lover. In his blind fury he almost
strangles her. But he calms down; he comes of a
race, he says, whose qualities are curiously blended—
made up partly of passion, partly of prudence; and
now he will have done with passion. Whereupon, he
turns Iris out of the house—shouting, " This is your
punishment; to drift back into the condition in which
I found you a few months since; this is your reward "
—and is last seen, as the curtain comes down, madly
sweeping the china from the mantelpiece and smashing
the furniture—the wild beast in 'him, the *bête à quatre
pattes*, let loose.

Iris is a very powerful, very painful, play, a characteristic specimen of Mr. Pinero's art, a piece of
literature and at the same time a piece of solid, living,
throbbing drama.

LETTY

(DUKE OF YORK'S, *October* 1903)

IN *Letty* Mr. Pinero reverts to an earlier manner. It is a play of incident and character—that is to say, it just tells you a story for the story's sake—it is not a contribution to the "drama of ideas." I do not, of course, mean that it is "unidea'd." By no means; it may even be said to have its little thesis, just as every baby in *Utopia Limited* had "its little prospectus." But the little thesis is quite unpretentious; it has almost the air of an afterthought, of a mere curtain "tag." It is better to resign yourself to orthodox domesticity in your own humble station in life than to sell your peace of mind for a career of "guilty splendour." It would have been better for Emma Bovary had she reconciled herself to a placid, if humdrum, existence with Charles. Quite so. It is a thesis, as the French say, "like another," if as a thesis it "do not over-stimulate." But it is not to be supposed that the thesis of *Letty* is the element in the play with which Mr. Pinero has been at all seriously concerned. His chief aim has been to tell us a straightforward story for its own sake; to embody for us in a dramatic form what in the cant phrase is called "knowledge of the human heart"; and his aim has been fully realised. *Letty* is not a great, but it is an extremely interesting, play.

Letty is a clerk in a " bucket-shop," who has made
the acquaintance of a " swell," Nevill Letchmere, and
in her timid and fluttering little heart cherishes the
hope that he means to marry her.   She is a good little
girl, and never visits a gentleman's rooms unless
chaperoned by her comrades Hilda and Marion.   The
three girls have come to Letchmere's flat in Grafton
Street to celebrate Letty's birthday, and are making
merry over cake and wine when they are interrupted
by the entrance of Bernard Mandeville, Letty's
employer.   Mandeville is a " bounder," but he is
prepared to marry Letty, and comes to bid Letchmere
" keep off the grass."   For Letchmere, as he points out,
is only spoiling the girl's chances, seeing that there is
somewhere or other a Mrs. Letchmere.   The Letchmeres
have " separated by mutual disagreement."   For a man
about town Letchmere is remarkably sententious and
didactic ; but simple little Letty is fascinated by his
fine language, as well as by his fine furniture.   She
yearns for romance, for luxury, for a life in which
people do not drop their " h's "—or preach the Gospel
of Work, like Marion, or like Hilda, talk of " chaps "
and gorge themselves on tinned lobster and bottled
stout.   Oh, Emma Bovary !   Letchmere obtains
permission to follow the girls to their lodgings.   He
has something important to say to Letty—alone.
Something important ?   Letty is in the seventh
heaven of feverish anticipation.   She thinks she
knows what Letchmere will have to say to her.
She does not know there is a Mrs. Letchmere.   And
that is the first act.

Act II. passes on the roof—in a humble sort of way
the roof-garden—of a house in Langham Street.   The
girls are giving a little party to some men of their own

set, a commercial traveller, an insurance agent, and a
photographer. Please observe the photographer, because
he is more important than he looks. He is a good
little fellow, with a passion for flowery language. Mr.
Pinero gets a great deal of fun out of these three men ;
honest, unsophisticated fun. The traveller is jocular,
the insurance agent lugubrious, the photographer
flowery. They propitiate Letty with gifts of sausage-
rolls and the other comic "properties" of the stage.
Altogether a gay little (and rather Middle Victorian)
roof-garden. But Letty's whole soul revolts from the
sordid vulgarity of her surroundings—as symbolised by
sausage-rolls. Will Letchmere never come? Come at
last he does, but only to shatter poor Letty's dream.
He cannot marry her ; his acquaintance is only doing
her harm ; on the whole she had better make up her
mind to marry Mandeville. While she is still reeling
under the shock Mandeville himself arrives, and duly
makes his offer of marriage. At first the girl turns
from him with loathing. But she is in debt and she
is ill ; Mandeville dangles a victoria before her eyes
and the delights of Trouville. Half beside herself
Letty accepts him, and the whole party sets off for an
evening out at the Alhambra. And that is the second
act.

In the third act we are in a *cabinet particulier* at the
Café Régence. Three people are over their coffee and
cigarettes after dinner—Letchmere, his sister, Mrs. Ivor
Crosbie, and his sister's admirer, Coppinger Drake, to
whom she is about to say good-bye. She has a brute
of a husband, and Drake would like nothing better
than to elope with her, but Letchmere hopes to keep
one respectable member in the family, and determines
that the "good-bye" between his sister and her admirer

12

shall be final. The farewell is duly taken, and then
the room is suddenly filled by the other party,
Mandeville, Letty, and the rest, who have come on to
supper from the Alhambra. Details of a "spread"
with a wonderful *consommé*, a *sole Dieppoise*, and
innumerable bottles of Moet 1892. More comic
business from the traveller, the insurance agent, and
the photographer; comic insolence from Mandeville;
comic vulgarity from Hilda. But Letty's position is
terrible. Letchmere has remained behind, and is
compelled to endure the sight of Mandeville's outrage-
ous behaviour. The girl's agony comes to an
unendurable pitch when Mandeville, filled with Moet
1892, assaults the proprietor of the restaurant. "You
will never be able to stand life with this man," says
Letchmere. "Come to my rooms to-night, and see if
we can try another plan." And that is the third
act.

In Letchmere's flat, at midnight, with her spirit
utterly crushed, Letty gives up the struggle. The pair
map out a Continental tour—Venice in the moonlight,
a new hat every day, and *la joie de vivre, ohé ohé!*
But a message arrives from Letchmere's sister. She
has "bolted" with Drake after all. Letchmere cannot
forgive himself. If he had escorted his sister home as
he had promised, instead of staying behind at the
restaurant with Letty and her friends, the mischief
would not have happened. A woman has fallen, and
a woman whom he could have saved. "Then save a
woman now," says Letty, in a revulsion of feeling, "be
kind to me; let me go home." And he lets her go—
and that is the fourth act.

An epilogue shows what has happened to all the
parties after an interval of a couple of years. Letty

has married the photographer. Emma Bovary has
settled down half-contentedly with Charles. Marion
and the ex-insurance agent help in the business.
Hilda has gone on the stage. Drake has married
the woman he ran away with, and turns out as
unsatisfactory a husband as her first. Letchmere is
in a consumption, marked for death. Letty's last
word to him is " Thanks." She thanks him for having
saved her for a reasonable marriage in her own station.
The photographer is " funny," she knows, but good.
And she has her baby. It is not until Letchmere
has left the room that her face drops. She cannot
forget.

It is, then, a story-play, but the story has no dull
moments, and the play is admirably played. Miss
Irene Vanbrugh's picture of the weak, romantic, timid,
loving little heroine is a picture not to be forgotten.
The girl is, as one of the people says in the play, " alive
all over." That is the prime quality of Miss Irene
Vanbrugh's acting; it is always alive, alive all over.
Mr. Irving, too, is very good, making a really fine thing
of his dramatic scene in the fourth act; but he is
a little too solemn. Some of his speeches in Grafton
Street are delivered as it were *ex cathedra*, in the style
of a lecture at the Royal Institution round the corner.
The fault is partly Mr. Pinero's, who is too fond of
making Letchmere (and not only Letchmere) " talk
like a book."

This matter of Mr. Pinero's dialogue is worth
looking into: for it is a question in which, of course,
not only the drama is concerned, but all literature and,
indeed, the daily commerce of practical life. It would
seem as though nearly all writers—and absolutely all
those who are learning to write—are in deadly terror

of being caught writing just as they would naturally talk. And many of them, no doubt, have this justification, that they talk badly. But, in point of fact, they are just as much afraid of what is simple and fresh and direct in their talk as they are of what is slipshod or slangy. When the sporting reporter of a bygone generation wrote of " Old Sol " or " Jupiter Pluvius," he was making a concession to what he supposed in a vague sort of way to be the dignity of literature; he rejected the words "sun" and "rain," because these were the words that he would use in the bosom of his family—they were not fit for "company." You have the same feeling at work in the Asiatic prose of the auctioneer's rostrum, the feeling that you must put on fine language as you put on a fine coat, for public display. Mr. Borthrop Trumbull in *Middlemarch* is the great exemplar of auctioneer English. Trumbullism, if one may coin a word, is one of the strongest and most persistent forces in literature. At its best it is, of course, a very fine thing—as we can all see when we take up *Rasselas* or *The Decline and Fall*, or *Vathek*. At its worst it is the abomination of desolation — the horrible jargon of the East End melodrama and the penny novelette on the one hand, and the equally horrible jargon, on the other, of the "precious" critic and the Dellacruscan essayist. In the one case as in the other it is an attempt to disguise something of which the writer is, perhaps foolishly, ashamed. He feels that his natural self will not bear inspection. " An underbred, fine-spoken fellow was he "—in his first epithet Goldsmith hit the real offence of Trumbullism.

Are we to maintain, then, that the best literature is always modelled on the best conversation? Are we to condemn by implication, the vast—and in English literature peculiarly rich—field of ornate or "chiselled" or idiosyncratic prose? That would be a foolhardy enterprise, indeed, in a generation which is still under the spell of Ruskin and Meredith and Pater and Stevenson. Non-natural prose may have nothing to do with what I have called Trumbullism ; far from being a cloak for the *mauvaise honte* of inferiority, it may be the inevitable expression of majestic supremacy, of transcendent genius. But the fact remains that a delicate and fastidious feeling for *realism* in language is an extremely rare thing. It is as rare in the world of affairs as it is in the world of art. Anyone who read, for instance, a recently published correspondence between the Prime Minister and the Duke of Devonshire must have seen that Mr. Balfour has this rare feeling to his finger-tips, while the Duke has it not at all. Though the Duke wrote a dignified letter, it was not a letter couched in language which a duke or any man would naturally speak; but Mr. Balfour replied in the exact tone of one man of parts and breeding conversing with another. Strangely enough, the rarity of this particular feeling for language is most conspicuous just where it is most disastrous— in the dialogue of the stage. Whatever may be said as regards other departments of literature, absolute realism of language is indispensable in a play of contemporary life. Yet many of the foremost modern dramatists have been curiously deficient in it. I say "modern dramatists," because accurate realism of language was not expected in the old or rhetorical theatre, and would, indeed, have been out of place there. The theory of that theatre was that the personages of the play, while ostensibly talking to

one another, were really talking *at* the audience. The
public came to hear them make speeches — " in
character," to be sure—but to hear them make
speeches. Modern drama is based upon the theory
that the audience " overhears " the conversation of the
people on the stage. Yet how many even among
first-rate dramatists have attained this ideal of absolutely realistic language, the exact tone of conversation
" overheard"? Dumas *fils* conspicuously failed in this.
Even Ibsen's language—heresy though it may be to
say so—often strikes one as unnatural. The fault
has sometimes been laid at the door of his English
translators—unjustly, however, for I find Edmond de
Goncourt noting in the French translation precisely
the same characteristic, the excess of " mots livresques,"
the habit of " talking like a book." De Goncourt, by
the way, claimed to be himself the inventor of the true
stage dialogue—what he called " la langue littéraire
parlée." Whatever we may think of his claim, we may
take his phrase as an excellent definition. Stage
language should always be " literary "—*i.e.* the outcome of design, selection, rejection, arrangement to
an artistic end ; but it should always be " spoken "
language—*i.e.* selected from the repertory of natural,
colloquial, appropriate speech.

The wind bloweth where it listeth, and this feeling
for natural, appropriate speech has been denied to
many of our best playwrights. Mr. Barrie has it ;
but who else ? Certainly not the author of *Letty.*
In the main arts of the playwright, the art of
character-building and the art of story-telling, Mr.
Pinero is without a rival. But I am not discussing
Mr. Pinero's total equipment for dramatic work ; I
content myself with pointing out a curious defect in

that equipment—the lack of a nice feeling for realism
in language. The defect is a curious one, because it
is evident that Mr. Pinero is fully alive to the whims
and humours of eccentric character as exhibited in
speech. Unlike many of his *confrères*, he is no mere
floundering Trumbullist. Sometimes, to be sure, he
will Trumbullise deliberately and for the fun of the
thing—as in the flowery periods of his comic
photographer. That character is conceived in a vein
of playful exaggeration, and the language assigned to
it is quite conceivably appropriate. So, when he deals
with a vulgar personage, like the shop-girl Hilda, he
can make that character, too, talk with quite appropriate vulgarity. But what man about town ever
talked like his hero, Nevill Letchmere? Listen to
Nevill describing an " outside stockbroker " in a quiet
tête-à-tête with his sister :—

" An arrant brigand, thriving mainly upon the shame-
faced gambling propensities of the respectable classes.
The credulous parson, the sanguine widow, and the
struggling professional man are his chief victims—
although his transactions are occasionally spiced by
a soiled flimsy from an adventurous *demi-mondaine*."

Note how each substantive gets its adjective—the
parson is " credulous," the widow " sanguine," and so
on—and the stiff vocabulary—" transactions," " *demi-
mondaine*." This is not conversation ; it is " spouting."
A few lines lower you read :—

" The austere Marion shares a stuffy lodging in the
most depressing locality conceivable."

Obviously Nevill would never have used the last three
words ; they belong to the comic photographer.

When Letty faints, in the same scene, Nevill blandly remarks :—

"The heat in this room is insufferable. My man must have neglected to lower the sun-blinds."

This, as a speech obviously without ironical intention, is *impayable*. At first you may have thought that in assigning this stilted, bookish language to Nevill Letchmere, Mr. Pinero had the deliberate design of portraying character; that he wished to make Nevill a prig, after the pattern of the young prig (played by the same actor) in *The Princess and the Butterfly*. But nothing in the subsequent development of the character serves to justify this view, and you abandon it when you find that not only the hero spouts, but the heroine as well. Here is a speech which Letty makes to two girl-friends :—

"To my imperfect intelligence, it seems that the first essential is to be capable of resigning oneself to a scheme of things which ordains that some women shall spend their lives in perpetual fag, while others— our more fortunate sisters as they are styled—enjoy freedom and luxury galore. . . ."

There is no need to labour the point further. That word "galore" settles it.

HIS HOUSE IN ORDER

(ST. JAMES'S, *February* 1906)

WHEN Mr. Pinero is at his best you may reckon yourself as close upon the high-water mark of theatrical enjoyment. In *His House in Order* he is at his very best. His master quality, by which I mean the quality specifically called "dramatic," is here seen at its *maximum* of energy. This or that playwright may show more "heart" than Mr. Pinero or a more delicate subtlety, a third may easily outclass him in intellectual gymnastic, but in his command of the resources of the stage for the legitimate purposes of the stage he is without a rival. The art of drama is, quintessentially, the art of story-telling, as the sculptors say, "in the round." Mr. Pinero is supreme as a story-teller of that sort. We are always keenly interested in what his people are doing at the moment; we always have the liveliest curiosity about what they are going to do a moment later. He knows it is the dramatist's main business to "get along," and he gets along in *His House in Order* at a "record" pace. The play tells a plain tale plainly, with the directness of a novel of Defoe; there are no suspensions, no digressions. It displays a richly comic invention, it culminates in a situation of tremendous seriousness, it reveals that quasi-classic element of drama the "purging" of a will, and it has a perpetual undertone of almost mocking irony. Not, of course, that this work, any more than any other work, is flawless. Mr. Pinero, though he has subdued, has not completely conquered his weakness for talking like a book. And there is one passage which seems to suggest that he has neglected Johnson's advice to Boswell to " clear his mind of cant." But, take it for all in all, *His House in Order* is a very choice specimen of Pinero work; in other words a play yielding the highest possible measure of delight.

Distaste for the obvious must not deter me from saying what will be said by everyone—that the play ought to have been called *The Second Mrs. Jesson.* That title, indeed, would be far more appropriate for the new play than was *The Second Mrs. Tanqueray* for the old. I mean that in the earlier play the contrast between the first and second wife, though indicated, was not worked out; whereas that contrast may be said to be the main *motif* of the new play. The character of the first Mrs. Tanqueray had no bearing on the fortunes of the second. The stern lady " with marble arms " was dead, and there, dramatically, was an end of her. But the first Mrs. Jesson, though dead, may be said in a sense to be a protagonist in *His House in Order*; the cult of her memory is what the mathematicians call an " effective force " in the action ; she suffers, posthumously, a change of character which determines the fortunes of the living people in the play. More than that, the evolution in the character of the first wife determines, as by a mathematical law, the evolution of character in the second. It is a case of " contrary motion." When wife No. 1 is morally " up," wife No. 2 is morally " down "—I do not mean merely seems to others, by dint of contrast, but really *is* an inferior creature. When, through a sudden discovery, wife No. 1 sinks as low as she formerly stood high, wife No. 2 goes up like a rocket—again I do not mean merely in the opinion of the rest, but she actually *becomes* a superior creature. And the very discovery which reveals the inferiority of the dead woman is the means by which the living woman finds her own better self. There is a symmetry about this scheme which should captivate the geometrician in us; it has the "elegance" of a theorem by Housel or Chasles. But it must not be supposed that there is anything so arid as formal geometry, any suspicion of a blackboard demonstration, in the way Mr. Pinero tells his story.

Act I. A journalist who has come to "interview" Mr. Filmer Jesson, M.P. for a Midland county division, on the occasion of his opening a new park, presented to the neighbouring town in memory of his deceased wife Annabel, has a preliminary talk with the M.P.'s private secretary, which is the means of at once bringing the audience acquainted with the names and relationship of all the people in the play. The ceremony is to be graced by the presence of the Ridgeleys, father and mother, brother and sister, of the deceased lady. Geraldine Ridgeley, the sister, is a permanent inmate of the house; is, in fact, its martinet ruler. Then there is little Derek Jesson, the son, and Major Maurewarde, an old friend of the Jesson family. Finally, there is Hilary Jesson, Filmer's elder brother, a diplomat on leave. But, asks the reporter, have you not forgotten the present Mrs. Jesson? Oh yes, to be sure! We see at once that Nina, the present Mrs. Jesson, counts for nothing in the establishment. A conversation between Filmer and his brother Hilary

soon tells us why.   Filmer is a prig, whose watchwords
are method and order; rigid "correctness" is his fetish.
The late Mrs. Jesson lived up to his ideals in these
matters; his present wife merely exists to outrage
them.   In a moment of impulse he has married his
child's governess, a clergyman's daughter (note that
detail, please), and finds he has made a mistake.
Nina smokes cigarettes, brings her dogs into the
drawing-room, and is absolutely deficient in those
qualities of order which illustrated her dead prede-
cessor.   But order is essential to Filmer, and so he has
had to call in the dead lady's sister to restore it.
Hilary, who has a marked talent for preaching, which,
as we shall soon find, is apt to get the better of him,
advances the thesis that we should take women as we
find 'em, God bless 'em, and not ask from one the
virtues special to another.   All very well for you, a
bachelor, with an easy temper, is Filmer's contemptu-
ous reply.   Presently Hilary gets a *tête-à-tête* with
Nina, and learns her side of the story.   She recognises
her deficiencies, and would have tried to mend them
if only she had had a little encouragement.   But the
Ridgeleys coldly snub her, and have the ear of her
husband.   The worship of Annabel has got on Nina's
nerves.   Treated as a naughty child she can only
behave as one.   Hilary listens sympathetically; and
the pair forthwith become fast friends.

In Act II. we make the acquaintance of the
Ridgeley family: old Sir Daniel a pompous bore,
Lady Ridgeley a dragon, Pryce Ridgeley a solemn ass.
Geraldine Ridgeley, the *de facto* ruler of the household,
we have already seen.   These, with Filmer Jesson,
constitute what Nina calls the Society of Annabel
Worshippers.   Hilary advises her, for the sake of

domestic harmony, to join that society, and she promises to try. An opportunity occurs over the question of the memorial park. There is a suggestion of
adding a bandstand (rejected by the Ridgeley family
because open-air music is un-English) or a fountain.
Nina begs to be allowed to contribute a fountain, an
artistic fountain. Artistic fountains are also vetoed as
un-English—and Nina flounces out of the room in a
rage. Hilary seizes the opportunity to recite to the
puzzled Ridgeleys a rather too lengthy apologue about
a French cook who succeeded another French cook
and, because of unfavourable comparison, blew up the
kitchen boiler. Nina returns, and apologises for her
misbehaviour. But the discovery that Annabel's
boudoir, reopened to-day for the first time after its
owner's death, is to be allotted to little Derek instead
of to herself provokes a more serious outburst of anger.
She flatly declines to attend the opening ceremony at
the park on the morrow, and is in open revolt. The
Ridgeleys throughout this act have been extremely
droll. Master Derek has shown himself a charming
little boy, and (again, please note) there is an extra-
ordinarily warm affection between him and Major
Maurewarde.

Act III. Nina still in full revolt. She defiantly
puts on a dress of flaming red, just to scandalise the
Ridgeleys, who are all in deep black to celebrate the
third anniversary of Annabel's death. To Hilary's
friendly remonstrances she turns a deaf ear; with her
husband she declares open war. And then, at the
moment when Nina's case is touching bottom, comes the
great discovery. Little Derek, rummaging in his dead
mother's boudoir, has unearthed a handbag from a
" secret " drawer. Nina unsuspectingly opens it—and

finds some faded letters from Maurewarde to Annabel.
These letters show that Annabel, far from being a saint,
was Maurewarde's mistress and that Derek is his child.
Annabel was on the point of eloping with Maurewarde
when she met her death in a carriage accident.   So
now the tables are turned !   Nina has it in her power
to dethrone the sacred image of Annabel, and to
humiliate the tyrannical Ridgeleys.   She means, she
tells Hilary, to use her power.   But Hilary also has
his power, the power of preaching, and he uses—indeed,
abuses—it.   Let her think of Annabel, her remorse,
her misery.   Why, interjects Nina, she was on the
point of eloping when she met her death !   Just so,
replies Hilary ;   do you not (being a clergyman's
daughter) there recognise the hand of God ?   And he
appeals to her " belief in the doctrine of Divine interposition in the ordinary affairs of life."   I just quote
that phrase—I might quote many more—to support
the statement that Mr. Pinero has not yet got over
his weakness for talking like a book.   But Hilary's
reference to the " hand of God " in the carriage accident
is an instance of a less venial weakness ; it is the lapse,
to which I have already alluded, into cant.   Hilary is
represented as a sensible man of the world, not a fool.
Why then is he made to put forward the singular
theory of a God who ignores clandestine adultery but
intervenes when the secret sin threatens to become an
open scandal ?   And it is done so seriously, with so
evident a bid for our " sympathy " !   Mr. Pinero should
have given us some little sign, at least, to make it clear
that he is not the dupe of his own sophistry.   Anyhow,
he puts a sensible reply into Nina's mouth : " Oh, yes,
and it was also the hand of God that brought the
letters to light and delivered them to me."   Thereupon

Hilary tries another tack, and this time a successful one. The really heroic people are the people who have learnt to renounce. " Nina, be among those who wear the halo. Burn Maurewarde's letters, my dear." After a silent struggle, Nina hands him the letters. What is more, she volunteers to go to the park-opening after all, and rushes off to put on a black dress. And that closes a stirringly dramatic third act.

But we have not yet done with thrills. In Act IV., after Hilary has quietly turned Maurewarde out of the house, the party come back from the ceremony, and the Ridgeleys treat the now submissive Nina more contemptuously than ever. There is a fine irony in the scene to the spectator who knows that the woman is bending her neck to the yoke just when she could, if she chose, turn and rend her persecutors. The sight is, however, too much for Hilary. He resolves that there shall be an end of it—and puts the fatal letters in his brother's hands. Nina, horrified, snatches and burns them. But they have been read, and Filmer Jesson's eyes are at length opened—opened to his own weakness, and his wife's sterling worth. The astounded Ridgeleys are politely bowed out of the house, and Hilary quietly shuts the door as Filmer and Nina sit affectionately, and at last with true understanding, side by side. Hilary's silent exit, by the way, is his best effect—far more eloquent than the prolix speeches which Mr. Pinero has lavished upon the part. If Hilary can only be persuaded to be more terse (and to reconsider his " doctrine of Divine interposition in the ordinary affairs of life ") there will be no reasonable fault to find with *His House in Order*. For it would be hypercriticism to object to a certain exaggeration in the handling of the Ridgeley family. Though they exist, dramatically, as a squad, rather than as individual agents, they are cleverly differentiated in details; the slight touch of convention in their treatment is legitimate and indeed inevitable; they remain always in the true key of comedy.

But since there is this trace of exaggeration, however slight, of convention, however legitimate, in the drawing of the Ridgeley family, all the more is it incumbent on the players to go delicately. "Glissez, mais n'appuyez pas" is the proverb, of which Mlle. Thomé, little Derek's French governess, might remind them. Fortunately they need no reminder. It would be difficult to better the tact, the artistic restraint, with which Miss Bella Pateman and Mr. Lyall Swete, Miss Beryl Faber and Mr. Lowne, present the humorous aspects of this family so monumentally humorless. They all four show triumphantly, as they are intended to show, the vast power for evil, for cruelty, for downright tyranny, of complacent, conscientious narrow-mindedness. Mr. Pinero makes, I submit, one little mistake over this group. He allows Hilary, the *raisonneur* of his play, to have an indignant explosion and to declare that the type, as a social pest, ought to be swept off the face of the earth. And this after Mr. Pinero has been turning them to such handsome account, forcing them to contribute to the public stock of harmless pleasure! No, Hilary, as a man of the world, ought to have learnt to suffer solemn bores gladly; where would *His House in Order* be without them? And, for that matter, the denunciation of bores comes with a peculiarly ill grace from Hilary. May one whisper it? He comes at times perilously near to being a bore himself. He loves the sound of his own voice. He is a perfect martyr to dictionary English; even in the most intimate *tête-à-tête* he is careful to "admit that your allegations are not unfounded," or to "point out that matters will eventually adjust themselves." Well, as he himself would say, God bless him; he represents a little weakness of Mr. Pinero's, and so we must accept him with philosophic tolerance. Mr. Alexander plays him with manifest gusto; the more wordy the speech the more the actor seems to revel in it. Again, God bless him. At any rate, he is an excellent foil to the wayward, impulsive Nina of Miss Irene Vanbrugh, with her rapid *staccato* utterance, her febrile restlessness. In the great scene of the third act, when the woman stands out for revenge and the man pleads for renunciation, the acting of both rises to a high level of passionate sincerity.

.

J. M. BARRIE

QUALITY STREET

(VAUDEVILLE, *September* 1902)

THE charm of a genuine Barrie, while it is undeniable, is at the same time not very easily
explicable. In the ultimate analysis I believe that
the pleasure of a genuine Barrie will be found not so
much in what the work—whether novel or play—says
as in what it implies. That, of course, is true in a
sense of any work of art; what we admire or dislike
in it is, in the last resort, the artist behind it. Behind
any genuine Barrie, by which I mean any work in
which the man allows himself freely "to abound," as
the French say, "in his own sense," lets himself go, as
we English say, we are conscious of a sweet nature.
There is ozone in the air; we are once more young
barbarians, all at play; all things for us become
seemly and of good report. It may look like
æsthetic disparagement of Mr. Barrie's work thus to
dwell on its ethical aspect; and I shall run the risk of
exciting prejudice against him, in a certain order of
minds if I say that he is one of the most moral
writers I know. Yet so it is. Mr. Barrie justifies the
simple, natural life; he demonstrates the essential
virtuousness of cakes and ale and even of ginger hot
i' the mouth. *Quality Street* is a case in point. Its

theme, to speak generally, is the joy of living—of living, as the pedants would say, κατὰ φύσιν. More particularly the theme is the desire of women to love tenderly and to be honourably loved in return. That desire is never more charmingly exhibited than it is in young spinsters verging on an age when love seems in danger of passing them by. It is the theme of Jane Austen's *Persuasion*. If that classic instance comes automatically to the pen it is because Mr. Barrie's play chooses Jane Austen's period, and his characters speak the delightfully stilted language of Jane Austen's people.

It is true they all speak that language a little too emphatically; they are more royalist than the king, more Austenite than Jane herself. There are too many "ma'ams," and "vastlys," and "elegant females," and "vowings," and "protestings." Jane Austen's idiom was much more like our own than Mr. Barrie would have us suppose. And there are incongruities which grate on the ear. Jane Austen would never have talked of "object-lessons" or of a lady being "gown'd." To say "This will be a great year for females" and "I long to dazzle a male" is to burlesque her style. In harping on Jane Austen I am paying Mr. Barrie the greater compliment. He gives us something very like her delicate sampler-work, her pomander fragrance. And the story he tells might have been told by her.

Only she would have told it more quietly. *Quality Street* is always, what Jane Austen's work was never, a trifle jerky. It is Jane a little out of breath and flustered, just as Miss Susan Throssell's dear "white and blue" room is a little too garish for the period of the Brothers Adam. Miss Susan's younger sister Phœbe, aged twenty-one, expects a proposal of marriage from

Mr. Valentine Brown. He once kissed her cheek on
the pretext that it was wet. But he only meant
friendship, and, instead of proposing marriage, calls to
say he is going to the wars. Then, for nine weary
years, the dear "white and blue" room is turned into a
school, and Phœbe's brightness becomes dimmed in the
effort to master the rudiments of algebra for beginners.
Let me say in passing that the fun of the scholars
and the difficult algebra occupy nearly a whole act of
the play. That is Mr. Barrie's way; he follows his
humour wherever it leads him; and it sometimes leads
him very far from the business in hand. Then, after
nine years, Mr. Valentine Brown returns from the wars,
at length convinced that what he thought was friendship was really love. The interval is significant; it is
that for which Horace advised poets to bottle up their
verses; and we may say, in Mr. Brown's case, that
love, like poetry, is improved by observation of the
maxim,

> ". . . nonumque prematur in annum."

But Mr. Brown is not yet allowed to realise the full
meaning of his feeling for Phœbe, for we are only at
the end of Act II., and what would become of the
play? Accordingly the interest is prolonged by a
fantastic device. That also is Mr. Barrie's way; his
plots are apt to be thin, and he spins them out by the
first artifice that comes to hand. Phœbe pretends to
be an imaginary niece of hers, one Livy, in order that
she may reassume her well-nigh vanished youth without
let or hindrance, and in order, too, that she may flirt
violently with Mr. Valentine Brown at the officers'
ball. Mr. Brown has a moment of mad love for the
supposed Livy; but only a moment, for a revulsion of

feeling against the lively, forward Livy shows him that
it is the shy modesty of Phœbe that he really adores.
That is a delicious scene—a passage of Marivaux
turned into Austenite English—wherein Brown, thinking that he is telling Livy why he does not love
her, is really telling her why he does. Perhaps it is
rather subtle for the footlights. That, once more, is
Mr. Barrie's way: the way of supersubtlety, of
emotional casuistry, which is rather the method of
the novelist than of the playwright. And, finally, it is
Mr. Barrie's way to prolong the story after the story is
really at an end by a last act which is much ado about
nothing. But we leave everything and everybody
quite happy and cosy in the " white and blue " room ;
Mr. Brown has kissed Phœbe again—and has even
kissed Miss Susan, who had never before in her life
been kissed by a male.

It is all very pretty and sweet, but, as Matthew
Arnold was never tired of quoting from Sainte-Beuve,
every literary *genre* has its *écueil particulier* ; and the
écueil particulier of the pretty and sweet is the namby-
pamby. Here and there *Quality Street* verges on the
namby-pamby, so that we almost sigh for a wolf in the
little sheep-fold. Here and there, too, it is a little
garrulous—as garrulous, shall we say ? as Jane Austen's
Miss Bates. But the fact remains that it is a genuine
Barrie, and, being a genuine Barrie, has an irresistible
charm. It shows us the sweetness of life as lived by
old maids, and by young maids who are honestly
determined not to be old maids if they can help it.
It makes us, like St. Augustine in his youth, in love
with love. It has laid us up in lavender.

THE ADMIRABLE CRICHTON

(Duke of York's, *November* 1902)

I T has been whispered here and there that the root-idea of *The Admirable Crichton* is to be traced to a German play, *Robinsons Eiland*, by Ludwig Fulda. I mention the rumour, but feel quite indifferent as to its accuracy of fact. The root-idea of Mr. Barrie's "Fantasy in Four Acts" is really common property, an idea as old as the hills. But *difficile est proprie communia dicere*, and the point is what exactly an author makes of a common idea—whether he can appropriate it to himself by giving it an individual turn, the turn peculiar to his genius. Now on this point there cannot be the slightest doubt in the case of *The Admirable Crichton*. It is signed "Barrie" over and over again; hold it up to the light and you see "Barrie" in the watermark. And therefore it seems absurd to be reminded by it of some *Conte Philosophique* of Voltaire, because no one will accuse Mr. Barrie of being a Voltairean. But if we are to seek a literary analogy I would assuredly rather find it in eighteenth-century Gallic wit and philosophy than in the Teutonisms of Herr Fulda. In form a brilliant extravaganza, in substance a piece of hard logic, of close-packed thought, this play of Mr. Barrie's is in reality something which Voltaire could never have succeeded in writing had he tried till he was black in the face. Let me take another glance at the eighteenth-century philosophers, and say the theme of this play comes straight from Rousseau. It deals with Rousseau's perpetual subject, " the return to nature." But it deals with that subject in a whimsical, pathetic, ironic, serious way which would have driven Rousseau crazy. Perhaps it takes a little too long in the telling. Perhaps the actors are a little slow. But when all discount has been allowed, the play is to my thinking as delightful a play as the English stage has produced in our generation ; always fresh and exhilarating, yet always giving *furieusement à penser.*

The " return to nature." That is the theme, and in Act I. we find the Earl of Loam expounding it. His lordship believes in equality—once a month—and once a month invites his servants into the drawing-room, where, much to their discomfort, they are treated as honoured guests. In vain his lordship's daughters pout and protest ; if any one of them is not properly polite, threatens the Earl, she shall be condemned to recite. Mr. Crichton, his lordship's butler, does not protest—he is too perfect a butler for that—but he does venture to hint that treating the servants as equals is not really a " return to nature." In London, he says, it is " natural " for earls to be earls and for servants to be servants. The butler alone, then, maintains the calm of philosophic resignation, while the domestics of the household strike attitudes of ludicrous discomposure. This scene of the servants in the drawing-room is a little masterpiece in the presentation of Low Life above Stairs. Dominating the scene is the austere figure of the butler, knowing his place, remembering, not without pride, that he is the son of a butler and a lady's-maid, " perhaps the happiest of all combinations."

Act II. shows us what the "return to nature" really is. The Earl and his family, yachting in the South Seas, have been wrecked on a desert island; and, as by a turn of the kaleidoscope, all the relative positions of the parties are changed. Crichton proves to be a born "handy man," full of invention, able to fashion needles out of hairpins, and to light fires by catching the sun's rays on a watch-glass. He also proves born to command. The rest of the party struggle feebly against his authority, but in vain. They even give him "notice," and retire to another part of the island. But he presides over the cooking-pot, and he knows that hunger will bring them back. The scene wherein they crawl humbly and silently back and gather in the darkness round the cooking-pot, over which Crichton is thoughtfully smoking his philosophic pipe, is the "return to nature" in dumb show. And the point is that Crichton has assumed his ascendency not by willing it, not by domineering, but by sheer force of circumstance. He is the one strong man on the spot; the rest follows by a "natural" law. Nothing could be more droll—and nothing more deeply suggestive—than the impotence of the weaklings to assert themselves on the old social basis. "Nature" on an island establishes a different social hierarchy from that which is settled by "nature" in Mayfair. Crichton does nothing of set policy to further the change; he is indeed quite sorry for it; he simply cannot help it.

Two years have passed before the curtain rises on Act III., and in that interval an extraordinary transformation has been effected. Crichton, beginning as the pioneer and founder, has become the veritable king of the little community. The Earl has cheerfully descended to menial offices. His daughters wait humbly upon King Crichton (and find they have insensibly acquired the trick of "washing their hands with invisible soap" which *he* had when a butler). The Earl's nephew has been trained to useful work by getting a ducking in a bucket whenever he lapses into one of his old Mayfair epigrams. The greatest change is in the character of Crichton himself. He suffers from megalomania, he condescends to the Earl's daughter, as King Cophetua to the beggar maiden. Everyone trembles at his slightest word.

But hark! What was that? A gun! A ship has by accident touched at the island, and a British naval party lands to carry the little community back to civilisation. (Farewell, a long farewell to all Crichton's greatness!) He could, at one moment, have allowed the ship's boat to return from the island without the discovery that it was inhabited. But he is too much of a man to suffer that; he will "play the game." And, as the rescue party enters, and the menials are once more addressed as lords and ladies and the nephew begins to think once more of his Mayfair epigrams, Crichton once more falls into his old respectful butler attitude.

In the last act they are all at home again. The nephew has brought out a book about their adventure, in which he figures as the hero, though he pays Crichton "a kindly tribute in a footnote." All the efforts of the family are now directed to hushing up the truth about what happened on the island. An old busybody, Lady Brocklehurst, is within an ace of discovering the facts, but Crichton holds his tongue, and settles down with the serving-wench who has been faithful to him all along in a little public-house in the Harrow Road, "at the more fashionable end."

I have spoken of the play as a *fantasia* on the theme of the " return to nature." Sir Leslie Stephen once said that he never saw the word " nature " without instinctively putting himself on his guard against some bit of slipshod criticism or sham philosophy, and that he heartily wished the word could he turned out of the language. This is all very well; but what would become of drama? Ever since the days of Thespis and his cart the drama has busied itself with the question, What is nature? and that, of course, in no mere dispassionate spirit of inquiry, but with the practical object of exalting nature, when " located " in any given set of circumstances, as the true guide of conduct. The conflict of forces which is at the root of all drama has been, nearly always, a conflict of nature on the one side against the various restraints—moral, social, political, religious, or merely formal—which the human race has imposed upon nature. And just here, one may say parenthetically, is to be found the real explanation of the antagonism displayed through all the Christian ages by all the Churches, by the Puritan spirit, by the Nonconformist conscience, by all the ascetic sects, to the theatre ; because it is the mission of the theatre, willy-nilly, to exalt and glorify nature, while for all these other institutions nature is something to be checked and chastened and trampled under foot. The simple creed of Crichton in Mr. Barrie's play, " Whatever is natural is right," has always been the creed of the drama. Terence preached it as well as Molière ; it is the common ground of authors otherwise so dissimilar as Sheridan and Dumas *fils*, as (with a more searching analysis of " nature ") Henrik Ibsen and Henri Becque. Indeed, it is the great element of continuity in dramatic literature, this thesis that nature will have her way, that though you expel her with a fork she will yet recur. Take this simple application of the thess—that brides resist all schemes of education elaborated for them by elderly men and fly naturally into the arms of the first young gallant who comes in at the window. That is the story of *L'École des Femmes*; it is also the story of Mrs. Ryley's *Mice and Men*. Nature will not be denied is the implied thesis of the *Adelphi*; it is also, however differently worked out, the implied thesis of Mrs. Humphry Ward's *Eleanor*. All Mr. Gilbert's work in its various forms may be said to be a plea for nature—with a homely, rather prosaic, view of nature. So also may the work of M. Alfred Capus—who takes nature more easily, with a Rabelaisian liberality. No modern dramatist has been more anxiously concerned with nature than Mr. Bernard Shaw; we may not agree with him as to what shall be called "natural"—indeed, it is his deliberate purpose to upset the current views about that—but when once he has settled upon the "natural" he bids us follow it. He, like all his predecessors, holds Crichton's creed, Whatever is natural is right.

Virtually all the dramatists, then, have treated this "nature" theme in their several ways—as Hot-gospellers (Dumas *fils*), or as "the plain man" (Molière), or satirically (Gilbert), or with irony (moral, Shaw; unmoral Becque; immoral, Capus). It has been reserved for Mr. Barrie to work out the theme in several moods at once; he is at once ironic, playfully satirical—as "detached" as you please—and yet very much in earnest, contemplating all forms of creed, and yet making it quite plain that he holds firmly to one. The simplicity and straightforwardness of *The Admirable*

Crichton as a play must not blind us to the subtlety and complexity of the ideas underlying it.

And, first, there is the question, What is nature? Equality, answers Lord Loam; all men are by nature equal. To be sure, his lordship's notions of equality are a little odd. He confutes in the very act of explaining himself. "I'll soon show you if I am not your equal," he says testily to his butler Crichton; "hold your tongue." Also his equality is subject, like comets, to the law of periodicity; all men are equal —once a month, when the servants take tea in the drawing-room. Crichton, on the other hand, declares for inequality as the law of nature. There will always be a social hierarchy, always the *régime* of master and servant. And the system extends further than his lordship suspects. Even were equality established in the drawing-room, it would never obtain in the servants' hall. "Little fleas have lesser fleas." A butler never "walks out" with a servant-girl, is never engaged; he may "cast a favourable eye." Between cook at one end of the kitchen table and John and Thomas at the other is the "tweeny" to pass the dishes. All are but parts of one stupendous whole, and the system is to Crichton not merely inevitable, but æsthetically gratifying and best for everyone. "To me," he cries, "the most beautiful thing in the world is a haughty aristocratic English house with everyone kept in his place. Though I were equal to you, what would be the pleasure to me? It would be counter-balanced by the pain of feeling that John and Thomas were equal to *me*."

At bottom Crichton's conception of nature is the evolutionist's: the perfect adaptation of organism to environment; and at once there arises the further question, What happens with a change of environment

—say, from Mayfair to a South Sea Island? To answer that question in action is the main object of the play—which, be it observed, would be a good play merely from the superficial drollery of its action, the humours of drawing-room and kitchen in Mayfair and the humours of castaways on a desert island, but which is a thousand times better play because underneath the drolleries at the surface is a logical *nexus* of ideas. What happens with the changed environment is an inversion of the old hierarchy; servants (being inured to practical work) become masters, and masters (being useless outside civilisation) become servants. And, mark, it is by no conscious volition that the change comes about, but by a natural law, "something not ourselves which makes for" the new inequality. Lord Loam sinks "naturally" to the bottom, just as Crichton rises "naturally" to the top. All the conscious effort there is is devoted by all concerned to the maintenance of the old order; but in vain. When Crichton lays down the rule "no work, no dinner," he did not invent it, he "seemed to see it growing on the island." And when the aristocrats, after giving Crichton "notice," humbly creep back to him, he has not summoned them; it is their hunger drawing them to the cooking-pot. I have already described this scene of the return of the party to the cooking-pot as giving the gist of the play in dumb show. It is precisely this faculty of inventing such silent yet all-expressive actions which is the test faculty of the dramatist. After the "curtain" of *The Admirable Crichton*, Act II., no one can again question Mr. Barrie's instinct for drama.

But Act III. is *the* act. It is not too much to say that it has a real philosophical significance. For it shows not only how well a new environment, a

new hierarchy, gets established, but how the features
common to all hierarchies come "naturally" into
being—a sort of kinship, the discipline of fear, a
servile class, the curious effects of what we call
"prestige." Power becomes so "natural" to Crichton
that we even see the first germ of a "divine right"
theory working in him. And not only have the
others abandoned all idea of resistance; they are
battus et contents, like George Dandin in very different
circumstances. Lord Loam is content to pluck
Crichton's poultry. Lady Mary is content to be
Crichton's parlourmaid. And, more, we are shown
how the dyer's hand is subdued to what it works in;
how the new servants not only perform the duties,
but acquire the very tricks of the old. The Earl
finds himself repeating Crichton's old catchword,
"Thank *you*, Sir," and Lady Mary, when waiting at
table, mechanically rubs her hands as Crichton used
to do. Thus we see that not only will there always,
as Crichton declared in Act I., be masters and
servants, but the two classes will always "naturally"
behave "as sich," and in each will come out the
"natural" *stigmata* of their employment.

Further, it is in this remarkable third act—almost
disquieting by the reach of its intellectual suggestion
—that Mr. Barrie, hitherto so detached, so playfully
ironic, lets his own sincere conviction peep out. His
conviction is that though all lives are "natural,"
when appropriate to their circumstances, the best
"nature" is that of the wild island life. Under the
influence of open air, hard exercise, and strict
discipline—"no work, no dinner"—all the castaways
are for the first time in their lives thoroughly happy.
You are reminded of Thoreau at Walden Pond or

of Tusitala in Samoa. It is the old Abernethian
recipe for happiness: live on sixpence a day—and
earn it. And the lesson is pointed by the obvious
falling-off in happiness when they all return in the
last act to Mayfair, where the Earl is worried by
his collars and Lady Mary has painfully to check
herself from running up three stairs at a time. What
a dismal contrast to their enjoyment when they
were " barbarians all at play"! Indeed, the conclusion of the piece is the only portion of it which
leaves a somewhat bitter flavour in the mouth. The
aristocrats, who began by being merely fools, are
driven in the end into being consummate liars. And
they lie not only for self-preservation, but wantonly—
publishing a book ascribing all Crichton's heroic acts
to themselves, and barely mentioning " the servants "
in a footnote. The most cruel thing is the dwindling
of Crichton to his original proportions; and, what is
more serious, it is an incredible thing. Dramatically,
I admit, it must so befall; Mr. Barrie's scheme
involves symmetry and contrast, the return of all
concerned to their precise starting-point—after the
fashion of those " biographs " at the music-halls which
show the successive stages of a pillow-fight and then
show those stages reversed. But while it was
" natural " for Crichton to develop into the hero, or
" overman " of Acts II. and III., it was not " natural "
for him to shrink back into his old self. For " nature "
—if I may hazard something about her on my own
account—never forgets. As the island life turned a
butler into a ruler, says Mr. Barrie, so civilisation
turned the ruler back into a butler. That is rather
too savage an indictment of civilisation.

However, there is the play, brimful of ideas, and,

quite apart from your delight in the sheer amusement of the thing, you welcome it with gratitude for its ideas. For what the English stage most sorely needs at this time of the day is ideas; and the advent of a dramatist who like Mr. Barrie can *play* with ideas, can (as Dr. Johnson said, "the dogs," his opponents, could not) "write trifles with dignity," is a rare piece of luck.

PETER PAN

(DUKE OF YORK'S, *December* 1904)

THERE has always been much of the frank
and trusting simplicity of the child in Mr.
Barrie's work, of the child for whom romance is the
true reality and that which children of a larger growth
call knowledge, something divined to be not worth
knowing. It was certain, therefore, in advance that
when he set himself to write a play for children and
about children he would give us of his very best,
his most fanciful, and his most tender. *Peter Pan*
is from beginning to end a thing of pure delight.
Mr. and Mrs. Darling are a young couple with three
little children, Wendy, John, and Michael, and, strange
to say, the children have a four-footed nurse, the
dog Nana, who turns on the " hot " and " cold " taps in
the bath with his teeth, lays out their night-clothes to
dry before the nursery fire, and, what is more, sees
that they take their medicine at the proper time. In
this matter of medicine Mr. Darling affects to set the
children an example by bravely taking the nauseous
draught himself; but Mr. Darling, I am sorry to say,
is a humbug, and he surreptitiously pours the stuff
into Nana's milk, thereby earning and richly deserving
the contempt of Wendy, John, and Michael. By
and by, when father and mother have gone off to
their dinner-party (Mr. Darling giving a sad exhibition

14

of grown-up " temper " over a white tie) and the children
have gone off to sleep, Peter Pan comes in at the window.
Peter Pan is a prose Puck, a twentieth-century Ariel, who
has come to the children's nursery to recover his shadow,
which had been unfortunately caught tight in the
window-sash.   He is accompanied by the fairy Tinker
Bell, though we are only aware of her presence by
her tintinnabulation and by a will-o'-the-wisp gleam of
light on the wall.   The tintinnabulation awakes Miss
Wendy, who graciously offers Peter a kiss.   But as
Peter doesn't know what a kiss is she gives him a
thimble instead, so that ever afterwards Peter calls
thimbles " kisses " and kisses " thimbles."   Then John
and Michael wake up too, and Peter teaches all three
how to fly.   But whither shall they fly?   Why not
to Peter's home, the Never-Never-Land, peopled by
children who, when infants, have been dropped out of
their perambulators by careless nursemaids and have
not been claimed within seven days?   Out then
they all float through the nursery window, and we
follow them to the Never-Never-Land, where they
live underground, descending through the hollow
trunks of trees, and using a big mushroom as a
chimney for their kitchen fire.   Besides the young
inhabitants who began life by dropping out of a
perambulator, the Never-Never-Land is peopled by
Red Indians and Pirates, who lose no time in showing
us that they know how to " behave as sich."   The
Red Indians always lay their ear to the ground, then
give vent to unearthly yells, and prepare for scalping
somebody—a Pirate, for choice.   At the head of the
Pirates is the terrible James Hook, so-called because
he has a formidable hook in lieu of a right hand.   The
hand, we learn, has been bitten off by a crocodile, who

liked it so much that he has been ever since in quest
of James Hook, in order to make a meal off the rest
of him. Fortunately the crocodile has swallowed a
clock, so that his presence is always announced by a
loud tick. Some day the clock must run down, and
James Hook dreads that day with a deadly fear.
Meanwhile, the Pirates go a-pirating and the Redskins
a-redskinning with gusto and many choruses. These
are not the only perils that beset the children. There
are fierce wolves who decline to be driven away until
someone luckily remembers that you may frighten
away a wolf by looking at him with your head between
your legs.

The plot, which may be said to have hitherto been
"in solution," now begins to crystallise round Miss
Wendy. The motherless boys who fell out of the
perambulators have unanimously adopted her as their
little mother. (Note, in passing, this latest instance of
Mr. Barrie's fondness for the idea of a child playing
mother to other children—an idea used in *The Wedding
Guest* as well as in *Little Mary*.) This arouses the
jealousy of the Pirates, for they, too, have never known
a mother's love, and they resolve to kidnap Wendy in
order that she may be a mother to them, instead of to
the little boys. But the motherhood of Wendy
involves the fatherhood of Peter Pan, and that corollary
is extremely distasteful, not only to the Pirates, but
also to the Redskins, and even to the fairy Tinker
Bell. For the chief maiden of the Redskin tribe wants
Peter for herself; so does the fairy; while the
Pirates have clearly no use for Peter. Thereupon
James Hook resolves to murder Peter with poison
double-distilled from a plum-cake, and would have
succeeded, had not the fairy drunk off the poison

instead. Then shall the fairy die?   No, for Peter Pan appeals to the audience—to " all you who believe in fairies "—to save her by their cheers, and of course does not appeal in vain.   But James Hook and his buccaneers have, in the meantime, kidnapped Wendy and the other children, gagging and binding them as they severally ascend from underground through the trunks of the trees; just as the Spanish soldiers are severally gagged and bound in M. Sardou's *Patrie*. It shall be Peter Pan's task to rescue them.

This peripety brings us to the deck of the Pirate Ship. The children are under hatches, while the Pirates dance hornpipes overhead and James Hook paces the quarter-deck, giving a continuous burlesque of old nautical melodrama.   It is now time for the unhappy children to walk the plank—though two of them shall be spared to serve as cabin-boys if only they will cry " Down with King Edward."   Proudly the dauntless boys reply with " God save the King," and " Rule Britannia," and so the dread plank is run out over the side.   But hush! What is that sound? Tick-tick-tick!   It is the crocodile, the implacable enemy of James Hook, who cowers in a corner, bidding the rest to hide him.   And now what do we see? Yes, no, yes—it is Peter Pan and no crocodile, who has ingeniously provided himself with a clock.   Swiftly he unlooses the children's bonds, and as swiftly armed to the teeth they fall upon the astonished Pirates.   To throw the scoundrels overboard is the work of a moment.   Into the deep they go, sending up great splashes of real water, till Hook and Peter are left face to face.   " James Hook, you have to reckon with me—Peter Pan, the Avenger."   The combat is brief but fierce, and of course in the end the wicked

Hook goes over the side—splash!—to his watery grave. Then down with the Jolly Roger, and up with the Union Jack, and three hearty cheers, with three cheers more, for Peter Pan, the Avenger!

After seeing more of the crocodile, and more of the Redskins, and even more of the Pirates (for they are not all so dead as had been supposed), we begin to wonder how poor bereaved Mr. and Mrs. Darling are getting on. So do Wendy, John, and Michael, who accordingly return home, to find their father living, in token of remorse, in Nana's kennel (in which he gets invited out to "smart" parties, and makes a speech to the members of the Stock Exchange). Then they rush into their mother's arms (in a scene suggesting a famous one from *La Joie fait Peur*), and everybody lives happy ever afterwards—except, I am afraid, poor Peter Pan, who has no mother to go home to, and is last seen gazing very, very sadly and wistfully through the nursery window. The whole affair is a delicious frolic, touched with the lightest of hands, full of quiet wisdom and sweet charity, under its surface of wild fun, and here and there not without a place for a furtive tear.

BERNARD SHAW

CANDIDA

(COURT, *April* 1904)

FANTASY has its place in the theatre, as well as realism, and that is one reason why the theatre has room for Mr. Bernard Shaw. His method of travestying life is to eliminate from it everything but the pure intelligence. Just as Mr. H. G. Wells amuses us by supposing a world where the laws of gravity are suspended, or where there is no such thing as time, or where space is of x dimensions, so Mr. Shaw amuses us by representing a world where conduct is regulated by thought, and men love women, as the civil servant in *Pickwick* ate crumpets, on principle. There are, no doubt, such people in real life, people who choose their diet, their clothes, and their wives on principle; people, even, who in flat defiance of Scripture do by taking thought add a cubit to their stature. I forget how many millions of inhabitants there are on the Planet Terra, but evidently there are quite enough to realise all thinkable things in actual facts. If you will only go on dealing for ever, you are bound one day to hold thirteen trumps. All the same, if you choose that day for the " period " of a whist-drama, you will present fantasy, not realism. So it is with ideas. Ideas count for next to nothing in the fundamental human relationships. Our little exploits in coherent thought are mere bobbing corks on the great stream of life. Ideas, like dukes in Mr. Gilbert's opera, are two a penny. We are such stuff as dreams, not manuals of logic, are made of. " Why did I love my friend ? " asks Montaigne, and gives the only true answer : " Because it was he, because it was I." By systematically ignoring this all-important side of life, all its subconscious and unconscious elements, by representing life in general and love in particular as based upon ratiocination, Mr. Shaw obtains most amusing results.

Thus in *Candida* he takes the familiar dramatic situation of a woman between two men, but his peculiar treatment makes the familiar situation something quite new and strange and diverting. The lady is beloved by her clerical husband, who has a clergyman's ideas, and also by a young poet, who has a poet's ideas. At a given moment the clergyman takes the poet by the coat-collar and gives him a good shaking. The poet, so soon as he has recovered his breath, shouts out: " I'm not afraid of a clergyman's ideas. I'll fight your ideas. I'll rescue her [Candida, the parson's wife] from her slavery to them ; I'll pit my own ideas against them. You are driving me out of the house because you daren't let her choose between your ideas and mine." In an ordinary play, of course, in a representation of life, this would merely be a speech " in character "— the speech of a man who, being hit, cannot hit back with his fists, but hits back with his rhetoric. But Mr. Shaw actually means it; it is the very thesis of his play. The parson's ideas *do* waver, break, and flee before the poet's ideas ; the lady *is* asked to choose between the two sets of ideas, and gravely, without irony, makes her choice accordingly. It is an amusing game, worked out with the "elegance" of a mathematical demonstration. To crown the joke, Mr. Shaw takes care to give his fantasy a certain admixture of reality. While his dramatic conflict is a conflict of pure ideas, it is ostensibly carried out by people who are, externally at any rate, familiar types in the world around us. We know the East End parson, a "muscular Christian," a bit of a socialist, a "strenuous" worker of good works. We know the poet, with some traits borrowed from Shelley and others from De Quincey. As for Candida herself, we know her only too well. She is the managing, mothering, thoroughly competent woman, who carries about innumerable bags and parcels, with an aggressive air of brisk usefulness, and cannot talk to a man without patting him on the back, or retying his cravat, or picking bits of cotton off his coat. In real life she is what American slang calls a "holy terror." In Mr. Shaw's fantasy she attracts the love and admiration of every man who comes near her. She is the star and they are the moths. Whole sets of ideas—parsonical ideas and poetical ideas—gyrate furiously around her. That is part of Mr. Shaw's fun, but this time it is not intentional fun. As a rule, he keeps his sympathies well in hand. He treats both parson and poet calmly and dispassionately. But he cannot conceal his conviction that the Candidas of this world are angels in petticoats.

There is nothing in all this that one could not have told from the printed play. What further impressions do we get from the acted play? Mainly a heightening of the fun, a sharper sense of the incongruity between the external reality of the people

and the internal fantasy of their actions. We *see*
Candida flicking the cotton off the gentleman's coat
and carrying the little parcels and bags, we *hear* her
gravely "opting" between parson and poet: "I give
myself to the weaker of the two." And the minor
characters, who are unalloyed reality—the parson's
typist and his curate and his father-in-law—become, of
course, more solidly real on the stage, present a more
startling contrast to the essentially fantastic protagonists.
Further, we have the pleasure of an actual performance,
the pleasure of seeing what the players make of their
parts and how their notions of them correspond or not
with our own preconceived notions. In this respect
one has no disappointment to record. Miss Rorke's
Candida, like Mr. McKinnell's parson and Mr. Granville
Barker's poet, was the very thing; while Miss Sydney
Fairbrother revealed much more in Proserpine than
one ever guessed to be there, and both the father-in-law
of Mr. A. G. Poulton and the curate of Mr. Athol Stewart
were as good as could be. The fact is, intelligent
actors must revel in Mr. Shaw's plays; they are never
called upon to open their mouths without saying
something worth saying, and whatever they are called
upon to do there can be no doubt in their minds as
to what, precisely, it is.

On the other hand, the stage-presentation of *Candida*
adds nothing to what is the chief delight of the play
—the chief delight of every one of Mr. Shaw's plays—
its brilliant dialectic. And in one respect the spectator
is actually deprived of a pleasure enjoyed by the
reader. The book gives characteristic fragments of
exegesis which necessarily disappear on the stage.
One example is the account — as good as any
"portrait" of La Bruyère —of the father-in-law,

Mr. Burgess. Another occurs at the fall of the curtain. The stage direction is "They (husband and wife) embrace. But they do not know the secret in the poet's heart." On the stage the actors can, and do, embrace ; but they have no possible means of telling the spectator, by their actions, whether they do or do not know the secret in the poet's heart. On the whole, however, *Candida* on the stage is capital sport. Mr. Shaw maintains that he is quite serious, an out-and-out realist ; in short, that in saluting him as a merry sportsman one is like the young lady who, when Sydney Smith said grace, shook him by the hand with a " Thank you so much, Mr. Smith ; you are always so amusing." If so, one is evidently in the ignorant position of Candida and her husband when they embrace at the fall of the curtain ; one does not know the secret in the playwright's heart.

JOHN BULL'S OTHER ISLAND

(COURT, *November* 1904)

" I T'S all rot," says Broadbent, the Englishman, of some speech by his Irish friend, Larry Doyle, " it's all rot, but it's so brilliant, you know." Here, no doubt, Mr. Shaw is slyly taking a side-glance at the usual English verdict on his own works. That verdict will need some slight modification in the case of *John Bull's Other Island*. For, in the first place, the play is not *all* rot. Further, it has some other qualities than mere brilliancy. It is at once a delight and a disappointment. It delights by its policy of pin-pricks. Mr. Shaw takes up the empty bladders of life, the current commonplaces, the cant phrases, the windbags of rodomontade, the hollow conventions, and the sham sentiments; quietly inserts his pin; and the thing collapses with a pop. Occasionally, he indulges in fiercer onslaughts with more formidable weapons. Like Johnson, after a certain conversation described by Garrick, he has " tossed and gored several persons." The play delights, again, by its able dialectic. Its interlocutors never shirk a point or swerve from it; every side gets a fair hearing, and though, in the end, all parties are dismissed with costs, you have a conviction that justice has been done. Englishmen and Irishmen alike get credit for their qualities as well as their defects. As an Irishman Mr. Shaw, perhaps,

permits himself to tell us more than any English writer
could venture to say about his countrymen's weaknesses.
There he speaks with authority. Add that Mr. Shaw
has, for once, succeeded in depicting a natural and
delightful woman. On the other hand the play is a
disappointment because of its wilful, perverse disregard
of anything like construction. It is written on the "go-
as-you-please" principle, without beginning, middle, or
end. People wander in and out quite casually and say
whatever happens to come into Mr. Shaw's head at the
moment. A rivulet of "story" meanders through a
meadow of "Shawisms" and trickles dry long before
the curtain descends. There is no reason whatever
why the play should end when it does—except that
Mr. Shaw has had enough of it. Some of us may
perhaps wish he had got tired just a little (say half an
act) sooner.

Broadbent is a typical John Bull Englishman. With
a native fund of "horse-sense," indefatigable energy, an
incurable optimism, and a total incapacity to sympathise
with any other *ethos* or understand any other point of
view than his own, he lives mainly upon shibboleths—
Free Trade, Home Rule, Championship of Oppressed
Nationalities, the Sacred Memory of Our Grand Old
Man, and Reform. Asked to define Reform he replies
that it is the pious conservation of such existing
reforms as have been brought about by the Great
Liberal Party. If anyone is sick or sorry, he cheers
them with the assurance that it will be all right after
the next election. I have said that he is a Home
Ruler. He is now minded to study Ireland on the
spot, and desires to take with him his Irish friend Larry
Doyle. Larry contemplates the trip without enthusiasm,
for he is an Anglicised Irishman who knows things

about Ireland which do not quite accord with Broadbent's anticipations. Broadbent appeals to Larry's Irish heart. "Oh, never mind my heart," says Larry, "an Irishman's heart is nothing but his imagination." Then Broadbent puts down his friend's gloom to "the melancholy of the Celtic race." "Celtic" has nothing to do with it, is the reply, it is the Irish climate and landscape and humdrum surroundings. Anyway, retorts Broadbent, there is the charm of the Irish voice and the Irish brogue. Larry explains that the voice is only the result of a frugal diet, while, as to the brogue, his friend does not know the real thing from the sham article, brought from Glasgow or the Scotland Road Division of Liverpool for consumption in cockney music-halls. After this conversation the pair set out for Ireland.

Here, in the village of Roscullen, we make the acquaintance of native types: the peasant with local superstitions that are really Pagan; the parish priest, who reproves the peasant's superstitions, but displays worse Catholic ones of his own; and a certain Keegan, an unfrocked priest, who passes for a madman and is really a mystic. Keegan, an Irish St. Francis, talks with grasshoppers, calls the donkey and the pig " my brother," has been taught by a dying Hindu to believe in metempsychosis, and asserts (with the devil in *Dr. Faustus*) that this earth of ours is really hell. Broadbent, who is the first of the two visitors to arrive, meets with Miss Nora, an old sweetheart of Larry's who has been pining for him through all the years in which he has neglected her. The Englishman at once falls in love; but the Irish girl tells him it is only the native potheen, which is too strong for his head, and gently but firmly leads him home to bed. Next morning there is a village conclave, composed of Larry's father, the priest,

and a couple of small farmers, who concoct a scheme for
turning Larry into a member of Parliament. Larry's
principles are not theirs, he explains, but they make
light of so absurd a reason. " What we want is to get
a new class of man into Parliament—a man who can
afford to live in London and pay his own way until
Home Rule arrives." Larry still declines the offer,
which is then transferred to Broadbent, who eagerly
accepts it, and begins to spout all the English Home
Rule shibboleths. So great is his admiration for the
country that he firmly believes that, if once Home
Rule is established, the whole Liberal party will become
"naturalised Irishmen." The real Irishmen laugh at
him in their sleeves, and fool him to the top of his bent.
To get " popularity " he offers to take a farmer's pig
home on his motor-car. The landlord question and
Church question are debated, and Mr. Shaw hits out
all round. There is a little gem in the way of a
dialogue between Broadbent's cockney valet and an
embittered Irish farmer, in which the valet tells the
farmer that there are worse evictions in Lambeth than
ever there were in Roscullen. But, thank goodness,
Englishmen are free. Ay, retorts the farmer, it's little
use muzzling sheep.

Broadbent's motor-car has run over the farmer's pig
and knocked the window out of the Roscullen china-
shop; but, unabashed, the Englishman again deluges
the sniggering villagers with Home Rule shibboleths—
and again makes love to Nora, who, this time, accepts
him. She accepts him on finding that Larry does not
really care for her. (Larry, who has not seen her for
eighteen years, can only hum a tune and talk about the
weather, and admits that what should have been a
romantic occasion is a dismal failure. " All these great

sentimental events usually are failures.") Nora, however, who has a fortune of £40 a year, is much disgusted
to find that, for electioneering purposes, she will have
to shake hands with the " common people " in Roscullen.
She is met by the remark that " For an M.P.'s wife, no
one is common whose name is on the register." Finally,
there is a discussion about heaven, in which the
Englishman talks of a dream of " blue satin " and
Keegan delivers a mystical oration about various
idealistic trinities ; and with Broadbent's announcement
that he will build a big hotel in Roscullen, make golf-
links, and " restore " the old round tower, the curtain
descends upon what is, of course, not a play but a
thoroughly characteristic " Shavian " entertainment.

MAN AND SUPERMAN

(COURT, *May* 1905)

IT has been bruited abroad that Mr. Bernard Shaw
is a somewhat lukewarm admirer of Shakespeare.
If this be so, it is only one more illustration of the
familiar gnomic saying of Euripides that there is no
enmity so fierce as that of brother against brother.
For Mr. Shaw and Shakespeare have at least one conspicuous bond of fraternal relationship; they both use
the same stage technique.   To Mr. Shaw as to Shakespeare organic plot-development is a matter of indifference, as compared with the systematic exhibition of
ideas.   They both ignore the *liaison des scènes* with
a splendid carelessness, and ruthlessly sacrifice imitation
of external life to any passing velleity for propagandism.
It is not the same propagandism, of course.   Shakespeare's is the propagandism of current morality or
beauty or sheer poetry; Mr. Shaw's is the propagandism of paradox or inconoclasm or sheer
antinomianism.   But the effect on the dramatic form
is the same.   Hamlet interrupts the action on the platform at Elsinore to expatiate on alcoholism, Gertrude
keeps Ophelia's bier waiting in the wings while she
gives a " word picture " of a river bank, John Tanner
brings everybody and everything to a standstill (always
" talking," as Ann pithily puts it) in order to give forth
so much of Nietzsche and Schopenhauer as Mr. Shaw

has chanced to assimilate. Thus for the sake of something which may be very fine, but certainly is not drama, both dramatists cheerfully let the quintessential drama go hang. Neither of them is, for stage purposes, a man "looking before and after"; they are both playhouse Cyrenaics, living in the moment for the moment's sake. This identical result has arisen from very different causes. For Shakespeare there were the limitations and the licence of the platform-stage, together with a tremendous energy of creation which was perpetually driving him outside the bounds of drama. For Mr. Shaw there are his own limitations; he, too, is perpetually energising outside the bounds of drama, and if for a moment he gets inside them it is by a mere fluke. It is piquant to find identity of form so absolute with such a world-wide difference of content. No need, is there, to account for that difference? On the one hand a born dramatist, and that the greatest; on the other a man who is no dramatist at all. Let me not be misunderstood. When I venture to say that Mr. Shaw is no dramatist I do not mean that he fails to interest and stimulate and amuse us in the theatre. Many of us find him more entertaining than any other living writer for the stage. But that is because he is bound to be an entertaining writer in any art-form—essay or novel or play. All I mean is that when he happens to choose the play as the form in which he shall entertain us there is a certain artistic waste. There is waste, because Mr. Shaw neglects, or more probably is impotent to fulfil, what Pater calls the responsibility of the artist to his material. You forgive the waste for the sake of the pleasure. Nevertheless, in the interests of good drama it is one's duty to be dis-

15

satisfied.   We want a play that shall be a vehicle for
the Shavian philosophy and the Shavian talent and, at
the same time, a perfect play.   Shall we ever get
it?   Probably not, in this imperfect world.   We
certainly do not get it in *Man and Superman.*

Were it not for the typographical inconvenience of
the arrangement one might draw up a balance-sheet
of this play in two parallel columns.   The left-hand
column would display the action-plot.   I use the term
action, of course, in its widest sense, so as to cover
not merely the external incident but the psychologic
and, more particularly, the emotional movement and
"counterpoint" of the play.   The right-hand column
would give the idea-plot—that is to say, the more or
less logical *nexus* of concepts in the author's mind
which form the stuff, the real *raison d'être* of the play.
Only by that method of sharp visual contrast could
one hope to bring to light the masked interde-
pendence of the action-plot and idea-plot and the
curious way in which the one is warped and maimed
in being made to serve as the vehicle for the other.
One would have been better able to show by the
method of parallel columns that the action-plot is
well-nigh meaningless without the key of the idea-
plot; that regarded as an independent entity it is
often trivial and sometimes null; and that it is because
of this parasitic nature of the action-plot, because of
its weakness, its haphazardness, its unnaturalness,
considered as a "thing in itself," that one finds the
play as a play unsatisfying.

The idea-plot I am not called upon to criticise.
In the playhouse a dramatist's ideas are postulates
not to be called in question.   Theories of Schopenhauer
about woman and the sex-instinct or of Nietzsche

about a revised system of conduct are most assuredly open to discussion, but not by the dramatic critic. His business is, first and foremost, with the action-plot. For that is what we *see* ; it is in fact the play itself, in the sense that it is what is being played under our noses; it is the sum of all the direct appeals to our sensations, before we start the secondary process of inferring and concluding. Now what do we see on the stage of the Court Theatre? What is it that we are asked to accept for an hour or two as part and parcel of our daily human life? We see, first of all, a smug, bald-headed old gentleman who proceeds, *à propos de bottes*, to spout the respectable middle-class Mill-Spencer-Cobden Liberalism of the mid-Victorian age. Then we see him vivaciously " cheeked " by a youngish, excitable, voluble gentleman, who evidently stands for the latest intellectual " advance." The younger man tells us, by and by, that he is a product of Eton and Oxford; but those of us who think we know that product will nourish a secret conviction that he is really, like his *chauffeur*, a product of the Board School and the Polytechnic. He has steeped himself in those fragments of the newest German philosophy which find their way into popular English translations, and he spends his time—mark, the *whole* of his time—in spouting these precious theories. He does this, as he admits, because he has no sense of shame; to put it more simply, he is a young person of rather bad manners. We note—for in the theatre the most trivial detail that we *see* outweighs the most important philosophy that we deduce—that he wears a beard which in a few years' time will resemble Mr. Shaw's; and he has already acquired Mr. Shaw's habit (an apparently deliberate piece of " business," and there-

fore one stands excused for mentioning it) of combing
his beard with his fingers. It is not unfair to assume
that there is as much of Mr. Shaw in Jack Tanner as
there is of Shakespeare in Hamlet; and that (if
Professor Bradley only knew it!) is saying a good
deal. Casually, this young man lets fall the remark
that he is descended from Don Juan. Why? What
is Don Juan doing *dans cette galère*? That you soon
discover when you are introduced to Miss Ann. For
Miss Ann is the new Don Juan, the huntress of men—
no, of one man (that is to say, no Don Juan at all,
but for the moment let that pass), the one man being
Jack Tanner. Miss Ann means to marry Jack, though
he does not yet know it. What he does know (from
the German) is that man is the helpless prey of the
"mother woman" through the influence of the "life
force." This Tanner expounds, in good set Schopen-
hauerian terms, to a sentimental young man, half
engaged to Ann, alleged to be a "poet." "Alleged" is
the word, because this young man's profession of poet
is, for stage purposes, a non-effective force. So far
as the play is concerned the "poet" might just as well
be a drysalter. And thus it is that, busied as in the
theatre we must be with the action-plot, we are
perpetually baffled and pulled up—wondering why
Tanner is descended from Don Juan and why Octavius
is alleged to be a poet. Also we wonder why Tanner
lectures poor mild milksopish Octavius about the
devastating egoism of the "artist man"—how the
"artist man" is (apparently) the masculine of the
"mother woman," how they are twin creators, she of
children, he of mind, and how they live only for that
act of creation, so that there is the devil to pay
(examples from literary history) when they happen to

become man and wife. This, we say to ourselves, may be all very true; but why does Tanner say it all, just at that moment, to the alleged poet but obvious barber's-block Octavius? While we are thus racking our brain we are interrupted by a new diversion. Octavius's sister (whom we have never seen or heard of) is suddenly reported to have "gone wrong." Agony of Octavius; glaring reprobation of the "respectable" types ; and coruscation of Nietzschean fireworks from Tanner. Conventional morality, humbug! Is mother-hood less holy—I beg pardon, less helpful—because it is motherhood without "marriage lines"? Etc., etc. (I say "etc., etc.," because the worst of Mr. Shaw's cheap German philosophic baggage is that when you see the first article you know all the rest of the set beforehand.) But stop; you may spare all trouble over the argument. For lo! it is a mistake, a false scent. Octavius's sister proves to be really and truly married. And the curtain of the first act descends upon a group cowering, as Tanner says, before the wedding ring.

Now this, the first section of the action-plot, is of course on the face of it a mere *pot-pourri*, a Caucus race, chaos come again. You have been immensely amused, Cyrenaically enjoying the moment for the moment's sake, but looking before and after (as you cannot help looking in the theatre) you have been disconcerted. What is the key to the mystery? The key is the idea-plot. Glance at that for a moment and you will see why Octavius is alleged to be a poet and why his sister is falsely alleged to be no better than she should be. (*a*) Fundamental idea : the irresistible power of woman over man in carrying out the aim of nature (or the "life force") to make her a mother. (*b*) Development : partly in Ann's actions, mainly in

Tanner's talk. And there, in that disproportion, at once you touch a dramatic weakness of the play. The properly dramatic development would have thrown all the onus upon Ann—we should have seen Ann energising as the " mother woman," and nothing else— and would have hept Tanner's mouth shut. But Mr. Shaw cannot exhibit, or can only feebly exhibit, by character and action; his native preference is for exposition by dialectic and ratiocination—*i.e.* by abstract talk; which is one of the reasons why you conclude he is no dramatist. (*c*) Corollary of the fundamental idea : if motherhood is nature's aim, then marriage is a detail—our morality which brands motherhood *minus* a wedding ring is false. Hence the " false scent" about Octavius's sister's baby. (*d*) Antithetical question suggested by the fundamental idea : is there not a male counterpart to the " mother woman "? Mr. Shaw hunts about. Yes, no, yes—it must be, the " artist man." Hence the alleged poetic vocation of Octavius, in order that Tanner may have a cue for haranguing him about the " artist man " and the " mother woman." Not otherwise do they insert cues in " musical comedies " when the time has come for a song or dance. That is one reason why " musical comedies " are like Mr. Shaw's comedies—*not* comedies. If Mr. Shaw's play were a real play there would be no need to explain the action-plot by laborious reference to the idea-plot. The one would be the natural garment of the other ; or rather the one would be the flesh of which the other was the bones. Octavius would be a real poet in the dramatic action (as is, for instance, the case with the poet in *Candida*) ; there would be no false alarm about Octavius's sister ; Ann would exhibit Mr. Shaw's thesis " on her own," instead of by the help of Mr. Jack Tanner's lecture-wand and gift of the gab. In that way we should miss many diverting moments; but only in some such way as that could we get a real play.

There is little or no dramatic development in Acts II. and III. For look again at the idea-plot and you will see that it soon exhausts itself, so that the action-plot, being as I have said a mere parasite of the other, is bound very rapidly to give out. Tanner can only continue to Schopenhauerise, and the moment of his falling into the lady's arms will synchronise with that in which the author is tired of his game and brings down the curtain. The so-called poet peters out; indeed, never existed. His sister is provided with an American husband. Why? *Vide*, once more, idea-plot. The super-chivalric American view of woman, being a contrast to the Schopenhauerian, obviously calls for mention. Hence Mr. Hector Malone. Hence also, indirectly, Mr. Malone senior, American millionaire and ex-Irish emigrant (opportunity for short *bravura* episode about wrongs of Ireland)——a character which—— rare mischance with Mr. Shaw!——hovers on the outer edge of the tiresome. All that is left to be done is to emphasise in Ann woman's talent for lying (type-example: Raina in *Arms and the Man*), at the same time getting it neatly hooked on to the Schopen-hauerian "mother woman" theory. Two subordinate characters — Ann's mother, middle-aged, querulous, helpless in her daughter's hands, and the cockney *chauffeur*, the *fine fleur* of Board School education, Henry Straker. These two small parts, from the point of view of genuine and fresh observation, are among the best things in the play. In them Mr. Shaw has been content to reproduce, instead of deducing. Would that he more often fell a victim to the same weakness !

The acting is quite admirable. Never was playwright more lucky in finding a born interpreter of his talent than Mr. Shaw in the case of Mr. Granville Barker. He is so alert, so exuberant, so "brainy," so engagingly impudent, so voluble in his patter! The Straker of Mr. Edmund Gwenn is a little masterpiece of truthful portraiture. Miss Sarah Brooke, as Octavius's maligned sister, is deliciously cool and trim and "smart." If Miss Lillah McCarthy does not bring home to us the full, irresistible seduction of the "mother woman," it is no fault of hers. Mr. Shaw has conceived Ann not as a character, but as a pure idea, a walking theory; Miss McCarthy turns her almost into a genuine character, and entirely into an agreeable woman. How voluptuous she might have been, how credible a female Don Juan, if Mr. Shaw had only given her the chance! But examination of Mr. Shaw's *théâtre complet* shows us that it is not in him to "do" a voluptuary. His present play, *ex hypothesi*, was concerned with the World, the Flesh, and the Devil. The Devil (a delightfully prominent person in the printed version) has unhappily had to be omitted on the stage. As for the Flesh, it never began to be warm, but is merely an intellectual category. Mr. Shaw is no flesh-painter.

MAJOR BARBARA

(COURT, *November* 1905)

M. AUGUSTIN FILON has said the right thing about Mr. Bernard Shaw. " L'enfant terrible est devenu un enfant gâté." Mr. Shaw has become the fashion, and in becoming the fashion he has given way to the besetting sin of the fashionable; he has become a law, or rather a caprice, unto himself. He exaggerates his own perversities, revels in his own weaknesses, parades his own prejudices. And it is all so naïvely done ! You are reminded of what Sterne said to the lady. " Pooh, pooh, ma'am, look at your child there, lolling on the carpet. He shows much that we conceal, but in perfect innocence, my dear ma'am, in perfect innocence." In perfect innocence Mr. Shaw puts his apology into the mouth of one of the people in *Major Barbara*. " Andrew, this is not the place for making speeches;" and Andrew replies, " I know no other way of expressing myself." Exactly ! Here is a dramatist who knows no other way of expressing himself in drama than the essentially un- dramatic way of speech-making. He never knew any other way, but in his earlier plays he did make an effort to conceal the fact. In his earlier plays there was some pretence of dramatic form, unity, coherence. In *Major Barbara* there is none. His motto is that of his own Andrew Undershaft—" Unashamed." And

the worst of it is, this innocence of Mr. Shaw's, the
shameless innocence of the child, is more effective than
the wisdom of the serpent. " Faiblesse qui est une
force," as Professor Bellac says of something else. All
the time the innocent Mr. Shaw is taking a mean
advantage of playwrights far less guileless than himself.
Many of our playwrights have skill, one or two have
even thoughts, but unfortunately their skill is wasted
on rubbish, and their thoughts are never concerned
with things worth thinking about. Now Mr. Shaw has
no dramatic skill, has apparently no dramatic instinct,
but he is a thinker who from first to last deals with
things worth thinking about. And so you turn with
relief, nay, with positive joy, from the intellectual
commonplaces of the average English playwright to
the intellectual eccentricity of Mr. Shaw. Though a
dramatist he is not, he is a first-class pleasure-monger.
That is why he has become the fashion in a pleasure-
seeking world. But one word of warning. He must
not abuse his vogue. Amusing as he is, he is perhaps
not amusing for quite so long as he supposes. The
truth is, he doesn't know when to stop. He lapses
into *longueurs*. There is a Professor of Greek in the
play who might quote to Mr. Shaw a familiar line
about that. " A yawn," says Euripides, " silently
rebukes the garrulous poet."

But for two at least of his three acts Mr. Shaw's
garrulity is never tiresome. The play opens with a
delightful conversation between Lady Britomart Undershaft and her son Stephen. Lady Britomart (daughter
of a Whig Earl, firm in the principles of mid-Victorian
Liberalism, and fond of ordering everybody about) asks
Stephen for advice, dictating to him what he shall
advise. Her difficulty is to get money to provide

dowries for her two marriageable daughters, Sarah—
who is colourless, and engaged to an ordinary " society "
fool without final " g's," Charles Lomax—and Barbara
—a Salvationist major, engaged to Adolphus Cusins, a
Professor of Greek, who has joined the Salvation Army
(as big drum) in order to be near his beloved. (Greek
scholars, we are told, are privileged ; few of them know
Greek, and none of them know anything else ; but
Professor Cusins knows how to win the way to Barbara's
heart.) Lady Britomart in the end advises herself to
apply for the necessary funds to her husband Andrew,
millionaire and manufacturer of torpedoes, guns, aerial
battleships, explosives, and all known implements of
destruction. She has separated from Andrew because
she cannot agree with him as to the future disposal of
the Undershaft business. Stephen is her candidate ;
but Andrew feels bound by the time-honoured tradition
of the Undershafts, which is to leave the business to
an adopted foundling. In this he proudly likens the
line of Undershafts to the Antonine Emperors, who
always adopted their successors. Another cause of
dissension between husband and wife is Andrew's queer
attitude in regard to morality. While all the rest of
the world practise immorality, but own themselves in
the wrong by preaching morality, Andrew practises
morality and preaches immorality. This is only the
Whig and mid-Victorian way of stating that Andrew,
as we shall by and by see, is a Nietzschean. Andrew
visits Lady Britomart at her invitation, and is introduced to the family which has grown up in his absence.
Of course he takes every gentleman in the room for his
son except the right one (this is Mr. Shaw's little gibe
at the old *voix du sang*), and finds the right one quite
uninteresting when he does know him. His interest is,

in fact, concentrated on Barbara. Himself the master
of a vast concern, he would like to know all about the
organisation of the Salvation Army. Barbara, on her
side, catches fire at the idea of "saving" her father's
"soul," and invites him to the Barracks. Agreed;
provided that, in return, she will visit her father's
workshops. And the question is — Will Barbara
convert Andrew to Salvationism or Andrew convert
Barbara to the Gospel of Power? Barbara is confident
of her own success and waxes enthusiastic over her
faith. "Really, Barbara," interrupts Lady Britomart,
"you speak as if religion were a pleasant subject"—
and, as a wholesome corrective, orders family prayers.
But all the children follow Andrew to the drawing-room,
and the poor mother is left alone lamenting the decline
and fall of sound mid-Victorian principles. And that
is the first Act.

Act II. passes in the West Ham Shelter of the
Salvation Army. We are introduced to various types
of converts. There are a pair of hypocrites who invent
past wickedness in order to get more credit for the
present regeneration. "Where would they get the
money from if we were to let on as we're no worse
than other people?" The male hypocrite has the
glory of "confessing" on platforms. The female one
jealously deplores that "*our* confession 'as to be
whispered." A third convert is a freethinker and an
honest workman, turned out of his job because his hair
is (prematurely) grey; he accepts charity only as a
loan, but cannot help admiring the missionary zeal of
the Salvation major. "Ah, if you'd only read Tom
Paine in a proper spirit!" A fourth convert is a
drunken brute who "bashes" women before our eyes
—so brutally that one wishes Professor Cusins had

inculcated Mr. Shaw with the Aristotelian principle about τὸ μιάρον. Well, the Salvationist lasses, cruelly smitten, turn the other cheek and pray for the smiter, and Professor Cusins, " a sort of collector of religions, and inclined to believe in them all," delivers a panegyric on Salvationism, which he compares to the worship of Dionysos. Andrew Undershaft, not to be outdone by a wealthy distiller, gives the army a cheque for £5000, and is even preparing to join the procession with a trombone—when Barbara suddenly stops the way. She has seen the army, in terrible straits for money, take alms from the distiller and the gun manufacturer. It is in vain that her father preaches the beneficent influences of war. It is in vain that he defends alcohol —alcohol which "enables Parliament to do at eleven o'clock at night what no sane person would do at eleven o'clock in the morning." Barbara cannot believe in a religion even indirectly based on drunkenness and murder. And that is the second act.

In the third we start with a discussion between Lady Britomart and her husband as to their son Stephen's future profession. " He knows nothing and thinks he knows everything." " That, clearly," says Andrew, " points to a political career." But Stephen interpolates some fine stereotyped phrases about the British character. "Ah," says Stephen, "now we know what to do with you, my boy; you are a born journalist." Whereupon they all depart to inspect the Undershaft machine-shops and model-town (with everything up-to-date, including Ethical Societies and a William Morris Labour Church), and to listen to interminable speeches from Undershaft himself on the Armourer's Faith, the Gospel of Power, and other Nietzschean gimcracks. We learn how poverty is the

worst of all crimes, how rent (and half a dozen other
economic things which I forget) are the Seven Deadly
Sins, and how we ought to treat the old morality as
Undershaft treats outworn battleships or obsolete guns.
"Morality that doesn't fit the facts — 'scrap' it!"
Finally, when they have all talked themselves out (it
is at this stage that you begin to feel tired), Professor
Cusins is taken into the Undershaft business (if not
exactly a "foundling" he is the next thing to it, as
his father married his deceased wife's sister) and gets
the hand of Barbara. Though Barbara has renounced
Salvationism, we are to understand that she still retains
her missionary zeal. She will convert her father's
model-town to some faith or other, one knows not
exactly what. For, as she candidly warns her
Adolphus, she would never make a stay-at-home wife.
"There are larger loves and diviner dreams than the
fireside ones." And that is the end.

Mr. Shaw has certainly justified his sub-title of
"discussion," and he has discussed everything under
the sun : Salvationism, Whiggism, Parliament, the Press,
University education, the choice of a profession, the
philosophy of war, alcohol, charity, Donizetti's music,
Greek scholarship, English slang, courtship and matrimony, the manufacture of explosives, *quicquid agunt
homines*. It is all very "Shavian," very bewildering,
very suggestive in its flashes of shrewd sense, very
amusing in its long stretches of March-hare madness
(until they become too long), and absolutely undramatic
throughout.

THE DOCTOR'S DILEMMA

(COURT, *November* 1906)

" I 'VE lost the thread of my remarks," says one of
Mr. Shaw's physicians; "what was I talking
about?" Mr. Shaw himself might say this, or something very like it. True, he does not helplessly lose
the thread of his play. But he is continually dropping
it, in order that he may start a fresh topic. This
foible of discursiveness has been steadily gaining on
him. *John Bull* was more discursive than *Man and
Superman*. *Major Barbara* was more discursive than
John Bull. *The Doctor's Dilemma* is more discursive
than *Major Barbara*. Needless to point out that this
discursiveness is not a new method, but a " throwing
back " to a very old method. It was, for instance,
the method of Shakespeare. A certain unity of idea
does, however, underlie Mr. Shaw's new play, and
that is to be found in its satire of the medical profession. Therein he has been anticipated by Brieux
in his *L'Évasion*. But of course the theme belongs,
as of right, to Molière. Is there not something piquant
in the spectacle of Mr. Shaw applying Shakespearian
treatment to a Molièrean theme? After all, there is
no such thoroughgoing classicist as your professed
iconoclast.

Superficially, no doubt, we seem to have travelled
a long way from the buffooneries of M. Purgon and

M. Diafoirus. Only superficially, however. For the
old mock-Latin, for the clysters, for the instruments
which modern delicacy does not permit to be named,
we now have barbarous Greek—opsonin and phago-
cytosis—surgical saws and " nuciform sacs." *Plus ça
change plus c'est la même chose.* That, by the way,
is the criticism which, in effect, the oldest of Mr.
Shaw's physicians, Sir Patrick Cullen, is always
applying to the new-fangled discoveries of his fellow-
practitioners. He has seen all these " novelties "
before; they have their law of periodicity—say, once
in every fifteen years—and nothing is altered but the
names. Sir Patrick, who stands for bluff cynical
comment on scientific affectation, heads a group of
half a dozen medical types. There is Sir Ralph
Bloomfield Bonnington — familiarly known as " old
B. B."—Court physician (much liked by what he
invariably calls " the Family ") and platitudinously
pompous bungler. He is, as you see, an entirely
Molièresque figure. Good easy man, he does not
know the difference between a vaccine and an antitoxin, and is all for stimulating the phagocytes.
There is Sir Colenso Ridgeon—just knighted as the
curtain rises for his great " opsonin " discovery—who
is all for buttering the bacilli. There is the great
surgeon, Cutler Walpole, who in every human ill
sees blood-poisoning, and is all for cutting out the
" nuciform sac." Physic he bluntly characterises as
" rot"; the physicians, in return, dismiss surgery as
mere " manual labour." There remain two types not
anticipated by Molière; Leo Schutzmacher, who has
made a fortune in the East End by selling advice and
drugs for sixpences, under the sign " cure guaranteed,"
and Dr. Blenkinsop, a hard-working general practitioner

who has never succeeded in making both ends meet and begs fashionable consultants for their cast-off frock-coats. All these people display their several humours in a Queen Anne Street consulting-room, whither they have come to congratulate Sir Colenso Ridgeon on his Birthday Honour. The irony of the thing is that Sir Colenso's knighthood is the fruit of one of "old B. B.'s" most glaring blunders in treating one of "the Family." The disheartened and disgusted Ridgeon remarks, in an "aside," "Ours is not a profession, but a conspiracy."

Why not call it, rather, a procession? For that is what it turns out to be in the conduct of Mr. Shaw's play. Our bevy of doctors career through the play, always together (one wonders what becomes of their unfortunate patients), like the wedding guests in the *Chapeau de Paille d'Italie.* From Queen Anne Street their line of march takes them to the Star and Garter at Richmond, and thence to Louis Dubedat's studio. But who is Louis Dubedat? It is time that he was mentioned here, though it is a whole hour by the clock—an hour devoted to the exhibition and discussion of medical humours—before you hear of him in the theatre. Louis Dubedat is an artist with a tuberculous lung. Please keep one eye fixed on the art and the other on the lung, for these are the two separate elements out of which Mr. Shaw makes his play. Examine the lung first, for that *motif* still continues the original thesis—medical humbug. Louis Dubedat is the *corpus vile* on which the medical experiments are to be made. Jennifer Dubedat, Louis's wife, has sought out Sir Colenso Ridgeon, and, with great difficulty, secured his promise to undertake the case. When Ridgeon consents it is

16

really out of his profound (but entirely discreet)
admiration for Jennifer, an idealist from Cornwall, a
child of nature, to whom belief in Louis's genius is a
religion.   But Ridgeon's consent at once places him
in a dilemma.   He has only staff and accommodation
for ten cases, and all his beds are full.   If he takes
in Louis, he must dismiss (practically to certain death)
one of the original ten; life for life.   Nevertheless,
knowing what he does of Jennifer, and knowing
as yet nothing of Louis, he consents.   As soon as
he gets to know Louis the case is altered.   Now is
the time for you to remember that Louis is an
artist as well as a sick man.   You find that he is
a particular kind of artist—the non-moral artist, a
man without any sense of conduct, to whom the words
"right" and "wrong," as ordinarily understood, have
no meaning.   Think of him as a Pierrot, or as a Faun.
Imprimis, he belongs to Elia's great race of borrowers.
Invited to meet the doctors (in a body, of course) he
"touches" each of them for a loan.   *Item*, he is a
bigamist.   *Item*, he is a blackmailer.   That people
should reprobate these practices is a thing he cannot
even begin to understand.   When the doctors arrive
(always in a body) to upbraid him, he sits down and
quietly sketches them.   He gaily declares himself to
be a disciple of Bernard Shaw, a celebrity unknown
to Sir Patrick Cullen, who, however, promptly finds
in him a moral likeness to John Wesley.

    And now Sir Colenso is in a worse dilemma than
ever.   For he finds that his poor *confrère*, the morally
irreproachable Dr. Blenkinsop, has also a tuberculous
lung.   Which is he to save?   The good Blenkinsop,
who is a social failure, or the bad Dubedat, who paints
good pictures?   Good men are fairly common, he

argues. Good pictures are very rare. And he decides in favour of Dubedat. But here there is a fresh complication. Jennifer Dubedat's whole life consists in the worship of Louis. If Louis ceased to be her hero, she would commit suicide—has, indeed, already marked out a certain cliff in Cornwall for that purpose. To prolong Dubedat's life is to ensure that his wife shall sooner or later find him out, and so have her religion shattered and lose her own life into the bargain. Therefore, for Jennifer's sake (even although, to the vulgar mind, it may look like murdering a man in the hope of marrying his widow) Sir Colenso must let Louis die. " Rather hard that a lad should be killed because his wife has too high an opinion of him " is old Sir Patrick's comment; " fortunately very few of us are in that predicament."

Killed, however, Louis is. Killed because he is handed over by Sir Colenso, the only man who could save him (with magical opsonin butter for the bacilli), to " old B. B.," who doesn't know the difference between a vaccine and an antitoxin. Louis dies, or fades away, before our eyes, with his head on Jennifer's breast (as Duse dies on Armand's in the last act of *La Dame*), dies like one of Montaigne's Emperors " in a jest," chaffing the doctors all round and uttering his artist's *credo* with his last breath— " I believe in Michael Angelo and Rembrandt and Velasquez and the Message of Art." Incorrigible Pierrot, unregenerate Faun ! *Qualis artifex pereo*, he might have said. But instead of that he says let there be no horrible crape, let not his wife mar her beauty with tears ; he hates widows, she must promise him to marry again. Also he gives a plain hint that he understands Sir Colenso's game. So does Jennifer, who coldly dismisses Sir Colenso from the death-chamber. Amateurs of the morbid will revel in this realistic death-scene. Other people will dislike it as bad taste and cheap art. Bad taste in its punctuation of solemnity by jokes (for there is a touch of the Pierrot and the Faun in Mr. Shaw himself). Cheap art in its employment of such a fact as death (realistic, not poetised death) to secure an emotional thrill; a thrill which, from the very constitution of human nature, is bound to come without any reference to the skill of the artist. Mr. Shaw made a like mistake in the face "bashing" scene of *Major Barbara.* But it is useless to argue with him over these things. He will do them. All we can do is to be sorry.

There is a brief, quaint, not entirely comprehensible, epilogue. Jennifer and Sir Colenso meet at Louis Dubedat's posthumous "One man show." Sir Colenso, treated with cold disdain, is driven to try and open Jennifer's eyes to the truth about her dead hero. He fails utterly. The secret of his love for her pops out. She mocks at the idea of love in this "elderly gentleman"—a new view of himself for Sir Colenso. Besides, in deference to her hero's dying injunction, she has already married again. The curtain descends while we are still wondering who is Jennifer's second husband. Can it be the well-groomed manager of the Art Gallery?

A thoroughly "Shavian" play, this, stimulating and diverting for the most part, occasionally distressing, now and then bewildering. O philosopher! O humorist! you mutter with gratitude. And then you whisper, with a half sigh, O Pierrot! O Faun!

THE PHILANDERER

(COURT, *February* 1907)

MR. SHAW never shirks a challenge. A friend challenged him to write about Don Juan, and he produced *Man and Superman*. Another friend challenged him to write about death, and he produced *The Doctor's Dilemma*. Has he no friend who will challenge him to produce a wordless play? It would be a wholesome discipline for him and might be a joy for us. His people would then be forced to show us what they are, and from their conduct we should judge them. At present they only tell us what they are, explain their own conduct with the aid of a lecturer's wand or by the process of question and answer, or else jump out of their skins and deliver impartial judgments on themselves as though they were somebody else. Now and then Shakespeare's people did that—as when Richard Crookback said, " I am determined to be a villain." But what Shakespeare did out of inadvertence Mr. Shaw does deliberately. He has yet to learn that action and emotion do not exist dramatically just because someone says that he has done this or felt that. His people analyse their passions with a logic so complete as to convince you that they have no passions to analyse. The great passions are mute ; the others are only semi-articulate, and never auto-analytical. In the club scene of *The Philanderer* Dr.

Paramore says to Charteris, who is plaguing him with
inopportune talk, "Allow me to call your attention to
that." "That" is the word SILENCE placarded on the
wall. It would do Mr. Shaw a world of good to keep
that placard on his desk. Let him try to invent a few
people who hold their tongues, at any rate about
themselves.

Are, then, self-expository characters to be entirely
banished from the stage? By no means. There are,
at least, two legitimate uses for them. Their first
legitimate use is in a fantastic play, where every
character shamelessly reveals itself for exactly what
it is or naïvely gives itself away. See *The Palace
of Truth* and the Gilbertian theatre *passim.* Mr.
Gilbert made his people do this precisely because it is
what real people do not do; the essence of this kind of
art is a surprising and grotesque departure from life.
Mr. Shaw makes his people do it because he cannot
help it, and in situations which are intended not to
depart from life but to adhere closely to it, to give its
very form and pressure. Raina Petkoff does it. Mrs.
Warren does it. The hero of *Man and Superman*
does it. Louis Dubedat does it. Charteris in *The
Philanderer* does it. They all do it. And why?
Because Mr. Shaw does it himself. In his letters to
the newspapers, in his platform addresses, in his prefaces, on every occasion on which he speaks in his own
person he speaks as a man who with unblushing frankness gives himself away. That is the secret of his
method, the quintessence of Shavianism. And what
Mr. Shaw does in his own person, he cannot help
doing through the persons of his plays.

But there is another legitimate use for the self-
expository character, and legitimate, this time, in the

drama of adherence to real life. There is a certain
type of person in real life who *is* self-expository, whose
nature may hardly be said to exist until it has come to
the stage of being expounded, whose feelings do not
come into play so much for their own sake as for the
sake of being analysed. Of this type, as we have seen,
Mr. Shaw is himself a brilliant example. As, then,
self-expository men exist, Mr. Shaw may say he is
entitled to put their images on the stage. Yes. Mr.
Shaw is fully entitled to make a stage-hero of the self-
expository man ; but he does it at his risks and perils.
For we, his audience, are also entitled to say that the
type is not well chosen, that it is not suitable to the
subject-matter of the play, that we get no pleasure out
of seeing it just where it is and doing just what it does.
That is my own feeling about the eponymous hero
of *The Philanderer.* I get no pleasure out of him.
Charteris is a man perpetually shilly-shallying between
two women, or rather pursued by one woman while he
pursues another. Yesterday he was "carrying on"
with Julia, but is now tired of her and is "making up"
to Grace. I say "carrying on" and "making up"
because I do not quite know in what category of
amorous relation I am to place the two pairs.
Perhaps "walking out" would be a more apt phrase,
for the behaviour of the parties too often suggests the
manners of "downstairs." There is a good deal of
hugging and kissing, but apparently everybody's intentions are to be understood as conventionally "honourable." Charteris sometimes alludes to his proceedings
as "philandering," sometimes as "sweethearting." Julia,
on the other hand, talks of having been "the slave of
his passion" for her. Queer as the behaviour of these
very osculatory ladies is, we are to understand that

they are technically virtuous.   We do not quite know
where we are ; but let us be charitable and take it to
be all an affair of " courtship "—courtship with a rather
unusual allowance of caressing.   Charteris, then, is
courting Grace, in order to escape being courted by
Julia.   He talks of " loving " Grace, but evidently loves
no one but himself.   But what he loves even better
than himself is the sound of his own voice.   He is for
ever expounding, now to Julia, now to Grace, now to
both together, the nature of the emotions which they,
individually and collectively, have inspired, do inspire,
or may possibly inspire in him.

Mr. Shaw says that this is just the sort of thing the
women like.   Tired of being treated with the respect
" due to their sex," they are fascinated by any man
who will treat them on frank and equal terms.
Charteris's idea of frank and equal terms is for the
man to punctuate long and argumentative discourses
with perfunctory kisses.

" Was ever woman in this humour woo'd ? "

Perhaps this is a specimen of *l'amour psychique* that
Professor Bellac used to talk about.   The Duchess
did not believe Bellac, and we do not believe Charteris.
We do not believe a word he says, and, further, we find
him a bore.   That is the worst of putting your self-
expository man on the stage.   The glibness of the
self-exposition soon ceases to amuse us, and we look
for our interest to the quality of the self-expounded.
Now the fact is, the self in this case, the true inward-
ness of Charteris, is not interesting.   He might have
been interesting if he had had enough stuff in him to
be a real blackguard.   But he has not " betrayed "
Julia, he has simply been " philandering " with her—

some sort of grown-up boy and girl nonsense. He might be interesting if he had a spark of real love for Grace ; but he has not. He is simply a kind of voluble jackass who has wasted his time dangling round women or letting them dangle round him in order that he may chatter to them about emotions which he does not, in fact, feel. Well, says Mr. Shaw, that is just the sort of man a " philanderer " *is*, and I have put him on the stage for you to see. We answer that the sight of him gives us no pleasure, that his chatter wearies us, and that the empty insincerity of the principal character spoils the whole play.

Nor are the other characters of any compensating importance. Julia stands for the " womanly woman " ; she is not, she is merely one of Mr. Shaw's shrews. Grace stands for the late Victorian " new woman," a type now so utterly forgotten that one looks upon the character to-day as rather more outrageously fantastic than one of Molière's *précieuses ridicules*. (There is an " Ibsen Club " in the play, and much talk of " Ibsenism " —oh! those remote 'nineties ! Here is a play hardly more than a dozen years old, and yet already out of date and even *rococo* !) The only amusing characters are those who stand outside the " philandering " story —two heavy fathers, one of whom is an anti-Ibsenite sentimentalist (a caricature, not unkind, of a real person, now dead) and the other the luckless victim of a medical blunder. Dr. Paramore has discovered a new disease of the liver, and diagnoses its fatal presence in Colonel Craven. The colonel gives up meat and drink and resigns himself to a speedy death from " Paramore's disease." By and by it is conclusively proved that there is no such disease. Rage and despair of Paramore, aggravated by what he considers the indecent joy of the Colonel — a scene that tells us, what we knew before, that Mr. Shaw has a true gift for Molièresque comedy. On the whole, however, the play is one of Mr. Shaw's least happy experiments.

ELEONORA DUSE

LA GIOCONDA

(May 1900)

GABRIELE D'ANNUNZIO dedicates his tragedy of *La Gioconda* to Eleonora Duse "dalle belle mani," and it is in these beautiful hands that the fate of the tragedy lies. Hardly has Silvia Settala entered when attention is directed to her hands. "Care mani," says Silvia's old friend Lorenzo Gaddi, the sculptor, "coraggiose e belle, sicure e belle!" They rival the famous hands of the "donna dal mazzolino" of Verrocchio. Her husband should carve them in marble and hang them up as an *ex-voto* for his rescue from death. For he, too, Lucio Settala, is a sculptor, and it is to his wife's loving care that he owes his recovery from the wound he has inflicted on himself. It was in a moment of passionate despair. He was the victim of a love bordering on frenzy for Gioconda Dianti, his model, and the inspiration of his art. Was? Perhaps he still is, notwithstanding his renewed love, born of gratitude, for his wife, who is in an agony of doubt because she knows the other woman is still at hand, implacable, waiting to draw Lucio back into her net. For the moment Silvia's doubt is set at rest by her husband's protestation of devotion, but we see, what she does not, that the fever of the old love is still upon him. In a scene with his friend Cosimo Dalbo

—D'Annunzio does not disdain the employment of confidants—Lucio confesses the truth. He adores his wife. Hers is a soul of inestimable price. " Ma io non scolpisco le anime," he cries ; he is not a sculptor of souls. This woman with the beautiful soul was not meant for him. Whereas the other will furnish him, not with one statue, but with thousands. When he saw her he thought of all the blocks of marble in the flanks of distant mountains, " per la volontà di fermare in ciascuno un suo gesto." And Lucio pours forth the fervour of his love for Gioconda, which to him means love for his art, the worship of plastic beauty, everything, in short, for which he lives. Even now, it seems, Gioconda is serving the cause of Lucio's art. She comes every day to his deserted studio to preserve his last unfinished statue by keeping the clay wet. But, interjects his friend, while Gioconda has been saving your statue, Silvia has been saving your life ! Lucio's reply reveals the " absolute artist ": " Quale delle due cose ha maggior pregio ? " It is not permissible to argue with sculptors, or it might have been pointed out that the saving of an unfinished statue would be useless unless the sculptor's life had been saved too.

At this stage Silvia's instinct warns her that her husband is not safe so long as the other woman still holds the key of the studio. She determines then to confront her, wrest the key from her, and drive her forth. The second act has now closed, and, save for one brief minute, we shall see the husband no more. It is the turn of the two women, rivals for the man's love, to come face to face and to fight it out. A great scene it should be—a *scène-à-faire*, as M. Sarcey would have called it, if ever there was one—and a great scene it is. The wife stands, silent, posed as nobly as any

of the statues around her, while the other woman opens
the studio door.   There is a moment's pause, then
" Io sono Silvia Settala," says the wife.   " Voi ? "
" Which of us is the intruder ?   Is it I, perhaps ? "
" Perhaps," answers the other woman ; and proceeds to
make good her retort.   For this studio is not the home
of the domestic virtues.   It is outside common laws
and rights.   Here a sculptor makes his statues.
" And I, Gioconda, am naught here save an instrument
of his art."   Nature has sent her to him to bring him
a message and to serve him.   She is here to serve him
at this moment.   This is no vulgar quarrel, it will be
seen.   D'Annunzio fairly assigns to each side in the
struggle its point of view and its complete case.   And
now a sudden temptation comes to the baffled and
tortured Silvia ; a temptation which D'Annunzio calls
" la fatalità antica della menzogna."   Silvia lies.   She
tells her rival that she has been sent to dismiss her by
Lucio himself, and she lies so thoroughly that Gioconda
is convinced.   " Then," cries Gioconda, roused in her
turn to fury, " I will destroy the statue, *my* statue,
made with the life he wrung out of me drop by drop."
As Gioconda rushes to destroy the statue, Silvia follows
her to save it.   She does save it, but at terrible cost.
Her hands, her beautiful, sure hands, are crushed into
a shapeless mass.   Clumsy or brutal stage-management, it need hardly be said, might have made this
incident a thing of horror ; but Signora Duse keeps it
rigidly within the limits of true art.   It is the pity of
the tragedy which smites the heart, not the horror.

After this terrible scene we must have peace, and
the last act is strangely peaceful, touched with poetic
fantasy, infinitely pathetic.   The poor maimed creature,
in a robe which conceals her handless wrists, is alone

by the sea, conversing with a half-crazed peasant girl,
La Sirenetta, who tells her the rhyme of the Seven
Sisters and their fates :—

> "Eravamo sette sorelle
> Ci specchiamo alle fontane :
> Eravamo tutte belle."

But where are her hands, asks La Sirenetta, the
beautiful hands she had so often kissed? "I have
given them," is the answer, "to my love." La
Sirenetta would offer Silvia her own hands, were they
not so rough and brown; and Silvia's reply shows that
D'Annunzio is true poet as well as playwright—"Sono
felice le tue mani," they can touch the leaves and the
flowers and earth and water and the stones and the
children and animals and all innocent things. And
now Silvia is waiting. Not for her husband; he has
left her—since the "absolute artist" can be a miserable
cur—for La Gioconda. It is for her child Beata that
Silvia is waiting—Beata whom she has not seen since
the loss of her hands. When Beata runs in she offers
her mother flowers, which the poor woman cannot take.
"Why don't you take me in your arms, mother, and
clasp me tight?" And the mother sinks slowly upon
her knees in speechless agony.

D'Annunzio's style has marmorean dignity and purity
and polish. There are passages of prose in it which
are a sheer delight as beautiful sound, apart from the
feeling and thought which have their own beauty too.
And one must use the same word for Signora Duse's performance; it is entirely beautiful. In the crises of tragic
frenzy, as in the interspaces of pure pathos, she never
forsakes the eternal principle of great art, the principle
of beauty.

FRANCESCA DA RIMINI

(ADELPHI, *October* 1903)

*D*U *Sang, de la Volupté et de la Mort* — the strange name which Maurice Barrès has given to one of his strange books—might serve as a sub-title for the *Francesca da Rimini* of Gabriele d'Annunzio. The play reeks of blood. The roses over which Francesca bends in the first scene are dyed a deeper red with blood.

"È il miracolo del sangue !"

she cries. Rose-red and blood-red—there you have the colours of the whole play. For this vivid colour scheme there must, of course, be maintained a pitch of violent emotion. The men, all save Paolo, are wild beasts. Ostasio, Francesca's brother, cannot question a harmless, necessary jester without half-strangling him. For a sneering word he stabs his bastard-brother Bannio in the cheek. (It is Bannio's blood which stains Francesca's roses. Smaragdi, the slave, has mopped it up and poured it into the Byzantine sarcophagus that holds them.) Paolo's younger brother Malatestino is a demon of cruelty. He tortures a prisoner, then cuts off his head and carries it about in a ghastly bundle. All this violence and "human gore" cunningly prepares one for the final slaughter. We are to feel that Gianciotto's murder of his wife and her lover, almost by the same sword-stroke, was just a typical thirteenth-century affair.   Francesca herself is quite used to violence and blood.   On the battlements she plays with Greek fire, will not go away when the arrows begin to fall round her, and declares her love for a good fight—

"È bello il combattente alla battaglia."

She buckles on her husband's gorget as one quite used to it.   Blood-red, then, is the dominant colour of the tragedy.

Blood-red — but also rose-red.   For against the violence of the passions, the general ferocity and cruelty, you have to set the suavity of D'Annunzio's verse—rich and even (like Mr. Fred Bayham's conversation) " sumptuous," but always beautiful, always a feast for the ear.   Beauty the whole play assuredly has, the beauty of roses and the beauty of blood. Even young Malatestino, with his chopper and with only one eye, is not without a certain savage beauty. To the beauty of every form of energy D'Annunzio has always shown himself peculiarly susceptible, and this feeling for beauty he gives to all his characters.   Not only Paolo, but Gianciotto and Malatestino are the slaves of Francesca's beauty.   The most passionate speech of her brother Ostasio is a panegyric of that. When she herself plays with the Greek fire it is not for the sport of danger, but that she may intoxicate herself with its beauty—

"Questa fiamma è tanto
bella che me ne sento inebriata."

See, too, how voluptuously she caresses the rich stuffs which the merchant has brought her.   Musicians are in

her train. She lives for beauty. What is the glory
for her of Paolo if it be not that he is " Il Bello " ? Do
not the pair (in Hedda Gabler's phrase) " die beautifully " ? D'Annunzio, then, in this play always makes
for beauty—the beauty of suavity and the beauty of
violence and death. The red of the rose and the red
of blood. It is a blend peculiarly Italian and, what is
more, peculiarly D'Annunzian.

Next to this primary sensation, the sensation of a
rich, sensuous, multicoloured and flamboyant beauty,
one gets a sensation of drama. That order, it will be
said, is a covert condemnation of the play, inasmuch
as the essence of great drama is, before everything, to
make a dramatic appeal. The truth—surely an obvious
truth—is, that the story of Francesca da Rimini
and Paolo il Bello is not a first-rate subject for drama.
Of course, the catastrophe—like any other scene of
sudden death—is dramatic enough ; but a catastrophe
is only the end of a play, not the play itself. The
play itself must be the story of a gradual drifting into
a guilty passion, and, do what you will, you cannot
make that drifting dramatic in itself. Do what you
will, you cannot make Paolo anything but a stick, a
beautiful stick. Further, your cardinal scene must be
a transfer to the stage of the famous passage from
Dante about the lovers' kiss over the book. You
cannot escape that scene ; the play without that scene
would be *Hamlet* without the Prince of Denmark.
You may make that scene a thing of beauty, as
D'Annunzio does ; but neither D'Annunzio nor anyone else can make that scene dramatic. But
D'Annunzio's handling of the whole story is more
dramatic than the handling of anyone else. The
sudden confrontation of Francesca and Paolo at the

17

end of the first act, with never a word spoken, is
highly dramatic.   There is no need for words.   The
twain stand spellbound.   The woman hands the man
a rose, a blood-stained rose.   All the story to come is
there.   The second act, the fighting on the ramparts,
if not dramatic, is full of bustle and excitement.   Its
one *raison d'être* as drama is that it reveals to Paolo,
supposed to be wounded, the secret of Francesca's
passion.   Only half-dramatic, again, the third act; but
it had to be there, as I have said, for the sake of the
cardinal scene, the scene of the kiss and the book.   In
the fourth act the dramatic pulse beats hot and fierce.
It is the act of Malatestino's lust for blood and
his treacherous betrayal of Francesca.   D'Annunzio's invention of this one-eyed traitor, Malatestino
"dall'occhio," is an admirable invention.   What more
natural than his jealous denunciation of his sister, after
he has been himself repulsed by her?   He strikes the
note of drama, then, as well as the note of horror.
The scene of his avowal to his brother, when Gianciotto,
all in armour, nearly crushes the life out of him in his
fierce eagerness to know the truth, is the finest in the play.
When people say, as many people do, that Gabriele
d'Annunzio lacks the true faculty of the dramatist,
I would ask them what other name than true dramatist
is to be found for the man who conceived and wrote
this scene?   The final scene, too, following the
authentic story in which Paolo, seeking to escape, is
caught by his tunic in the trap-door, is the most
dramatic arrangement of any that one has seen.   Of
course, the original intractability of the subject remains.
It cannot be turned into first-rate drama—the drama
of uninterrupted and cumulative interest.   D'Annunzio
has done the next best thing—he has filled out the

story with the *maximum* number of poignantly
dramatic episodes. His rose-red and his blood-red are
never " still-life " colours. There is no stagnation.

As for Signora Duse, it is the beauty of the play
rather than the drama of it that she fastens upon and
chiefly illustrates. In passages of beauty she is
perfection itself. There is such a passage in the first
act, wherein Francesca describes her little sister
Samaritana the " piccola colomba," and one again in
the second, wherein Francesca describes the wild beauty
of Greek fire and her joy in it—to listen to these
was to hear the most exquisite music. In the scene
over the lectern it was wonderful to watch the changes
of her face and the " passions de l'amour," to use
Pascal's phrase, following fast upon one another there.
But when she had a passage not so much of beauty as
of dramatic force to deliver, as in her description to the
slave Smaragdi of her terrible dream, she was far less
satisfactory—dwelling almost exclusively on the musical
beauty of the lines and almost ignoring the force and
terror of them. If the truth must out, a simple semi-
archaic type, a Francesca, a figure of little else than
plastic and musical beauty, does not enable her to put
forth her best and truest powers. This is by no means
to say that her Francesca is not in its way a supremely
exquisite thing.

LA SECONDA MOGLIE

(WALDORF, *May* 1905)

SIGNORA DUSE is in London once again, and once again revitalises our theatrical emotions for us and resumes from the moment she enters the scene all her old spell. There may be changes to be noted by the curious in this our great enchantress, but they are merely trivial, external changes—a slightly heightened complexion, perhaps, and a more luxuriant *coiffure*. These are details for the gossips. All one cares about is the welcome certainty that there is no loss of magic—the magic of the thrilling voice and the nervous gesture, and the wonderful play of glance and feature. Out of compliment to her audience, or, maybe, with the aim of being more readily understood by those who have no Italian, Signora Duse makes her re-entry in an English play. For my part I should have welcomed any other choice. *The Second Mrs. Tanqueray* is, no doubt, a first-rate specimen of our modern English drama, but I have a vague feeling that Signora Duse in this English drama is like a 'Varsity oar in a College eight—somewhat too magnificent an instrument for a comparatively humble piece of work. To vary the figure, one does not care to see a great virtuoso performing on a cottage piano. Was Paula Tanqueray, the ex-Mrs. Jarman, really so splendid, so romantic a figure as this? I cannot believe it. She would have set all Surrey by the ears, or, rather, have turned it into some poetic place of the South, an Alban lake or a Borromean isle. This is no Mrs. Tanqueray, who "adores fruit, especially when it is expensive," but an exotic orchidaceous creature with the enigmatic smile of a Da Vinci portrait and tones in her voice that are echoed from a Straduarius. It is not Paula fondling and caressing Aubrey, but some Vivien beguiling Merlin. In a word Signora Duse inevitably poetises the prose of the play, and so warps it from its real nature; making it, to be sure, something much more glorious, but at the same time much less true. Paula Tanqueray was a vulgar "fast" woman, promoted from a "shy" villa to Anglican respectability, whereas this is some beautiful strange monster let loose among mortal men. When she is joyous there are "harps in the air," when sad, her weeping is like a convulsion of nature. She has rapid tragic moments that seem like acted readings in Dante. As when Paula, cast once more into the presence of Ardale, and with her secret divined by her step-daughter, declares that her past is written indelibly upon her face—and accompanies her words with a sudden gesture that chills the blood of the onlooker. Such art, or rather such a temperament, as this seems to cry aloud for the ample scope of some part of high romance, where everything shall inevitably be "in the grand style." In the grand style all that Eleonora Duse does is inevitably done; so that, as I have said, she drives this prosaic English part out of its nature, and you are reminded throughout of the feat which Goldsmith attributed to Johnson of "making little fishes talk like big whales." It is a wonderful thing to see, a kaleidoscopic show of varying emotions that each communicate to the spectator their little thrill of pity or terror or delight ; but it is no more Mrs. Tanqueray than the Colossus of Rhodes is one of the frock-coated statues on the Thames Embankment.

LA LOCANDIERA

(WALDORF, *June* 1905)

NO doubt it is as a great tragic actress that
Signora Duse will pass into history. Hers is
the tragic mask, with its knitted brow and its mouth
drawn down at the corners. She has gestures of
physical disgust and revolt, as when she rubs the
ignoble Gaston's kisses from her hand in *Visita di
Nozze,* or the pinched face and "dead" voice of blank
despair, as in the penultimate scene of *Seconda Moglie,*
that are almost stifling with their tragic oppression.
Yet those of us who have seen her as the Mirandolina
of Goldoni will always put that memory of her before
everything else; we shall say that, tragic actress
though she may be by temperament and choice, it is
in her one brief moment of comedy that she casts over
us her most potent spell. For my own part, I count it
a unique thing. Night after night, year after year, I
have gone to theatre after theatre, and, though I have
not found all barren, yet on the whole I should be
inclined to sigh over a misspent life were it not for the
thought of Duse in *La Locandiera.* For the sake of
that one supreme pleasure I might be tempted to go
through it all again. . . . It would be a great comfort
if one could stop at this simple statement of fact. But
it is the business of criticism to try to account for just
such facts as these, to trace pleasure to its source, to

separate the components of the charm. Hopeless as
such an adventure is in the present case, I must not
shirk it.

The place is Florence. The time, mid-eighteenth
century. Gentlemen, in the rich dress of the period,
wear wigs of a higher arch over the brow than was
our general English fashion. Our "macaronis"
adopted it, however, evidently getting their perukes
where they got their name. This little detail of the
wig at once gives a touch of local colour. It may be
said that, laid as the action is entirely within four
walls, there is no sensation of place. But that is a
mistake; you are always aware of the *genius loci* in
Goldoni. A Venetian (whether by birth or not I
forget, but certainly by frequentation), he generally
affects Venice for his scene. This comedy, however,
is too light and cheerful and innocent a thing for
the decadent Venice of the period—that Venice of
Casanova which Théophile Gautier had a morbid
longing to have lived in. No; though you do not
see it, you feel that the clear air of Florence is on the
other side of those inn-walls, and that the gentlemen
before you, the Count and the Marquis and the
Cavaliere, may be on visiting terms with Sir Horace
Mann. Count and Marquis, both in love with the
hostess, Mirandolina, are snarling at one another.
"Contea comprata!" sneers the Marquis. "Yes, I
bought my county when you sold your marquisate"
is the retort. The snuffy old Marquis, "povero e
superbo," with his perpetual refrain of "Son chi sono,"
is delightfully played by Ettore Mazzanti; the Count
has little more to do than to give him his cue. They
amuse you until Mirandolina appears, and then you
straightway forget them. She is in flowered brocade,

with a *sacque*—rather sumptuous attire, perhaps, for
the landlady of an inn; I liked better the plain,
chocolate-coloured gown, with a stiff hoop, in which
she used to dress the part. But she wears the same
coquettish little cap. You at once see that this is a
landlady in a thousand—respectful without a tinge of
servility, not above her business, and yet a perfect
little lady, of the frank Italian sort. Between her two
admirers she steers a clear course, not caring a fig for
either of them, but too adroit to turn a too cold
shoulder to "gentlefolk" customers. Her tact is
perfect. Though her childlike delight in pretty toys
breaks out unrestrainedly in hand-clapping and "belli,
belli," over the diamond earrings offered her by the
Count, she is not overwhelmed by the magnificence of
the gift; and when the Marquis, in his turn, offers her
a common red handkerchief, though her eyes dance
with fun, she shows no offended dignity. Her dignity
is not tried until the Cavaliere appears—the bear, the
professed woman-hater. He grumbles rudely at the
inn-linen. She replies with quiet good-breeding,
showing by look, not by speech, that she expects
complaints of this sort to be made to the servants.
She keeps her smile—the frankest, pleasantest smile
I know—and, under her smile, resolves to teach the
bear a lesson. For the honour of her outraged sex
she will tame him and bring him to her feet.

This she announces, formally, to the audience, as she
is seated alone on the stage. (Deliciously naïve, blandly
artificial, Goldoni!) A little touch of this kind gives
one all the joy of a genuine Chippendale chair-leg or a
piece of *pâte tendre*. How can one hope to set down
in printer's ink the details of Mirandolina's adventure?
As well try to explain the mood of a midsummer day

in the humming blazing countryside by pointing to the
Ordnance map! But, groaning over what one cannot
do, one must do what one can. First, then, she breaks
down the outer barrier of the man's surliness by bringing him fresh linen herself—caressing its smooth surface,
expatiating on the elegance of its pattern, till he finds it
useless to try and silence her, and listens with a shrug.
By and by he listens with attention; she has begun to
interest him. Then she asks him to give her his hand.
Grudgingly he gives it, and, slyly looking into his face,
she says, "'tis the first time I have the honour to take
the hand of a man *che pensa veramente da uomo.*" The
flattery begins to work. He sits at table, and she
brings him dishes prepared by her own fair hand. He
smacks his lips; never was there such cookery! She
must take a chair, and drink with him. Never was
there such burgundy! (They drink it out of delightful
squat decanters and gilt-edged stemless goblets that
make the collector's mouth water.) For a moment the
poor victim struggles against his fate. His only safety,
he knows, is in flight; and he keeps on muttering to
himself, "domani a Livorno!" He calls for his bill,
but Mirandolina brings it with neatly simulated tears,
and at the sight of her tears all his resolution fails.
He calls her "cara," to his own dismay ("io *cara* ad
una donna!"), and you can see her laughing on the side
of her face which he cannot see.

And now she has had enough of it. She will show
the man how he has been fooled. And so, when he
comes to confess his love, he finds her at the ironing
table, intent upon her work and receiving him with
blank indifference. When he would utter impassioned
speeches, she calls loudly for Fabrizio, the head-waiter,
to bring another iron, and with the hot iron she contrives

to burn the Cavaliere's fingers. The Count and the
Marquis enter, to find their woman-hating friend in a
state of amorous frenzy. In his hot fit he would slay the
Count for a gibe. It is time, thinks Mirandolina, to bring
matters to an end. She blandly explains that she
intends to marry Fabrizio, and *exit* the Cavaliere in a
rage. "Mirandolina," says the Count, resuming the
moral of the little tale, "voi siete una gran donna; voi
avete l'abilità di condur gli uomini dove volete." Yes,
"gran donna" is not too fine a style for this bewitching
coquette. The delicious quality of it is that the
coquetry is without any of the elaborate artifice, the
leering archness, that the stage generally exhibits.
Though Mirandolina absolutely pushes her little nose
into the Cavaliere's face, leans caressingly against him,
seems on the point of throwing herself into his arms,
yet you feel throughout that it is all pure childlike fun ;
the woman is essentially modest and innocent. Mr.
Meredith's phrase, now hackneyed, must be used once
more ; for it might have been invented for Signora
Duse in Mirandolina. She is a "dainty rogue." In
the epilogue which she speaks as they all join hands
and come forward to the footlights (the old-fashioned
conventionality of the play, its soliloquies, its "tags," and
its epilogue only add to its charm), she speaks of things
"dear to her within the limits *della convenienza e dell'
onestà*." It is Signora Duse's triumph to have guided
the part always delicately and beautifully within those
limits.

SARAH BERNHARDT

THE MORALIST

THE editor of the *Cornhill Magazine* [1] has accomplished a wonderful feat. He has induced
Mme. Sarah Bernhardt to write an article, a real article
fifteen pages long from title to facsimile signature, the
only article she has ever written. You admire his
business enterprise, and still more do you admire the
intrepidity of his emissary, who has effected her purpose
amid the most bewildering distractions. She found
the actress under the electric light in her beautiful room
of cream and gold (whither she had been transported in
her original-looking little carriage drawn by chestnuts),
clothed in a long white clinging ermine-trimmed dress,
and surrounded by flowers, jewels, rich draperies, an
image of Buddha, a bronze of Christ, M. Victorien
Sardou in the flesh, a terrier, a greyhound, and a
secretary. It was the secretary who first regained
speech when the demand for an article fell into the
midst of this dazzling scene like a thunderbolt. An
article? "Never, never, has Madame done such a
thing; articles have been written *on* her, but never *by*
her [the italics are the secretary's]—it is impossible in
her busy life for her to find the time to write herself."
Yet the impossible has happened, and " Madame Sarah "

[1] December 1902, Art. "The Moral Influence of the Theatre."

(as her company always call her, with a blend of affection and respect which recalls the case of the Cabinet Ministers and " Mr. G.") has written her article.

Well, I have every desire to be impressed. I have read the article backwards and forwards and upside down, under the electric light, but all to no purpose: do what I will, I cannot find it impressive. I am driven to surmise that it lacks the proper surroundings; the flowers, and the jewels, and the long white clinging ermine-trimmed dress. Read without these enchanting accompaniments it falls flat. Platitudes which need no demonstration are mingled with judgments demonstrably false, or personal anecdotes which have nothing to do with the case. The interstices are filled with critical " howlers." It is all the fault of the enterprising magazine editor. He has destroyed a generous illusion. The world had willingly believed that, like Habakkuk according to Voltaire, Mme. Sarah was *capable de tout*, and now it appears that there is one thing she cannot do; she cannot make a contribution of real value to that old question " The Moral Influence of the Theatre."

She starts with a sweeping proposition. The influence of the theatre on morals has never been anything but beneficial. Evidently she has never heard of the Restoration drama or of the plays of Mrs. Aphra Behn, and has never found time to visit the Palais Royal. She supports her proposition by a pompous generality which proves nothing. " Beneficial it must always be to see the evolution of the human soul; and the more intelligently this evolution of the human soul is shown, the more effectual is the lesson drawn by those privileged to witness it." The evolution of some human souls is intelligently shown in *The Way*

of the World and *The Country Wife*, in *Une Parisienne*
and *La Sensitive*. Is therefore its effect on those
privileged to witness it beneficial? Mme. Bernhardt
knows, like everybody else, that it is not, for she
proceeds to deplore the existence of "so many pieces
which do so much harm, as they familiarise the mind
with vice without showing its immorality." She has
thus triumphantly refuted herself.

The fact is that you cannot hope to defend the
moral influence of the drama, unless you know something of the grounds on which it has been attacked;
and you may search Mme. Bernhardt's article through
without fiuding any trace of this knowledge. For
certain types of mind and temper—types as various as
Plato's and Charles Kingsley's, Pascal's and Dr. Parker's
—the drama has always been immoral because it is not
deliberately and directly moral. The religious enthusiast and the austere moralist, the saint and the Puritan,
will always distrust a force which does not work in the
sphere of direct morality. In the most moral drama
its morality is a by-product; "disinterestedness" is an
essential condition of æsthetic feeling; and "disinterestedness" will never be palatable to men who hold
that the active will, the choice of strenuous and right
conduct, should fill every moment of life. They cannot
abide the "play-mood," the suspension of the serious
business of living, which is the mood demanded by the
drama. And even as a by-product the morality of the
drama, as Coleridge pointed out, is seldom the higher
morality, is seldom distinguishable from worldly
prudence—and to the austere moralist that is only
another name for immorality. The deadliest attacks
on the theatre have come not from men like Jeremy
Collier, who were simply content to prove that this or

that play was immoral, but from those who urged that
the drama as an art, in its essence, was immoral.
Mme. Bernhardt, it so chances, mentions one of these
men, and she mentions him in such a way as to show
herself innocent of any suspicion as to the " true inward-
ness" of his attack. " Jean Jacques Rousseau " she
naïvely says, " appears not to have liked the theatre."
So one might say that King Jamie appears not to have
liked tobacco, or that Hampden appears not to have
liked Ship-money, or that Borrow appears not to have liked
the Jesuits. Rousseau's famous letter to D'Alembert
" Sur les Spectacles " is, despite its crotchets and
exaggerations, one of the most formidable cases against
the theatre ever penned. He pointed out the objection
to dramatic emotion—the tragic " purging " of pity and
terror—as an emotion which is an end in itself, an
emotion which does not lead to action but makes a
luxury of grief. The theatre, he said, flatters the
passions; it changes neither feelings nor manners, it
only reproduces them. What? It renders virtue
amiable and vice odious? But reason could do that
without it. We go to a tragedy because of the pleasure
we take in seeing others suffer, so long as we do not
suffer ourselves; we go to comedy because of the low
pleasure we take in the consciousness of one another's
infirmities. Then the theatre is a perpetual spectacle
of love, and so inflames the most dangerous of the
passions. It is a school of gallantry for men; and
certainly not a school of modesty for women. Well,
all this is, as we say nowadays, a little " steep "; but it
would be idle to pretend that it is all nonsense. And
it is certainly not to be disposed of by Mme. Bernhardt's
quaint statement that Jean Jacques in reality " adored
dramatic literature " until this taste " paled under

Diderot's cold and deadening influence." That exuberant sentimentalist Diderot "cold and deadening"!
That enthusiast for the "moral theatre," the author of
the *Fils Naturel* and the *Père de Famille*, Diderot, the
man who deluded Rousseau into the belief that the
theatre was immoral! Why, a mere consideration of
dates—the letter to D'Alembert was published in the
same year as the *Père de Famille* (1758)—but one
must not be so clumsy as to import dates into that
brilliant white and gold apartment, with its flowers and
its jewels and its electric light.

In fact one is conscious of cutting a ludicrous figure
in attempting to argue this subject on its merits with a
charming lady (in a long white clinging ermine-trimmed
dress) who gravely contends that *La Dame aux Camélias*
is a piece which every young girl ought to be taken to
see, that M. Sardou's *Fédora* is "a powerful sermon
against revenge," not to be equalled by "many pages
of philosophy," while M. Sardou, it appears, holds
undisputed sway as Master of his Art. One is driven
to turn to things more profitable, irrelevant though they
are—Mme. Bernhardt's little personal anecdotes and
confessions. She remembers that, when she first played
Iphigénie at the Comédie Française and she held up
her long thin arms for the sacrifice, the audience burst
out laughing. She still feels nervous on the stage—
especially over a new piece. She likes American and
English audiences, because they take the theatre
seriously, whereas the Latin nations do not. Nevertheless, the courtesy of the Spaniards is very charming,
and "France retains the place of honour for literary
works." Nor must one, in international comparisons,
forget the society of the Entente Cordiale "at whose
soirée I assisted in London," or the wild Iroquois in

Canada who once gave a *fête* in Mme. Sarah's honour. Also, "as a young girl I had serious thoughts of becoming a *réligieuse*. It seemed an outlet for my soul, overflowing with exalted sentiment, in spite of my wayward and passionate temperament." But, fortunately, as things have turned out, instead of the cloister, you have the *boudoir* of cream and gold, with the flowers and the jewels and the image of Buddha and the terrier and the greyhound and "the fine intellectual rugged face of the great author" (who but M. Sardou?) expanding in "grateful acknowledgment to the grand interpreter of his artistic pen." Yes, the wayward and passionate temperament has done wonders, which we can all gratefully acknowledge—but it is too wayward a temperament to run into the mould of the magazine article.

ANDROMAQUE

(ADELPHI, *July* 1903)

WE English have especial cause for gratitude to
Racine for writing *Andromaque*. Namby-
pamby Philips translated it into *The Distrest Mother*,
a poor version—"poor but honest," however, like the
parents of old-fashioned melodramatic heroines—and
Namby-pamby Philips was a friend of Joseph Addison,
who puffed the play in the *Spectator* and made it the
pretext of an entirely delightful evening with Sir Roger
de Coverley. Who can forget Sir Roger's remark
about the heroine? "You can't imagine, sir, what
it is to have to do with a widow." Or his comment
on Hermione? "On my word, a notable young
baggage." Or his views on Astyanax, who is always
being heard of but never seen? "He owned he should
have been very glad to have seen the little boy, who,
says he, must needs be a very fine child by the account
that is given of him." Before taking Sir Roger Mr.
Spectator had gone to see *The Distrest Mother* with
Will Honeycombe, who "feared the play was not busy
enough for the present taste" and "recommended that
every part should be perfectly new dressed." Will, it
is perhaps unnecessary to remark, was not advocating
"correct" costumes. I chance to possess a picture of
"Mrs. Hartley in the character of Andromache." Mrs.
Hartley wears hoops, paniers, and a sweeping train.

Her sleeves are trimmed with ermine, and her skirts are festooned with the aid of cords as heavy as the old-fashioned bell-pull. Add a tiara with tall plumes and you have a remarkable set of "weeds" for the widow of Hector.

Archæologists may smile, but really this fashion of dressing *Andromaque* accorded very happily with the stateliness of Racine. There is much to be said for reviving the "powder and patch" presentation of Racinian tragedy, much more than is to be said for the nondescript dresses worn by Mme. Bernhardt and her companions. M. de Max, as Oreste, looked as though he had strayed out of the Coronation Durbar. Hermione had obviously modelled herself on Becky Sharp as Clytemnestra, and the attendants of Pyrrhus had borrowed the clothes of Jos Sedley's hookabadar. Absurdity for absurdity, I prefer Mrs. Hartley's bell-pulls. After all, it matters very little, perhaps, what costumes are worn in *Andromaque* so long as they do not distract attention from the play itself, and play-goers who cannot attend to *Andromaque*, who are not absorbed and fascinated by it, who are not intoxicated with the beauty of it, can hardly count as human beings. For one thing, it is certain that they can never have been in love, never have been jealous, never have been jilted.

Everybody in the play is in love, and everybody is in love with the wrong person. Oreste loves Hermione, who will have none of him, but longs for Pyrrhus. Pyrrhus is betrothed to Hermione, but will have none of her and pursues Andromaque. Andromaque "never, never will desert" the memory of her dead Hector. The game is kept afoot by shilly-shallying. Pyrrhus, repulsed by Andromaque, thinks

he will take Hermione after all. Then he jilts
Hermione and returns to Andromaque. Oreste ex-
horts Pyrrhus to relinquish his pursuit of Andromaque
and his protection of her child, and is beside himself
with wrath when taken at his word. What especially
angers him is the thought that his own passion for
Hermione has caused Pyrrhus to veer round to her.
Hermione, enraged when Pyrrhus finally prefers
Andromaque, offers her hand to Oreste if only he will
kill Pyrrhus. He does (or his Greeks do), and then it
is Hermione's turn to be beside herself with grief
because she has been taken at her word. As for
Andromaque, after rejecting Pyrrhus again and again,
she suddenly agrees to marry him. We know, of
course, that she does this thinking to ensure the safety
of her child, and purposing to kill herself immediately
after the ceremony. But (as was remarked early in
the eighteenth century) this is a very poor scheme, as
it will leave the child to the mercy of a stepfather who
has been " sold " by the child's mother. The obvious
truth of the matter is that the fate of the child is a
mere pretext for a plot. It is Andromaque's love for
Hector, not her love for her child, which is her master
passion. Philips should have called his play *The
Distrest Widow* rather than *The Distrest Mother*.
Another point in Andromaque's character has been the
subject of much curious speculation. Does Racine
intend to suggest that she " flirts " with Pyrrhus, or
does he not? Years ago Nisard professed to find in
or between the lines of her part evidence of a certain
coquetterie vertueuse. It was a happy phrase, and
many controversialists have played with it, but M.
Emile Faguet has discovered that it was not invented
by Nisard, but by Geoffroy, of the *Débats*, in 1803.

The late M. Sarcey was strong for the "flirting" theory; M. Faguet is dead against it. So, for that matter, is Mme. Bartet, the incomparable Andromaque of our time.

It has been suggested that Mme. Bernhardt ought to have played the part rather than Hermione, but I think she has chosen wisely. Andromaque is a part of pathos, while Hermione is a part of passion. Andromaque is a purely classical part, and Hermione is largely a romantic part; there is more colour in it, more "modernity" even. Andromaque is all of a piece, Hermione is everything by turns. Yes, Mme. Bernhardt has chosen wisely; Hermione gives her, as Andromaque could not, opportunity for her displays of "nerves," her hoarse cries, her seductive scenes, her whirlwinds of passion. But I do not understand her whim for playing so much of this part in a recumbent posture. Does she wish to rival Mme. Réjane in the first act of *Ma Cousine*? Whatever the reason, this Hermione is, more often than not, a horizontal Hermione. M. Desjardins is only a respectable Pyrrhus; he woos Andromaque without fire, and listens to the fierce invectives of Hermione without apparent attention. It is all very well for Pyrrhus to treat Hermione as a scold, but it will hardly do for him to treat her as a bore. The Oreste is M. de Max, who, as most people know, comes from Rumania, and would seem to suggest that the son of Agamemnon was a compatriot. One feels tempted to mutter over this youth who purports to be a Greek, but obviously is not, the old joke about "si jeune et déjà Moldo-Valache!" M. de Max is all for violent colour, febrile intensity, passion which vents itself in growls and groans. In short, his method strikes one as too flamboyant for Racine. Racinian passion never for a moment forgets to express itself nobly. It may burn with a white heat, it never sputters. Indeed, *Andromaque* is a miracle of "elegance." It shows men and women hungering for one another like wild beasts, and yet draping their desires in a style of delicate reticence as fastidious as Jane Austen's.

ADRIENNE LECOUVREUR

(CORONET, *June* 1905)

THE *Adrienne Lecouvreur* of Mme. Sarah Bernhardt has bewildered me on many points, but it has left me quite clear about one. It has compelled my admiration for the *Adrienne Lecouvreur* of MM. Scribe and Legouvé. I had hitherto attached little value to that ancient melodrama. I had thought it stilted, artificial, and long-winded. But then I had not become acquainted with the *Adrienne Lecouvreur* of Mme. Sarah Bernhardt. What caprice tempted the actress to rewrite the old subject is beyond conjecture. Is there not a proverb that it is well to let sleeping melodramas lie? Surely common gratitude might have induced Mme. Bernhardt to respect the mortal remains of MM. Scribe and Legouvé. Time after time she has triumphantly appeared as the heroine of their unimpeachably respectable work. But, apparently, her familiarity with it has bred contempt. She has got to feel that, in Mrs. Poyser's phrase, " it ought to be born again—and born different." Different, indeed, it now is! I do not say that the lady found it marble and left it brick; let me rather say that she found it stucco and left it *carton-pierre*. Where the deceased Academicians were long-winded, she is interminably prolix; where they were merely dull, she is appallingly tiresome; where they were slightly vague, she is absolutely

incomprehensible. They, too, had now and then a
gleam of fun; Mme. Bernhardt is as solemn as a
mausoleum. Why, one asks again, was she not
satisfied with the old work? Perhaps I shall be told
that her historical conscience revolted at it, that she
had gone to the original documents, and was determined to present us with the unvarnished facts. Well,
it may be so. Just as Mr. Wegg admitted that he had
not read Gibbon slap through just lately, "being
otherwise engaged, Mr. Boffin," so I confess that, for a
like reason, I have not recently consulted the original
documents about Adrienne Lecouvreur. Consequently,
if Mme. Bernhardt chooses to assert that the famous
actress's life was mixed up with the queer proceedings
of the humpbacked Abbé whom M. de. Max thrusts
upon our attention, I am unable to offer any denial.
But there credulity stops. I draw the line at Voltaire.
Not all the documents in all the archives shall persuade
me that every crisis in Adrienne's existence was
witnessed and provided with appropriate reflections by
Voltaire. Further, most of us have read some of
Voltaire's writings, and I for one utterly decline to
believe that his conversation can have sunk to the
level indicated by Mme. Bernhardt. "Oh, ce Voltaire,"
says the schoolgirl in *Le Monde où l'on s'ennuie*, "quel
génie!" If she had seen this play she would have
said "quel raseur!"

You first see Voltaire in Adrienne's dressing-room
at the theatre. Adrienne wafts him a kiss from behind
the curtain, and Voltaire remarks that a woman's
kisses are magical, even behind a curtain. When
Maurice de Saxe enters Voltaire discreetly retires, but
only to bide his time, for he knows full well that it
is he and not Maurice who in the long run will get the

lion's share of the play. He took no prominent part
in the next scene, a reception at the Duchess de
Bouillon's, but no doubt he was lurking somewhere in
the background—always with his ironic smile—biding
his time. In the foreground was the humpbacked
Abbé, already mentioned, painting Adrienne's portrait
and indulging in melancholy reflections on his hump.
The *grandes dames* fondled his hump for luck, and his
vexation became more marked than ever. Meanwhile,
there had been a furious quarrel over Maurice between
Adrienne and the Duchess de Bouillon, and the
Duchess, vowing vengeance, hissed into the ear of the
humpbacked Abbé that he must become her tool.
In the next scene you were in the Luxembourg
gardens, whither the Abbé came to inform Adrienne
that the Duchess had commissioned him to poison her.
" Poison her within a week or—the Bastille ! " The
week being now up, the police appeared to carry off
the Abbé. Where was Voltaire ? I began to wonder
—till, sure enough, one found him, still ironically
smiling, in the Abbé's cell at the Bastille, comforting
the Abbé, exchanging polite repartees with Adrienne,
and calmly telling the Duke de Bouillon all about his
wife's infidelities. Voltaire then restored the Abbé to
liberty. Was he not the champion of Calas ? But he
was too late to save Adrienne. The implacable
Duchess told the poor woman that she was poisoned,
and had only a day or two to live. In the final act
you saw her die. So, of course, did Voltaire. He
retired respectfully into a corner, in order that she
might have room to die, and she said to him, almost
with her dying breath, " Your smile has lost its irony."
Maurice de Saxe and the humpbacked Abbé also
arrived in the nick of time to see her die. Very likely

her death is "documentary." It is certainly very touching. She whirls round and round, as in a dance, until she stops short when confronted by the hump-backed Abbé. Then she sinks slowly into Maurice's arms, and expires. Voltaire strikes a Voltairean attitude in his corner. " Oh, ce Voltaire ! Quel poseur ! "

If I have insisted upon the Voltairean element in this play, it is because I suspect that therein is to be found the true explanation of its origin. Mme. Bernhardt felt, I conjecture, that MM. Scribe and Legouvé had no business to write a play about Voltaire's period and to leave Voltaire out of it. And so she has repaired the omission—given Voltaire his ironic smile and then killed Adrienne in his presence in order to purge the smile of its irony. But she cannot purge my smile in that way. It may be wrong to indulge in an ironic smile over a work which has evidently cost the actress great pains and much—far too much—ink ; but I really cannot help it. I fully recognise the fine acting of Mme. Bernhardt herself in the eponymous part. But all the fine acting in the world cannot blind one to the fact that the Duchess de Bouillon is a mere mechanical *traîtresse* of melo-drama, that Adrienne in the new play is not the poetic, suavely beautiful figure of the old, that the hump-backed Abbé is a grotesque nuisance, and that Voltaire, for all the wit he shows, might be—Fréron. When he let the irony die out of his smile—with Mme. Bernhardt's play still under his nose—he gave the final twist to one's conviction that he was an arrant impostor.

RÉJANE

LA PARISIENNE

(Coronet, *June* 1901)

TO say that *La Parisienne* is a clever piece would be true but inadequate. It is diabolically clever. It purports to have been written by the late M. Henry Becque, single-handed, but I suspect Old Nick to have been at his elbow, an unseen collaborator. At least, there must have been brimstone in M. Becque's inkpot. No one with the slightest sense of humour can see the piece without laughing, or rather, I fear it must be admitted, without sniggering. But that is only the superficial effect. The play cuts deep. Its irony bites like vitriol. And the ultimate impression is of something grim, cruel, malignant. It tends to make us loathe ourselves, or, at any rate, our next-door neighbours. This is a strange impression to receive from a comedy, from Mme. Réjane's face of impish mischief, her ravishing gowns. It is a strange blend, this whiff of sulphur combined with *odeur de femme*. But, then, *La Parisienne* is a strange piece.

It begins with one of the most complete hoaxes ever devised by a playwright. The curtain rises upon an empty stage. Madame enters and hastily conceals a letter under a blotting-pad. Close upon her heels follows Monsieur in a jealous fury. " Give me that

letter!" "No!" And then a long scene of bullying
and bickering. The man, tortured with suspicion,
plies the woman with questions. "Where have you
been?" "Do you still love me?" Madame at first
enjoys the man's agony, and is then exasperated by
it. It is the familiar scene of jealous husband and
teazing wife. They calm down, and Monsieur begs
Madame to be more prudent in her conduct. "En
me restant fidèle, vous restez digne et honorable." As
he utters the words the door opens and another
gentleman enters. "Prenez garde," whispers Madame
to Monsieur—"voilà mon mari." And, lo! we find
that our quarrelling couple, so conjugal in every detail
of their quarrel, are not husband and wife, after all, but
lover and mistress. How, then, comes it that the
jealous gentleman is so like a husband? That is the
point, or a point, of the play. Lafont, the lover, has
assumed by usage and temperament and the inevitable
tendency of things, *quasi*-marital qualities. "Un
second mari, autant dire," is Clotilde's way of putting
it. And so she finds herself between Lafont, the
husband *de facto*, and Du Mesnil, the husband *de jure*.
If anyone is shocked by the situation it is certainly
not Clotilde. She does not see the irony of it, for
she cannot see herself as she is. No more does
Lafont, for the same reason. No more does Du
Mesnil, for Du Mesnil sees nothing at all, not even
when it passes under his very nose.

But the irony is there, and its teeth drive sharp
into our poor human flesh. It consists in the spectacle
of two people carrying on irregular relations with
precisely the same set of feelings and prejudices which
would be operative were their relations regular. The
"immoral" is shown to labour under the same condi-

tions as the "moral." Lafont is exigent, querulous, jealous, and tiresome. He is even prudish. He forbids Clotilde to visit in a household of somewhat doubtful reputation. He is shocked to hear that one of her married friends is a faithless wife. In sum— "un second mari, autant dire."

And Clotilde, with all her irregularity of conduct, is entirely conventional in her ideas. She declares herself a Conservative in politics, because she inclines to the party of social "order." She is indignant at the thought that her lover might leave her for another mistress who is "without religious principles." As a matter of fact, she has no moral sense whatever. She is absolutely without conscience. Things are for her merely pleasant or unpleasant, conduct is merely expedient or inexpedient. She is a Nietzschean, a Nietzschean without knowing it, a Nietzschean in frills and furbelows of the most fashionable cut. She has lovers, but no passions, hardly even appetites, only caprices. A monster, then, something merely perverse and noxious? Yes—and No. Yes, according to any accepted standard of ethics. No, by virtue of her reality. There is a great deal of ordinary human nature in Clotilde. She desires to hurt no one, she merely means to "have a good time." She is good-humoured, patient, reasonable, tactful. Mark that she is a capable woman—indeed, the one capable member of the triangular household. She gets her fool of a husband into a good post. It would be ungenerous to inquire too closely into the means; the point is that she can do for her husband what he cannot do for himself. If Lafont were not so tiresomely jealous, she could get on excellently with him, too. This, after all, is an eminently companionable sort of monster. And, though she has a wonderful gift of fiction, she does not tell unnecessary lies. According to M. Anatole France, that, in a woman, may be called veracity.

Nor is she without her little chastening experience. When she has dismissed Lafont she tries another lover, who bores her to death and then leaves her in the lurch. The lesson is not thrown away. There was something in the "second mari" after all. She takes him back into favour, and we leave the three people of the first scene all comfortably together again in the last. Do you not hear a chuckle as the curtain descends? It must be M. Becque's unseen collaborator. Evidently on this occasion there is no need, with the charitable lady in the Scotch ancedote, to "pity the puir deil." He has had it all his own way. And he could not conceivably have found a more bewitching, tantalising, irresistible interpreter than Mme. Réjane. Her performance of Clotilde is one of the most comic—and one of the most disquieting—things to be seen on the stage of our time.

ZAZA

(IMPERIAL, *May* 1902)

IN Paris they have an expression that may be said to speak volumes, very trashy volumes — the *littérature de concierge.* It is not difficult to conjecture the sort of literature beloved by the autocrat of the street-door. It must be sentimental at all costs, even at the cost of dwelling upon illicit passion, provided that the superior respectability of family life be vindicated in the end. It must have the glitter of the gay world ; indeed, the *concierge* will not object should it verge on the garish. As many people as possible in it must be splendidly dressed. The facile contrast of tortured hearts beating under heavily bejewelled bodices must be rigorously insisted on. No direct and original observation of life is needed ; indeed, it would be resented by the *concierge,* who prefers- the conventional emotions and situations which are passed on as " common form " from one hack-writer to another. In an American version of *Zaza* by Mr. Belasco the word *concierge* has, I note, been translated, presumably in accordance with American idiom, as janitor. I thank Mr. Belasco for that word. It provides a convenient and comprehensive label for this play. *Zaza* is pre-eminently janitorious. The doorkeepers of all nations—if I may use the word in a Pickwickian and metaphorical sense—will revel in it. It shows

how spangles and a career of music-hall songs are not
incompatible with true love. It presents violent contrasts of households in Bohemia and "correct" homes
in the most expensively respectable quarters of Paris.
It gives several of its personages the opportunity of
being absurdly overdressed. It toys with vice and yet
pays complete, if tardy, homage to virtue. In short,
it is a perfect specimen of the janitorious drama.

The play, which is in five acts (for what *concierge*
does not know the orthodox number of acts required
for a theatrical masterpiece ?), opens behind the scenes
of a concert hall in a French country town. Zaza is
the "star" and, of course, has a jealous rival. They
are both petulant and vixenish and, at one moment,
come to blows. Zaza dresses and "makes up" for her
part in view of the audience. The company come and
go. Privileged gentlemen in the glossiest evening dress
present bouquets. Ah! that life behind the scenes!
How the doorkeeping mind revels in its gay wickedness! But Zaza, it need hardly be said, is no common
"star." She has a heart—and she has lost it to one
of the gentlemen in glossy evening dress, M. Bernard
Dufresne, who promptly falls a victim to her wiles. In
the next act—each act turning a different facet of the
heroine to the limelight—shows Zaza playing at simple
domestic bliss with M. Dufresne in a country cottage.
The *concierge* remembers the parallel case of Marguérite
Gauthier and Armand Duval, and is happy. But
Zaza's bliss is shortlived. She learns from one of her
theatrical comrades that M. Dufresne has a wife in
Paris. The pair have been seen at the play together,
drinking chocolate. "I'll spoil their chocolate," cries
the infuriated Zaza, and starts for Paris. Now comes
the opportunity for that family sentiment which the

doorkeeper feels to be his due. Intent on making a disturbance in the Dufresne household, Zaza is confronted by a little girl, and in the presence of childish innocence she retires humbled and in silence. Then passion has its turn. Zaza turns upon her lover and rends him, works herself into a frenzy of hysteria, and smashes the china on the mantelshelf. A woman shouting at the top of her voice and beside herself with fury is just the sort of woman the *concierge* can understand. " Women, poor things, are like that," he reflects, being in his way a philosopher and ready to take broad views of human nature. Besides, he is well aware that in all these plays a *scène de rupture* is the proper thing. Next to noise—of which in the penultimate act the *concierge* it will have been seen gets his fill—he loves worldly success, gaudy success, symbolised by extravagant costumes, the homage of the multitude, and a smart victoria. Zaza duly provides him with all this. In order to forget her lover she has devoted herself to her profession, and is now an artist of world-wide reputation and boundless wealth. When M. Dufresne comes to seek a reconciliation she parts from him more in sorrow than in anger, bidding him go back to his child, while with dignified simplicity she orders her coachman to drive her "home." A play which ends on the word "home" is bound to captivate the guardian of every street-door in both hemispheres.

Some people, not engaged in doorkeeping, may wonder why such plays as *Zaza* are written. The answer in this case is very simple. *Zaza* was constructed by MM. Berton and Simon to encircle the talent of Mme. Réjane. It is quite certain that, if Mme. Réjane had not been Mme. Réjane, there would have been no *Zaza*. That would not have been a

19

serious calamity.   But we must take the world as we
find it, and Mme. Réjane as Mme. Réjane.   She must
be allowed to have her fling.   Where is there another
actress who can be so *canaille* and frisky and senti-
mentally   grotesque   and   grotesquely   sentimental?
Where is there another actress who can speak so
comically through her nose or blow that impudent little
organ so realistically after a fit of tears?   Where is
there another actress who can so cleverly reproduce
the gradual *crescendo* from nervous irritation to suffocat-
ing or shrieking hysteria?   The answer is that there
is no other such actress, and that therefore Mme.
Réjane must do all these things and be all these things
for us in her own inimitable way, and have her fling
which is like nobody else's fling.   That is the explanation, though not the excuse, of such a play as *Zaza*.
Surely such a combination of opposites as this play
exhibits—external reality and internal falsity—never
was seen before.   False, its implied suggestion that the
courtesan is "redeemed" by a sincere passion.   False,
the glamour it throws over the vulgar music-hall "star,"
who, purged by grief, ends as a person of lofty sentiments and elegant language.   False, the sentimental
excuses of Zaza for her—let us say Bohemian—life, on
the score of parental neglect.   False, the conversion
of Zaza from a virago bent on revenge to a humbled
penitent, all on account of a talk with a pert little child.
False, the character of Zaza's lover—or, rather, not false,
but null, as this personage is a mere automaton, a mere
whetstone for Zaza to grind her various axes upon.
False, intolerably false, the whole atmosphere of the
play, its representation of love—and such love!—as
sanctifying   everything,   accounting   for   everything,
indeed, constituting everything.   Looked at from the

point of view of the mind and the feelings, the heart and the brain, *Zaza* is a miracle of falsity.

And yet, externally, how real! Watch the music-hall "artist" at her toilet——how she rubs in the grease-paint, unpins her false hair, dabs the powder-puff over her shoulders, putting on a pinafore the while in order not to soil her skirt. Not a detail is missed. Even when the corset is unlaced, Zaza is careful to go through the pantomime of holding her breath. All the world and his wife have been shown exactly how the "artist" dresses and undresses; we feel that the sum of human knowledge has been appreciably augmented. But on the principle that you cannot have too much of a good thing, Zaza does it all, or nearly all, over again. Having combed her hair in Act I., she combs it once more in Act IV., and offers you a further piece of minute realism by removing the loose ends of hair from the comb and throwing them out of the window. Then she dusts the chair with her uplifted petticoats, cleans the wine-glasses by blowing into them and giving them a wipe with her dressing-gown, and performs other choice little Bohemian-domestic exploits to which only the pen of a Swift could do full justice. Or watch Zaza discovering a hole in the tablecloth, making faces at the *bonne* about it, and trying to hide it with a plate. What a "convincing" spectacle, what a marvellous application of another player's famous theory about holding the mirror up to nature! When you have done with these mechanical details, these "fireside concerns" as Elia would have called them, you may turn to examine Zaza in an attack of nerves. See her mouth twitching, her hands clenched, listen to the shrill note gradually coming into her voice. Then sit tight in your seat for the final explosion, the total physical

abandonment and degradation.   It is the very thing.
Coleridge had a mock apostrophe to

"Inoculation !   Heavenly maid !"

So Mme. Réjane—for Mme. Réjane and Zaza are one
—so Mme. Réjane is the muse of hystero-epilepsy.

And when you have wallowed in the crapulous, and
been dragged through the sordid, and shocked with the
frantic, and fooled by the sham-sentimental for five acts,
at the end of it all the question occurs—Is even Mme.
Réjane "worth it"?   She does it all to the life—seems,
in fact, to *live* the character.   But *Zaza* is rather a
heavy price to pay even for this incomparable talent.

What really saves Mme. Réjane and the play is her
unfailing sense of humour.   Her winks of intelligence,
her droll intonations, her irrepressible playfulness do
relieve the character of some of its grossness.   You
come back to the old position.   Because Réjane is
Réjane, the disagreeable play has been written ; and if,
on occasion, you cannot help being pleased in spite of
yourself, that also is because Réjane is Réjane.

LA ROBE ROUGE

(IMPERIAL, *June* 1902)

M. EUGÈNE BRIEUX has been called a second Augier, because of his aim to make the drama an instrument of moral and social action. The dramatist, he maintains, should be the bagman of the intellectual world. Perhaps that is why you discern a touch of Herbert Spencer in *La Robe Rouge.* The English philosopher has shown the impediments to clear thinking in what he calls the " professional bias." The French playwright shows you that bias in its tragic consequences, in the wrecking of homes and the shedding of blood. But it is the picture of the bias itself rather than that of its results which is the really valuable part of *La Robe Rouge,* because a study of manners and motives is more important than the exhibition of violent acts. The professional bias selected for exposure is that of the French magistracy. M. Brieux deals seriously with the men of the law, the official lawyers, those who sit on the Bench and those who prosecute for the State, as Molière dealt humorously with the men of physic. It is desirable to be precise. You are not shown that "the law is a hass"; you are not shown that those who administer it are conscious and deliberate rogues. What you are shown is the working of the law to unjust ends through inevitable professional instincts, rivalries, practice, and traditions.

Things that are life and death, or honour and dishonour,
for the accused are for the lawyers merely details of
"*le métier*." The people in the dock, innocent or
guilty, are for the lawyers merely pawns in the game
of professional advancement. And for the moment
let me also treat the accused persons of the particular
story as pawns and consider solely the dramatist's
picture of "*le métier*." A remote provincial criminal
Court of the third class desires to be raised to the
second class. Its promotion will depend on its output
—the number of cases and the percentage of convictions. Every acquittal is a misfortune for it, every
prospect of a capital sentence a piece of good luck.
Hence the interest of every official lawyer in finding
accused persons guilty. Mark the psychological con-
sequence; the wish is father to the thought, and every
official lawyer tends in advance to believe every accused
person guilty. Mouzon, the *juge d'instruction*, or examining magistrate, typifies this frame of mind. A
murder has been committed; he believes he has laid
his hand on the assassin. Note the next psychological
stage. Self-interest originated his desire to prove the
man guilty, and that desire creates his belief in the
man's guilt; but his belief is strengthened and becomes
a fixed idea by the tendency which we all have to make
good a theory when we have once pledged ourselves to
it. This mental process is worked out, step by step, in
the second act of *La Robe Rouge*. Unconsciously—
remember that it is unconsciously, through professional
bias—the magistrate twists every answer given by A.,
the accused person, into evidence of guilt. Possessed
by his preconceived theory, he finds it monstrous that
A. should profess innocence. He bullies, lays traps,
even begs for a confession—a process which merely

drives A. out of his senses. Then A.'s wife is brought in and subjected to the same torture, and, bewildered in her turn by the magistrate, she herself half believes in her husband's guilt. The examination is, however, abortive, and A. is sent for trial.

Another side of the case. Mouzon has got into trouble with a disreputable woman, and is requested by his superior officer, the Procureur-Général, to resign his post. The local deputy, who knows the Minister of Justice, intervenes in his favour. Scandal must be avoided, especially with a shaky Ministry. So let Mouzon be sent away by all means—but to a higher post. Mouzon's misbehaviour, then, is the direct cause of his promotion.

Act III. exhibits a fresh aspect of the professional bias. The Procureur, Vagret, who has to prosecute A., is a simple, honest man, without " push " and without influence. His promotion depends on his getting a verdict, and the thought nerves him to a great effort. The jury, it is clear, have been convinced by his eloquence, and he is congratulated by everyone on a foregone conclusion. All of a sudden Vagret asks for a brief suspension of the trial, and makes a confession to his wife. He had honestly believed in A.'s guilt— for he too had his preconceived theory—but at the moment of his loudest thunders doubts began to occur to him. There were two men in him, one accumulating argument on argument against the accused, the other silently criticising these arguments and finding them faulty. He has now swung round to belief in A.'s innocence, and, at the sacrifice of his promotion, he feels he must move for an acquittal. He will " do his duty as an honest man." Here you have the lawyer whose conscience conquers his professional bias—in other words, the unsuccessful magistrate.

Is the theme of professional bias exhausted? Not yet. There is the President of Assize, who also depends for his advancement upon a conviction. Has not a Paris journalist come all the way to the Pyrenees to report the case? Quick, *greffier*, get him a good seat! And there is the Procureur-Général, who holds that it is the duty of procureurs to prosecute, and to leave questions of innocence to the counsel for the defence. Anyhow, he refuses to discuss Vagret's qualms of conscience, lest he might compromise his own interests. What would the local Deputy say? And what the Deputy's friend, the Minister of Justice? The only magistrate who can afford to look at the facts impartially is the one who has no professional interest in them, because he has reached the age-limit and is about to take his pension.

So much for the professional bias. You have seen it on every side and in every shade. M. Brieux omits nothing and makes every word, every action, tell towards his end. The scene of the examination by the Juge d'Instruction is a masterpiece at once of dramatic completeness and of dramatic economy. The scene of the procureur's "case of conscience" is a masterpiece of dramatic sincerity. Beyond all cavil, M. Brieux is a born dramatist "of ideas." He has set out to examine and to exhibit a professional bias, not as an abstraction, but as a basis for the natural actions of living people. And what he set out to do he has thoroughly done.

But he is also a dramatist in the lower, and more popular, sense. He can invent and develop an interesting story. For even were the "ideas" of the play eliminated, even were all the gentlemen of the long robe mere dummies instead of links in a logical chain, the story of the man whom I have called A. would be an exciting piece of drama. To use the Aristotelian lingo, the *muthos* of *La Robe Rouge* is as good as its *ethos* and its *dianoia*. A. is wholly innocent, yet the lawyer's questions are so adroit that the audience is almost tempted, like A.'s wife, to believe in his guilt. While he is in prison awaiting trial his neighbours rob him, his men leave his fields, and he is a ruined man. But that is not the worst. Some past irregularity of his wife's, long dead and buried, and redeemed by many years of irreproachable conduct, is incidentally brought to light at the trial. For the lawyers it was a mere " point," a minor move in the judicial game. But it wrecks A.'s happiness for ever. He casts off his wife and takes her children from her. Despair prompts the woman to frenzy ; she seizes a knife and plunges it into the breast of the man who is responsible for her misery, the Juge d'Instruction Mouzon. A concession to the old-fashioned " poetic justice " ? Perhaps ; but not forced. A picture so uniformly sombre needed the relieving splash of blood-red, the sudden catastrophe of tragedy.

Mme. Réjane is the wife, hot-headed, an " instinctive " creature, in the end a wild beast ; and in that sort of part this versatile actress can do just as well as in the coquetry of *Ma Cousine* or in the *canaillerie* of *Zaza*.

THE VOYSEY INHERITANCE

(COURT, *November* 1905)

YES, decidedly the Court is our "Shavian" theatre. Mr. Shaw's own plays are shown there nightly, and in the afternoons they give you new plays by the younger men, all different in essentials, but all alike in the one particular that there clings to them a faint aroma of Mr. Shaw. It is in the air of the Court Theatre, just as a vague odour of patchouli is in the air of the Burlington Arcade or as the ballroom in *La Cagnotte*, when entered by the gentleman who had had his swallow-tail coat cleaned, smelt of benzine. Mr. St. John Hankin's *Return of the Prodigal* had been delicately scented with a Shaw *sachet*, and now *The Voysey Inheritance* of Mr. Granville Barker gratifies your nostrils with *triple extrait de* Shaw. You recognise the subtle perfume whenever the personages fall to giving solemnly nonsensical or nonsensically solemn explanations of life, morality, and one another. Mr. Barker has a story to tell, an interesting story in itself, and so long as he lets the facts speak for themselves all is plain sailing. But at periodical intervals, overcome by the atmosphere of the Court Theatre, he feels compelled to offer you a gloss, a "Shavian" gloss, on the facts. Then all is confusion, "new" morality, Nietzschean "transvaluation," and goodness knows what. It is legitimate enough for Mr. Shaw himself

298

to indulge in this game. He invented it. His dramatic works are so many pretexts for playing it. It would never do for *him* to let his facts speak for themselves, because observation of external facts is not his strong point. He never allows himself the chance of looking fairly and squarely at the facts, because of his haste to be evolving a theory from them. In so far as he sees them at all, he sees them only in the light of his preconceived explanation. It is quite otherwise with Mr. Barker, who shows in this play a real gift of keen, minute, relentless observation. If only he had been content with that! If only he had let us enjoy in peace, and without comment, the curious little spectacle of life, or a certain corner of it, which he has had the skill to put before us! But no; he must get to work with the "Shavian" scent-spray. "Conventional" morality must be made to stand on its head, and things that need no explanation must be explained all wrong. I venture to commend to him an example from China. When two mandarins are engaged in conversation they pause at intervals to exchange little scraps of paper, inscribed with jokes. Thus they fulfil the recognised duty of mingling grave thoughts with refined pleasantry. In a similar fashion the Court dramatists might serve up that admixture of Shaw which the etiquette of the place demands. The story might go on in a plain way, and at fixed intervals the personages might retire in pairs to the background and converse for a few moments *sotto voce*. We should not be bothered by hearing their remarks; but it would be an understood thing that these were the "Shavian" explanations. Another recommendation, and I have done with advice. Mr. Barker should remember the French proverb: *Qui trop embrasse mal étreint*. He

sets out to tell not one story but several—the story of
old Voysey's rascality, of Edward Voysey's trials, of
Hugh Voysey's matrimonial experiences. He sketches
for us a round dozen of Voyseys or people allied to the
Voysey family by marriage. This is a scheme of almost
Balzacian dimensions, a little *Comédie Humaine*. Even
with the liberal allowance of five acts and three hours
it is hardly possible to handle so much matter without
crowding, diffuseness, lack of perspective. At times
you can hardly see the wood for the trees.

All this notwithstanding, *The Voysey Inheritance* has
great merits. It has fresh and true observation, subtle
discrimination of character, sub-acid humour, an agreeable irony, and a general air of *reality*. That is the
important thing. We have got miles away from the
theatrical. We do genuinely feel that the roof has
been lifted off an office in Lincoln's Inn or a suburban
mansion and that the people disclosed to view behave
and talk ("Shavian" explanations always excepted) in
a perfectly natural way. One supremely realistic effect
Mr. Barker has adopted from a far greater master than
Mr. Shaw. I refer to his gradual unfolding of the
principal character by leaving parts of it at first
enigmatic and then clearing them up by the method of
retrospection. You have to piece this and that bit of
evidence together till at last you have something like
a complete picture of the man and his motives. This,
of course—hats off, please!—is the famous "Ibsen
touch." When you first hear Mr. Voysey's confession
and *apologia*—which he makes to his son almost as
soon as the curtain is up—you do not quite know how
much of it to believe. Ostensibly a prosperous solicitor,
of the highest respectability, a liberal father of a family,
a generous parishioner, altogether one of the brightest

ornaments of our great middle-class, Voysey is in truth a thief. He has been living all these years on his clients' money, using their trust funds while regularly paying them their interest. But how, asks his horrified son (and newly-made partner) did he come to embark on his frauds? He answers that his own father began it and, like a dutiful son, he took up the burden of the inheritance. Beginning, then, as a martyr, he now considers himself something very like a hero. He has played a difficult and dangerous game successfully. It is he, the confessed swindler, who exults, while it is his as yet clean-handed son who is abashed—the son who has fed himself on books of ethics ("the kind of garden oats," says the father contemptuously, "you young men sow nowadays"). Voysey is the Borkman of Lincoln's Inn. But why does the father confess to his son? He says it is because he feels his time is getting short and he hopes his son will take up the Voysey inheritance from him as he took it up from his own father. But is this true? Someone suggests, later, another reason, a generalisation of criminal psychology. Men who succeed at the dangerous game played by Voysey, senior, feel an overmastering impulse to disclose their secret—an instance of perverted pride. A further doubt; did the grandfather really begin the swindling? Ultimately the most probable conclusion seems to be that he did, but to an extent so slight that the son in a few years was able to replace the stolen funds, and *after that*, seeing how easy the thing was and eager for wealth, began stealing on his own account and on a large scale.

And now what will the son do? Wash his hands of the dirty business? Or take up the Voysey inheritance? If he takes it up, it shall only be in order to devote his life to restitution. Hardly has he made up his mind to the latter course when the father gets a chill and dies. The son, Edward, tells the truth to the assembled family as soon as they have come home from the funeral. Here come in some capital scenes depicting the several members of the Voysey family— Booth Voysey, the military fool, who cannot understand, but bullies everybody in a loud voice; Trenchard Voysey, a cautious K.C.; Hugh Voysey, exponent of the unpractical "artist temperament"; Honor Voysey, the old maid of the family; and the several wives or sweethearts of the sons. They are all shocked by the disclosure (save poor deaf Mrs. Voysey, who knew something of the truth already, and now, with the insensibility of age, is unmoved); but none of them will help Edward. He at first resolves to publish the truth and take the consequences—among them, prison. His sweetheart dissuades him, not without "Shavian" reflections. Then he will carry on the old game— gradually setting aside the profits of the business to replacing the smaller sums. Thus the poorer clients will at any rate be recouped; the rich ones must wait. But suppose if, in carrying on the game, he should become demoralised, like his father, and steal, not from the rich for the poor, but for himself? His sweetheart says she will take that risk. But very soon the game is up. One of the bigger clients comes to withdraw his funds, and has to be told the truth. "And now prosecute, do prosecute," says Edward, "prison would be a rest from this harassing toil." The client wavers, finally decides not to prosecute, but tells other clients. What will be the end? We never know. Prison perhaps? Then Edward's sweetheart will be more proud of him than ever. Anything rather than a life of slavery, in the hopeless attempt to make restitution. The debate, nebulous with " Shawisms," is cut short by the final curtain. I have an idea that the pair were discussing a case of conscience from the point of view of an entirely revised system of ethics (perhaps Nietzschean—on the principle of *omne ignotum pro Nietzscheano*); but I am not sure.

THE WAY OF THE WORLD

(MERMAID SOCIETY, *April* 1904)

PLEASURE-SEEKERS ought to be grateful to
the Mermaid Society for reviving *The Way of
the World.* I say pleasure-seekers advisedly. For it
is the primary business of dramatic entertainments,
old or new, to entertain. A classic is a classic not
because it is old, not (as Stendhal petulantly said)
because it pleased our grandfathers, but because it
pleases us. When it ceases to please it is only a
ci-devant classic. It may still have its proper place on
the museum shelf, but the theatre has no use for it.
The Mermaid Society has demonstrated *The Way of
the World* to be still a live classic. Lady Wishfort
and Mrs. Millamant and Sir Wilfull Witwoud are
brimming over with life. Congreve is still capable of
giving you a vivid sense of reality. You may have
suspected that as likely; but it is only through the
Mermaid Society that you know it for certain. And
how have they enabled you to know it? Through the
quite straightforward and familiar, yet magical and
inscrutable, influence of flesh and blood.

It is, I suggest, just because this influence is so
familiar that its importance in the theatre is commonly
underestimated. What are the elements of an acted
drama? Apart from the costumes and scenery, there
is the contribution of the dramatist and the contribution

of the players. The dramatist "invents" the story and characters and dialogue. The players contribute their skill; the propriety with which they speak the words set down for them and the art with which they assume their imaginary character. But they also contribute something infinitely more important—something which marks off an acted drama from every other work of art, and something with which art has nothing to do—flesh and blood, their bodies, gestures, glance and voices. It is, probably, because this element has nothing to do with art that we hear so little about it from the artists. They hardly like to admit, or even to think, that they owe so much of their effect to the brute forces of nature, to the simple fact that they are, as Lady Wishfort would say, "persons." Yet there is nothing more certain. The fascination of what is vaguely called "temperament"—which, whatever else it may mean, means something physical and innate—is supreme in the theatre. A player who has it may warp and maim his part to suit it and yet give the spectator greater pleasure than the merely skilful "mime" who has it not. Eleonora Duse is a case in point. So, it is evident, was Edmund Kean. The curious psychical influence of bodily presence, the invisible currents that pass between one human being and another, are now the subject of a scientific research still only in its first beginnings. When more is known about them, then more will be known about the peculiar energies of the acted drama. But, though the causes are as yet obscure, the effects are plain enough. There is all the difference in the world between certain lines of printed dialogue headed "Millamant," supplemented by the reader's imagination, and the same words spoken by a real woman, with a certain smile, a certain

20

toss of the head, a certain gait. It is a difference not of degree but of kind. What Congreve has done for an imaginary woman called Millamant suddenly springs into life through everything that nature has done for a real woman called Ethel Irving. Of course this flesh-and-blood element, so enormous an aid to the dramatist, may also turn and rend him. Many a speech or action will pass muster in print but stand forth as false or inadequate when actually uttered or performed before us. The character must hold together before, so to speak, the human body is put into it. Congreve's characters stand this test. Therefore *The Way of the World* is still a " live " classic.

Pursue this analysis a little further and you find the flesh-and-blood element contributing to the total effect in two rather different ways. An old play will present permanent features of human nature—scenes of love and jealousy and hate, or, it may be, a coquette's airs, or, perhaps, an old matron's vain affectations—and temporary transitory features, manners, or language now obsolete. A reader would mentally distinguish between them as the " actual " and the " historical " features. What happens, precisely, when they are presented on the stage by means of flesh and blood ? The " actual " features merely become more actual. Their effect of reality is deepened. Such a scene, for instance, as that between Fainall and Mrs. Marwood in the Mall, when the guilty lovers fall out, taste something of the bitterness of a clandestine *amour* with its eternal hovering on the edge of hate, and then kiss again with tears, gains enormously in reality, though it was real enough in the printed page. It was real enough, but now it becomes " modern "; its close resemblance to sides of life that we know or divine positively startles us. To see a beautiful, highly-strung woman, in the person of Miss Edyth Olive, before our eyes in this plight is a much more poignant thing than to read about the same situation in the book as concerning an imaginary Mrs. Fainall. Still, the difference of impression is only one of degree. So with Millamant's scenes and Lady Wishfort's scenes. These women are eternally true; Miss Ethel Irving and Mrs. Theodore Wright only come in to reinforce the author. Now turn to the "historical" features—as, for example, Sir Wilfull's tipsy scene or the dialogue between Witwoud and Petulant — and you find the flesh-and-blood element not deepening the impression, but transforming it. What was "historical" now becomes "actual." The things said and done are strange, but the fact that they are said and done by real people makes them credible. While you laughed at Sir Wilfull in the printed page, you scarcely believed in him; it is impossible not to believe in Mr. Lennox Pawle. *Could* there have been such a creature as Witwoud? the reader asks himself. Yes, answers the spectator, for there the fellow really *is*, with the voice and strut and grin of Mr. Nigel Playfair. About Petulant, perhaps, you may still have a lingering doubt; he is an untractable character, and Mr. Ian Maclaren hardly succeeds in dragging him out of the "historical" limbo. But of one thing this revival must quite convince you. It has knocked the bottom out of Lamb's plea for Congreve's immoral world as something conventional and fantastic. So soon as the characters are put solidly before you by living men and women you are absolutely appalled by their grim reality. To say that you are appalled is only another way of saying that you are pleased; you snatch a fearful joy.

I have dwelt on the impression of reality given by
the revival of this play and the causes of it because
one gets tired of the nonsense talked about Congreve as
now fit only for the "closet." One need not examine
the reasons why his *Way of the World* is so weak in
plot. It is customary to say that Congreve could not
invent a plot; it would be much more accurate to say
that, given the existing conditions of the "platform"
stage at the time, there was no particular need for him
to try. The Congrevean stage was not a stage of
plots, but a stage of "turns." This is the very feature
which sends Londoners of to-day flocking to "musical
comedy"; why, then, complain of it in Congreve? By
the way, it was an actress hitherto associated with
"musical comedy" who played Millamant. Miss
Ethel Irving affords another illustration of what I have
said about the supremacy of "temperament." She may
not quite harmonise with your preconceived notions of
Congreve's *grande coquette*, who is majestic, almost awe-
inspiring. Miss Irving is rather the "dainty rogue,"
but so dainty a rogue, so "magnetic," so real a piece
of womanhood, such a delight to ear and eye, that it
would be affectation to profess any disappointment
over her failure in exact coincidence with the ideal
character.

THE IRISH NATIONAL THEATRE

(*May*, 1903)

STENDHAL said that the greatest pleasure he
had ever got from the theatre was given him by
the performance of some poor Italian strollers in a
barn. A little band of Irish men and women, strangers
to London and to Londoners, playing in a suburban
hall succeeded in giving some constant frequenters
of the regular playhouses an hour or two of calm
delight quite outside the range of anything which
those houses have to offer. The Irish National
Theatre Society is understood to consist of amateurs,
all engaged in daily work, who can devote only their
leisure time to the stage. That was the case, it will
be remembered, with the enthusiasts who helped
Antoine to found his Théâtre Libre; but there is
this difference, that, while the French enterprise was
an artistic adventure and nothing else, the Irish
Theatre is that and something more. It is part of
a national movement, it is designed to express the
spirit of the race, the "virtue" of it, in the medium of
acted drama. That is obviously an excellent design.
If the peculiarities of Irish thought and feeling can
be brought home to us through drama we shall all be
the better for the knowledge; and the art of drama,
too, cannot but gain by a change of air, a new outlook,
a fresh current of ideas. Meanwhile, it will suffice to
record the keen pleasure which an afternoon with the

Irish National Theatre has afforded, and try to analyse that pleasure.

First and foremost, there is the pleasure of the ear. This, of course, is an accidental pleasure; it has nothing to do with the æsthetic aims of the Society, nothing to do with the dramatic theories or poetic gifts of its President, Mr. W. B. Yeats, nothing to do with art at all; it results from the nature of things, from the simple fact that Irish speakers are addressing English listeners. It is none the less a very exquisite pleasure. I, for one, had never realised the musical possibilities of our language until I heard these Irish people speak it. Most Englishmen, I fancy, get their notions of Irish pronunciation from Thackeray, and though, no doubt, Thackeray's version was always good-natured enough, yet the talk of Costigan and the Mulligan and the O'Dowd tends to burlesque the truth. The association is always one of drollery, whereas the English of these Irish players gives you an impression, not of drollery at all, but of elegance. " Fool " is pronounced " fule " (with the thin French " u "), " philosophy " is " philosoph*ee*," " argument " is " argu-mént," and the words look funny when so written; but they do not sound funny, they sound charming. The unexpected emphasis on the minor syllables has an air of not ungraceful pedantry or, better still, of an old-world courtliness. You are listening to English spoken with watchful care and slightly timorous hesitation, as though it were a learned language. That at once ennobles our mother-tongue, brings it into relief, gives it a daintiness and distinction of which, in the rough workaday use of it, one had never dreamed. But the charm does not stop there. These Irish people *sing* our language—and always in a minor key. It becomes in very fact "most musical, most melancholy." Rarely, very rarely, the chant degenerates into a whine. But, for the most part, the English ear is mildly surprised and entirely charmed. Talk of *lingua Toscana in bocca Romana*! The English tongue on Irish lips is every whit as melodious.

The next pleasure is for the eye. These Irish gentlemen and ladies are good to look at; the men are lithe, graceful, bright-eyed, and one at least of the maidens, with the stage name of Maire Nic Shiubhlaigh, is of a strange, wan, "disquieting" beauty. But I am not thinking so much of what Elia's Scotch friend would call their "pairsonal pretensions" as of their postures and movements. As a rule they stand stock-still. The speaker of the moment is the only one who is allowed a little gesture—just as in the familiar convention of the Italian marionette theatre the figure supposed to be speaking is distinguished from the others by a slight vibration. The listeners do not distract one's attention by fussy "stage business," they just stay where they are and listen. When they do move it is without premeditation, at haphazard, even with a little natural clumsiness, as of people who are not conscious of being stared at in public. Hence a delightful effect of spontaneity. And in their demeanour generally they have the artless impulsiveness of children—the very thing which one found so enjoyable in another exotic affair, the performance of Sada Yacco and her Japanese company. Add that the scenery is of Elizabethan simplicity—sometimes no more than a mere backcloth—and you will begin to see why this performance is a sight good for sore eyes—eyes made sore by the perpetual movement and glitter of the ordinary stage.

But it is time to say something of the vital part of
one's pleasure, the pleasure of mind and mood.   That,
too, is largely a pleasure of rest—and resignation.
The mind is steeped in seriousness; the mood is
uniformly sad.   For anything of the same kind one
would have to go to some of Maeterlinck's earlier
plays.   But that is an imperfect comparison; the Irish
theatre is really of its own kind and of none other.
Its sustained note of subdued gravity, with here and
there faint harmonics of weird elfish freakishness
("harps in the air," Hilda Wangel would have called
them) is entirely Irish and entirely delightful.   Take
Mr. Yeats's " morality," *The Hour-Glass*.   An angel gives
a man a few moments wherein to try and find means
of salvation before he dies with the last running out
of the sand.   Imagine how the ordinary dramatist
would treat this, how largely the hour-glass would bulk
in the foreground, how the man would writhe and
shriek in the frenzied horror of imminent death.
Indeed, you need not imagine it; this very situation
fills the final act of Sardou's *Dante*.   Tick, tick! goes
the pendulum clock.   Lo! the pendulum is the figure
of Death with his scythe.   (Oh, symbolism! oh
Sardou!)   Remark the practical actor conscientiously
emptying out under the limelight the whole contents
of the theatrical bag of tricks labelled " Death Scenes."
Then turn for a refreshing contrast to the behaviour of
Mr. Yeats's "Wise Man."   He is agitated, to be sure,
but quietly agitated.   He hardly so much as glances
at the hour-glass.   What you are asked to contemplate
is the inner rout of his mind.   A moment ago he had
been so proud of his knowledge!   How immeasurably
superior he had seemed to Teigue the Fool!   In what
impassioned prose he had exulted over the folly he

thought he had overthrown! "Though they call him
Teigue the Fool, he is not more foolish than everyone
used to be, with their dreams and their preaching and
their three worlds. But I have overthrown their three
worlds with the seven sciences. With philosophy that
was made from the lonely star I have taught them to
forget theology . . . and with music the fierce planet's
daughter whose hair is always on fire, and with
grammar, that is the moon's daughter, I have shut
their ears to the imaginary harpings and speech of the
angels." And now one of the angels (it is the beautiful Maire Nic Shiubhlaigh) with a little word has cast
him low. To be saved he must find one whom his
teaching has not corrupted. In vain he summons his
pupils (one of them a King's son, no less); they
think he merely wishes to dispute with them. In vain
he calls in wife and children; he has taught them not
to pray. And at last it is Teigue the Fool who saves
the Wise Man, Teigue who has seen scores of angels,
who knows the hilltops where the country-folk spread
nets to catch the angels' feet, and who always cuts the
nets so that the angels shall not be caught. The
whole tone of the thing, as we have said, is grave and
subdued, its whole texture such stuff as dreams are
made of. A little thing, it may be, but it haunts the
mind long afterwards. I can still see the virginal face
of the angel, who has stepped out of some Irish Book
of Hours, and still hear the wheedling chant of Teigue
the Fool—"Give me a pen-nee! Give me some
pen-nees!"

Another play by Mr. Yeats, *Kathleen Ni Houlihan*,
gives us a whiff—or rather a sigh—of '98. Young
Michael Gillan is going to wed Delia Cahel, and old
Peter, Michael's father, sits lovingly caressing the

golden sovereigns which Delia brings as her dowry.
It should be a merry family gathering, but gradually
there steals over all present an uncomfortable feeling
that something, they know not what, is going to
happen. The vague fear of something impending,
unseen—what is that but the " note " of *L'Intruse* and
of many another Maeterlinck " early manner " ?   An old,
sad-faced woman enters, begs a moment's shelter, and
is received with a simple courtesy by these Irish
peasants which is as " elegant " as their English
pronunciation. They ask quietly among themselves
who the stranger is, and no one can tell. She sits by
the fire wailing and singing strange scraps of song.
Many have loved her, but those who love her must
die for her. And young Michael is strangely drawn
towards her (one thinks here of Little Eyolf and the
Rat Wife), and when she goes out leaves father and
mother and bride and silently follows her. Then the
people outside are heard joyfully shouting the news
that the French have landed, and someone who has
met the stranger now sees her with the face of a radiant
girl. She symbolises the spirit of Ireland. In this
beautiful little piece you have the same dream-feeling
as in the other ; in this as in the other, the people
move about silently, as fearing to break the dream,
and speak with bated breath.

In Lady Gregory's *Twenty-Five* there is more solid
matter of fact, more of human nature's daily food.
Christie Henderson comes home from America, with sixty
pounds in his pocket, to claim the girl he left behind
him. But she, who has heard never a word from him, is
married to Michael Ford. The Fords have been sold
up and are just starting for exile in England. Will not
the wife take her old friend's sixty pounds to save her

husband? No, not a penny of it. Then a way must be found to make her, so Christie gets Michael to sit down to cards, and they play the game of "twenty-five," and by the strangest run of ill luck the whole of Christie's little fortune passes into Michael's hands. Then they all fall to dancing, save the wife, who silently weeps, and Christie starts on his return to America without a wife and without a penny, and yet well content. Mr. W. G. Fay plays Christie in a vein of mingled sadness and fun, but always *pianissimo*.

Yes, they are all from the outset to the end playing *pianissimo*, all hushed as in some sick-room, all grave and, as it were, careworn. No doubt there is a touch of affectation in their methods; they have something of the self-importance of children surpliced for service at the altar or "dressed up" for a grand domestic occasion. A style "deliberately adopted" is the harmless little boast of their prospectus. Well, that is a matter of course. All new movements in art are self-conscious, abound in little exaggerations and affectations. Is there not an Irish precept, " Be aisy; and if ye can't be aisy, be as aisy as ye can"? One may commend that to the Irish National Theatre Society. And for ourselves we may be quite "aisy"; for the "deliberate" methods of these enthusiasts will surely lose their stiffness in due course of time. Meanwhile one is sincerely grateful to them for an hour or two of real refreshment, a train of curious suggestions, a series of new "thrills."

WARP AND WOOF

(CAMDEN, *June* 1904)

OF course Mrs. Alfred Lyttelton's play abounds in faults. Of course her stage-craft is amateurish. Of course she overstates her case. What else, pray, did anyone expect from a novice? More important than her degree of skill or the precise measure of her accuracy is the question of her impulse and her choice of theme. It is a comfort to know, in these days of dramas manufactured for the market, that "indignation" not only "makes verses," but sometimes also makes plays. And a play which, avoiding the beaten track of amorous or domestic adventure, deals fearlessly with some actual remediable evil of our social system, however naïve in conception that play may be, however clumsily written—and *Warp and Woof* is both naïve and clumsy—is, just now, a valuable playhouse asset. The fact is, Mrs Lyttelton, in a jejune prentice fashion, has attempted to do for a corner of London life what Brieux has done for many corners of France. She sees something wrong, something which outrages her sense of justice, and she would do her best to right the wrong by exposing it before a whole playhouse. One knows all that is to be said about the difficulty of reconciling art with propagandism. One is quite aware that· the best plays are written by people whose overmastering impulse is, first and last, to write a play and not a tract. Nevertheless, the moralists and the thesis-mongers are invaluable in the theatre. They keep it real, keep it in touch with the life that we know. The English theatre especially needs them, for it is the most unreal of all theatres, the most frivolous, the most devoid of ideas. Mrs. Lyttelton's little experiment in thesis-mongering, then, crude and faulty as it is, is really more helpful than many a conventional " story " play of impeccable workmanship.

Mrs. Lyttelton sees a wrong. Being a woman, she naturally sees a wrong done by women to women. She sees that mundane and modish women are apt to be in too great a hurry to get their smart frocks home from the dressmakers, and that the dressmakers, under stress of their customers' impatience, are apt to prefer to the alternative of an enlargement of staff the cheaper expedient of " overtime." Thus, between the thoughtlessness of one set of women and the greed of another set of women, a third set— the workgirls — become white slaves, live without proper meals, proper air, proper leisure, proper sleep, so that the coarser among them become benumbed and brutalised and the more delicate perish miserably. Further than that, if the workgirl have beauty and a natural, healthy desire for the *joie de vivre*, she is like to fall an easy victim to unprincipled men. But has the law nothing to say in this matter? Yes, of course, there are the stringent regulations of the Factory Acts, and there are the surprise visits of his Majesty's inspector. But laws can be ignored and inspectors humbugged. The root of the evil is not a thing which " kings or laws can cause or cure ";

it is the thoughtlessness of some women acting upon
the greed of other women to the detriment of many
more.   Well, Mrs. Lyttelton sees all this, and is angry
—and what does she do ?   She flings all that she has
seen in a heap on the stage, pell-mell, upside-down,
anyhow.   She shows us the thoughtless women being
thoughtless, demanding their frocks within an hour
or two of the order, gabbling childish slang ("divvy,"
"spity," and other odious words which ought to be
left to the vulgar tittle-tattle of "our society corre-
spondent "), or rehearsing absurd songs and dances in
fancy dress while workgirls faint and die.   She shows
us the greedy dressmaker being greedy, cringing to
her customers, bullying, starving, and overworking her
girls, and lying through thick and thin to his Majesty's
factory inspector.   The inspection scene, by the way,
with the girls, working "after hours," huddled away into
the next room, then discovered, but lying or keeping
mute when questioned, is the one really effective thing
in *Warp and Woof.*   There is some attempt to differentiate the types of workgirl—the girl who is too
stupid to speak, the girl who won't blab "for the
honour of the firm," the girl who is afraid of dismissal
if she speaks, and so forth.   But then this crucial scene
of the play does not touch the real *crux* of the thesis.
The real business of the thesis-monger here is not to
show an "adventure," the attempted deception of a
factory inspector, but to expose and to *explain* the root
of the evil—mundane thoughtlessness acting upon
commercial greed.   And just there, I think, is the
weakness of Mrs. Lyttelton's play.   She exhibits
certain surface facts ; she does not go beneath the
surface and explain them.   If she will look at the
work of any practised thesis-monger—the aforesaid

M. Brieux, for example—she will see that all facets
of the thesis are turned one after another to the light,
the *cons* as well as the *pros* are discussed, every point
of view is allowed for. There are always several points
of view in these questions of social or economic
injustice. Evils of this nature seldom arise from
sheer, unadulterated wickedness. Grinding employers,
unreasonable customers, are acting according to their
lights, have something to say for themselves, or, more
often than not, know not what they do. There is
often (as Ibsen knows, even better than Brieux) a
biting irony in the contrast between good, even benev-
olent, intentions and bad social or economic results.
Now you get no hint of this in Mrs. Lyttleton's play.
Her personages are all of a piece, all black or all white.
Her mundane customer is an elegant, her dressmaker
an inelegant, monster; her workgirl is the ideal
"victim." This is at once felt to be no true picture
of human nature. People are not like that, and the
hardships of workers are not to be explained on the
simple principle that employers are ogres. The thesis,
in short, has not been *approfondie*, and the result is
that you have a sense of exaggeration, of the exception
being presented as the rule, and of the whole affair
being left unexplained. The details external to the
thesis—Mrs. Lyttelton's little sentimentalities, little
love-scenes, little thumb-nail sketches of (I hope and
believe) impossible "journalists"—one need not consider. For, to be frank, these things are not
considerable. "Let us go into the boudoir," says
a swain (in uniform and gigantic top-boots) to his
lady-love. Mrs. Lyttelton would have been well
advised to have popped her lovers, her journalist,
and all the rest of her "extras" into the boudoir

before the curtain rose, and to have kept them there, under lock and key, to the end.

It appears that some dressmakers have protested against Mrs. Lyttelton's Mme. Stéfanie, declaring that this sketch of a fashionable dressmaker, tyrant, bully, and " sweater," " does injustice to dressmakers as a class." " But," replies Lady Frances Balfour in a letter to the papers, " Mrs Lyttelton does not profess to be describing a class, and had a right, for dramatic purposes, to take an extreme case. All jealousy does not lead to murder, nor all just indignation on the part of defenders of their country who meet with ingratitude to rebellion and invasion ; yet in writing a drama of jealousy, or revolt against ingratitude, the dramatist may fairly give us an Othello or Coriolanus. Mme. Stéfanies may, and do exist." This specious passage, I venture to think, bolsters up a fallacy by a false analogy.

Lady Frances's primary proposition is that the dramatist has a right, for dramatic purposes, to take an extreme case. The answer is that it all depends. It depends upon the kind of drama attempted. If you are writing a romantic drama upon the heroic plane you may certainly take an extreme case. It is the very essence of your business to take an extreme case. You are showing passions in excess, great forces of nature let loose. You are picturing human beings at their *maximum* of volition and suffering, in the acutest crises of their fate. Othello is an extreme case. Coriolanus is an extreme case. Hamlet is an extreme case. Macbeth is an extreme case. But even here there are limits to your choice of extremes. You must make it clear that you are presenting human beings. You must see that they act naturally and logically according to the law of their natures and the pressure of the particular environment which you invent for them. What is the test of that? The inherent truthfulness of the picture, the impression created in the spectator's mind that just thus and not otherwise would the thing have befallen. The test of truth, then, in this case is an internal test. It is nothing to you whether there was ever a real Coriolanus or a real Macbeth, or whether men are often or seldom placed in the predicaments of these men. The play in which they figure is self-contained, you judge it on its merits, not in relation to any set of external facts. Verisimilitude is all you bargain for, not actuality; you are dealing with poetry, not history. In this kind of drama you may go further. You may stretch your extreme case beyond the limits of humanity. You may bring in a Ghost or a Caliban—provided always that your fantastic inventions fit logically and naturally into the scheme of your play. This, by the way, is what the author of the *Poetics* had in mind when he said that "probable impossibilities" were preferable to "improbable possibilities." And this is what Victor Hugo misunderstood when he argued (in the preface to *Cromwell*) for a drama of nothing but contrasted extremes. Caliban is a "probable impossibility." Quasimodo is an "improbable possibility." To sum up: extreme cases are the legitimate subject of romantic drama on the heroic plane, are indeed its proper subject—always with the reservation of verisimilitude, of justification not by reference to external fact but to the internal logic of the play itself. Again, extreme cases are the legitimate subject of pure comedy. Malvolio is an extreme case. Lady Wishfort is an extreme case. Bob Acres is an extreme case. For this comedy makes

21

its account—partially, by no means entirely—out of
human eccentricity. And again there is the same
reservation ; the extreme characters must satisfy the
internal test.

But what has all this to do with such a play as
Warp and Woof ? Absolutely nothing. Is this play
a work of pure " disinterested " art, aiming at interesting
us in its characters and conduct for their own sake ?
Of course it is nothing of the kind. It is a play with
a purpose, and that purpose is not the mere offer of
artistic pleasure, but the awakening of the social
conscience by what purports to be a faithful picture of
a particular set of contemporary facts. At once we
see that the internal test ceases to be adequate. It is
not inapplicable ; the play, whatever else it may
achieve, has first of all to hang together as a play.
But it is far from being, as in the other kinds of drama,
the final test. The final test is now the test of external
fact ; the " poetry " is sunk in " history." Are there
such people as Mme. Stéfanie ? Are her relations to
her customers and workgirls a true picture of the actual
relations of real employers to real workgirls and real
customers ? It is upon the answers to these questions
that the ultimate value of the play depends. " Mrs.
Lyttelton does not profess to be describing a class,"
says Lady Frances Balfour. Does she not ? Then
she is doing something very futile, figuring as *chimæra
bombinans in vacuo*. For if we are to understand that
Mme. Stéfanie is a mere exception, this at once gives
away the dramatist's " case." What is the use of
painting a picture of employers and employed, and
then explaining that it has no general validity, that it
does not in fact represent a state of things, but only
some individual, accidental thing ? Does not Lady

Frances perceive that her contention, if just, would really knock the bottom out of the play? I suspect that she does, for she has no sooner advanced it than she qualifies it, and almost withdraws it. " Mrs. Lyttelton does not profess to be describing a class." Nevertheless, " Mme. Stéfanies may, and do exist." They may? That is not the point; that does not help us in the least. But they " do exist." Well, there you have it. And the question is, to what extent do they exist? Is Mme. Stéfanie typical of a class? If she is, *Warp and Woof* is a useful (not a good; that is quite another matter, but a useful) play. If not, not. One must leave the statisticians, the experts in the Factory Acts, and other practical persons to settle that point.

A *CINDERELLA* BALLET

(EMPIRE, *February* 1906)

THERE are many worthy burgesses who seem dead
to the charms of ballet. The dumb show
oppresses them; they are for ever wishing that "somebody would say something." The rhythm of the
dance, now suavely undulating, now heavily beaten out
as with hammer-strokes, by turns austere and voluptuous, stately-processional and frenzied-bacchantic, leaves
them unmoved. To tolerate ballet at all these people
must have the vulgar element which their jargon calls
the "up-to-date"; an odious mimicry of the pavement-
life outside, to say nothing of the gutter. But a ballet
that condescends to matter-of-fact has abdicated its true
functions. The ballet is, in essence, the most abstract
of the arts that work in the medium of flesh and blood,
the most remote from actual life, the most thoroughly
"purged," as Schopenhauer would have said, "of the
will-to-live." It should transfer us to the region of pure
sensation, where things are neither good nor bad, neither
true nor untrue, but merely beautiful in line and mass
and motion. And yet it has a moral appeal, of a sort;
that you may find in the happy faces, the irrepressible
tendency to gambolling of the dancers, bespeaking that
joy of the artist in his work which to a Ruskinian is the
moralising element in all art.

The worst of ballet, from the reviewer's standpoint,

is that it defies review. A blend of various wordless
arts, action and plastic and music, it is not reducible
to words. If only one could *dance* a criticism of
Cinderella! One's sense of the exquisite would be
signified by a pirouette; praise would have its graduated
scale of *entrechats*; one would perorate in a *pas de
fascination*. Words can in no way reproduce the direct
sensations created by ballet; the best one can hope to
do with them is to set forth the resultant mental state,
the dream-like mood. You begin in *Cinderella* with
a dream of Watteau. There is a park with a lake, a
classic temple in the distance, a hint or two of florid
stonework in the foreground—very much the scene of
" L'Embarquement pour Cythère." A little company
of perfectly attired Watteau figures dance a languid
minuet. Even more Watteau-ish are their attitudes in
repose : youths in satin, with cloak hanging loosely from
one shoulder, lute in hand, bending over ladies with
long wasp-waists, sacque and panier, and those little
turned-up cockaded hats which, by a happy revival of
fashion, are to be seen at this moment in the shop-
windows of the Rue de la Paix. And all the Watteau
sentiment is there, the atmosphere that is a little sickly
in its sweetness, a melancholy as of lovers (it is
D'Annunzio who has said this of the Watteau sentiment) about to love no more. A dainty child in white,
with hair *à la Pompadour* and roses over the ears,
makes her little timid yet elegant curtsey to the Prince.
Even the programme has caught the right Watteau
tone. The courtiers are called Mutine and Celadon,
Mignonne and Bel Amour. "Designed and produced,"
you read, "by C. Wilhelm." I could almost have
fancied I read " par Antoine Watteau." The perfect
taste, restraint, harmony of this scene are beyond

praise—one of the most beautiful things I can call to mind—either at the Empire or elsewhere.

Cinderella herself is mimed and danced by Mlle. Adeline Genée. It is a flawless performance. Perhaps performance is not the best word, because that suggests a conscious art, whereas Mlle. Genée's quiet charm is something wholly apart from her technical skill, wonderful as that is. It is a charm of native, even homely simplicity; a charm that is never mutinous, coquettish, "disquieting," as the French say; the charm of a child blithely yielding, without a thought of onlookers, to the play-impulse. See her when Cinderella is left alone in the kitchen, after the others have gone to the ball! At first she sits forlorn; then the picture of the ballroom takes hold of her and her face beams with delight at the idea of improvising a little ballroom scene all to herself. Up she jumps, plucks a couple of feathers from her broom and sticks them in her hair, snatches up the tablecloth to make a train, and whirls round with her broom for an imaginary partner. The dainty grace with which she makes believe to eat an ice, to bow to her partner, to yield to a pressing invitation for just one dance more! To every little endearing detail she brings some quaint touch of humour, some ingenuity of invention. As to her technical skill, I have called it wonderful, out of sheer inability to appraise it with proper knowledge. It is dancing without the slightest trace of effort, every step—in reality, no doubt, calculated to a hair's breadth and assiduously practised—having the air of a happy impromptu.

The next best dancer to Mlle. Genée is Mr. Sundberg. Towards male dancers as a rule most of us have a feeling for which the word dislike is too mild a name.

But with Mr. Sundberg's dancing I have only one fault to find; there is not enough of it. He has just one scene—wherein he gives a lesson, as Court Dancing Master, to Cinderella's stepmother. He enters, fiddle in hand, tripping on one foot and swaying the other rhythmically to and fro—a sort of glorified hop-scotch. From entry to exit he never stops dancing, and every movement is grace itself. At the same time he contrives to give to the whole thing a burlesque air, a mock solemnity, quite in the tradition of "le Diou de la Danse." His coat, with its ballooning skirts, his macaroni wig, seem to have come straight out of "*Mariage à la mode.*" This Court Dancing Master is my own particular joy. But for those who like it there is plenty of grotesque dancing of the ordinary "cellar-flap" sort, from Mr. Fred Farren (in a *pas seul*) as well as from Mr. W. Vokes, who, with two others, has a clever "act" under a huge umbrella. Nor can one forget the monkey-like antics of little Black Sambo, the page, who also seems to have been cut from some canvas of Hogarth. The music of the ballet is a *pot-pourri* of tunes and scraps of tunes from Mozart and Mendelssohn to Humperdinck and Messager and Tchaikovsky; an arrangement which one may be permitted to like far better than "specially composed" music from some inferior hand. This Empire *Cinderella* is, for the moment, the most beautiful stage entertainment in London. Even those who are lukewarm about the ballet must feel the fascination of the scene, with the little curtseying Pompadourish maid in white (is it Mutine or Mignonne?) and the silk-clad page with the lute (is it Celadon or Bel Amour?). It will give them, more surely even than any picture of Mr. Charles Conder's, the true Watteau "thrill."

THE DÉBUTANTE

(EMPIRE, *January* 1907)

IT has been bruited abroad that Mlle. Geneé is going to America. In the native home of the Washington Post and the Cake Walk she will be like a philosopher at a barbarian Court. Is it too late to buy her off? Perhaps another First Folio would do it. London without Adeline Genée will be a mere huddle of pedestrians, a benighted place where tiptoeing is only known by hearsay. If and when Genée departs she will have to leave London her white satin shoes, to be deposited in the British Museum. Théophile Gautier, so long ago as 1868, revealed to the brothers De Goncourt the significance of the ballet-dancers' shoes. "He describes," records the Diary, "the white satin shoe which, for each of them, is strengthened by a little cushion of silk in the place where the dancer feels that she bears and presses most—a cushion which would indicate to an expert the name of the dancer." Thus we should reconstruct the wearer from the shoe. *Ex pede Adelinam.*

Meanwhile the wearer as well as the shoe has been bewitching the town in *The Débutante*, a ballet divertissement in three tableaux by C. Wilhelm. The scene is the Paris Opera House; and the period is 1835 —the "palmy days," that is to say, the period of Taglioni the sylph-like, who was, however, not a bit

slimmer than Mlle. Genée, and, very likely, no better
dancer. It was a delightful period for the eye, both in
its everyday clothes and in its romantic travesties.
The gentlemen had tight waists, high-rolled collars,
enormous "toppers," trousers strapped tight under the
boot, and "frogged" cloaks ; the ladies wore dainty little
aprons, huge bonnets, and remarkable *coiffures*. That
was the costume of private life, and you have it all
duly reproduced in Scene I. of *The Débutante*, the
Rehearsal Room, whither comes Mlle. Delphine to join
M. Pirouette's dancing class. The pupils are all in
long white muslin Taglioni skirts and loll on benches
in easy attitudes, like so many pictures by Degas. It
is a world—and a whirl—of white muslin chequered by
the brilliantly coloured coats of the gentlemen, amateurs
of the ballet, who happen to have just looked in. You
like to fancy that the crowd contains—as surely a
crowd of the period would have contained—all the gay
lions of Balzac—Rastignac and De Marsay and Lucien
de Rubempré. The military gentleman with the flat
cap and "ducks" must be Colonel Philippe Bridau.
There, at any rate, is "The Baron" (Nucingen, you
hope, rather than Hulot), and the Baron it is who puts
forward Mlle. Delphine for the new ballet now in
rehearsal, *The Odalisque*, when the première danseuse,
Mlle. Florita, throws up her part. Despair of M.
Pirouette who tears his Paganini hair ; delirious delight
of M. Pirouette (who is Mr. Fred Farren, at his most
grotesque) when he discovers that Mlle. Delphine can
dance like Mlle. Genée, who in fact she is. You, the
spectator, are delighted by Mlle. Genée's dancing too,
but still more by her freshness, her girlish simplicity,
her spontaneity, her "petitionary" grace. There you
have the true secret of Genée's charm : the purely

physical charm of perfect grace in attitude and movement, the specific charm, that is to say, of the dancer,
plus the charm of native temperament unconsciously
revealed, the charm of the woman. In speaking of
players I have suggested that their ultimate appeal
rests rather upon what they are than upon what they
do. I have no wish to ride a theory to death, but
cannot refrain from pointing out that it is just as true
of the great dancers as of the great players. And now
the ballet that you have seen rehearsed is actually
performed. Of course, it is an Oriental ballet. All
romance was Oriental in 1835. The *locus classicus* of
the subject is to be found in a certain " Roundabout
Paper " concerning " William IV.'s time." " Even in
William IV.'s time, when I think of Duvernay prancing
in as the Bayadère. . . . How well I remember the
tune to which she used to appear ! Kaled used to say
to the Sultan, ' My Lord, a troop of those dancing and
singing gurls called Bayadères approaches,' and to the
clash of cymbals, and the thumping of my heart, in
she used to dance ! " That is just what you get at the
Empire. There is the Sultan (Mr. Fred Farren, again,
in a wonderful turban), and there is the troop of
dancing (fortunately *not* singing) gurls called Bayadères,
and to the clash of cymbals Mme. Genée as the chief
Odalisque comes prancing in. The Sultan obviously
suffers from senile decrepitude, as a Sultan should, but
he still knows good dancing when he sees it, and with
heavy bags of gold he purchases the fair Odalisque
from the wicked slave-dealer Mustafa—the incomparable
Mr. Sundberg—who expresses the utmost turpitude of
slave-dealing by extraordinary high jumps and twirls.
But, of course, it would never do for youth to be
sacrificed to crabbed age in this way, and, accordingly,

the Captain of the Guard comes to the rescue, only to be cast into chains for his temerity. Then the Odalisque sues for the gallant captain's pardon in a *pas de fascination*, and all ends happily.

Delightful, then, this ballet of *The Débutante*; delightful, in that it offers a compound pleasure—the purely sensuous pleasure of the ballet supplemented and made more exquisite by the pleasure of historico-literary suggestion. It gives us a glimpse of our grandfathers' generation and the ways of 1835, and shows us, in particular, the way they were accustomed to *visualise* romance in the full tide of the Romantic Movement. And mark the advantage of ballet for suggestion of this kind. A play presenting the period would monopolise your attention; whereas the placid semi-hypnotic state in which you look on at ballet invites to reverie. You have one eye on the stage and the other, as it were, on the well-loved back of this or that volume in your library. You are reading Thackeray to orchestral music. Balzac peeps out at you through a maze of muslin skirts and twirling satin shoes. It is the old story—*que de choses dans un menuet !*

A CATALOGUE OF BOOKS
PUBLISHED BY METHUEN
AND COMPANY: LONDON
36 ESSEX STREET
W.C.

CONTENTS

NOVEMBER 1907

A CATALOGUE OF

MESSRS. METHUEN'S
PUBLICATIONS

Colonial Editions are published of all Messrs. METHUEN'S Novels issued at a price above 2s. 6d., and similar editions are published of some works of General Literature. These are marked in the Catalogue. Colonial editions are only for circulation in the British Colonies and India.

I.P.L. represents Illustrated Pocket Library.

PART I.—GENERAL LITERATURE

Abbott (J. H. M.). Author of 'Tommy Cornstalk.' AN OUTLANDER IN ENGLAND: BEING SOME IMPRESSIONS OF AN AUSTRALIAN ABROAD. *Second Edition.* Cr. 8vo. 6s.
A Colonial Edition is also published.

Acatos (M. J.). See Junior School Books.

Adams (Frank). JACK SPRATT. With 24 Coloured Pictures. *Super Royal 16mo.* 2s.

Adeney (W. F.), M.A. See Bennett and Adeney.

Æschylus. See Classical Translations.

Æsop. See I.P.L.

Ainsworth (W. Harrison). See I.P.L.

Alderson (J. P.). MR. ASQUITH. With Portraits and Illustrations. *Demy 8vo.* 7s. 6d. net.

Aldis (Janet). MADAME GEOFFRIN, HER SALON, AND HER TIMES. With many Portraits and Illustrations. *Second Edition. Demy 8vo.* 10s. 6d. net.
A Colonial Edition is also published.

Alexander (William), D.D., Archbishop of Armagh. THOUGHTS AND COUNSELS OF MANY YEARS. *Demy 16mo.* 2s. 6d.

Aiken (Henry). THE NATIONAL SPORTS OF GREAT BRITAIN. With descriptions in English and French. With 51 Coloured Plates. *Royal Folio. Five Guineas net.* The Plates can be had separately in a Portfolio. £3, 3s. net.
See also I.P.L.

Allen (C. C.) See Textbooks of Technology.

Allen (Jessie). See Little Books on Art.

Allen (J. Romilly), F.S.A. See Antiquary's Books.

Almack (E.). See Little Books on Art.

Amherst (Lady). A SKETCH OF EGYPTIAN HISTORY FROM THE EARLIEST TIMES TO THE PRESENT DAY. With many Illustrations. *Demy 8vo.* 7s. 6d. net.

Anderson (F. M.). THE STORY OF THE BRITISH EMPIRE FOR CHILDREN. With many Illustrations. *Cr. 8vo.* 2s.

Anderson (J. G.), B.A., Examiner to London University, NOUVELLE GRAMMAIRE FRANÇAISE. *Cr. 8vo.* 2s.
EXERCICES DE GRAMMAIRE FRANÇAISE. *Cr. 8vo.* 1s. 6d.

Andrewes (Bishop). PRECES PRIVATAE. Edited, with Notes, by F. E. BRIGHTMAN, M.A., of Pusey House, Oxford. *Cr. 8vo.* 6s.

Anglo-Australian. AFTER-GLOW MEMORIES. *Cr. 8vo.* 6s.
A Colonial Edition is also published.

Anon. FELISSA; OR, THE LIFE AND OPINIONS OF A KITTEN OF SENTIMENT. With 12 Coloured Plates. *Post 16mo.* 2s. 6d. net.

Aristotle. THE NICOMACHEAN ETHICS. Edited, with an Introduction and Notes, by JOHN BURNET, M.A., Professor of Greek at St. Andrews. *Cheaper issue. Demy 8vo.* 10s. 6d. net.

Atkins (H. G.). See Oxford Biographies.

Atkinson (C. M.). JEREMY BENTHAM. *Demy 8vo.* 5s. net.

Atkinson (T. D.). A SHORT HISTORY OF ENGLISH ARCHITECTURE. With over 200 Illustrations. *Second Edition. Fcap. 8vo.* 3s. 6d. net.
A GLOSSARY OF TERMS USED IN ENGLISH ARCHITECTURE. Illustrated. *Second Ed. Fcap. 8vo.* 3s. 6d. net.

Auden (T.), M.A., F.S.A. See Ancient Cities.

Aurelius (Marcus) and Epictetus. WORDS OF THE ANCIENT WISE: Thoughts from. Edited by W. H. D. ROUSE, M.A., Litt.D. *Fcap. 8vo.* 3s. 6d. net. See also Standard Library.

Austen (Jane). See Little Library and Standard Library.

Bacon (Francis). See Little Library and Standard Library.

Baden-Powell (R. S. S.), Major-General. THE DOWNFALL OF PREMPEH. A Diary of Life in Ashanti 1895. Illustrated. *Third Edition. Large Cr. 8vo.* 6s.
A Colonial Edition is also published.

THE MATABELE CAMPAIGN, 1896. With nearly 100 Illustrations. *Fourth Edition. Large Cr. 8vo. 6s.*
A Colonial Edition is also published.

Bailey (J. C.), M.A. See Cowper.

Baker (W. G.), M.A. See Junior Examination Series.

Baker (Julian L.), F.I.C., F.C.S. See Books on Business.

Balfour (Graham). THE LIFE OF ROBERT LOUIS STEVENSON. *Third and Cheaper Edition, Revised. Cr. 8vo. 6s.*
A Colonial Edition is also published.

Ballard (A.), B.A., LL.B. See Antiquary's Books.

Bally (S. E.). See Commercial Series.

Banks (Elizabeth L.). THE AUTO-BIOGRAPHY OF A 'NEWSPAPER GIRL.' *Second Edition. Cr. 8vo. 6s.*
A Colonial Edition is also published.

Barham (R. H.). See Little Library.

Baring (The Hon. Maurice). WITH THE RUSSIANS IN MANCHURIA. *Third Edition. Demy 8vo. 7s. 6d. net.*
A Colonial Edition is also published.
A YEAR IN RUSSIA. *Second Edition. Demy 8vo. 7s. 6d.*

Baring-Gould (S.). THE LIFE OF NAPOLEON BONAPARTE. With over 150 Illustrations in the Text, and a Photogravure Frontispiece. *Royal 8vo. 10s.6d.net.*
THE TRAGEDY OF THE CÆSARS. With numerous Illustrations from Busts, Gems, Cameos, etc. *Sixth Edition. Royal 8vo. 10s. 6d. net.*
A BOOK OF FAIRY TALES. With numerous Illustrations by A. J. GASKIN. *Third Edition. Cr. 8vo. Buckram. 6s.*
OLD ENGLISH FAIRY TALES. With numerous Illustrations by F. D. BEDFORD. *Third Edition. Cr. 8vo. Buckram. 6s.*
THE VICAR OF MORWENSTOW. Revised Edition. With a Portrait. *Third Edition. Cr. 8vo. 3s. 6d.*
A BOOK OF DARTMOOR: A Descriptive and Historical Sketch. With Plans and numerous Illustrations. *Second Edition. Cr. 8vo. 6s.*
A BOOK OF DEVON. Illustrated. *Second Edition. Cr. 8vo. 6s.*
A BOOK OF CORNWALL. Illustrated. *Second Edition. Cr. 8vo. 6s.*
A BOOK OF NORTH WALES. Illustrated. *Cr. 8vo. 6s.*
A BOOK OF SOUTH WALES. Illustrated. *Cr. 8vo. 6s.*
A BOOK OF BRITTANY. Illustrated. *Cr. 8vo. 6s.*
A BOOK OF THE RIVIERA. Illustrated. *Cr. 8vo. 6s.*
A Colonial Edition is also published.
A BOOK OF THE RHINE: From Cleve to Mainz. Illustrated. *Second Edition. Crown 8vo. 6s.*
A Colonial Edition is also published.
A BOOK OF THE PYRENEES. With 24 Illustrations. *Crown 8vo. 6s.*
A Colonial Edition is also published.

A BOOK OF GHOSTS. With 8 Illustrations by D. MURRAY SMITH. *Second Edition. Cr. 8vo. 6s.*
OLD COUNTRY LIFE. With 67 Illustrations. *Fifth Edition. Large Cr. 8vo. 6s.*
A GARLAND OF COUNTRY SONG: English Folk Songs with their Traditional Melodies. Collected and arranged by S. BARING-GOULD and H. F. SHEPPARD. *Demy 4to. 6s.*
SONGS OF THE WEST: Folk Songs of Devon and Cornwall. Collected from the Mouths of the People. By S. BARING-GOULD, M.A., and H. FLEETWOOD SHEPPARD, M.A. New and Revised Edition, under the musical editorship of CECIL J. SHARP, Principal of the Hampstead Conservatoire. *Large Imperial 8vo. 5s. net.*
A BOOK OF NURSERY SONGS AND RHYMES. Edited by S. BARING-GOULD, and Illustrated by the Birmingham Art School. *A New Edition. Long Cr. 8vo. 2s. 6d. net.*
STRANGE SURVIVALS AND SUPERSTITIONS. *Third Edition. Cr. 8vo. 2s. 6d. net.*
YORKSHIRE ODDITIES AND STRANGE EVENTS. *New and Revised Edition. Cr. 8vo. 2s. 6d. net.*
See also Little Guides.

Barker (Aldred F.). See Textbooks of Technology.

Barker (E.), M.A. (Late) Fellow of Merton College, Oxford. THE POLITICAL THOUGHT OF PLATO AND ARISTOTLE. *Demy 8vo. 10s. 6d. net.*

Barnes (W. E.), D.D. See Churchman's Bible.

Barnett (Mrs. P. A.). See Little Library.

Baron (R. R. N.), M.A. FRENCH PROSE COMPOSITION. *Second Edition. Cr. 8vo. 2s. 6d. Key, 3s. net.*
See also Junior School Books.

Barron (H. M.), M.A., Wadham College, Oxford. TEXTS FOR SERMONS. With a Preface by Canon SCOTT HOLLAND. *Cr. 8vo. 3s. 6d.*

Bartholomew (J. G.), F.R.S.E. See C. G. Robertson.

Bastable (C. F.), M.A. THE COMMERCE OF NATIONS. *Fourth Ed. Cr. 8vo. 2s. 6d.*

Bastian (H. Charlton), M.D., F.R.S. THE EVOLUTION OF LIFE. Illustrated. *Demy 8vo. 7s. 6d. net.*

Batson (Mrs. Stephen). A CONCISE HANDBOOK OF GARDEN FLOWERS. *Fcap. 8vo. 3s. 6d.*

Batten (Loring W.), Ph.D., S.T.D. THE HEBREW PROPHET. *Cr. 8vo. 3s. 6d. net.*

Bayley (R. Child). THE COMPLETE PHOTOGRAPHER. With over 100 Illustrations. *Second Edition. Demy 8vo. 10s. 6d. net.*

Beard (W. S.). EASY EXERCISES IN ALGEBRA. *Cr. 8vo. 1s. 6d.* See Junior Examination Series and Beginner's Books.

Beckford (Peter). THOUGHTS ON HUNTING. Edited by J. OTHO PAGET, and Illustrated by G. H. JALLAND. *Second Edition. Demy 8vo. 6s.*

Beckford (William). See Little Library.

Beeching (H. C.), M.A., Canon of Westminster. See Library of Devotion.

Begbie (Harold). MASTER WORKERS. Illustrated. *Demy 8vo. 7s. 6d. net.*

Behmen (Jacob). DIALOGUES ON THE SUPERSENSUAL LIFE. Edited by BERNARD HOLLAND. *Fcap. 8vo. 3s. 6d.*

Bell (Mrs. A.). THE SKIRTS OF THE GREAT CITY. *Second Ed. Cr. 8vo. 6s.*

Belloc (Hilaire), M.P. PARIS. With Maps and Illustrations. *Second Edition, Revised. Cr. 8vo. 6s.*
HILLS AND THE SEA. *Second Edition. Crown 8vo. 6s.*

Bellot (H. H. L.), M.A. THE INNER AND MIDDLE TEMPLE. With numerous Illustrations. *Crown 8vo. 6s. net.*

Bennett (W. H.), M.A. A PRIMER OF THE BIBLE. *Fourth Ed. Cr. 8vo. 2s. 6d.*

Bennett (W. H.) and Adeney (W. F.). A BIBLICAL INTRODUCTION. *Fourth Edition. Cr. 8vo. 7s. 6d.*

Benson (Archbishop) GOD'S BOARD: Communion Addresses. *Fcap. 8vo. 3s. 6d. net.*

Benson (A. C.), M.A. See Oxford Biographies.

Benson (R. M.). THE WAY OF HOLINESS: a Devotional Commentary on the 119th Psalm. *Cr. 8vo. 5s.*

Bernard (E. R.), M.A., Canon of Salisbury. THE ENGLISH SUNDAY. *Fcap. 8vo. 1s. 6d.*

Bertouch (Baroness de). THE LIFE OF FATHER IGNATIUS. Illustrated. *Demy 8vo. 10s. 6d. net.*

Beruete (A. de). See Classics of Art.

Betham-Edwards (M.). HOME LIFE IN FRANCE. Illustrated. *Fourth and Cheaper Edition. Crown 8vo. 6s.*
A Colonial Edition is also published.

Bethune-Baker (J. F.), M.A. See Handbooks of Theology.

Bidez (M.). See Byzantine Texts.

Biggs (C. R. D.), D.D. See Churchman's Bible.

Bindley (T. Herbert), B.D. THE OECUMENICAL DOCUMENTS OF THE FAITH. With Introductions and Notes. *Second Edition. Cr. 8vo. 6s. net.*

Binns (H. B.). THE LIFE OF WALT WHITMAN. Illustrated. *Demy 8vo. 10s. 6d. net.*
A Colonial Edition is also published.

Binyon (Lawrence). THE DEATH OF ADAM, AND OTHER POEMS. *Cr. 8vo. 3s. 6d. net.*
See also W. Blake.

Birnstingl (Ethel). See Little Books on Art.

Blair (Robert). See I.P.L.

Blake (William). THE LETTERS OF WILLIAM BLAKE, TOGETHER WITH A LIFE BY FREDERICK TATHAM. Edited from the Original Manuscripts, with an Introduction and Notes, by ARCHIBALD G. B. RUSSELL. With 12 Illustrations. *Demy 8vo. 7s. 6d. net.*
ILLUSTRATIONS OF THE BOOK OF JOB. With a General Introduction by LAWRENCE BINYON. *Quarto. 21s. net.*
See also I.P.L. and Little Library.

Blaxland (B.), M.A. See Library of Devotion.

Bloom (J. Harvey), M.A. SHAKE-SPEARE'S GARDEN. Illustrated. *Fcap. 8vo. 3s. 6d.; leather, 4s. 6d. net.*
See also Antiquary's Books.

Blouet (Henri). See Beginner's Books.

Boardman (T. H.), M.A. See Textbooks of Science.

Bodley (J. E. C.), Author of 'France.' THE CORONATION OF EDWARD VII. *Demy 8vo. 21s. net.* By Command of the King.

Body (George), D.D. THE SOUL'S PILGRIMAGE: Devotional Readings from his writings. Selected by J. H. BURN, B.D., F.R.S.E. *Demy 16mo. 2s. 6d.*

Bona (Cardinal). See Library of Devotion.

Boon (F. C.). See Commercial Series.

Borrow (George). See Little Library.

Bos (J. Ritzema). AGRICULTURAL ZOOLOGY. Translated by J. R. AINSWORTH DAVIS, M.A. With 155 Illustrations. *Cr. 8vo. Third Edition. 3s. 6d.*

Botting (C. G.), B.A. EASY GREEK EXERCISES. *Cr. 8vo. 2s.* See also Junior Examination Series.

Boulting (W.) TASSO AND HIS TIMES. With 24 Illustrations. *Demy 8vo. 10s. 6d. net.*

Boulton (E. S.), M.A. GEOMETRY ON MODERN LINES. *Cr. 8vo. 2s.*

Boulton (William B.). THOMAS GAINSBOROUGH. With 40 Illustrations. *Demy 8vo. 7s. 6d. net.*
SIR JOSHUA REYNOLDS, P.R.A. With 49 Illustrations. *Demy 8vo. 7s. 6d. net.*

Bowden (E. M.). THE IMITATION OF BUDDHA: Being Quotations from Buddhist Literature for each Day in the Year. *Fifth Edition. Cr. 16mo. 2s. 6d.*

Boyd-Carpenter (Margaret). THE CHILD IN ART. Illustrated. *Second Edition. Large Crown 8vo. 6s.*

Boyle (W.). CHRISTMAS AT THE ZOO. With Verses by W. BOYLE and 24 Coloured Pictures by H. B. NEILSON. *Super Royal 16mo. 2s.*

Brabant (F. G.), M.A. See Little Guides.

Bradley (A. G.) ROUND ABOUT WILTSHIRE. With 30 Illustrations of which 14 are in colour by T. C. GOTCH. *Second Ed. Cr. 8vo. 6s.*

Bradley (J. W.). See Little Books on Art.

Braid (James) and Others. GREAT GOLFERS IN THE MAKING. By Thirty-Four Famous Players. Edited, with an Introduction, by HENRY LEACH. With 34 Portraits. *Demy 8vo. 7s. 6d. net.*
A Colonial Edition is also published.

Brailsford (H. N.). MACEDONIA: ITS RACES AND ITS FUTURE. Illustrated. *Demy 8vo.* 12s. 6d. net.

Brodrick (Mary) and Morton (Anderson). A CONCISE HANDBOOK OF EGYPTIAN ARCHÆOLOGY. Illustrated. *Cr. 8vo.* 3s. 6d.

Brooks (E. E.), B.Sc. See Textbooks of Technology.

Brooks (E. W.). See Byzantine Texts.

Brown (P. H.), LL.D., Fraser Professor of Ancient (Scottish) History at the University of Edinburgh. SCOTLAND IN THE TIME OF QUEEN MARY. *Demy 8vo.* 7s. 6d. net.

Brown (S. E.), M.A., Camb., B.A., B.Sc., London ; Senior Science Master at Uppingham School. A PRACTICAL CHEMISTRY NOTE-BOOK FOR MATRICULATION AND ARMY CANDIDATES: EASIER EXPERIMENTS ON THE COMMONER SUBSTANCES. *Cr. 4to.* 1s. 6d. net.

Browne (Sir Thomas). See Standard Library.

Brownell (C. L.). THE HEART OF JAPAN. Illustrated. *Third Edition. Cr. 8vo.* 6s. ; also *Demy 8vo.* 6d.

Browning (Robert). See Little Library.

Buckland (Francis T.). CURIOSITIES OF NATURAL HISTORY. Illustrated by H. B. NEILSON. *Cr. 8vo.* 3s. 6d.

Buckton (A. M.) THE BURDEN OF ENGELA : a Ballad-Epic. *Second Edition. Cr. 8vo.* 3s. 6d. net.
KINGS IN BABYLON. A Drama. *Crown 8vo.* 1s. net.
EAGER HEART : A Mystery Play. *Fifth Edition. Cr. 8vo.* 1s. net.

Budge (E. A. Wallis). THE GODS OF THE EGYPTIANS. With over 100 Coloured Plates and many Illustrations. *Two Volumes. Royal 8vo.* £3, 3s. net.

Bulot (H. Massac). THE MOTOR YEAR BOOK AND AUTOMOBILISTS' ANNUAL FOR 1906. *Demy 8vo.* 7s. 6d. net.

Bull (Paul), Army Chaplain. GOD AND OUR SOLDIERS. *Second Edition. Cr. 8vo.* 6s.

Bulley (Miss). See Lady Dilke.

Bunyan (John). THE PILGRIM'S PROGRESS. Edited, with an Introduction, by C. H. FIRTH, M.A. With 39 Illustrations by R. ANNING BELL. *Cr. 8vo.* 6s.
See also Library of Devotion and Standard Library.

Burch (G. J.), M.A., F.R.S. A MANUAL OF ELECTRICAL SCIENCE. Illustrated. *Cr. 8vo.* 3s.

Burgess (Gelett). GOOPS AND HOW TO BE THEM. Illustrated. *Small 4to.* 6s.

Burke (Edmund). See Standard Library.

Barn (A. E.), D.D., Rector of Handsworth and Prebendary of Lichfield.
See Handbooks of Theology.

Burn (J. H.), B.D. THE CHURCHMAN'S TREASURY OF SONG. Selected and Edited by. *Fcap 8vo.* 3s. 6d. net. See also Library of Devotion.

Barnand (Sir F. C.). RECORDS AND REMINISCENCES. With a Portrait by H. v. HERKOMER. *Cr. 8vo. Fourth and Cheaper Edition.* 6s.
A Colonial Edition is also published.

Burns (Robert), THE POEMS OF. Edited by ANDREW LANG and W. A. CRAIGIE. With Portrait. *Third Edition. Demy 8vo, gilt top.* 6s.

Burnside (W. P.), M.A. OLD TESTAMENT HISTORY FOR USE IN SCHOOLS. *Third Edition. Cr. 8vo.* 3s. 6d.

Burton (Alfred). See I.P.L.

Bussell (F. W.), D.D., Fellow and Vice-Principal of Brasenose College, Oxford. CHRISTIAN THEOLOGY AND SOCIAL PROGRESS: The Bampton Lectures for 1905. *Demy 8vo* 10s. 6d. net.

Butler (Joseph). See Standard Library.

Caldecott (Alfred), D.D. See Handbooks of Theology.

Calderwood (D. S.), Headmaster of the Normal School, Edinburgh. TEST CARDS IN EUCLID AND ALGEBRA. In three packets of 40, with Answers. 1s. each. Or in three Books, price 2d., 2d., and 3d.

Cambridge (Ada) [Mrs. Cross]. THIRTY YEARS IN AUSTRALIA. *Demy 8vo.* 7s. 6d.

Canning (George). See Little Library.

Capey (E. P. H.). See Oxford Biographies.

Careless (John). See I.P.L.

Carlyle (Thomas). THE FRENCH REVOLUTION. Edited by C. R. L. FLETCHER, Fellow of Magdalen College, Oxford. *Three Volumes. Cr. 8vo.* 18s.
THE LIFE AND LETTERS OF OLIVER CROMWELL. With an Introduction by C. H. FIRTH, M.A., and Notes and Appendices by Mrs. S. C. LOMAS. *Three Volumes. Demy 8vo.* 18s. net.

Carlyle (R. M. and A. J.), M.A. See Leaders of Religion.

Channer (C. C.) and Roberts (M. E.). LACEMAKING IN THE MIDLANDS, PAST AND PRESENT. With 16 full-page Illustrations. *Cr. 8vo.* 2s. 6d.

Chapman (S. J.). See Books on Business.

Chatterton (Thomas). See Standard Library.

Chesterfield (Lord), THE LETTERS OF, TO HIS SON. Edited, with an Introduction by C. STRACHEY, and Notes by A. CALTHROP. *Two Volumes. Cr. 8vo.* 12s.

Chesterton (G. K.). CHARLES DICKENS. With two Portraits in photogravure. *Fourth Edition. Demy 8vo.* 7s. 6d. net.
A Colonial Edition is also published.

Childe (Charles P.), B.A., F.R.C.S. THE CONTROL OF A SCOURGE : OR, How CANCER IS CURABLE. *Demy 8vo.* 7s. 6d. net.

Christian (F. W.). THE CAROLINE ISLANDS. With many Illustrations and Maps. *Demy 8vo.* 12s. 6d. net.

Cicero. See Classical Translations.

Clarke (F. A.), M.A. See Leaders of Religion.

Clausen (George), A.R.A., R.W.S. AIMS AND IDEALS IN ART : Eight Lectures delivered to the Students of the Royal Academy of Arts. With 32 Illustrations. *Second Edition. Large Post 8vo.* 5s. net.
SIX LECTURES ON PAINTING. *First Series.* With 19 Illustrations. *Third Edition, Large Post 8vo.* 3s. 6d. net.

Cleather (A. L.). See Wagner.

Clinch (G.). See Little Guides.

Clough (W. T.). See Junior School Books and Textbooks of Science.

Clouston (T. S.), M.D., C.C.D., F.R.S.E., Lecturer on Mental Diseases in the University of Edinburgh. THE HYGIENE OF MIND. With 10 Illustrations. *Fourth Edition. Demy 8vo.* 7s. 6d. net.

Coast (W. G.), B.A. EXAMINATION PAPERS IN VERGIL. *Cr. 8vo.* 2s.

Cobb (W. F.), M.A. THE BOOK OF PSALMS : with a Commentary. *Demy 8vo.* 10s. 6d. net.

Coleridge (S. T.). POEMS OF. Selected and Arranged by ARTHUR SYMONS. With a photogravure Frontispiece. *Fcap. 8vo.* 2s. 6d. net.

Collingwood (W. G.), M.A. THE LIFE OF JOHN RUSKIN. With Portraits. *Sixth Edition. Cr. 8vo.* 2s. 6d. net.

Collins (W. E.), M.A. See Churchman's Library.

Colonna. HYPNEROTOMACHIA POLIPHILI UBI HUMANA OMNIA NON NISI SOMNIUM ESSE DOCET ATQUE OBITER PLURIMA SCITU SANE QUAM DIGNA COMMEMORAT. An edition limited to 350 copies on handmade paper. *Folio.* £3, 3s. net.

Combe (William). See I.P.L.

Conrad (Joseph). THE MIRROR OF THE SEA : Memories and Impressions. *Third Edition. Cr. 8vo.* 6s.

Cook (A. M.), M.A., and **Marchant (C. E.),** M.A. PASSAGES FOR UNSEEN TRANSLATION. Selected from Greek and Latin Literature. *Third Ed. Cr. 8vo.* 3s. 6d.
LATIN PASSAGES FOR UNSEEN TRANSLATION. *Third Ed. Cr. 8vo.* 1s. 6d.

Cooke-Taylor (R. W.). THE FACTORY SYSTEM. *Cr. 8vo.* 2s. 6d.

Corelli (Marie). THE PASSING OF THE GREAT QUEEN. *Second Ed. Fcap. 4to.* 1s.
A CHRISTMAS GREETING. *Cr. 4to.* 1s.

Corkran (Alice). See Little Books on Art.

Cotes (Everard). SIGNS AND PORTENTS IN THE FAR EAST. With 24 Illustrations. *Second Edition. Demy 8vo.* 7s. 6d. net.

Cotes (Rosemary). DANTE'S GARDEN. With a Frontispiece. *Second Edition. Fcap. 8vo.* 2s. 6d.; *leather,* 3s. 6d. net.
BIBLE FLOWERS. With a Frontispiece and Plan. *Fcap. 8vo.* 2s. 6d. net.

Cowley (Abraham). See Little Library.

Cowper (William), THE POEMS OF. Edited with an Introduction and Notes by J. C. BAILEY, M.A. Illustrated, including two unpublished designs by WILLIAM BLAKE. *Demy 8vo.* 10s. 6d. net.

Cox (J. Charles), LL.D., F.S.A. See Little Guides, The Antiquary's Books, and Ancient Cities.

Cox (Harold), B.A., M.P. LAND NATIONALISATION AND LAND TAXATION. *Second Edition revised. Cr. 8vo.* 3s. 6d. net.

Crabbe (George). See Little Library.

Craigie (W. A.). A PRIMER OF BURNS. *Cr. 8vo.* 2s. 6d.

Craik (Mrs.). See Little Library.

Crane (Capt. C. P.). See Little Guides.

Crane (Walter). AN ARTIST'S REMINISCENCES. *Second Edition.*

Crashaw (Richard). See Little Library.

Crawford (F. G.). See Mary C. Danson.

Crofts (T. R. N.), M.A. See Simplified French Texts.

Cross (J. A.), M.A. THE FAITH OF THE BIBLE. *Fcap. 8vo.* 2s. 6d. net.

Cruikshank (G.). THE LOVING BALLAD OF LORD BATEMAN. With 11 Plates. *Cr. 16mo.* 1s. 6d. net.

Crump (B.). See Wagner.

Cunliffe (Sir F. H. E.), Fellow of All Souls' College, Oxford. THE HISTORY OF THE BOER WAR. With many Illustrations, Plans, and Portraits. *In 2 vols. Quarto.* 15s. each.

Cunynghame (H. H.), C.B. See Connoisseur's Library.

Cutts (E. L.), D.D. See Leaders of Religion.

Daniell (G. W.), M.A. See Leaders of Religion.

Danson (Mary C.) and Crawford (F. G.). FATHERS IN THE FAITH. *Fcap. 8vo.* 1s. 6d.

Dante. LA COMMEDIA DI DANTE. The Italian Text edited by PAGET TOYNBEE, M.A., D.Litt. *Cr. 8vo.* 6s.
THE PURGATORIO OF DANTE. Translated into Spenserian Prose by C. GORDON WRIGHT. With the Italian text. *Fcap. 8vo.* 2s. 6d. net.
See also Paget Toynbee, Little Library, Standard Library, and Warren-Vernon.

Darley (George). See Little Library.

D'Arcy (R. F.), M.A. A NEW TRIGONOMETRY FOR BEGINNERS. With numerous diagrams. *Cr. 8vo.* 2s. 6d.

Davenport (Cyril). See Connoisseur's Library and Little Books on Art.

Davey (Richard). THE PAGEANT OF LONDON. With 40 Illustrations in Colour by JOHN FULLEYLOVE, R.I. *In Two Volumes. Demy 8vo.* 15s. net.

Davis (H. W. C.), M.A., Fellow and Tutor of Balliol College, Author of 'Charlemagne.' ENGLAND UNDER THE NORMANS AND ANGEVINS : 1066-1272. With Maps and Illustrations. *Demy 8vo.* 10s. 6d. net.

Dawson (Nelson). See Connoisseur's Library.

Dawson (Mrs. N.). See Little Books on Art.

Deane (A. C.). See Little Library.

Dearmer (Mabel). A CHILD'S LIFE OF CHRIST. With 8 Illustrations in Colour by E. FORTESCOE-BRICKDALE. *Large Cr. 8vo. 6s.*

Delbos (Leon). THE METRIC SYSTEM. *Cr. 8vo. 2s.*

Demosthenes. AGAINST CONON AND CALLICLES. Edited by F. DARWIN SWIFT, M.A. *Second Edition. Fcap. 8vo. 2s.*

Dickens (Charles). See Little Library, I.P.L., and Chesterton.

Dickinson (Emily). POEMS. *Cr. 8vo. 4s. 6d. net.*

Dickinson (G. L.), M.A., Fellow of King's College, Cambridge. THE GREEK VIEW OF LIFE. *Sixth Edition. Cr. 8vo. 2s. 6d.*

Dilke (Lady), Bulley (Miss), and Whitley (Miss). WOMEN'S WORK. *Cr. 8vo. 2s. 6d.*

Dillon (Edward). See Connoisseur's Library and Little Books on Art.

Ditchfield (P. H.), M.A., F.S.A. THE STORY OF OUR ENGLISH TOWNS. With an Introduction by AUGUSTUS JESSOPP, D.D. *Second Edition. Cr. 8vo. 6s.*
OLD ENGLISH CUSTOMS: Extant at the Present Time. *Cr. 8vo. 6s.*
ENGLISH VILLAGES. Illustrated. *Second Edition. Cr. 8vo. 2s. 6d. net.*
THE PARISH CLERK. With 31 Illustrations. *Third Edition. Demy 8vo. 7s. 6d. net.*

Dixon (W. M.), M.A. A PRIMER OF TENNYSON. *Second Edition. Cr. 8vo. 2s. 6d.*
ENGLISH POETRY FROM BLAKE TO BROWNING. *Second Edition. Cr. 8vo. 2s. 6d*

Doney (May). SONGS OF THE REAL. *Cr. 8vo. 3s. 6d. net.*
A volume of poems.

Douglas (James). THE MAN IN THE PULPIT. *Cr. 8vo. 2s. 6d. net.*

Dowden (J.), D.D., Lord Bishop of Edinburgh. See Churchman's Library.

Drage (G.). See Books on Business.

Driver (S. R.), D.D., D.C.L., Canon of Christ Church, Regius Professor of Hebrew in the University of Oxford. SERMONS ON SUBJECTS CONNECTED WITH THE OLD TESTAMENT. *Cr. 8vo. 6s.*
See also Westminster Commentaries.

Dry (Wakeling). See Little Guides.

Dryhurst (A. R.). See Little Books on Art.

Du Buisson (J. C.), M.A. See Churchman's Bible.

Duguid (Charles). See Books on Business.

Dumas (Alexander). MY MEMOIRS. Translated by E. M. WALLER. With Portraits. *In Six Volumes. Cr. 8vo. 6s. each.*
Volume I.

Dunn (J. T.), D.Sc., and Mundella (V. A.). GENERAL ELEMENTARY SCIENCE. With 114 Illustrations. *Second Edition. Cr. 8vo. 3s. 6d.*

Dunstan (A. E.), B.Sc. See Junior School Books and Textbooks of Science.

Durham (The Earl of). A REPORT ON CANADA. With an Introductory Note. *Demy 8vo. 4s. 6d. net.*

Dutt (W. A.). THE NORFOLK BROADS. With coloured Illustrations by FRANK SOUTHGATE. *Cr. 8vo. 6s.*
WILD LIFE IN EAST ANGLIA. With 16 Illustrations in colour by FRANK SOUTHGATE, R.B.A. *Second Edition. Demy 8vo. 7s. 6d. net.*
See also Little Guides.

Earle (John), Bishop of Salisbury. MICROCOSMOGRAPHIE, OR A PIECE OF THE WORLD DISCOVERED. *Post 16mo. 2s net.*

Edmonds (Major J. E.). See W. B. Wood.

Edwards (Clement), M.P. RAILWAY NATIONALIZATION. *Second Edition Revised. Crown 8vo. 2s. 6d. net.*

Edwards (W. Douglas). See Commercial Series.

Egan (Pierce). See I.P.L.

Egerton (H. E.), M.A. A HISTORY OF BRITISH COLONIAL POLICY. New and Cheaper Issue. *Demy 8vo. 7s. 6d. net.*
A Colonial Edition is also published.

Ellaby (C. G.). See Little Guides.

Ellerton (F. G.). See S. J. Stone.

Ellwood (Thomas), THE HISTORY OF THE LIFE OF. Edited by C. G. CRUMP, M.A. *Cr. 8vo. 6s.*

Epictetus. See Aurelius.

Erasmus. A Book called in Latin ENCHIRIDION MILITIS CHRISTIANI, and in English the Manual of the Christian Knight.
From the edition printed by Wynken de Worde, 1533. *Fcap. 8vo. 3s. 6d. net.*

Fairbrother (W. H.), M.A. THE PHILOSOPHY OF T. H. GREEN. *Second Edition. Cr. 8vo. 3s. 6d.*

Farrer (Reginald). THE GARDEN OF ASIA. *Second Edition. Cr. 8vo. 6s.*

Fea (Allan). SOME BEAUTIES OF THE SEVENTEENTH CENTURY. With 82 Illustrations. *Second Edition. Demy 8vo. 12s. 6d. net.*

Ferrier (Susan). See Little Library.

Fidler (T. Claxton), M.Inst. C.E. See Books on Business.

Fielding (Henry). See Standard Library.

Finn (S. W.), M.A. See Junior Examination Series.

Firth (J. B.). See Little Guides.

Firth (C. H.), M.A. CROMWELL'S ARMY: A History of the English Soldier during the Civil Wars, the Commonwealth, and the Protectorate. *Cr. 8vo. 6s.*

Fisher (G. W.), M.A. ANNALS OF SHREWSBURY SCHOOL. Illustrated. *Demy 8vo.* 10s. 6d.

FitzGerald (Edward). THE RUBÁIYÁT OF OMAR KHAYYÁM. Printed from the Fifth and last Edition. With a Commentary by Mrs. STEPHEN BATSON, and a Biography of Omar by E. D. ROSS. *Cr. 8vo.* 6s. See also Miniature Library.

FitzGerald (H. P.). A CONCISE HANDBOOK OF CLIMBERS, TWINERS, AND WALL SHRUBS. Illustrated. *Fcap. 8vo.* 3s. 6d. net.

Fitzpatrick (S. A. O.). See Ancient Cities.

Flecker (W. H.), M.A., D.C.L., Headmaster of the Dean Close School, Cheltenham. THE STUDENT'S PRAYER BOOK. THE TEXT OF MORNING AND EVENING PRAYER AND LITANY. With an Introduction and Notes. *Cr. 8vo.* 2s. 6d.

Flux (A. W.), M.A., William Dow Professor of Political Economy in M'Gill University, Montreal. ECONOMIC PRINCIPLES. *Demy 8vo.* 7s. 6d. net.

Fortescue (Mrs. G.). See Little Books on Art.

Fraser (David). A MODERN CAMPAIGN; OR, WAR AND WIRELESS TELEGRAPHY IN THE FAR EAST. Illustrated. *Cr. 8vo.* 6s. A Colonial Edition is also published.

Fraser (J. F.). ROUND THE WORLD ON A WHEEL. With 100 Illustrations. *Fifth Edition. Cr. 8vo.* 6s.

French (W.), M.A. See Textbooks of Science.

Freudenreich (Ed. von). DAIRY BACTERIOLOGY. A Short Manual for the Use of Students. Translated by J. R. AINSWORTH DAVIS, M.A. *Second Edition. Revised. Cr. 8vo.* 2s. 6d.

Fulford (H. W.), M.A. See Churchman's Bible.

Galleher (D.) and Stead (W. J.). THE COMPLETE RUGBY FOOTBALLER, ON THE NEW ZEALAND SYSTEM. With an Account of the Tour of the New Zealanders in England. With 35 Illustrations. *Demy 8vo.* 10s. 6d. net.

Gallichan (W. M.). See Little Guides.

Gambado (Geoffrey, Esq.). See I.P.L.

Gaskell (Mrs.). See Little Library and Standard Library.

Gasquet, the Right Rev. Abbot, O.S.B. See Antiquary's Books.

George (H. B.), M.A., Fellow of New College, Oxford. BATTLES OF ENGLISH HISTORY. With numerous Plans. *Fourth Edition.* Revised, with a new Chapter including the South African War. *Cr. 8vo.* 3s. 6d.

A HISTORICAL GEOGRAPHY OF THE BRITISH EMPIRE. *Second Edition. Cr. 8vo.* 3s. 6d.

Gibbins (H. de B.), Litt.D., M.A. INDUSTRY IN ENGLAND : HISTORICAL OUTLINES. With 5 Maps. *Fifth Edition. Demy 8vo.* 10s. 6d.

THE INDUSTRIAL HISTORY OF ENGLAND. *Thirteenth Edition.* Revised. With Maps and Plans. *Cr. 8vo.* 3s.

ENGLISH SOCIAL REFORMERS. *Second Edition. Cr. 8vo.* 2s. 6d. See also Commercial Series and R. A. Hadfield.

Gibbon (Edward). THE DECLINE AND FALL OF THE ROMAN EMPIRE. Edited with Notes, Appendices, and Maps, by J. B. BURY, M.A., Litt.D., Regius Professor of Greek at Cambridge. *In Seven Volumes. Demy 8vo. Gilt top,* 8s. 6d. *each. Also, Cr. 8vo.* 6s. *each.*

MEMOIRS OF MY LIFE AND WRITINGS. Edited by G. BIRKBECK HILL, LL.D. *Cr. 8vo.* 6s. See also Standard Library.

Gibson (E. C. S.), D.D., Lord Bishop of Gloucester. See Westminster Commentaries, Handbooks of Theology, and Oxford Biographies.

Gilbert (A. R.). See Little Books on Art.

Gloag (M. R.) and Wyatt (Kate M.). A BOOK OF ENGLISH GARDENS. With 24 Illustrations in Colour. *Demy 8vo.* 10s. 6d. net.

Godfrey (Elizabeth). A BOOK OF REMEMBRANCE. Edited by. *Fcap. 8vo.* 2s. 6d. net.

Godley (A. D.), M.A., Fellow of Magdalen College, Oxford. LYRA FRIVOLA. *Third Edition. Fcap. 8vo.* 2s. 6d.

VERSES TO ORDER. *Second Edition. Fcap. 8vo.* 2s. 6d.

SECOND STRINGS. *Fcap. 8vo.* 2s. 6d.

Goldsmith (Oliver). THE VICAR OF WAKEFIELD. *Fcap. 32mo.* With 10 Plates in Photogravure by Tony Johannot. *Leather,* 2s. 6d. *net.* See also I.P.L. and Standard Library.

Goodrich-Freer (A.). IN A SYRIAN SADDLE. *Demy 8vo.* 7s. 6d. net. A Colonial Edition is also published.

Gorst (Rt. Hon. Sir John). THE CHILDREN OF THE NATION. *Second Edition. Demy 8vo.* 7s. 6d. net.

Goudge (H. L.), M.A., Principal of Wells Theological College. See Westminster Commentaries.

Graham (P. Anderson). THE RURAL EXODUS. *Cr. 8vo.* 2s. 6d.

Granger (F. S.), M.A., Litt.D. PSYCHOLOGY. *Third Edition. Cr. 8vo.* 2s. 6d.

THE SOUL OF A CHRISTIAN. *Cr. 8vo.* 6s.

Gray (E. M'Queen). GERMAN PASSAGES FOR UNSEEN TRANSLATION. *Cr. 8vo.* 2s. 6d.

Gray (P. L.), B.Sc. THE PRINCIPLES OF MAGNETISM AND ELECTRICITY : an Elementary Text-Book. With 181 Diagrams. *Cr. 8vo.* 3s. 6d.

Green (G. Buckland), M.A., late Fellow of St. John's College, Oxon. NOTES ON GREEK AND LATIN SYNTAX. *Second Edition. Crown 8vo.* 3s. 6d.

Green (E. T.), M.A. See Churchman's Library.

Greenidge (A. H. J.), M.A. A HISTORY OF ROME: From 133-104 B.C. *Demy 8vo. 10s. 6d. net.*

Greenwell (Dora). See Miniature Library.

Gregory (R. A.). THE VAULT OF HEAVEN. A Popular Introduction to Astronomy. Illustrated. *Cr. 8vo. 2s. 6d.*

Gregory (Miss E. C.). See Library of Devotion.

Grubb (H. C.). See Textbooks of Technology.

Gwynn (M. L.). A BIRTHDAY BOOK. New and cheaper issue. *Royal 8vo. 5s. net.*

Haddon (A. C.), Sc.D., F.R.S. HEAD-HUNTERS BLACK, WHITE, AND BROWN. With many Illustrations and a Map. *Demy 8vo. 15s.*

Hadfield (R. A.) and Gibbins (H. de B.). A SHORTER WORKING DAY. *Cr. 8vo. 2s. 6d.*

Hall (R. N.) and Neal (W. G.). THE ANCIENT RUINS OF RHODESIA. Illustrated. *Second Edition, revised. Demy 8vo. 10s. 6d. net.*

Hall (R. N.). GREAT ZIMBABWE. With numerous Plans and Illustrations. *Second Edition. Royal 8vo. 10s. 6d. net.*

Hamilton (F. J.), D.D. See Byzantine Texts.

Hammond (J. L.). CHARLES JAMES FOX. *Demy 8vo. 10s. 6d.*

Hannay (D.). A SHORT HISTORY OF THE ROYAL NAVY, 1200-1688. Illustrated. *Demy 8vo. 7s. 6d. each.*

Hannay (James O.), M.A. THE SPIRIT AND ORIGIN OF CHRISTIAN MONASTICISM. *Cr. 8vo. 6s.* THE WISDOM OF THE DESERT. *Fcap. 8vo. 3s. 6d. net.*

Hardie (Martin). See Connoisseur's Library.

Hare (A. T.), M.A. THE CONSTRUCTION OF LARGE INDUCTION COILS. With numerous Diagrams. *Demy 8vo. 6s.*

Harrison (Clifford). READING AND READERS. *Fcap. 8vo. 2s. 6d.*

Harvey (Alfred), M.B. See Ancient Cities.

Hawthorne (Nathaniel). See Little Library. HEALTH, WEALTH AND WISDOM. *Cr. 8vo. 1s. net.*

Heath (Frank R.). See Little Guides.

Heath (Dudley). See Connoisseur's Library.

Hello (Ernest). STUDIES IN SAINT-SHIP. Translated from the French by V. M. Crawford. *Fcap 8vo. 3s. 6d.*

Henderson (B. W.), Fellow of Exeter College, Oxford. THE LIFE AND PRINCIPATE OF THE EMPEROR NERO. Illustrated. *New and cheaper issue. Demy 8vo. 7s. 6d. net.* AT INTERVALS. *Fcap 8vo. 2s. 6d. net.*

Henderson (T. F.). See Little Library and Oxford Biographies.

Henderson (T. F.), and Watt (Francis). SCOTLAND OF TO-DAY. With many Illustrations, some of which are in colour. *Cr. 8vo. 6s.*

Henley (W. E.). ENGLISH LYRICS. *Second Edition. Cr. 8vo. 2s. 6d. net.*

Henley (W. E.) and Whibley (C.) A BOOK OF ENGLISH PROSE. *Cr. 8vo. 2s. 6d. net.*

Henson (H. H.), B.D., Canon of Westminster. APOSTOLIC CHRISTIANITY: As Illustrated by the Epistles of St. Paul to the Corinthians. *Cr. 8vo. 6s.* LIGHT AND LEAVEN: HISTORICAL AND SOCIAL SERMONS. *Cr. 8vo. 6s.*

Herbert (George). See Library of Devotion.

Herbert of Cherbury (Lord). See Miniature Library.

Hewins (W. A. S.), B.A. ENGLISH TRADE AND FINANCE IN THE SEVENTEENTH CENTURY. *Cr. 8vo. 2s. 6d.*

Hewitt (Ethel M.) A GOLDEN DIAL. A Day Book of Prose and Verse. *Fcap. 8vo. 2s. 6d. net.*

Heywood (W.). PALIO AND PONTE: A Book of Tuscan Games. Illustrated. *Royal 8vo. 21s. net.* See also St. Francis of Assisi.

Hill (Clare). See Textbooks of Technology.

Hill (Henry), B.A., Headmaster of the Boy's High School, Worcester, Cape Colony. A SOUTH AFRICAN ARITHMETIC. *Cr. 8vo. 3s. 6d.*

Hind (C. Lewis). DAYS IN CORNWALL. With 16 Illustrations in Colour by WILLIAM PASCOE, and 20 Photographs. *Second Edition. Cr. 8vo. 6s.* A Colonial Edition is also published.

Hirst (F. W.) See Books on Business.

Hoare (J. Douglas). ARCTIC EXPLORATION. With 18 Illustrations and Maps. *Demy 8vo, 7s. 6d. net.*

Hobhouse (L. T.), Fellow of C.C.C., Oxford. THE THEORY OF KNOWLEDGE. *Demy 8vo. 10s. 6d. net.*

Hobson (J. A.), M.A. INTERNATIONAL TRADE: A Study of Economic Principles. *Cr. 8vo. 2s. 6d. net.* PROBLEMS OF POVERTY. *Sixth Edition. Cr. 8vo. 2s. 6d.* THE PROBLEM OF THE UNEMPLOYED. *Third Edition. Cr. 8vo. 2s. 6d.*

Hodgkin (T.), D.C.L. See Leaders of Religion.

Hodgson (Mrs. W.) HOW TO IDENTIFY OLD CHINESE PORCELAIN. *Second Edition. Post 8vo. 6s.*

Hogg (Thomas Jefferson). SHELLEY AT OXFORD. With an Introduction by R. A. STREATFEILD. *Fcap. 8vo. 2s. net.*

Holden-Stone (G. de). See Books on Business.

Holdich (Sir T. H.), K.C.I.E. THE INDIAN BORDERLAND: being a Personal Record of Twenty Years. Illustrated. *Demy 8vo. 10s. 6d. net.* A Colonial Edition is also published.

Holdsworth (W. S.), M.A. A HISTORY OF ENGLISH LAW. *In Two Volumes.* *Vol. I. Demy 8vo. 10s. 6d. net.*

Holland (H. Scott), Canon of St. Paul's See Library of Devotion.

Holt (Emily). THE SECRET OF POPU-LARITY: How to Achieve Social Success. *Cr. 8vo. 3s. 6d. net.*
A Colonial Edition is also published.

Holyoake (G. J.). THE CO-OPERATIVE MOVEMENT TO-DAY. *Fourth Edition. Cr. 8vo. 2s. 6d.*

Hone (Nathaniel J.). See Antiquary's Books.

Hoppner. See Little Galleries.

Horace. See Classical Translations.

Horsburgh (E. L. S.), M.A. WATERLOO: A Narrative and Criticism. With Plans. *Second Edition. Cr. 8vo. 5s.*
See also Oxford Biographies.

Horth (A. C.). See Textbooks of Technology.

Horton (R. F.), D.D. See Leaders of Religion.

Hosie (Alexander). MANCHURIA. With Illustrations and a Map. *Second Edition. Demy 8vo. 7s. 6d. net.*
A Colonial Edition is also published.

How (F. D.). SIX GREAT SCHOOL-MASTERS. With Portraits and Illustrations. *Second Edition. Demy 8vo. 7s. 6d.*

Howell (A. G. Ferrers). FRANCISCAN DAYS. Translated and arranged by. *Cr. 8vo. 3s. 6d. net.*

Howell (G.). TRADE UNIONISM—NEW AND OLD. *Fourth Edition. Cr. 8vo. 2s. 6d.*

Hudson (Robert). MEMORIALS OF A WARWICKSHIRE PARISH. Illustrated. *Demy 8vo. 15s. net.*

Huggins (Sir William), K.C.B., O.M., D.C.L., F.R.S. THE ROYAL SOCIETY; OR, SCIENCE IN THE STATE AND IN THE SCHOOLS. With 25 Illustrations. *Wide Royal 8vo. 4s. 6d. net.*

Hughes (C. E.). THE PRAISE OF SHAKESPEARE. An English Anthology. With a Preface by SIDNEY LEE. *Demy 8vo. 3s. 6d. net.*

Hughes (Thomas). TOM BROWN'S SCHOOLDAYS. With an Introduction and Notes by VERNON RENDALL. *Leather. Royal 32mo. 2s. 6d. net.*

Hutchinson (Horace G.) THE NEW FOREST. Illustrated in colour with 50 Pictures by WALTER TYNDALE and 4 by LUCY KEMP-WELCH. *Third Edition. Cr. 8vo. 6s.*

Hutton (A. W.), M.A. See Leaders of Religion and Library of Devotion.

Hutton (Edward). THE CITIES OF UMBRIA. With many Illustrations, of which 20 are in Colour, by A. PISA. *Second Edition. Cr. 8vo. 6s.*
A Colonial Edition is also published.
THE CITIES OF SPAIN. *Second Edition.* With many Illustrations, of which 24 are in Colour, by A. W. RIMINGTON. *Demy 8vo. 7s. 6d. net.*

FLORENCE AND NORTHERN TUS-CANY. With Coloured Illustrations by WILLIAM PARKINSON. *Cr. 8vo. 6s.*
A Colonial Edition is also published.

ENGLISH LOVE POEMS. Edited with an Introduction. *Fcap. 8vo. 3s. 6d. net.*

Hutton (R. H.). See Leaders of Religion.

Hutton (W. H.), M.A. THE LIFE OF SIR THOMAS MORE. With Portraits. *Second Edition. Cr. 8vo. 5s.*
See also Leaders of Religion.

Hyde (A. G.) GEORGE HERBERT AND HIS TIMES. With 32 Illustrations. *Demy 8vo. 10s. 6d. net.*

Hyett (F. A.). A SHORT HISTORY OF FLORENCE. *Demy 8vo. 7s. 6d. net.*

Ibsen (Henrik). BRAND. A Drama. Translated by WILLIAM WILSON. *Third Edition. Cr. 8vo. 3s. 6d.*

Inge (W. R.), M.A., Fellow and Tutor of Hertford College, Oxford. CHRISTIAN MYSTICISM. The Bampton Lectures for 1899. *Demy 8vo. 12s. 6d. net.* See also Library of Devotion.

Innes (A. D.), M.A. A HISTORY OF THE BRITISH IN INDIA. With Maps and Plans. *Cr. 8vo. 6s.*
ENGLAND UNDER THE TUDORS. With Maps. *Demy 8vo. 10s. 6d. net.*

Jackson (C. E.), B.A. See Textbooks of Science.

Jackson (S.), M.A. See Commercial Series.

Jackson (F. Hamilton). See Little Guides.

Jacob (F.), M.A. See Junior Examination Series.

James (W. H. N.), A.R.C.S., A.I.E.E. See Textbooks of Technology.

Jeans (J. Stephen). TRUSTS, POOLS, AND CORNERS. *Cr. 8vo. 2s. 6d.*
See also Books on Business.

Jeffreys (D. Gwyn). DOLLY'S THEATRI-CALS. Described and Illustrated with 24 Coloured Pictures. *Super Royal 16mo. 2s. 6d.*

Jenks (E.), M.A., Reader of Law in the University of Oxford. ENGLISH LOCAL GOVERNMENT. *Second Edition. Cr. 8vo. 2s. 6d.*

Jenner (Mrs. H.). See Little Books on Art.

Jennings (Oscar), M.D., Member of the Bibliographical Society. EARLY WOOD-CUT INITIALS, containing over thirteen hundred Reproductions of Pictorial Letters of the Fifteenth and Sixteenth Centuries. *Demy 4to. 21s. net.*

Jessopp (Augustus), D.D. See Leaders of Religion.

Jevons (F. B.), M.A., Litt.D., Principal of Bishop Hatfield's Hall, Durham. RE-LIGION IN EVOLUTION. *Cr. 8vo. 3s. 6d. net.*
See also Churchman's Library and Hand-books of Theology.

Johnson (Mrs. Barham). WILLIAM BOD-HAM DONNE AND HIS FRIENDS. Illustrated. *Demy 8vo. 10s. 6d. net.*

Johnston (Sir H. H.), K.C.B. BRITISH CENTRAL AFRICA. With nearly 200 Illustrations and Six Maps. *Third Edition. Cr. 4to. 18s. net.*
A Colonial Edition is also published.
Jones (R. Crompton), M.A. POEMS OF THE INNER LIFE. Selected by. *Thirteenth Edition. Fcap. 8vo. 2s. 6d. net.*
Jones (H.). See Commercial Series.
Jones (H. F.). See Textbooks of Science.
Jones (L. A. Atherley), K.C., M.P. THE MINERS' GUIDE TO THE COAL MINES REGULATION ACTS. *Cr. 8vo. 2s. 6d. net.*
COMMERCE IN WAR. *Royal 8vo. 21s. net.*
Jonson (Ben). See Standard Library.
Juliana (Lady) of Norwich. REVELATIONS OF DIVINE LOVE. Ed. by GRACE WARRACK. *Second Edit. Cr. 8vo. 3s. 6d.*
Juvenal. See Classical Translations.
'Kappa.' LET YOUTH BUT KNOW: A Plea for Reason in Education. *Cr. 8vo. 3s. 6d. net.*
Kaufmann (M.). SOCIALISM AND MODERN THOUGHT. *Second Edition. Cr. 8vo. 2s. 6d. net.*
Keating (J. F.), D.D. THE AGAPE AND THE EUCHARIST. *Cr. 8vo. 3s. 6d.*
Keats (John). THE POEMS OF. Edited with Introduction and Notes by E. de Selincourt, M.A. *Second Edition. Demy 8vo. 7s. 6d. net.*
REALMS OF GOLD. Selections from the Works of. *Fcap. 8vo. 3s. 6d. net.*
See also Little Library and Standard Library.
Keble (John). THE CHRISTIAN YEAR. With an Introduction and Notes by W. LOCK, D.D., Warden of Keble College. Illustrated by R. ANNING BELL. *Third Edition. Fcap. 8vo. 3s. 6d. ; padded morocco, 5s.*
See also Library of Devotion.
Kelynack (T. N.), M.D., M.R.C.P., Hon. Secretary of the Society for the Study of Inebriety. THE DRINK PROBLEM IN ITS MEDICO - SOCIOLOGICAL ASPECT. Edited by. With 2 Diagrams. *Demy 8vo. 7s. 6d. net.*
Kempis (Thomas à). THE IMITATION OF CHRIST. With an Introduction by DEAN FARRAR. Illustrated by C. M. GERE. *Third Edition. Fcap. 8vo. 3s. 6d.; padded morocco. 5s.*
Also Translated by C. BIGG, D.D. *Cr. 8vo. 3s. 6d.* See also Library of Devotion and Standard Library.
Kennedy (Bart.). THE GREEN SPHINX. *Cr. 8vo. 3s. 6d. net.*
A Colonial Edition is also published.
Kennedy (James Houghton), D.D., Assistant Lecturer in Divinity in the University of Dublin. ST. PAUL'S SECOND AND THIRD EPISTLES TO THE CORINTHIANS. With Introduction, Dissertations and Notes. *Cr. 8vo. 6s.*
Kimmins (C. W.), M.A. THE CHEMISTRY OF LIFE AND HEALTH. Illustrated. *Cr. 8vo. 2s. 6d.*

Kinglake (A. W.). See Little Library.
Kipling (Rudyard). BARRACK-ROOM BALLADS. *80th Thousand. Twenty-second Edition. Cr. 8vo. 6s.*
A Colonial Edition is also published.
THE SEVEN SEAS. *63rd Thousand. Eleventh Edition. Cr. 8vo. 6s.*
A Colonial Edition is also published.
THE FIVE NATIONS. *41st Thousand. Second Edition. Cr. 8vo. 6s.*
A Colonial Edition is also published.
DEPARTMENTAL DITTIES. *Sixteenth Edition. Cr. 8vo. 6s.*
A Colonial Edition is also published.
Knight (Albert E.). THE COMPLETE CRICKETER. Illus. *Demy 8vo. 7s. 6d. net.*
Knight (H. J. C.), M.A. See Churchman's Bible.
Knowling (R. J.), M.A., Professor of New Testament Exegesis at King's College, London. See Westminster Commentaries.
Lamb (Charles and Mary), THE WORKS OF. Edited by E. V. LUCAS. Illustrated. *In Seven Volumes. Demy 8vo. 7s. 6d. each.*
See also Little Library and E. V. Lucas.
Lambert (F. A. H.). See Little Guides.
Lambros (Professor). See Byzantine Texts.
Lane-Poole (Stanley). A HISTORY OF EGYPT IN THE MIDDLE AGES. Fully Illustrated. *Cr. 8vo. 6s.*
Langbridge (F.), M.A. BALLADS OF THE BRAVE: Poems of Chivalry, Enterprise, Courage, and Constancy. *Third Edition. Cr. 8vo. 2s. 6d.*
Law (William). See Library of Devotion and Standard Library.
Leach (Henry). THE DUKE OF DEVONSHIRE. A Biography. With 12 Illustrations. *Demy 8vo. 12s. 6d. net.*
See also James Braid.
GREAT GOLFERS IN THE MAKING. With 34 Portraits. *Demy 8vo. 7s. 6d. net.*
Le Braz (Anatole). THE LAND OF PARDONS. Translated by FRANCES M. GOSTLING. Illustrated in colour. *Second Edition. Demy 8vo. 7s. 6d. net.*
Lee (Captain L. Melville). A HISTORY OF POLICE IN ENGLAND. *Cr. 8vo. 3s. 6d. net.*
Leigh (Percival). THE COMIC ENGLISH GRAMMAR. Embellished with upwards of 50 characteristic Illustrations by JOHN LEECH. *Post 16mo. 2s. 6d. net.*
Lewes (V. B.), M.A. AIR AND WATER. Illustrated. *Cr. 8vo. 2s. 6d.*
Lewis (Mrs. Gwyn). A CONCISE HANDBOOK OF GARDEN SHRUBS. Illustrated. *Fcap. 8vo. 3s. 6d. net.*
Lisle (Fortunéede). See Little Bookson Art.
Littlehales (H.). See Antiquary's Books.
Lock (Walter), D.D., Warden of Keble College. ST. PAUL, THE MASTER-BUILDER. *Second Ed. Cr. 8vo. 3s. 6d.*
THE BIBLE AND CHRISTIAN LIFE. *Cr. 8vo. 6s.*
See also Leaders of Religion and Library of Devotion.

Locker (F.). See Little Library.
Lodge (Sir Oliver), F.R.S. THE SUB-STANCE OF FAITH ALLIED WITH SCIENCE: A Catechism for Parents and Teachers. *Eighth Ed. Cr. 8vo. 2s. net.*
Lofthouse (W. F.), M.A. ETHICS AND ATONEMENT. With a Frontispiece. *Demy 8vo. 5s. net.*
Longfellow (H. W.). See Little Library.
Lorimer (George Horace). LETTERS FROM A SELF-MADE MERCHANT TO HIS SON. *Sixteenth Edition. Cr. 8vo. 3s. 6d.*
 A Colonial Edition is also published.
OLD GORGON GRAHAM. *Second Edition. Cr. 8vo. 6s.*
 A Colonial Edition is also published.
Lover (Samuel). See I. P. L.
E. V. L. and C. L.'G. ENGLAND DAY BY DAY : Or, The Englishman's Handbook to Efficiency. Illustrated by GEORGE MORROW. *Fourth Edition. Fcap. 4to. 1s. net.*
Lucas (E. V.). THE LIFE OF CHARLES LAMB. With 25 Illustrations. *Third Edition. Demy 8vo. 7s. 6d. net.*
 A Colonial Edition is also published.
A WANDERER IN HOLLAND. With many Illustrations, of which 20 are in Colour by HERBERT MARSHALL. *Seventh Edition. Cr. 8vo. 6s.*
 A Colonial Edition is also published.
A WANDERER IN LONDON. With 16 Illustrations in Colour by NELSON DAWSON, and 36 other Illustrations. *Fifth Edition. Cr. 8vo. 6s.*
 A Colonial Edition is also published.
FIRESIDE AND SUNSHINE. *Third Edition. Fcap. 8vo. 5s.*
THE OPEN ROAD : a Little Book for Way-farers. *Eleventh Edition. Fcap. 8vo. 5s. ; India Paper, 7s. 6d.*
THE FRIENDLY TOWN : a Little Book for the Urbane. *Third Edition. Fcap. 8vo. 5s. ; India Paper, 7s. 6d.*
CHARACTER AND COMEDY. *Second Edition.*
Lucian. See Classical Translations.
Lyde (L. W.), M.A. See Commercial Series.
Lydon (Noel S.). See Junior School Books .
Lyttelton (Hon. Mrs. A.). WOMEN AND THEIR WORK. *Cr. 8vo. 2s. 6d.*
Macaulay (Lord). CRITICAL AND HIS-TORICAL ESSAYS. Edited by F. C. MON-TAGUE, M.A. *Three Volumes. Cr. 8vo. 18s.*
 The only edition of this book completely annotated.
M'Allen (J. E. B.), M.A. See Commercial Series.
MacCulloch (J. A.). See Churchman's Library.
MacCunn (Florence A.). MARY STUART. With over 60 Illustrations, in-cluding a Frontispiece in Photogravure. *Second and Cheaper Edition. Cr. 8vo. 6s.*
 See also Leaders of Religion.
McDermott (E. R.). See Books on Business.
M'Dowall (A. S.). See Oxford Biographies.
Mackay (A. M.). See Churchman's Library.

Macklin (Herbert W.), M.A. See Anti-quary's Books.
Mackenzie (W. Leslie), M.A., M.D., D.P.H., etc. THE HEALTH OF THE SCHOOL CHILD. *Cr. 8vo. 2s. 6d.*
Mdlle Mori (Author of). ST. CATHER-INE OF SIENA AND HER TIMES. With 28 Illustrations. *Demy 8vo. 7s. 6d. net.*
Magnus (Laurie), M.A. A PRIMER OF WORDSWORTH. *Cr. 8vo. 2s. 6d.*
Mahaffy (J. P.), Litt.D. A HISTORY OF THE EGYPT OF THE PTOLEMIES. Fully Illustrated. *Cr. 8vo. 6s.*
Maitland (F. W.), LL.D., Downing Professor of the Laws of England in the University of Cambridge. CANON LAW IN ENG-LAND. *Royal 8vo. 7s. 6d.*
Malden (H. E.), M.A. ENGLISH RE-CORDS. A Companion to the History of England. *Cr. 8vo. 3s. 6d.*
THE ENGLISH CITIZEN : HIS RIGHTS AND DUTIES. *Seventh Edition. Cr. 8vo. 1s. 6d.*
 See also School Histories.
Marchant (E. C.), M.A., Fellow of Peter-house, Cambridge. A GREEK ANTHO-LOGY *Second Edition. Cr. 8vo. 3s. 6d.*
 See also A. M. Cook.
Marr (J. E.), F.R.S., Fellow of St John's Col-lege, Cambridge. THE SCIENTIFIC STUDY OF SCENERY. *Second Edition.* Illustrated. *Cr. 8vo. 6s.*
AGRICULTURAL GEOLOGY. Illustrated. *Cr. 8vo. 6s.*
Marriott (J. A. R.). FALKLAND AND HIS TIMES. With 20 Illustrations. *Second Ed. Demy 8vo. 7s. 6d. net.*
 A Colonial Edition is also published.
Marvell (Andrew). See Little Library.
Masefield (John). SEA LIFE IN NEL-SON'S TIME. Illustrated. *Cr. 8vo. 3s. 6d. net.*
ON THE SPANISH MAIN. With 22 Illustrations and a Map. *Demy 8vo. 10s. 6d. net.*
A SAILOR'S GARLAND. Edited and Selected by. *Cr. 8vo. 3s. 6d. net.*
Maskell (A.). See Connoisseur's Library.
Mason (A. J.), D.D. See Leaders of Religion.
Massee (George). THE EVOLUTION OF PLANT LIFE : Lower Forms. Illustrated. *Cr. 8vo. 2s. 6d.*
Masterman (C. F. G.), M.A., M.P. TENNYSON AS A RELIGIOUS TEACHER. *Cr. 8vo. 6s.*
Matheson (Mrs. E. F.). COUNSELS OF LIFE. *Fcap. 8vo. 2s. 6d. net.*
May (Phil). THE PHIL MAY ALBUM. *Second Edition. 4to. 1s. net.*
Mellows (Emma S.). A SHORT STORY OF ENGLISH LITERATURE. *Cr. 8vo. 3s. 6d.*
Methuen (A. M. S.). THE TRAGEDY OF SOUTH AFRICA. *Cr. 8vo. 2s. net. Also Cr. 8vo. 3d. net.*
 A revised and enlarged edition of the author's 'Peace or War in South Africa.'

ENGLAND'S RUIN : Discussed in Six-teen Letters to the Right Hon. Joseph Chamberlaih, M.P. *Seventh Edition. Cr. 8vo. 3d. net.*

Miles (Eustace), M.A. LIFE AFTER LIFE, OR, THE THEORY OF REIN-CARNATION. *Cr. 8vo. 2s. 6d. net.*

Millais (J. G.). THE LIFE AND LET-TERS OF SIR JOHN EVERETT MILLAIS, President of the Royal Academy. With many Illustrations, of which 2 are in Photogravure. *New Edition. Demy 8vo. 7s. 6d. net.*
See also Little Galleries.

Millin (G. F.). PICTORIAL GARDEN-ING. Illustrated. *Cr. 8vo. 3s. 6d. net.*

Millis (C. T.), M.I.M.E. See Textbooks of Technology.

Milne (J. G.), M.A. A HISTORY OF ROMAN EGYPT. Fully Illus. *Cr. 8vo. 6s.*

Milton (John). A DAY BOOK OF. Edited by R. F. Towndrow. *Fcap. 8vo. 3s. 6d. net.*
See also Little Library and Standard Library.

Minchin (H. C.), M.A. See R. Peel.

Mitchell (P. Chalmers), M.A. OUTLINES OF BIOLOGY. Illustrated. *Second Edition. Cr. 8vo. 6s.*

Mitton (G. E.). JANE AUSTEN AND HER TIMES. With many Portraits and Illustrations. *Second and Cheaper Edition. Cr. 8vo. 6s.*
A Colonial Edition is also published.

Moffat (Mary M.). QUEEN LOUISA OF PRUSSIA. With 20 Illustrations. *Fourth Edition. Demy 8vo. 7s. 6d. net.*

'Moll (A.).' See Books on Business.

Moir (D. M.). See Little Library.

Molinos (Dr. Michael de). See Library of Devotion.

Money (L. G. Chiozza), M.P. RICHES AND POVERTY. *Third Edition. Demy 8vo. 5s. net.*

Montagu (Henry), Earl of Manchester. See Library of Devotion.

Montaigne. A DAY BOOK OF. Edited by C. F. Pond. *Fcap. 8vo. 3s. 6d. net.*

Montmorency (J. E. G. de), B.A., LL.B. THOMAS A KEMPIS, HIS AGE AND BOOK. With 22 Illustrations. *Second Edition. Demy 8vo. 7s. 6d. net.*

Moore (H. E.). BACK TO THE LAND. An Inquiry into Rural Depopulation. *Cr. 8vo. 2s. 6d.*

Moorhouse (E. Hallam). NELSON'S LADY HAMILTON. With 51 Portraits. *Second Edition. Demy 8vo. 7s. 6d. net.*
A Colonial Edition is also published.

Moran (Clarence G.). See Books on Business.

More (Sir Thomas). See Standard Library.

Morfill (W. R.), Oriel College, Oxford. A HISTORY OF RUSSIA FROM PETER THE GREAT TO ALEXANDER II. With Maps and Plans. *Cr. 8vo. 3s. 6d.*

Morich (R. J.), late of Clifton College. See School Examination Series.

Morris (J.). THE MAKERS OF JAPAN. With 24 Illustrations. *Demy 8vo. 12s. 6d. net.*
A Colonial Edition is also published.

Morris (J. E.). See Little Guides.

Morton (Miss Anderson). See Miss Brod-rick.

Moule (H. C. G.), D.D., Lord Bishop of Dur-ham. See Leaders of Religion.

Muir (M. M. Pattison), M.A. THE CHEMISTRY OF FIRE. Illustrated. *Cr. 8vo. 2s. 6d.*

Mundella (V. A.), M.A. See J. T. Dunn.

Munro (R.), LL.D. See Antiquary's Books.

Naval Officer (A). See I. P. L.

Neal (W. G.). See R. N. Hall.

Newman (Ernest). HUGO WOLF. *Demy 8vo. 6s.*

Newman (George), M.D., D.P.H., F.R.S.E., Lecturer on Public Health at St. Bartholo-mew's Hospital, and Medical Officer of Health of the Metropolitan Borough of Finsbury. INFANT MORTALITY, A Social Problem. With 16 Diagrams. *Demy 8vo. 7s. 6d. net.*

Newman (J. H.) and others. See Library of Devotion.

Nichols (J. B. B.). See Little Library.

Nicklin (T.), M.A. EXAMINATION PAPERS IN THUCYDIDES. *Cr. 8vo. 2s.*

Nimrod. See I. P. L.

Norgate (G. Le Grys). THE LIFE OF SIR WALTER SCOTT. Illustrated. *Demy 8vo. 7s. 6d. net.*

Norregaard (B. W.). THE GREAT SIEGE : The Investment and Fall of Port Arthur. Illustrated. *Demy 8vo. 10s. 6d. net.*

Norway (A. H.). NAPLES. With 25 Col-oured Illustrations by Maurice Greiffen-hagen. *Second Edition. Cr. 8vo, 6s.*

Novalis. THE DISCIPLES AT SAIS AND OTHER FRAGMENTS. Edited by Miss Una Birch. *Fcap. 8vo. 3s. 6d.*

Oldfield (W. J.), M.A., Prebendary of Lincoln. A PRIMER OF RELIGION. Based on the Catechism of the Church of England. *Fcap. 8vo. 2s. 6d.*

Oldham (P. M.), B.A. See Textbooks of Science.

Oliphant (Mrs.). See Leaders of Religion.

Oman (C. W. C.), M.A., Fellow of All Souls', Oxford. A HISTORY OF THE ART OF WAR. The Middle Ages, from the Fourth to the Fourteenth Century. Illus-trated. *Demy 8vo. 10s. 6d. net.*

Ottley (R. L.), D.D. See Handbooks of Theology and Leaders of Religion.

Overton (J. H.). See Leaders of Religion.

Owen (Douglas). See Books on Business.

Oxford (M. N.), of Guy's Hospital. A HAND-BOOK OF NURSING. *Fourth Edition. Cr. 8vo. 3s. 6d.*

Pakes (W. C. C.). THE SCIENCE OF HYGIENE. Illustrated. *Demy 8vo. 15s.*

Palmer (Frederick). WITH KUROKI IN MANCHURIA. Illustrated. *Third Edition. Demy 8vo. 7s. 6d. net.*

Parker (Gilbert). A LOVER'S DIARY. *Fcap. 8vo. 5s.*

Parkes (A. K.). SMALL LESSONS ON GREAT TRUTHS. *Fcap. 8vo. 1s. 6d.*

Parkinson (John). PARADISI IN SOLE PARADISUS TERRESTRIS, OR A GARDEN OF ALL SORTS OF PLEASANT FLOWERS. *Folio. £3, 3s. net.*

Parmenter (John). HELIO-TROPES, OR NEW POSIES FOR SUNDIALS, 1625. Edited by PERCIVAL LANDON, *Quarto. 3s. 6d. net.*

Parmentier (Prof. Leon). See Byzantine Texts.

Parsons (Mrs. Clement). GARRICK AND HIS CIRCLE. With 36 Illustrations. *Second Edition. Demy 8vo. 12s. 6d. net.*
A Colonial Edition is also published.

Pascal. See Library of Devotion.

Paston (George). SOCIAL CARICATURE IN THE EIGHTEENTH CENTURY. With over 200 Illustrations. *Imperial Quarto. £2, 12s. 6d. net.*
See also Little Books on Art and I.P.L.

LADY MARY WORTLEY MONTAGU. With 24 Portraits and Illustrations. *Second Edition. Demy 8vo. 15s. net.*
A Colonial Edition is also published.

Paterson(W. R.)(Benjamin Swift). LIFE'S QUESTIONINGS. *Cr. 8vo. 3s. 6d. net.*

Patterson (A. H.). NOTES OF AN EAST COAST NATURALIST. Illustrated in Colour by F. SOUTHGATE. *Second Edition. Cr. 8vo. 6s.*

NATURE IN EASTERN NORFOLK. A series of observations on the Birds, Fishes, Mammals, Reptiles, and Stalkeyed Crustaceans found in that neighbourhood, with a list of the species. With 12 Illustrations in colour, by FRANK SOUTHGATE. *Second Edition. Cr. 8vo. 6s.*

Peacock (N.). See Little Books on Art.

Peake (C. M. A.), F.R.H.S. A CONCISE HANDBOOK OF GARDEN ANNUAL AND BIENNIAL PLANTS. With 24 Illustrations. *Fcap. 8vo. 3s. 6d. net.*

Peel (Robert), and Minchin (H. C.), M.A. OXFORD. With 100 Illustrations in Colour. *Cr. 8vo. 6s.*

Peel (Sidney), late Fellow of Trinity College, Oxford, and Secretary to the Royal Commission on the Licensing Laws. PRACTICAL LICENSING REFORM. *Second Edition. Cr. 8vo. 1s. 6d.*

Petrie (W.M.Flinders), D.C.L., LL.D., Professor of Egyptology at University College. A HISTORY OF EGYPT, FROM THE EARLIEST TIMES TO THE PRESENT DAY. Fully Illustrated. *In six volumes. Cr. 8vo. 6s. each.*

VOL. I. PREHISTORIC TIMES TO XVITH DYNASTY. *Sixth Edition.*

VOL. II. THE XVIITH AND XVIIITH DYNASTIES. *Fourth Edition.*

VOL. III. XIXTH TO XXXTH DYNASTIES.

VOL. IV. THE EGYPT OF THE PTOLEMIES. J. P. MAHAFFY, Litt.D.

VOL. V. ROMAN EGYPT. J. G. MILNE, M.A.

VOL. VI. EGYPT IN THE MIDDLE AGES. STANLEY LANE-POOLE, M.A.

RELIGION AND CONSCIENCE IN ANCIENT EGYPT. Illustrated. *Cr. 8vo. 2s. 6d.*

SYRIA AND EGYPT, FROM THE TELL EL AMARNA TABLETS. *Cr. 8vo. 2s. 6d.*

EGYPTIAN TALES. Illustrated by TRISTRAM ELLIS. *In Two Volumes. Cr. 8vo. 3s. 6d. each.*

EGYPTIAN DECORATIVE ART. With 120 Illustrations. *Cr. 8vo. 3s. 6d.*

Phillips (W. A.). See Oxford Biographies.

Phillpotts (Eden). MY DEVON YEAR. With 38 Illustrations by J. LEY PETHYBRIDGE. *Second and Cheaper Edition. Large Cr. 8vo. 6s.*

UP ALONG AND DOWN ALONG. Illustrated by CLAUDE SHEPPERSON. *Cr. 4to. 5s. net.*
A volume of poems.

Plarr (Victor G.). See School Histories.

Plato. See Standard Library.

Plautus. THE CAPTIVI. Edited, with an Introduction, Textual Notes, and a Commentary, by W. M. LINDSAY, Fellow of Jesus College, Oxford. *Demy 8vo. 10s. 6d. net.*

Plowden-Wardlaw (J. T.), B.A., King's College, Cambridge. See School Examination Series.

Podmore (Frank). MODERN SPIRITUALISM. *Two Volumes. Demy 8vo. 21s. net.*
A History and a Criticism.

Poer (J. Patrick Le). A MODERN LEGIONARY. *Cr. 8vo. 6s.*

Pollard (Alice). See Little Books on Art.

Pollard (A. W.). OLD PICTURE BOOKS. Illustrated. *Demy 8vo. 7s. 6d. net.*

Pollard (Eliza P.). See Little Books on Art.

Pollock (David), M.I.N.A. See Books on Business.

Potter (M. C.), M.A., F.L.S. A TEXTBOOK OF AGRICULTURAL BOTANY. Illustrated. *Second Edition. Cr. 8vo. 4s. 6d.*

Power (J. O'Connor). THE MAKING OF AN ORATOR. *Cr. 8vo. 6s.*

Prance (G.). See R. Wyon.

Prescott (O. L.). ABOUT MUSIC, AND WHAT IT IS MADE OF. *Cr. 8vo. 3s. 6d. net.*

Price (L. L.), M.A., Fellow of Oriel College, Oxon. A HISTORY OF ENGLISH POLITICAL ECONOMY. *Fourth Edition. Cr. 8vo. 2s. 6d.*

Primrose (Deborah). A MODERN BŒOTIA. *Cr. 8vo. 6s.*

Protheros (Ernest). THE DOMINION OF MAN. GEOGRAPHY IN ITS HUMAN ASPECT. With 32 full-page Illustrations. *Cr. 8vo. 2s.*

Pugin and Rowlandson. THE MICROCOSM OF LONDON, OR LONDON IN MINIATURE. With 104 Illustrations in colour. *In Three Volumes. Small 4to.* £3, 3s. net.

'Q' (A. T. Quiller Couch). THE GOLDEN POMP. A PROCESSION OF ENGLISH LYRICS. *Second Edition. Cr. 8vo.* 2s. 6d. net.

Quevedo Villegas. See Miniature Library.

G. R. and E.S. THE WOODHOUSE CORRESPONDENCE. *Cr. 8vo.* 6s.
A Colonial Edition is also published.

Rackham (R. B.), M.A. See Westminster Commentaries.

Ragg (Laura M.). THE WOMEN-ARTISTS OF BOLOGNA. With 20 Illustrations. *Demy 8vo.* 7s. 6d. net.

Ragg (Lonsdale). B.D., Oxon. DANTE AND HIS ITALY. With 32 Illustrations largely from contemporary Frescoes and Documents. *Demy 8vo.* 12s. 6d. net.

Rahtz (F. J.), M.A., B.Sc., Lecturer in English at Merchant Venturers' Technical College, Bristol. HIGHER ENGLISH. *Second Edition. Cr. 8vo.* 3s. 6d.

Randolph (B. W.), D.D. See Library of Devotion.

Rannie (D. W.), M.A. A STUDENT'S HISTORY OF SCOTLAND. *Cr. 8vo.* 3s. 6d.

Rashdall (Hastings), M.A., Fellow and Tutor of New College, Oxford. DOCTRINE AND DEVELOPMENT. *Cr. 8vo.* 6s.

Raven (J. J.), D.D. See Antiquary's Books.

Rawstorne (Lawrence, Esq.). See I.P.L.

Raymond (Walter). See School Histories.

A Real Paddy. See I.P.L.

Reason (W.), M.A. UNIVERSITY AND SOCIAL SETTLEMENTS. *Cr. 8vo.* 2s. 6d.

Redpath (H. A.), M.A. See Westminster Commentaries.

Reynolds. See Little Galleries.

Rhoades (J. F.). See Simplified French Texts.

Rhodes (W. E.). See School Histories.

Rieu (H.), M.A. See Simplified French Texts.

Roberts (M. E.). See C. C. Channer.

Robertson (A.), D.D., Lord Bishop of Exeter. REGNUM DEI. The Bampton Lectures of 1901. *Demy 8vo.* 7s. 6d. net.

Robertson (C. Grant). M.A., Fellow of All Souls' College, Oxford, Examiner in the Honours School of Modern History, Oxford, 1901-1904. SELECT STATUTES, CASES, AND CONSTITUTIONAL DOCUMENTS, 1660-1832. *Demy 8vo.* 10s. 6d. net.

Robertson (C. Grant) and Bartholomew (J. G.), F.R.S.E., F.R.G.S. A HISTORICAL AND MODERN ATLAS OF THE BRITISH EMPIRE. *Demy Quarto.* 4s. 6d. net.

Robertson (Sir G.S.), K.C.S.I. CHITRAL: THE STORY OF A MINOR SIEGE. *Third Edition.* Illustrated. *Cr. 8vo.* 2s. 6d. net.

Robinson (A. W.), M.A. See Churchman's Bible.

Robinson (Cecilia). THE MINISTRY OF DEACONESSES. With an Introduction by the late Archbishop of Canterbury. *Cr. 8vo.* 3s. 6d.

Robinson (F. S.). See Connoisseur's Library.

Rochefoucauld (La). See Little Library.

Rodwell (G.), B.A. NEW TESTAMENT GREEK. A Course for Beginners. With a Preface by WALTER LOCK, D.D., Warden of Keble College. *Fcap. 8vo.* 3s. 6d.

Roe (Fred). OLD OAK FURNITURE. With many Illustrations by the Author, including a frontispiece in colour. *Demy 8vo.* 10s. 6d. net.

Rogers (A. G. L.), M.A. See Books on Business.

Romney. See Little Galleries.

Roscoe (E. S.). See Little Guides.

Rose (Edward). THE ROSE READER. Illustrated. *Cr. 8vo.* 2s. 6d. *Also in 4 Parts. Parts I. and II.* 6d. *each; Part III.* 8d. *; Part IV.* 10d.

Rowntree (Joshua). THE IMPERIAL DRUG TRADE. A RE-STATEMENT OF THE OPIUM QUESTION. *Second and Cheaper Edition. Cr. 8vo.* 2s. net.

Royde-Smith (N. G.). THE PILLOW BOOK: A GARNER OF MANY MOODS. *Second Edition. Cr. 8vo.* 4s. 6d. net.

Ruble (A. E.), D.D. See Junior School Books.

Russell (W. Clark). THE LIFE OF ADMIRAL LORD COLLINGWOOD. With Illustrations by F. BRANGWYN. *Fourth Edition. Cr. 8vo.* 6s.

Sainsbury (Harrington), M.D., F.R.C.P. PRINCIPIA THERAPEUTICA. *Demy 8vo.* 7s. 6d. net.

St. Anselm. See Library of Devotion.

St. Augustine. See Library of Devotion.

St. Bernard. See Library of Devotion.

Sales (St. Francis de). See Library of Devotion.

St. Cyres (Viscount). See Oxford Biographies.

St. Francis of Assisi. THE LITTLE FLOWERS OF THE GLORIOUS MESSER ST. FRANCIS AND HIS FRIARS. Newly translated by WILLIAM HEYWOOD. With an Introduction by A. G. F. HOWELL, and 40 Illustrations from Italian Painters. *Demy 8vo.* 5s. net.
See also Standard Library and Library of Devotion.

'Saki' (H. Munro). REGINALD. *Second Edition. Fcap. 8vo.* 2s. 6d. net.

Salmon (A. L.). See Little Guides.

Sargeaunt (J.), M.A. ANNALS OF WESTMINSTER SCHOOL. Illustrated. *Demy 8vo.* 7s. 6d.

Sathas (C.). See Byzantine Texts.

Schmitt (John). See Byzantine Texts.

Scott (A. M.). WINSTON SPENCER CHURCHILL. With Portraits and Illustrations. *Cr. 8vo.* 3s. 6d.

Scudamore (Cyril). See Little Guides.

Sells (V. P.), M.A. THE MECHANICS OF DAILY LIFE. Illustrated. *Cr. 8vo. 2s. 6d.*

Selous (Edmund). TOMMY SMITH'S ANIMALS. Illustrated by G. W. ORD. *Ninth Edition. Fcap. 8vo. 2s. 6d. School Edition, 1s. 6d.*
TOMMY SMITH'S OTHER ANIMALS. With 12 Illustrations by AUGUSTA GUEST. *Third Edition. Fcap. 8vo. 2s. 6d.*

Settle (J. H.). ANECDOTES OF SOLDIERS. *Cr. 8vo. 3s. 6d. net.*

Shakespeare (William).
THE FOUR FOLIOS, 1623; 1632; 1664; 1685. Each £4, 4s. net, or a complete set, £12, 12s. net.
Folios 3 and 4 are ready.
Folio 2 is nearly ready.
See also Arden, Standard Library and Little Quarto Shakespeare.

Sharp (A.). VICTORIAN POETS. *Cr. 8vo. 2s. 6d.*

Sharp (Cecil). See S. Baring-Gould.

Sharp (Mrs. E. A.). See Little Books on Art.

Shedlock (J. S.) THE PIANOFORTE SONATA. *Cr. 8vo. 5s.*

Shelley (Percy B.). ADONAIS; an Elegy on the death of John Keats, Author of 'Endymion,' etc. Pisa. From the types of Didot, 1821. *2s. net.*

Sheppard (H. F.), M.A. See S. Baring-Gould.

Sherwell (Arthur), M.A. LIFE IN WEST LONDON. *Third Edition. Cr. 8vo. 2s. 6d.*

Shipley (Mary E.). AN ENGLISH CHURCH HISTORY FOR CHILDREN. A.D. 597-1066. With a Preface by the Bishop of Gibraltar. With Maps and Illustrations. *Cr. 8vo. 2s. 6d. net.*

Sime (J.). See Little Books on Art.

Simonson (G. A.). FRANCESCO GUARDI. With 41 Plates. *Imperial 4to. £2, 2s. net.*

Sketchley (R. E. D.). See Little Books on Art.

Skipton (H. P. K.). See Little Books on Art.

Sladen (Douglas). SICILY: The New Winter Resort. With over 200 Illustrations. *Second Edition. Cr. 8vo. 5s. net.*

Small (Evan), M.A. THE EARTH. An Introduction to Physiography. Illustrated. *Cr. 8vo. 2s. 6d.*

Smallwood (M. G.). See Little Books on Art.

Smedley (F. E.). See I.P.L.

Smith (Adam). THE WEALTH OF NATIONS. Edited with an Introduction and numerous Notes by EDWIN CANNAN, M.A. *Two volumes. Demy 8vo. 21s. net.*

Smith (Horace and James). See Little Library.

Smith (H. Bompas), M.A. A NEW JUNIOR ARITHMETIC. *Crown 8vo. 2s.* With Answers, *2s. 6d.*

Smith (R. Mudie). THOUGHTS FOR THE DAY. Edited by. *Fcap. 8vo. 3s. 6d. net.*

Smith (Nowell C.). See W. Wordsworth.

Smith (John Thomas). A BOOK FOR A RAINY DAY; Or, Recollections of the Events of the Years 1766-1833. Edited by WILFRED WHITTEN. Illustrated. *Wide Demy 8vo. 12s. 6d. net.*

Snell (F. J.). A BOOK OF EXMOOR. Illustrated. *Cr. 8vo. 6s.*

Snowden (C. E.). A HANDY DIGEST OF BRITISH HISTORY. *Demy 8vo. 4s. 6d.*

Sophocles. See Classical Translations.

Sornet (L. A.). See Junior School Books.

South (E. Wilton), M.A. See Junior School Books.

Southey (R.). ENGLISH SEAMEN. Edited by DAVID HANNAY.
Vol. I. (Howard, Clifford, Hawkins, Drake, Cavendish). *Second Edition. Cr. 8vo. 6s.*
Vol. II. (Richard Hawkins, Grenville, Essex, and Raleigh). *Cr. 8vo. 6s.*
See also Standard Library.

Spence (C. H.), M.A. See School Examination Series.

Spicer (A. D.). THE PAPER TRADE. With Maps and Diagrams. *Demy 8vo. 12s. 6d. net.*

Spooner (W. A.), M.A. See Leaders of Religion.

Staley (Edgcumbe). THE GUILDS OF FLORENCE. Illustrated. *Second Edition. Royal 8vo. 16s. net.*

Stanbridge (J. W.), B.D. See Library of Devotion.

'Stancliffe.' GOLF DO'S AND DONT'S. *Second Edition. Fcap. 8vo. 1s.*

Stead (W. J.). See D. Gallaher.

Stedman (A. M. M.), M.A.
INITIA LATINA: Easy Lessons on Elementary Accidence. *Tenth Edition. Fcap. 8vo. 1s.*
FIRST LATIN LESSONS. *Tenth Edition. Cr. 8vo. 2s.*
FIRST LATIN READER. With Notes adapted to the Shorter Latin Primer and Vocabulary. *Seventh Ed. revised. 18mo. 1s. 6d.*
EASY SELECTIONS FROM CÆSAR. The Helvetian War. *Third Edition. 18mo. 1s.*
EASY SELECTIONS FROM LIVY. The Kings of Rome. *18mo. Third Edition. 1s. 6d.*
EASY LATIN PASSAGES FOR UNSEEN TRANSLATION. *Eleventh Ed. Fcap. 8vo. 1s. 6d.*
EXEMPLA LATINA. First Exercises in Latin Accidence. With Vocabulary. *Third Edition. Cr. 8vo. 1s.*

EASY LATIN EXERCISES ON THE SYNTAX OF THE SHORTER AND REVISED LATIN PRIMER. With Vocabulary. *Eleventh and Cheaper Edition, re-written. Cr. 8vo. 1s. 6d. Original Edition. 2s. 6d.* KEY, *3s. net.*

THE LATIN COMPOUND SENTENCE: Rules and Exercises. *Second Edition. Cr. 8vo. 1s. 6d.* With Vocabulary. *2s.*

NOTANDA QUAEDAM : Miscellaneous Latin Exercises on Common Rules and Idioms. *Fifth Edition. Fcap. 8vo. 1s. 6d.* With Vocabulary. *2s.* Key, *2s. net.*

LATIN VOCABULARIES FOR REPETITION : Arranged according to Subjects. *Fourteenth Edition. Fcap. 8vo. 1s. 6d.*

A VOCABULARY OF LATIN IDIOMS. *18mo. Fourth Edition. 1s.*

STEPS TO GREEK. *Third Edition, revised. 18mo. 1s.*

A SHORTER GREEK PRIMER. *Second Edition. Cr. 8vo. 1s. 6d.*

EASY GREEK PASSAGES FOR UNSEEN TRANSLATION. *Fourth Edition, revised. Fcap. 8vo. 1s. 6d.*

GREEK VOCABULARIES FOR REPETITION. Arranged according to Subjects. *Fourth Edition. Fcap. 8vo. 1s. 6d.*

GREEK TESTAMENT SELECTIONS. For the use of Schools. With Introduction, Notes, and Vocabulary. *Fourth Edition. Fcap. 8vo. 2s. 6d.*

STEPS TO FRENCH. *Eighth Edition. 18mo. 8d.*

FIRST FRENCH LESSONS. *Eighth Edition, revised. Cr. 8vo. 1s.*

EASY FRENCH PASSAGES FOR UNSEEN TRANSLATION. *Sixth Edition, revised. Fcap. 8vo. 1s. 6d.*

EASY FRENCH EXERCISES ON ELEMENTARY SYNTAX. With Vocabulary. *Fourth Edition. Cr. 8vo. 2s. 6d.* KEY. *3s. net.*

FRENCH VOCABULARIES FOR REPETITION : Arranged according to Subjects. *Thirteenth Edition. Fcap. 8vo. 1s.* See also School Examination Series.

Steel (R. Elliott), M.A., F.C.S. THE WORLD OF SCIENCE. With 147 Illustrations. *Second Edition. Cr. 8vo. 2s. 6d.* See also School Examination Series.

Stephenson (C.), of the Technical College, Bradford, and **Suddards (F.)** of the Yorkshire College, Leeds. ORNAMENTAL DESIGN FOR WOVEN FABRICS. Illustrated. *Demy 8vo. Third Edition. 7s. 6d.*

Stephenson (J.), M.A. THE CHIEF TRUTHS OF THE CHRISTIAN FAITH. *Cr. 8vo. 3s. 6d.*

Sterne (Laurence). See Little Library.

Sterry (W.), M.A. ANNALS OF ETON COLLEGE. Illustrated. *Demy 8vo. 7s. 6d.*

Steuart (Katherine). BY ALLAN WATER. *Second Edition. Cr. 8vo. 6s.*

Stevenson (R. L.) THE LETTERS OF ROBERT LOUIS STEVENSON TO HIS FAMILY AND FRIENDS. Selected and Edited by SIDNEY COLVIN. *Third Edition. Cr. 8vo. 12s.*

LIBRARY EDITION. *Demy 8vo. 2 vols. 25s. net.* A Colonial Edition is also published.

VAILIMA LETTERS. With an Etched Portrait by WILLIAM STRANG. *Sixth Edition. Cr. 8vo. Buckram. 6s.* A Colonial Edition is also published.

THE LIFE OF R. L. STEVENSON. See G. Balfour.

Stevenson (M. I.). FROM SARANAC TO THE MARQUESAS. Being Letters written by Mrs. M. I. STEVENSON during 1887-8. *Cr. 8vo. 6s. net.*

LETTERS FROM SAMOA, 1891-95. Edited and arranged by M. C. BALFOUR. With many Illustrations. *Second Edition. Cr. 8vo. 6s. net.*

Stoddart (Anna M.). See Oxford Biographies.

Stokes (F. G.), B.A. HOURS WITH RABELAIS. From the translation of SIR T. URQUHART and P. A. MOTTEUX. With a Portrait in Photogravure. *Cr. 8vo. 3s. 6d.*

Stone (S. J.). POEMS AND HYMNS. With a Memoir by F. G. ELLERTON, M.A. With Portrait. *Cr. 8vo. 6s.*

Storr (Vernon F.), M.A., Lecturer in the Philosophy of Religion in Cambridge University ; Examining Chaplain to the Archbishop of Canterbury; formerly Fellow of University College, Oxford. DEVELOPMENT AND DIVINE PURPOSE. *Cr. 8vo. 5s. net.*

Straker (F.). See Books on Business.

Streane (A. W.), D.D. See Churchman's Bible.

Streatfeild (R. A.). MODERN MUSIC AND MUSICIANS. With 24 Illustrations. *Second Edition. Demy 8vo. 7s. 6d. net.*

Stroud (H.), D.Sc., M.A. PRACTICAL PHYSICS. With many Diagrams. *Second Edition. 3s. net.*

Strutt (Joseph). THE SPORTS AND PASTIMES OF THE PEOPLE OF ENGLAND. Illustrated by many Engravings. Revised by J. CHARLES COX, LL.D., F.S.A. *Quarto. 21s. net.*

Stuart (Capt. Donald). THE STRUGGLE FOR PERSIA. With a Map. *Cr. 8vo. 6s.*

Sturch (F.), Staff Instructor to the Surrey County Council. MANUAL TRAINING DRAWING (WOODWORK). Its Principles and Application, with Solutions to Examination Questions, 1892-1905. Orthographic, Isometric and Oblique Projection. With 50 Plates and 140 Figures. *Foolscap. 5s. net.*

Suddards (F.). See C. Stephenson.

Surtees (R. S.). See I.P.L.

Symes (J. E.), M.A. THE FRENCH REVOLUTION. *Second Edition. Cr. 8vo. 2s. 6d.*

Sympson (E. M.), M.A., M.D. See Ancient Cities.

Tacitus. AGRICOLA. With Introduction Notes, Map, etc., by R. F. DAVIS, M.A., *Fcap. 8vo.* 2s.
GERMANIA. By the same Editor. *Fcap. 8vo.* 2s. See also Classical Translations.
Tallack (W.). HOWARD LETTERS AND MEMORIES. *Demy 8vo.* 10s. 6d. net.
Tauler (J.), See Library of Devotion.
Taylor (A. E.). THE ELEMENTS OF METAPHYSICS. *Demy 8vo.* 10s. 6d. net.
Taylor (F. G.), M.A. See Commercial Series.
Taylor (I. A.). See Oxford Biographies.
Taylor (John W.). THE COMING OF THE SAINTS : Imagination and Studies in Early Church History and Tradition. With 26 Illustrations. *Demy 8vo.* 7s. 6d. net.
Taylor T. M.), M.A., Fellow of Gonville and Caius College, Cambridge. A CONSTITUTIONAL AND POLITICAL HISTORY OF ROME. *Cr. 8vo.* 7s. 6d.
Teasdale-Buckell (G. T.). THE COMPLETE SHOT. Illustrated. *Second Ed.*
Tennyson (Alfred, Lord). THE EARLY POEMS OF. Edited, with Notes and an Introduction, by J. CHURTON COLLINS, M.A. *Cr. 8vo.* 6s.
IN MEMORIAM, MAUD, AND THE PRINCESS. Edited by J. CHURTON COLLINS, M.A. *Cr. 8vo.* 6s. See also Little Library.
Terry (C. S.). See Oxford Biographies.
Thackeray (W. M.). See Little Library.
Theobald (F. V.), M.A. INSECT LIFE. Illustrated. *Second Edition Revised. Cr. 8vo.* 2s. 6d.
Thompson (A. H.). See Little Guides.
Tileston (Mary W.). DAILY STRENGTH FOR DAILY NEEDS. *Fourteenth Edition. Medium 16mo.* 2s. 6d. net. Also an edition in superior binding, 6s.
Tompkins (H. W.), F.R.H.S. See Little Guides.
Townley (Lady Susan). MY CHINESE NOTE-BOOK With 16 Illustrations and 2 Maps. *Third Ed. Demy 8vo.* 10s. 6d. net
Toynbee (Paget), M.A., D.Litt. See Oxford Biographies.
Trench (Herbert). DEIRDRE WEDDED AND OTHER POEMS. *Cr. 8vo.* 5s.
An episode of Thirty hours delivered by the three voices. It deals with the love of Deirdre for Naris and is founded on a Gaelic Version of the Tragical Tale of the Sons of Usnach.
Trevelyan (G. M.), Fellow of Trinity College, Cambridge. ENGLAND UNDER THE STUARTS. With Maps and Plans. *Second Edition. Demy 8vo.* 10s. 6d. net.
Troutbeck (G. E.). See Little Guides.
Tyler (E. A.), B.A., F.C.S. See Junior School Books.
Tyrrell-Gill (Frances). See Little Books on Art.
Vardon (Harry). THE COMPLETE GOLFER. Illustrated. *Eighth Edition. Demy 8vo.* 10s. 6d. net.
A Colonial Edition is also published.
Vaughan (Henry). See Little Library.

Vaughan (Herbert M.), B.A. (Oxon.). THE LAST OF THE ROYAL STUARTS, HENRY STUART, CARDINAL, DUKE OF YORK. With 20 Illustrations. *Second Edition. Demy 8vo.* 10s. 6d. net.
THE NAPLES RIVIERA. With 25 Illustrations in Colour by MAURICE GREIFFENHAGEN. *Cr. 8vo.* 6s.
A Colonial Edition is also published.
Voegelin (A.), M.A. See Junior Examination Series.
Waddell (Col. L. A.), LL.D., C.B. LHASA AND ITS MYSTERIES. With a Record of the Expedition of 1903-1904. With 155 Illustrations and Maps. *Third and Cheaper Edition. Demy 8vo.* 7s. 6d. net.
Wade (G. W.), D.D. OLD TESTAMENT HISTORY. With Maps. *Fifth Edition. Cr. 8vo.* 6s.
Wagner (Richard). MUSIC DRAMAS : Interpretations, embodying Wagner's own explanations. By A. L. CLEATHER and B. CRUMP. *In Four Volumes. Fcap 8vo.* 2s. 6d. each.
 VOL. I.—THE RING OF THE NIBELUNG. *Third Edition.*
 VOL. II.—PARSIFAL, LOHENGRIN, and THE HOLY GRAIL.
 VOL. III.—TRISTAN AND ISOLDE.
Wall (J. C.). DEVILS. Illustrated by the Author and from photographs. *Demy 8vo.* 4s. 6d. net. See also Antiquary's Books.
Walters (H. B.). See Little Books on Art and Classics of Art.
Walton (F. W.). See School Histories.
Walton (Izaac) and **Cotton (Charles).** See I.P.L., Standard Library, and Little Library.
Warren-Vernon (Hon. William), M.A. READINGS ON THE INFERNO OF DANTE, based on the Commentary of BENVENUTO DA IMOLA and other authorities. With an Introduction by the Rev. Dr. MOORE. In Two Volumes. *Second Edition, entirely re-written. Cr. 8vo.* 15s. net.
Waterhouse (Mrs. Alfred). WITH THE SIMPLE-HEARTED : Little Homilies to Women in Country Places. *Second Edition. Small Pott 8vo.* 2s. net.
See also Little Library.
Watt (Francis). See T. F. Henderson.
Weatherhead (T. C.), M.A. EXAMINATION PAPERS IN HORACE. *Cr. 8vo.* 2s. See also Junior Examination Series.
Webber (F. C.). See Textbooks of Technology.
Weir (Archibald), M.A. AN INTRODUCTION TO THE HISTORY OF MODERN EUROPE. *Cr. 8vo.* 6s.
Wells (Sidney H.). See Textbooks of Science.
Wells (J.), M.A., Fellow and Tutor of Wadham College. OXFORD AND OXFORD LIFE. *Third Edition. Cr. 8vo.* 3s. 6d.
A SHORT HISTORY OF ROME. *Eighth Edition.* With 3 Maps. *Cr. 8vo.* 3s. 6d.
See also Little Guides.
Wheldon (F. W.). A LITTLE BROTHER TO THE BIRDS. With 15 Illustrations,

¶ of which are by A. H. BUCKLAND. *Large Cr. 8vo.* 6s.

Whibley (C.). See W. E. Henley.

Whibley (L.), M.A., Fellow of Pembroke College, Cambridge. GREEK OLIGARCHIES: THEIR ORGANISATION AND CHARACTER. *Cr. 8vo.* 6s.

Whitaker (G. H.), M.A. See Churchman's Bible.

White (Gilbert). THE NATURAL HISTORY OF SELBORNE. Edited by L. C. MIALL, F.R.S., assisted by W. WARDE FOWLER, M.A. *Cr. 8vo.* 6s.
See also Standard Library.

Whitfield (E. E.). See Commercial Series.

Whitehead (A. W.). GASPARD DE COLIGNY. Illustrated. *Demy 8vo.* 12s. 6d. net.

Whiteley (R. Lloyd), F.I.C., Principal of the Municipal Science School, West Bromwich. AN ELEMENTARY TEXT-BOOK OF INORGANIC CHEMISTRY. *Cr. 8vo.* 2s. 6d.

Whitley (Miss). See Lady Dilke.

Whitten (W.). See John Thomas Smith.

Whyte (A. G.), B.Sc. See Books on Business.

Wilberforce (Wilfrid). See Little Books on Art.

Wilde (Oscar). DE PROFUNDIS. *Tenth Edition. Cr. 8vo.* 5s. net.
A Colonial Edition is also published.
THE DUCHESS OF PADUA. *Demy 8vo.* 12s. 6d. net.
POEMS. *Demy 8vo.* 12s. 6d. net.
INTENTIONS. *Demy 8vo.* 12s. 6d. net.
SALOME, AND OTHER PLAYS. *Demy 8vo.* 12s. 6d. net.
LADY WINDERMERE'S FAN. *Demy 8vo.* 12s. 6d. net.
A WOMAN OF NO IMPORTANCE. *Demy 8vo.* 12s. 6d. net.
AN IDEAL HUSBAND. *Demy 8vo.* 12s. 6d. net.
THE IMPORTANCE OF BEING EARNEST. *Demy 8vo.* 12s. 6d. net.
A HOUSE OF POMEGRANATES and THE HAPPY PRINCE. *Demy 8vo.* 12s. 6d. net.
LORD ARTHUR SAVILE'S CRIME and OTHER PROSE PIECES. *Demy 8vo.* 12s. 6d. net.

Wilkins (W. H.), B.A. THE ALIEN INVASION. *Cr. 8vo.* 2s. 6d.

Williams (A.). PETROL PETER: or Pretty Stories and Funny Pictures. Illustrated in Colour by A. W. MILLS. *Demy 4to.* 3s. 6d. net.

Williamson (M. G.). See Ancient Cities.

Williamson (W.). THE BRITISH GARDENER. Illustrated. *Demy 8vo.* 10s. 6d.

Williamson (W.), B.A. See Junior Examination Series, Junior School Books, and Beginner's Books.

Willson (Beckles). LORD STRATHCONA: the Story of his Life. Illustrated. *Demy 8vo.* 7s. 6d.
A Colonial Edition is also published.

Wilmot-Buxton (E. M.). MAKERS OF EUROPE. *Cr. 8vo. Eighth Ed.* 3s. 6d.
A Text-book of European History for Middle Forms.
THE ANCIENT WORLD. With Maps and Illustrations. *Cr. 8vo.* 3s. 6d.
See also Beginner's Books.

Wilson (Bishop.). See Library of Devotion.

Wilson (A. J.). See Books on Business.

Wilson (H. A.). See Books on Business.

Wilson (J. A.). See Simplified French Texts.

Wilton (Richard), M.A. LYRA PASTORALIS: Songs of Nature, Church, and Home. *Pott 8vo.* 2s. 6d.

Winbolt (S. E.), M.A. EXERCISES IN LATIN ACCIDENCE. *Cr. 8vo.* 1s. 6d.
LATIN HEXAMETER VERSE: An Aid to Composition. *Cr. 8vo.* 3s. 6d. KEY, 5s. net.

Windle (B. C. A.), F.R.S., F.S.A. See Antiquary's Books, Little Guides, Ancient Cities, and School Histories.

Winterbotham (Canon), M.A., B.Sc., LL.B. See Churchman's Library.

Wood (Sir Evelyn), F.M., V.C., G.C.B., G.C.M.G. FROM MIDSHIPMAN TO FIELD-MARSHAL. With 24 Illustrations and Maps. *Two Volumes. Fifth Edition. Demy 8vo.* 25s. net.
A Colonial Edition is also published.

Wood (J. A. E.). See Textbooks of Technology.

Wood (J. Hickory). DAN LENO. Illustrated. *Third Edition. Cr. 8vo.* 6s.
A Colonial Edition is also published.

Wood (W. Birkbeck), M.A., late Scholar of Worcester College, Oxford, and **Edmonds (Major J. E.),** R.E., D.A.Q.-M.G. A HISTORY OF THE CIVIL WAR IN THE UNITED STATES. With an Introduction by H. SPENSER WILKINSON. With 24 Maps and Plans. *Demy 8vo.* 12s. 6d. net.

Wordsworth (Christopher). See Antiquary's Books.

Wordsworth (W.). POEMS BY. Selected by STOPFORD A. BROOKE. With 40 Illustrations by EDMUND H. NEW. With a Frontispiece in Photogravure. *Demy 8vo.* 7s. 6d. net.
A Colonial Edition is also published.

Wordsworth (W.) and Coleridge (S. T.). See Little Library.

Wright (Arthur), D.D., Fellow of Queen's College, Cambridge. See Churchman's Library.

Wright (C. Gordon). See Dante.

Wright (J. C.). TO-DAY. *Demy 16mo.* 1s. 6d. net.

Wright (Sophie). GERMAN VOCABULARIES FOR REPETITION. *Fcap. 8vo.* 1s. 6d.

Wrong (George M.), Professor of History in the University of Toronto. THE EARL OF ELGIN. Illustrated. *Demy 8vo.* 7s. 6d. net.
A Colonial Edition is also published.

Wyatt (Kate M.). See M. R. Gloag.

Wylde (A. B.). MODERN ABYSSINIA. With a Map and a Portrait. *Demy 8vo.* 15*s. net.*
A Colonial Edition is also published.

Wyndham (Rt. Hon. George). M.P. THE POEMS OF WILLIAM SHAKESPEARE. With an Introduction and Notes. *Demy 8vo. Buckram, gilt top.* 10*s 6d.*

Wyon (R.) and **Prance (G.).** THE LAND OF THE BLACK MOUNTAIN. Being a Description of Montenegro. With 40 Illustrations. *Cr. 8vo.* 2*s. 6d. net.*

Yeats (W. B.). A BOOK OF IRISH VERSE. Selected from Modern Writers.

Revised and Enlarged Edition. Cr. 8vo. 3*s. 6d.*

Young (Filson). THE COMPLETE MOTORIST. With 138 Illustrations. *Seventh Edition. Demy 8vo.* 12*s. 6d. net.*
A Colonial Edition is also published.

THE JOY OF THE ROAD: An Appreciation of the Motor Car. *Small Demy 8vo.* 5*s. net.*

Young (T. M.). THE AMERICAN COTTON INDUSTRY: A Study of Work and Workers. *Cr. 8vo. Cloth,* 2*s. 6d. ; paper boards,* 1*s. 6d.*

Zimmern (Antonia). WHAT DO WE KNOW CONCERNING ELECTRICITY? *Fcap. 8vo.* 1*s. 6d. net.*

Ancient Cities

General Editor, B. C. A. WINDLE, D.Sc., F.R.S.

Cr. 8vo. 4*s. 6d. net.*

CHESTER. By B. C. A. Windle, D.Sc. F.R.S. Illustrated by E. H. New.

SHREWSBURY. By T. Auden, M.A., F.S.A. Illustrated.

CANTERBURY. By J. C. Cox, LL.D., F.S.A. Illustrated.

EDINBURGH. By M. G. Williamson, M.A. Illustrated by Herbert Railton.

LINCOLN. By E. Mansel Sympson, M.A., M.D. Illustrated by E. H. New.

BRISTOL. By Alfred Harvey. Illustrated by E. H. New.

DUBLIN. By S. A. O. Fitzpatrick. Illustrated by W. C. Green.

The Antiquary's Books

General Editor, J. CHARLES COX, LL.D., F.S.A.

Demy 8vo. 7*s. 6d. net.*

ENGLISH MONASTIC LIFE. By the Right Rev. Abbot Gasquet, O.S.B. Illustrated. *Third Edition.*

REMAINS OF THE PREHISTORIC AGE IN ENGLAND. By B. C. A. Windle, D.Sc., F.R.S. With numerous Illustrations and Plans.

OLD SERVICE BOOKS OF THE ENGLISH CHURCH. By Christopher Wordsworth, M.A., and Henry Littlehales. With Colored and other Illustrations.

CELTIC ART. By J. Romilly Allen, F.S.A. With numerous Illustrations and Plans.

ARCHÆOLOGY AND FALSE ANTIQUITIES. By R. Munro, LL.D. Illustrated.

SHRINES OF BRITISH SAINTS. By J. C. Wall. With numerous Illustrations and Plans.

THE ROYAL FORESTS OF ENGLAND. By J. C. Cox, LL.D., F.S.A. Illustrated.

THE MANOR AND MANORIAL RECORDS. By Nathaniel J. Hone. Illustrated.

ENGLISH SEALS. By J. Harvey Bloom. Illustrated.

THE DOMESDAY INQUEST. By Adolphus Ballard, B.A., LL.B. With 27 Illustrations.

THE BRASSES OF ENGLAND. By Herbert W. Macklin, M.A. With many Illustrations. *Second Edition.*

PARISH LIFE IN MEDIÆVAL ENGLAND. By the Right Rev. Abbott Gasquet, O.S.B. With many Illustrations. *Second Edition.*

THE BELLS OF ENGLAND. By Canon J. J. Raven, D.D., F.S.A. With Illustrations. *Second Edition.*

The Arden Shakespeare

Demy 8vo. 2*s. 6d. net each volume.*

General Editor, W. J. CRAIG.

An edition of Shakespeare in single Plays. Edited with a full Introduction, Textual Notes, and a Commentary at the foot of the page.

HAMLET. Edited by Edward Dowden.

ROMEO AND JULIET. Edited by Edward Dowden.

KING LEAR. Edited by W. J. Craig.

JULIUS CAESAR. Edited by M. Macmillan.

THE TEMPEST. Edited by Moreton Luce.

[Continued.

ARDEN SHAKESPEARE—*continued*.

OTHELLO. Edited by H. C. Hart.
TITUS ANDRONICUS. Edited by H. B. Baildon.
CYMBELINE. Edited by Edward Dowden.
THE MERRY WIVES OF WINDSOR. Edited by H. C. Hart.
A MIDSUMMER NIGHT'S DREAM. Edited by H. Cuningham.
KING HENRY V. Edited by H. A. Evans.
ALL'S WELL THAT ENDS WELL. Edited by W. O. Brigstocke.
THE TAMING OF THE SHREW. Edited by R. Warwick Bond.
TIMON OF ATHENS. Edited by K. Deighton.
MEASURE FOR MEASURE. Edited by H. C. Hart.
TWELFTH NIGHT. Edited by Moreton Luce.

THE MERCHANT OF VENICE. Edited by C. Knox Pooler.
TROILUS AND CRESSIDA. Edited by K. Deighton.
ANTONY AND CLEOPATRA. Edited by R. H. Case.
LOVE'S LABOUR'S LOST. Edited by H. C. Hart.
THE TWO GENTLEMAN OF VERONA. R, Warwick Bond.
PERICLES. Edited by K. Deighton.
THE COMEDY OF ERRORS. Edited by H. Cuningham.
KING RICHARD III. Edited by A. H. Thompson.
KING JOHN. Edited by Ivor B. John.

The Beginner's Books
Edited by W. WILLIAMSON, B.A.

EASY FRENCH RHYMES. By Henri Blouet. *Second Edition*. Illustrated. *Fcap. 8vo. 1s.*

EASY STORIES FROM ENGLISH HISTORY. By E. M. Wilmot-Buxton, Author of 'Makers of Europe.' *Third Edition. Cr. 8vo. 1s.*

EASY EXERCISES IN ARITHMETIC. Arranged by W. S. Beard. *Second Edition. Fcap.*

8vo. Without Answers, 1s. With Answers. 1s. 3d.

EASY DICTATION AND SPELLING. By W. Williamson, B.A. *Fifth Ed. Fcap. 8vo. 1s.*
AN EASY POETRY BOOK. Selected and arranged by W. Williamson, B.A., Author of 'Dictation Passages.' *Second Edition. Cr. 8vo. 1s.*

Books on Business
Cr. 8vo. 2s. 6d. net.

PORTS AND DOCKS. By Douglas Owen.
RAILWAYS. By E. R. McDermott.
THE STOCK EXCHANGE. By Chas. Duguid. *Second Edition.*
THE BUSINESS OF INSURANCE. By A. J. Wilson.
THE ELECTRICAL INDUSTRY: LIGHTING, TRACTION, AND POWER. By A. G. Whyte, B.Sc.
THE SHIPBUILDING INDUSTRY: Its History, Science, Practice, and Finance. By David Pollock, M.I.N.A.
THE MONEY MARKET. By F. Straker.
THE BUSINESS SIDE OF AGRICULTURE. By A. G. L. Rogers, M.A.
LAW IN BUSINESS. By H. A. Wilson.
THE BREWING INDUSTRY. By Julian L. Baker, F.I.C., F.C.S.

THE AUTOMOBILE INDUSTRY. By G. de H. Stone.
MINING AND MINING INVESTMENTS. By 'A. Moil.'
THE BUSINESS OF ADVERTISING. By Clarence G. Moran, Barrister-at-Law. Illustrated.
TRADE UNIONS. By G. Drage.
CIVIL ENGINEERING. By T. Claxton Fidler, M.Inst. C.E. Illustrated.
THE IRON TRADE OF GREAT BRITAIN. By J. Stephen Jeans. Illustrated.
MONOPOLIES, TRUSTS, AND KARTELLS. By F. W Hirst.
THE COTTON INDUSTRY AND TRADE. By Prof. S. J. Chapman, Dean of the Faculty of Commerce in the University of Manchester. Illustrated.

Byzantine Texts
Edited by J. B. BURY, M.A., Litt.D.

A series of texts of Byzantine Historians, edited by English and foreign scholars.

ZACHARIAH OF MITYLENE. Translated by F. J. Hamilton, D.D., and E. W. Brooks. *Demy 8vo. 12s. 6d. net.*

EVAGRIUS. Edited by Léon Parmentier and M. Bidez. *Demy 8vo. 10s. 6d. net.*

THE HISTORY OF PSELLUS. Edited by C. Sathas. *Demy 8vo. 15s. net.*
ECTHESIS CHRONICA. Edited by Professor Lambros. *Demy 8vo. 7s. 6d. net.*
THE CHRONICLE OF MOREA. Edited by John Schmitt. *Demy 8vo. 15s. net.*

The Churchman's Bible

General Editor, J. H. BURN, B.D., F.R.S.E.

Fcap. 8vo.   1s. 6d. *net each.*

A series of Expositions on the Books of the Bible, which will be of service to the general reader in the practical and devotional study of the Sacred Text.

Each Book is provided with a full and clear Introductory Section, in which is stated what is known or conjectured respecting the date and occasion of the composition of the Book, and any other particulars that may help to elucidate its meaning as a whole. The Exposition is divided into sections of a convenient length, corresponding as far as possible with the divisions of the Church Lectionary. The Translation of the Authorised Version is printed in full, such corrections as are deemed necessary being placed in footnotes.

THE EPISTLE OF ST. PAUL THE APOSTLE TO THE GALATIANS. Edited by A. W. Robinson, M.A. *Second Edition.*

ECCLESIASTES. Edited by A. W. Streane, D.D.

THE EPISTLE OF ST. PAUL THE APOSTLE TO THE PHILIPPIANS. Edited by C. R. D. Biggs, D.D. *Second Edition.*

THE EPISTLE OF ST. JAMES. Edited by H. W. Fulford M.A.

ISAIAH. Edited by W. E. Barnes, D.D. *Two Volumes.* With Map. 2s. *net each.*

THE EPISTLE OF ST. PAUL THE APOSTLE TO THE EPHESIANS. Edited by G. H. Whitaker, M.A.

THE GOSPEL ACCORDING TO ST. MARK. Edited by J. C. Du Buisson, M.A. 2s. 6d. *net.*

ST. PAUL'S EPISTLES TO THE COLOSSIANS AND PHILEMON. Edited by H. J. C. Knight, M.A. 2s. *net.*

The Churchman's Library

General Editor, J. H. BURN, B.D., F.R.S.E.

Crown 8vo.   3s. 6d. *each.*

THE BEGINNINGS OF ENGLISH CHRISTIANITY. By W. E. Collins, M.A. With Map.

THE KINGDOM OF HEAVEN HERE AND HEREAFTER. By Canon Winterbotham, M.A., B.Sc., LL.B.

THE WORKMANSHIP OF THE PRAYER BOOK: Its Literary and Liturgical Aspects. By J. Dowden, D.D. *Second Edition.*

EVOLUTION. By F. B. Jevons, M.A., Litt.D.

SOME NEW TESTAMENT PROBLEMS. By Arthur Wright, D.D. 6s.

THE CHURCHMAN'S INTRODUCTION TO THE OLD TESTAMENT. By A. M. Mackay, B.A.

THE CHURCH OF CHRIST. By E. T. Green, M.A. 6s.

COMPARATIVE THEOLOGY. By J. A. MacCulloch. 6s.

Classical Translations

Edited by H. F. FOX, M.A., Fellow and Tutor of Brasenose College, Oxford.

Crown 8vo.

A series of Translations from the Greek and Latin Classics, distinguished by literary excellence as well as by scholarly accuracy.

ÆSCHYLUS—Agamemnon Choephoroe, Eumenides. Translated by Lewis Campbell, LL.D. 5s.

CICERO—De Oratore I. Translated by E. N. P. Moor, M.A. 3s. 6d.

CICERO—Select Orations (Pro Milone, Pro Mureno, Philippic II., in Catilinam). Translated by H. E. D. Blakiston, M.A. 5s.

CICERO—De Natura Deorum. Translated by F. Brooks, M.A. 3s. 6d.

CICERO—De Officiis. Translated by G. B. Gardiner, M.A. 2s. 6d.

HORACE—The Odes and Epodes. Translated by A. D. Godley, M.A. 2s.

LUCIAN—Six Dialogues (Nigrinus, Icaro-Menippus, The Cock, The Ship, The Parasite, The Lover of Falsehood) Translated by S. T. Irwin, M.A. 3s. 6d.

SOPHOCLES—Electra and Ajax. Translated by E. D. A. Morshead, M.A. 2s. 6d.

TACITUS—Agricola and Germania. Translated by R. B. Townshend. 2s. 6d.

THE SATIRES OF JUVENAL. Translated by S. G. Owen. 2s. 6d.

Classics of Art

Edited by DR. J. H. W. LAING

THE ART OF THE GREEKS. By H. B. Walters. With 112 Plates and 18 Illustrations in the Text. *Wide Royal 8vo.* 12s. 6d. net.

VELAZQUEZ. By A. de Beruete. With 94 Plates. *Wide Royal 8vo.* 10s. 6d. net.

Commercial Series

Edited by H. DE B. GIBBINS, Litt.D., M.A.

Crown 8vo.

COMMERCIAL EDUCATION IN THEORY AND PRACTICE. By E. E. Whitfield, M.A. 5s.
An introduction to Methuen's Commercial Series treating the question of Commercial Education fully from both the point of view of the teacher and of the parent.

BRITISH COMMERCE AND COLONIES FROM ELIZABETH TO VICTORIA. By H. de B. Gibbins, Litt.D., M.A. *Third Edition.* 2s.

COMMERCIAL EXAMINATION PAPERS. By H. de B. Gibbins, Litt.D., M.A. 1s. 6d.

THE ECONOMICS OF COMMERCE. By H. de B. Gibbins, Litt.D., M.A. *Second Edition.* 1s. 6d.

A GERMAN COMMERCIAL READER. By S. E. Bally. With Vocabulary. 2s.

A COMMERCIAL GEOGRAPHY OF THE BRITISH EMPIRE. By L. W. Lyde, M.A. *Sixth Edition.* 2s.

A COMMERCIAL GEOGRAPHY OF FOREIGN NATIONS. By F. C. Boon, B.A. 2s.

A PRIMER OF BUSINESS. By S. Jackson, M.A. *Third Edition.* 1s. 6d.

COMMERCIAL ARITHMETIC. By F. G. Taylor, M.A. *Fourth Edition.* 1s. 6d.

FRENCH COMMERCIAL CORRESPONDENCE. By S. E. Bally. With Vocabulary. *Third Edition.* 2s.

GERMAN COMMERCIAL CORRESPONDENCE. By S. E. Bally. With Vocabulary. *Second Edition.* 2s. 6d.

A FRENCH COMMERCIAL READER. By S. E. Bally. With Vocabulary. *Second Edition.* 2s.

PRECIS WRITING AND OFFICE CORRESPONDENCE. By E. E. Whitfield, M.A. *Second Edition.* 2s.

A GUIDE TO PROFESSIONS AND BUSINESS. By H. Jones. 1s. 6d.

THE PRINCIPLES OF BOOK-KEEPING BY DOUBLE ENTRY. By J. E. B. M'Allen, M.A. 2s.

COMMERCIAL LAW. By W. Douglas Edwards. *Second Edition.* 2s.

The Connoisseur's Library

Wide Royal 8vo. 25s. net.

A sumptuous series of 20 books on art, written by experts for collectors, superbly illustrated in photogravure, collotype, and colour. The technical side of the art is duly treated. The first volumes are—

MEZZOTINTS. By Cyril Davenport. With 40 Plates in Photogravure.

PORCELAIN. By Edward Dillon. With 19 Plates in Colour, 20 in Collotype, and 5 in Photogravure.

MINIATURES. By Dudley Heath. With 9 Plates in Colour, 15 in Collotype, and 15 in Photogravure.

IVORIES. By A. Maskell. With 80 Plates in Collotype and Photogravure.

ENGLISH FURNITURE. By F. S. Robinson. With 160 Plates in Collotype and one in Photogravure. *Second Edition.*

EUROPEAN ENAMELS. By Henry H. Cunynghame, C.B. With 54 Plates in Collotype and Half-tone and 4 Plates in Colour.

GOLDSMITHS' AND SILVERSMITHS' WORK. By Nelson Dawson. With many Plates in Collotype and a Frontispiece in Photogravure. *Second Edition.*

ENGLISH COLOURED BOOKS. By Martin Hardie. With 28 Illustrations in Colour and Collotype.

GLASS. By Edward Dillon. With 37 Illustrations in Collotype and 12 in Colour.

The Library of Devotion

With Introductions and (where necessary) Notes.

Small Pott 8vo, cloth, 2s. ; leather, 2s. 6d. net.

THE CONFESSIONS OF ST. AUGUSTINE. Edited by C. Bigg, D.D. *Sixth Edition.*

THE CHRISTIAN YEAR. Edited by Walter Lock, D.D. *Third Edition.*

THE IMITATION OF CHRIST. Edited by C. Bigg, D.D. *Fourth Edition.*

A BOOK OF DEVOTIONS. Edited by J. W. Stanbridge. B.D. *Second Edition.*

[*Continued.*

THE LIBRARY OF DEVOTION—*continued.*

LYRA INNOCENTIUM. Edited by Walter Lock, D.D.

A SERIOUS CALL TO A DEVOUT AND HOLY LIFE. Edited by C. Bigg, D.D. *Fourth Edition.*

THE TEMPLE. Edited by E. C. S. Gibson, D.D. *Second Edition.*

A GUIDE TO ETERNITY. Edited by J. W. Stanbridge, B.D.

THE PSALMS OF DAVID. Edited by B. W. Randolph, D.D.

LYRA APOSTOLICA. By Cardinal Newman and others. Edited by Canon Scott Holland and Canon H. C. Beeching, M.A.

THE INNER WAY. By J. Tauler. Edited by A. W. Hutton, M.A.

THE THOUGHTS OF PASCAL. Edited by C. S. Jerram, M.A.

ON THE LOVE OF GOD. By St. Francis de Sales. Edited by W. J. Knox-Little, M.A.

A MANUAL OF CONSOLATION FROM THE SAINTS AND FATHERS. Edited by J. H. Burn, B.D.

THE SONG OF SONGS. Edited by B. Blaxland, M.A.

THE DEVOTIONS OF ST. ANSELM. Edited by C. C. J. Webb, M.A.

GRACE ABOUNDING. By John Bunyan. Edited by S. C. Freer, M.A.

BISHOP WILSON'S SACRA PRIVATA. Edited by A. E. Burn, B.D.

LYRA SACRA : A Book of Sacred Verse. Edited by H. C. Beeching, M.A., Canon of Westminster.

A DAY BOOK FROM THE SAINTS AND FATHERS. Edited by J. H. Burn, B.D.

HEAVENLY WISDOM. A Selection from the English Mystics. Edited by E. C. Gregory.

LIGHT, LIFE, and LOVE. A Selection from the German Mystics. Edited by W. R. Inge, M.A.

AN INTRODUCTION TO THE DEVOUT LIFE. By St. Francis de Sales. Translated and Edited by T. Barns, M.A.

MANCHESTER AL MONDO : a Contemplation of Death and Immortality. By Henry Montagu, Earl of Manchester. With an Introduction by Elizabeth Waterhouse, Editor of 'A Little Book of Life and Death.'

THE LITTLE FLOWERS OF THE GLORIOUS MESSER ST. FRANCIS AND OF HIS FRIARS. Done into English by W. Heywood. With an Introduction by A. G. Ferrers Howell.

THE SPIRITUAL GUIDE, which Disentangles the Soul and brings it by the Inward Way to the Fruition of Perfect Contemplation, and the Rich Treasure of Internal Peace. Written by Dr. Michael de Molinos, Priest. Translated from the Italian copy, printed at Venice, 1685. Edited with an Introduction by Kathleen Lyttelton. With a Preface by Canon Scott Holland.

The Illustrated Pocket Library of Plain and Coloured Books

Fcap 8vo.   3s. 6d. net each volume.

A series, in small form, of some of the famous illustrated books of fiction and general literature. These are faithfully reprinted from the first or best editions without introduction or notes. The Illustrations are chiefly in colour.

COLOURED BOOKS

OLD COLOURED BOOKS. By George Paston. With 16 Coloured Plates. *Fcap. 8vo. 2s. net.*

THE LIFE AND DEATH OF JOHN MYTTON, ESQ. By Nimrod. With 18 Coloured Plates by Henry Alken and T. J. Rawlins. *Fourth Edition.*

THE LIFE OF A SPORTSMAN. By Nimrod. With 35 Coloured Plates by Henry Alken.

HANDLEY CROSS. By R. S. Surtees. With 17 Coloured Plates and 100 Woodcuts in the Text by John Leech. *Second Edition.*

MR. SPONGE'S SPORTING TOUR. By R. S. Surtees. With 13 Coloured Plates and 90 Woodcuts in the Text by John Leech.

JORROCKS' JAUNTS AND JOLLITIES. By R. S. Surtees. With 15 Coloured Plates by H. Alken. *Second Edition.*

This volume is reprinted from the extremely rare and costly edition of 1843, which contains Alken's very fine illustrations instead of the usual ones by Phiz.

ASK MAMMA. By R. S. Surtees. With 13 Coloured Plates and 70 Woodcuts in the Text by John Leech.

THE ANALYSIS OF THE HUNTING FIELD. By R. S. Surtees. With 7 Coloured Plates by Henry Alken, and 43 Illustrations on Wood.

THE TOUR OF DR. SYNTAX IN SEARCH OF THE PICTURESQUE. By William Combe. With 30 Coloured Plates by T. Rowlandson.

THE TOUR OF DOCTOR SYNTAX IN SEARCH OF CONSOLATION. By William Combe. With 24 Coloured Plates by T. Rowlandson.

THE THIRD TOUR OF DOCTOR SYNTAX IN SEARCH OF A WIFE. By William Combe. With 24 Coloured Plates by T. Rowlandson.

THE HISTORY OF JOHNNY QUAE GENUS : the Little Foundling of the late Dr. Syntax. By the Author of 'The Three Tours.' With 24 Coloured Plates by Rowlandson.

THE ENGLISH DANCE OF DEATH, from the Designs of T. Rowlandson, with Metrical Illustrations by the Author of 'Doctor Syntax.' *Two Volumes.*

This book contains 76 Coloured Plates.

THE DANCE OF LIFE : A Poem. By the Author of 'Doctor Syntax.' Illustrated with 26 Coloured Engravings by T. Rowlandson.

[*Continued.*

LIFE IN LONDON: or, the Day and Night Scenes of Jerry Hawthorn, Esq., and his Elegant Friend, Corinthian Tom. By Pierce Egan. With 36 Coloured Plates by I. R. and G. Cruikshank. With numerous Designs on Wood.

REAL LIFE IN LONDON: or, the Rambles and Adventures of Bob Tallyho, Esq., and his Cousin, The Hon. Tom Dashall. By an Amateur (Pierce Egan). With 31 Coloured Plates by Alken and Rowlandson, etc. *Two Volumes.*

THE LIFE OF AN ACTOR. By Pierce Egan. With 27 Coloured Plates by Theodore Lane, and several Designs on Wood.

THE VICAR OF WAKEFIELD. By Oliver Goldsmith. With 24 Coloured Plates by T. Rowlandson.

THE MILITARY ADVENTURES OF JOHNNY NEWCOME. By an Officer. With 15 Coloured Plates by T. Rowlandson.

THE NATIONAL SPORTS OF GREAT BRITAIN. With Descriptions and 51 Coloured Plates by Henry Alken.

This book is completely different from the large folio edition of 'National Sports' by the same artist, and none of the plates are similar.

THE ADVENTURES OF A POST CAPTAIN. By A Naval Officer. With 24 Coloured Plates by Mr. Williams.

GAMONIA: or, the Art of Preserving Game; and an Improved Method of making Plantations and Covers, explained and illustrated by Lawrence Rawstorne, Esq. With 15 Coloured Plates by T. Rawlins.

AN ACADEMY FOR GROWN HORSEMEN: Containing the completest Instructions for Walking, Trotting, Cantering, Galloping, Stumbling, and Tumbling. Illustrated with 27 Coloured Plates, and adorned with a Portrait of the Author. By Geoffrey Gambado, Esq.

REAL LIFE IN IRELAND, or, the Day and Night Scenes of Brian Boru, Esq., and his Elegant Friend, Sir Shawn O'Dogherty. By a Real Paddy. With 19 Coloured Plates by Heath, Marks, etc.

THE ADVENTURES OF JOHNNY NEWCOME IN THE NAVY. By Alfred Burton. With 16 Coloured Plates by T. Rowlandson.

THE OLD ENGLISH SQUIRE: A Poem. By John Careless, Esq. With 20 Coloured Plates after the style of T. Rowlandson.

PLAIN BOOKS

THE GRAVE: A Poem. By Robert Blair. Illustrated by 12 Etchings executed by Louis Schiavonetti from the original Inventions of William Blake. With an Engraved Title Page and a Portrait of Blake by T. Phillips, R.A.

The illustrations are reproduced in photogravure.

ILLUSTRATIONS OF THE BOOK OF JOB. Invented and engraved by William Blake.

These famous Illustrations—21 in number —are reproduced in photogravure.

ÆSOP'S FABLES. With 380 Woodcuts by Thomas Bewick.

WINDSOR CASTLE. By W. Harrison Ainsworth. With 22 Plates and 87 Woodcuts in the Text by George Cruikshank.

THE TOWER OF LONDON. By W. Harrison Ainsworth. With 40 Plates and 58 Woodcuts in the Text by George Cruikshank.

FRANK FAIRLEGH. By F. E. Smedley. With 30 Plates by George Cruikshank.

HANDY ANDY. By Samuel Lover. With 24 Illustrations by the Author.

THE COMPLEAT ANGLER. By Izaak Walton and Charles Cotton. With 14 Plates and 77 Woodcuts to the Text.

This volume is reproduced from the beautiful edition of John Major of 1824.

THE PICKWICK PAPERS. By Charles Dickens. With the 43 Illustrations by Seymour and Phiz, the two Buss Plates, and the 32 Contemporary Onwhyn Plates.

Junior Examination Series

Edited by A. M. M. STEDMAN, M.A. *Fcap. 8vo.* 1s.

JUNIOR FRENCH EXAMINATION PAPERS. By F. Jacob, M.A. *Second Edition.*

JUNIOR LATIN EXAMINATION PAPERS. By C. G. Botting, B.A. *Fourth Edition.*

JUNIOR ENGLISH EXAMINATION PAPERS. By W. Williamson, B.A.

JUNIOR ARITHMETIC EXAMINATION PAPERS. By W. S. Beard. *Fourth Edition.*

JUNIOR ALGEBRA EXAMINATION PAPERS. By S. W. Finn, M.A.

JUNIOR GREEK EXAMINATION PAPERS. By T. C. Weatherhead, M.A.

JUNIOR GENERAL INFORMATION EXAMINATION PAPERS. By W. S. Beard.

A KEY TO THE ABOVE. 3s. 6d. *net.*

JUNIOR GEOGRAPHY EXAMINATION PAPERS. By W. G. Baker, M.A.

JUNIOR GERMAN EXAMINATION PAPERS. By A. Voegelin, M.A.

Junior School-Books

Edited by O. D. INSKIP, LL.D., and W. WILLIAMSON, B.A.

A CLASS-BOOK OF DICTATION PASSAGES. By W. Williamson, B.A. *Thirteenth Edition.* *Cr. 8vo. 1s. 6d.*

THE GOSPEL ACCORDING TO ST. MATTHEW. Edited by E. Wilton South, M.A. With Three Maps. *Cr. 8vo. 1s. 6d.*

THE GOSPEL ACCORDING TO ST. MARK. Edited by A. E. Rubie, D.D. With Three Maps. *Cr. 8vo. 1s. 6d.*

A JUNIOR ENGLISH GRAMMAR. By W. Williamson, B.A. With numerous passages for parsing and analysis, and a chapter on Essay Writing. *Third Edition. Cr. 8vo. 2s.*

A JUNIOR CHEMISTRY. By E. A. Tyler, B.A., F.C.S. With 78 Illustrations. *Fourth Edition. Cr. 8vo. 2s. 6d.*

THE ACTS OF THE APOSTLES. Edited by A. E. Rubie, D.D. *Cr. 8vo. 2s.*

A JUNIOR FRENCH GRAMMAR. By L. A. Sornet and M. J. Acatos. *Second Edition. Cr. 8vo. 2s.*

ELEMENTARY EXPERIMENTAL SCIENCE. PHYSICS by W. T. Clough, A.R.C.S. CHEMISTRY by A. E. Dunstan, B.Sc. With 2 Plates and 154 Diagrams. *Fifth Edition. Cr. 8vo. 2s. 6d.*

A JUNIOR GEOMETRY. By Noel S. Lydon. With 276 Diagrams. *Fifth Edition. Cr. 8vo. 2s.*

ELEMENTARY EXPERIMENTAL CHEMISTRY. By A. E. Dunstan, B.Sc. With 4 Plates and 109 Diagrams. *Second Edition. Cr. 8vo. 2s.*

A JUNIOR FRENCH PROSE. By R. R. N. Baron, M.A. *Second Edition. Cr. 8vo. 2s.*

THE GOSPEL ACCORDING TO ST. LUKE. With an Introduction and Notes by William Williamson, B.A. With Three Maps. *Cr. 8vo. 2s.*

THE FIRST BOOK OF KINGS. Edited by A. E. Rubie, D.D. With Maps. *Cr. 8vo. 2s.*

Leaders of Religion

Edited by H. C. BEECHING, M.A., Canon of Westminster.   *With Portraits.*

Cr. 8vo.   2s. net.

CARDINAL NEWMAN. By R. H. Hutton.

JOHN WESLEY. By J. H. Overton, M.A.

BISHOP WILBERFORCE. By G. W. Daniell, M.A.

CARDINAL MANNING. By A. W. Hutton, M.A.

CHARLES SIMEON. By H. C. G. Moule, D.D.

JOHN KEBLE. By Walter Lock, D.D.

THOMAS CHALMERS. By Mrs. Oliphant.

LANCELOT ANDREWES. By R. L. Ottley, D.D. *Second Edition.*

AUGUSTINE OF CANTERBURY. By E. L. Cutts, D.D.

WILLIAM LAUD. By W. H. Hutton, M.A. *Third Edition.*

JOHN KNOX. By F. MacCunn. *Second Edition.*

JOHN HOWE. By R. F. Horton, D.D.

BISHOP KEN. By F. A. Clarke, M.A.

GEORGE FOX, THE QUAKER. By T. Hodgkin, D.C.L. *Third Edition.*

JOHN DONNE. By Augustus Jessopp, D.D.

THOMAS CRANMER. By A. J. Mason, D.D.

BISHOP LATIMER. By R. M. Carlyle and A. J. Carlyle, M.A.

BISHOP BUTLER. By W. A. Spooner, M.A.

Little Books on Art

With many Illustrations.   Demy 16mo.   2s. 6d. net.

A series of monographs in miniature, containing the complete outline of the subject under treatment and rejecting minute details. These books are produced with the greatest care. Each volume consists of about 200 pages, and contains from 30 to 40 illustrations, including a frontispiece in photogravure.

GREEK ART. H. B. Walters. *Third Edition.*

BOOKPLATES. E. Almack.

REYNOLDS. J. Sime. *Second Edition.*

ROMNEY. George Paston.

GREUZE AND BOUCHER. Eliza F. Pollard.

VANDYCK. M. G. Smallwood.

TURNER. Frances Tyrrell-Gill.

DÜRER. Jessie Allen.

HOPPNER. H. P. K. Skipton.

HOLBEIN. Mrs. G. Fortescue.

WATTS. R. E. D. Sketchley.

LEIGHTON. Alice Corkran.

VELASQUEZ. Wilfrid Wilberforce and A. R. Gilbert.

COROT. Alice Pollard and Ethel Birnstingl.

RAPHAEL. A. R. Dryhurst.

MILLET. Netta Peacock.

ILLUMINATED MSS. J. W. Bradley.

CHRIST IN ART. Mrs. Henry Jenner.

JEWELLERY. Cyril Davenport.

[Continued.

LITTLE BOOKS ON ART—*continued.*

BURNE-JONES. Fortunée de Lisle. *Second Edition.*
REMBRANDT. Mrs. E. A. Sharp.

CLAUDE. Edward Dillon.
THE ARTS OF JAPAN. Edward Dillon.
ENAMELS. Mrs. Nelson Dawson.

The Little Galleries

Demy 16mo. 2s. 6d. net.

A series of little books containing examples of the best work of the great painters. Each volume contains 20 plates in photogravure, together with a short outline of the life and work of the master to whom the book is devoted.

A LITTLE GALLERY OF REYNOLDS.
A LITTLE GALLERY OF ROMNEY.
A LITTLE GALLERY OF HOPPNER.

A LITTLE GALLERY OF MILLAIS.
A LITTLE GALLERY OF ENGLISH POETS.

The Little Guides

With many Illustrations by E. H. NEW and other artists, and from photographs.

Small Pott 8vo, cloth, 2s. 6d. net.; leather, 3s. 6d. net.

Messrs. METHUEN are publishing a small series of books under the general title of THE LITTLE GUIDES. The main features of these books are (1) a handy and charming form, (2) artistic Illustrations by E. H. NEW and others, (3) good plans and maps, (4) an adequate but compact presentation of everything that is interesting in the natural features, history, archæology, and architecture of the town or district treated.

CAMBRIDGE AND ITS COLLEGES. By A. Hamilton Thompson. *Second Edition.*
OXFORD AND ITS COLLEGES. By J. Wells, M.A. *Seventh Edition.*
ST. PAUL'S CATHEDRAL. By George Clinch.
WESTMINSTER ABBEY. By G. E. Troutbeck.

THE ENGLISH LAKES. By F. G. Brabant, M.A.
THE MALVERN COUNTRY. By B. C. A. Windle, D.Sc., F.R.S.
SHAKESPEARE'S COUNTRY. By B. C. A. Windle, D.Sc., F.R.S. *Third Edition.*

BUCKINGHAMSHIRE. By E. S. Roscoe.
CHESHIRE. By W. M. Gallichan.
CORNWALL. By A. L. Salmon.
DERBYSHIRE. By J. Charles Cox, LL.D., F.S.A.
DEVON. By S. Baring-Gould.
DORSET. By Frank R. Heath.
HAMPSHIRE. By J. Charles Cox, LL.D., F.S.A.

HERTFORDSHIRE. By H. W. Tompkins, F.R.H.S.
THE ISLE OF WIGHT. By G. Clinch.
KENT. By G. Clinch.
KERRY. By C. P. Crane.
MIDDLESEX. By John B. Firth.
NORTHAMPTONSHIRE. By Wakeling Dry.
NORFOLK. By W. A. Dutt.
OXFORDSHIRE. By F. G. Brabant, M.A.
SUFFOLK. By W. A. Dutt.
SURREY. By F. A. H. Lambert.
SUSSEX. By F. G. Brabant, M.A. *Second Edition.*
THE EAST RIDING OF YORKSHIRE. By J. E. Morris.
THE NORTH RIDING OF YORKSHIRE. By J. E. Morris.

BRITTANY. By S. Baring-Gould.
NORMANDY. By C. Scudamore.
ROME By C. G. Ellaby.
SICILY. By F. Hamilton Jackson.

The Little Library

With Introductions, Notes, and Photogravure Frontispieces.

Small Pott 8vo. Each Volume, cloth, 1s. 6d. net; leather, 2s. 6d. net.

Anon. ENGLISH LYRICS, A LITTLE BOOK OF.
Austen (Jane). PRIDE AND PREJUDICE. Edited by E. V. Lucas. *Two Vols.*

NORTHANGER ABBEY. Edited by E. V. Lucas.
Bacon (Francis). THE ESSAYS OF LORD BACON. Edited by EDWARD WRIGHT.

[Continued.

THE LITTLE LIBRARY—*continued.*

Barham (R. H.). THE INGOLDSBY LEGENDS. Edited by J. B. ATLAY. *Two Volumes.*

Barnett (Mrs. P. A.). A LITTLE BOOK OF ENGLISH PROSE.

Beckford (William). THE HISTORY OF THE CALIPH VATHEK. Edited by E. DENISON ROSS.

Blake (William). SELECTIONS FROM WILLIAM BLAKE. Edited by M. PERUGINI.

Borrow (George). LAVENGRO. Edited by F. HINDES GROOME. *Two Volumes.*

THE ROMANY RYE. Edited by JOHN SAMPSON.

Browning (Robert). SELECTIONS FROM THE EARLY POEMS OF ROBERT BROWNING. Edited by W. HALL GRIFFIN, M.A.

Canning (George). SELECTIONS FROM THE ANTI-JACOBIN: with GEORGE CANNING's additional Poems. Edited by LLOYD SANDERS.

Cowley (Abraham). THE ESSAYS OF ABRAHAM COWLEY. Edited by H. C. MINCHIN.

Crabbe (George). SELECTIONS FROM GEORGE CRABBE. Edited by A. C. DEANE.

Craik (Mrs.). JOHN HALIFAX, GENTLEMAN. Edited by ANNE MATHESON. *Two Volumes.*

Crashaw (Richard). THE ENGLISH POEMS OF RICHARD CRASHAW. Edited by EDWARD HUTTON.

Dante (Alighieri). THE INFERNO OF DANTE. Translated by H. F. CARY. Edited by PAGET TOYNBEE, M.A., D.Litt.

THE PURGATORIO OF DANTE. Translated by H. F. CARY. Edited by PAGET TOYNBEE, M.A., D.Litt.

THE PARADISO OF DANTE. Translated by H. F. CARY. Edited by PAGET TOYNBEE, M.A., D.Litt.

Darley (George). SELECTIONS FROM THE POEMS OF GEORGE DARLEY. Edited by R. A. STREATFEILD.

Deane (A. C.). A LITTLE BOOK OF LIGHT VERSE.

Dickens (Charles). CHRISTMAS BOOKS. *Two Volumes.*

Ferrier (Susan). MARRIAGE. Edited by A. GOODRICH - FREER and LORD IDDESLEIGH. *Two Volumes.*

THE INHERITANCE. *Two Volumes.*

Gaskell (Mrs.). CRANFORD. Edited by E. V. LUCAS. *Second Edition.*

Hawthorne (Nathaniel). THE SCARLET LETTER. Edited by PERCY DEARMER.

Henderson (T. F.). A LITTLE BOOK OF SCOTTISH VERSE.

Keats (John). POEMS. With an Introduction by L. BINYON, and Notes by J. MASEFIELD.

Kinglake (A. W.). EOTHEN. With an Introduction and Notes. *Second Edition.*

Lamb (Charles). ELIA, AND THE LAST ESSAYS OF ELIA. Edited by E. V. LUCAS.

Locker (F.). LONDON LYRICS. Edited by A. D. GODLEY, M.A. A reprint of the First Edition.

Longfellow (H. W.). SELECTIONS FROM LONGFELLOW. Edited by L. M. FAITHFULL.

Marvell (Andrew). THE POEMS OF ANDREW MARVELL. Edited by E. WRIGHT.

Milton (John). THE MINOR POEMS OF JOHN MILTON. Edited by H. C. BEECHING, M.A., Canon of Westminster.

Moir (D. M.). MANSIE WAUCH. Edited by T. F. HENDERSON.

Nichols (J. B. B.). A LITTLE BOOK OF ENGLISH SONNETS.

Rochefoucauld (La). THE MAXIMS OF LA ROCHEFOUCAULD. Translated by Dean STANHOPE. Edited by G. H. POWELL.

Smith (Horace and James). REJECTED ADDRESSES. Edited by A. D. GODLEY, M.A.

Sterne (Laurence). A SENTIMENTAL JOURNEY. Edited by H. W. PAUL.

Tennyson (Alfred, Lord). THE EARLY POEMS OF ALFRED, LORD TENNYSON. Edited by J. CHURTON COLLINS, M.A.

IN MEMORIAM. Edited by H. C. BEECHING, M.A.

THE PRINCESS. Edited by ELIZABETH WORDSWORTH.

MAUD. Edited by ELIZABETH WORDSWORTH.

Thackeray (W. M.). VANITY FAIR. Edited by S. GWYNN. *Three Volumes.*

PENDENNIS. Edited by S. GWYNN. *Three Volumes.*

ESMOND. Edited by S. GWYNN.

CHRISTMAS BOOKS. Edited by S. GWYNN.

Vaughan (Henry). THE POEMS OF HENRY VAUGHAN. Edited by EDWARD HUTTON.

Walton (Izaak). THE COMPLEAT ANGLER. Edited by J. BUCHAN.

Waterhouse (Mrs. Alfred). A LITTLE BOOK OF LIFE AND DEATH. Edited by. *Tenth Edition.*

Also on Japanese Paper. *Leather.* 5s. *net.*

Wordsworth (W.). SELECTIONS FROM WORDSWORTH. Edited by NOWELL C. SMITH.

Wordsworth (W.) and Coleridge (S. T.). LYRICAL BALLADS. Edited by GEORGE SAMPSON.

The Little Quarto Shakespeare

Edited by W. J. CRAIG. With Introductions and Notes

Pott 16mo. In 40 Volumes. Leather, price 1s. net each volume. Mahogany Revolving Book Case. 10s. net.

Miniature Library

Reprints in miniature of a few interesting books which have qualities of humanity, devotion, or literary genius.

EUPHRANOR: A Dialogue on Youth. By Edward FitzGerald. From the edition published by W. Pickering in 1851. *Demy 32mo. Leather, 2s. net.*

POLONIUS: or Wise Saws and Modern Instances. By Edward FitzGerald. From the edition published by W. Pickering in 1852. *Demy 32mo. Leather, 2s. net.*

THE RUBÁIYÁT OF OMAR KHAYYÁM. By Edward FitzGerald. From the 1st edition of 1859, *Fourth Edition. Leather, 1s. net.*

THE LIFE OF EDWARD, LORD HERBERT OF CHERBURY. Written by himself. From the edition printed at Strawberry Hill in the year 1764. *Demy 32mo. Leather, 2s. net.*

THE VISIONS OF DOM FRANCISCO QUEVEDO VILLEGAS, Knight of the Order of St. James. Made English by R. L. From the edition printed for H. Herringman, 1668. *Leather. 2s. net.*

POEMS. By Dora Greenwell. From the edition of 1848. *Leather, 2s. net.*

Oxford Biographies

Fcap. 8vo. Each volume, cloth, 2s. 6d. net ; leather, 3s. 6d. net.

DANTE ALIGHIERI. By Paget Toynbee, M.A., D.Litt. With 12 Illustrations. *Second Edition.*

SAVONAROLA. By E. L. S. Horsburgh, M.A. With 12 Illustrations. *Second Edition.*

JOHN HOWARD. By E. C. S. Gibson, D.D., Bishop of Gloucester. With 12 Illustrations.

TENNYSON. By A. C. BENSON, M.A. With 9 Illustrations.

WALTER RALEIGH. By I. A. Taylor. With 12 Illustrations.

ERASMUS. By E. F. H. Capey. With 12 Illustrations.

THE YOUNG PRETENDER. By C. S. Terry. With 12 Illustrations.

ROBERT BURNS. By T. F. Henderson. With 12 Illustrations.

CHATHAM. By A. S. M'Dowall. With 12 Illustrations.

ST. FRANCIS OF ASSISI. By Anna M. Stoddart. With 16 Illustrations.

CANNING. By W. Alison Phillips. With 12 Illustrations.

BEACONSFIELD. By Walter Sichel. With 12 Illustrations.

GOETHE. By H. G. Atkins. With 12 Illustrations.

FENELON. By Viscount St Cyres. With 12 Illustrations.

School Examination Series

Edited by A. M. M. STEDMAN, M.A. *Cr. 8vo. 2s. 6d.*

FRENCH EXAMINATION PAPERS. By A. M. M. Stedman, M.A. *Fourteenth Edition.* A KEY, issued to Tutors and Private Students only to be had on application to the Publishers. *Fifth Edition. Crown 8vo. 6s. net.*

LATIN EXAMINATION PAPERS. By A. M. M. Stedman, M.A. *Thirteenth Edition.* KEY (*Sixth Edition*) issued as above. 6s. net.

GREEK EXAMINATION PAPERS. By A. M. M. Stedman, M.A. *Ninth Edition.* KEY (*Fourth Edition*) issued as above. 6s. net.

GERMAN EXAMINATION PAPERS. By R. J. Morich. *Sixth Edition.*

KEY (*Third Edition*) issued as above. 6s. net.

HISTORY AND GEOGRAPHY EXAMINATION PAPERS. By C. H. Spence, M.A. *Third Edition.*

PHYSICS EXAMINATION PAPERS. By R. E. Steel, M.A., F.C.S.

GENERAL KNOWLEDGE EXAMINATION PAPERS. By A. M. M. Stedman, M.A. *Sixth Edition.* KEY (*Fourth Edition*) issued as above. 7s. net.

EXAMINATION PAPERS IN ENGLISH HISTORY. By J. Tait Plowden-Wardlaw, B.A.

School Histories

Illustrated. Crown 8vo. 1s. 6d.

A SCHOOL HISTORY OF WARWICKSHIRE. By
B. C. A. Windle, D.Sc., F.R.S.
A SCHOOL HISTORY OF SOMERSET. By
Walter Raymond. *Second Edition.*
A SCHOOL HISTORY OF LANCASHIRE. by
W. E. Rhodes.

A SCHOOL HISTORY OF SURREY. By H. E.
Malden, M.A.

A SCHOOL HISTORY OF MIDDLESEX. By V.
G. Plarr and F. W. Walton.

Textbooks of Science

Edited by G. F. GOODCHILD, M.A., B.Sc., and G. R. MILLS, M.A.

PRACTICAL MECHANICS. By Sidney H. Wells.
Fourth Edition. Cr. 8vo. 3s. 6d.
PRACTICAL CHEMISTRY. Part I. By W.
French, M.A. *Cr. 8vo. Fourth Edition.*
1s. 6d. Part II. By W. French, M.A., and
T. H. Boardman, M.A. *Cr. 8vo.* 1s. 6d.
TECHNICAL ARITHMETIC AND GEOMETRY.
By C. T. Millis, M.I.M.E. *Cr. 8vo.*
3s. 6d.
EXAMPLES IN PHYSICS. By C. E. Jackson,
B.A. *Cr. 8vo.* 2s. 6d.
PLANT LIFE, Studies in Garden and School.
By Horace F. Jones, F.C.S. With 320
Diagrams. *Cr. 8vo.* 3s. 6d.

THE COMPLETE SCHOOL CHEMISTRY. By F.
M. Oldham, B.A. With 126 Illustrations.
Cr. 8vo.

AN ORGANIC CHEMISTRY FOR SCHOOLS AND
TECHNICAL INSTITUTES. By A. E. Dunstan,
B.Sc. (Lond.), F.C.S. Illustrated.
Cr. 8vo.

ELEMENTARY SCIENCE FOR PUPIL TEACHERS.
PHYSICS SECTION. By W. T. Clough,
A.R.C.S. (Lond.), F.C.S. CHEMISTRY
SECTION. By A. E. Dunstan, B.Sc. (Lond.),
F.C.S. With 2 Plates and 10 Diagrams.
Cr. 8vo. 2s.

Methuen's Simplified French Texts

Edited by T. R. N. CROFTS, M.A.

One Shilling each.

L'HISTOIRE D'UNE TULIPE. Adapted by T. R.
N. Crofts, M.A. *Second Edition.*
ABDALLAH. Adapted by J. A. Wilson.

LA CHANSON DE ROLAND. Adapted by H.
Rieu, M.A.
MÉMOIRES DE CADICHON. Adapted by J. F.
Rhoades.

Methuen's Standard Library

In Sixpenny Volumes.

THE STANDARD LIBRARY is a new series of volumes containing the great classics of the
world, and particularly the finest works of English literature. All the great masters will be
represented, either in complete works or in selections. It is the ambition of the publishers to
place the best books of the Anglo-Saxon race within the reach of every reader, so that the
series may represent something of the diversity and splendour of our English tongue. The
characteristics of THE STANDARD LIBRARY are four :—1. SOUNDNESS OF TEXT. 2. CHEAPNESS.
3. CLEARNESS OF TYPE. 4. SIMPLICITY. The books are well printed on good paper at a
price which on the whole is without parallel in the history of publishing. Each volume contains from 100 to 250 pages, and is issued in paper covers, Crown 8vo, at Sixpence net, or in
cloth gilt at One Shilling net. In a few cases long books are issued as Double Volumes
or as Treble Volumes.

THE MEDITATIONS OF MARCUS AURELIUS.
The translation is by R. Graves.

SENSE AND SENSIBILITY. By Jane Austen.

ESSAYS AND COUNSELS and THE NEW
ATLANTIS. By Francis Bacon, Lord
Verulam.

RELIGIO MEDICI and URN BURIAL. By
Sir Thomas Browne. The text has been
collated by A. R. Waller.

THE PILGRIM'S PROGRESS. By John Bunyan.

REFLECTIONS ON THE FRENCH REVOLUTION.
By Edmund Burke.

THE POEMS AND SONGS OF ROBERT BURNS.
Double Volume.

THE ANALOGY OF RELIGION, NATURAL AND
REVEALED. By Joseph Butler, D.D.

THE POEMS OF THOMAS CHATTERTON. In 2
volumes.
Vol. I.—Miscellaneous Poems.

[Continued.

METHUEN'S STANDARD LIBRARY—*continued.*

Vol. II.—The Rowley Poems.

THE NEW LIFE AND SONNETS. By Dante. Translated into English by D. G. Rossetti.

TOM JONES. By Henry Fielding. Treble Vol.

CRANFORD. By Mrs. Gaskell.

THE HISTORY OF THE DECLINE AND FALL OF THE ROMAN EMPIRE. By Edward Gibbon. In 7 double volumes.

The Text and Notes have been revised by J. B. Bury, Litt.D., but the Appendices of the more expensive edition are not given.

THE VICAR OF WAKEFIELD. By Oliver Goldsmith.

THE POEMS AND PLAYS OF OLIVER GOLDSMITH.

THE WORKS OF BEN JONSON.

VOL. I.—The Case is Altered. Every Man in His Humour. Every Man out of His Humour.

Vol. II.—Cynthia's Revels; The Poetaster. The text has been collated by H. C. Hart.

THE POEMS OF JOHN KEATS. Double volume. The Text has been collated by E. de Selincourt.

ON THE IMITATION OF CHRIST. By Thomas à Kempis.

The translation is by C. Bigg, DD., Canon of Christ Church.

A SERIOUS CALL TO A DEVOUT AND HOLY LIFE. By William Law.

PARADISE LOST. By John Milton.

EIKONOKLASTES AND THE TENURE OF KINGS AND MAGISTRATES. By John Milton.

UTOPIA AND POEMS. By Sir Thomas More.

THE REPUBLIC OF PLATO. Translated by Sydenham and Taylor. Double Volume. The translation has been revised by W. H. D. Rouse.

THE LITTLE FLOWERS OF ST. FRANCIS. Translated by W. Heywood.

THE WORKS OF WILLIAM SHAKESPEARE. In 10 volumes.

VOL. I.—The Tempest; The Two Gentlemen of Verona; The Merry Wives of Windsor; Measure for Measure; The Comedy of Errors.

VOL. II.—Much Ado About Nothing; Love's Labour's Lost; A Midsummer Night's Dream; The Merchant of Venice; As You Like It.

VOL. III.—The Taming of the Shrew; All's Well that Ends Well; Twelfth Night; The Winter's Tale.

Vol. IV.—The Life and Death of King John; The Tragedy of King Richard the Second; The First Part of King Henry IV.; The Second Part of King Henry IV.

Vol. V.—The Life of King Henry V.; The First Part of King Henry VI.; The Second Part of King Henry VI.

Vol. VI.—The Third Part of King Henry VI.; The Tragedy of King Richard III.; The Famous History of the Life of King Henry VIII.

THE POEMS OF PERCY BYSSHE SHELLEY. In 4 volumes.

Vol. I.—Alastor; The Dæmon of the World; The Revolt of Islam, etc. The Text has been revised by C. D. Locock.

THE LIFE OF NELSON. By Robert Southey.

THE NATURAL HISTORY AND ANTIQUITIES OF SELBORNE. By Gilbert White.

Textbooks of Technology

Edited by G. F. GOODCHILD, M.A., B.SC., and G. R. MILLS, M.A.

Fully Illustrated.

HOW TO MAKE A DRESS. By J. A. E. Wood. *Fourth Edition. Cr. 8vo. 1s. 6d.*

CARPENTRY AND JOINERY. By F. C. Webber. *Fifth Edition. Cr. 8vo. 3s. 6d.*

MILLINERY, THEORETICAL AND PRACTICAL. By Clare Hill. *Third Edition. Cr. 8vo. 2s.*

AN INTRODUCTION TO THE STUDY OF TEXTILE DESIGN. By Aldred F. Barker. *Demy 8vo. 7s. 6d.*

BUILDERS' QUANTITIES. By H. C. Grubb. *Cr. 8vo. 4s. 6d.*

RÉPOUSSÉ METAL WORK. By A. C. Horth. *Cr. 8vo. 2s. 6d.*

ELECTRIC LIGHT AND POWER: An Introduction to the Study of Electrical Engineering. By E. E. Brooks, B.Sc. (Lond.) Second Master and Instructor of Physics and Electrical Engineering, Leicester Technical School, and W. H. N. James, A.R.C.S., A.I.E.E., Assistant Instructor of Electrical Engineering, Manchester Municipal Technical School. *Cr. 8vo. 4s. 6d.*

ENGINEERING WORKSHOP PRACTICE. By C. C. Allen, Lecturer on Engineering, Municipal Technical Institute, Coventry. With many Diagrams. *Cr. 8vo. 2s.*

Handbooks of Theology

Edited by R. L. OTTLEY, D.D., Professor of Pastoral Theology at Oxford, and Canon of Christ Church, Oxford.

The series is intended, in part, to furnish the clergy and teachers or students of Theology with trustworthy Textbooks, adequately representing the present position of the questions dealt with ; in part, to make accessible to the reading public an accurate and concise statement of facts and principles in all questions bearing on Theology and Religion.

THE XXXIX. ARTICLES OF THE CHURCH OF ENGLAND. Edited by E. C. S. Gibson, D.D. *Fifth and Cheaper Edition in one Volume. Demy 8vo. 12s. 6d.*

AN INTRODUCTION TO THE HISTORY OF RELIGION. By F. B. Jevons. M.A., Litt.D. *Third Edition. Demy 8vo. 10s. 6d.*

THE DOCTRINE OF THE INCARNATION. By R. L. Ottley, D.D. *Second and Cheaper Edition. Demy 8vo. 12s. 6d.*

AN INTRODUCTION TO THE HISTORY OF THE CREEDS. By A. E. Burn, D.D. *Demy 8vo. 10s. 6d.*

THE PHILOSOPHY OF RELIGION IN ENGLAND AND AMERICA. By Alfred Caldecott, D.D. *Demy 8vo. 10s. 6d.*

A HISTORY OF EARLY CHRISTIAN DOCTRINE. By J. F. Bethune-Baker, M.A. *Demy 8vo. 10s. 6d.*

The Westminster Commentaries

General Editor, WALTER LOCK, D.D., Warden of Keble College, Dean Ireland's Professor of Exegesis in the University of Oxford.

The object of each commentary is primarily exegetical, to interpret the author's meaning to the present generation. The editors will not deal, except very subordinately, with questions of textual criticism or philology ; but, taking the English text in the Revised Version as their basis, they will try to combine a hearty acceptance of critical principles with loyalty to the Catholic Faith.

THE BOOK OF GENESIS. Edited with Introduction and Notes by S. R. Driver, D.D. *Sixth Edition Demy 8vo. 10s. 6d.*

THE BOOK OF JOB. Edited by E. C. S. Gibson, D.D. *Second Edition. Demy 8vo. 6s.*

THE ACTS OF THE APOSTLES. Edited by R. B. Rackham, M.A. *Demy 8vo. Third Edition. 10s. 6d.*

THE FIRST EPISTLE OF PAUL THE APOSTLE TO THE CORINTHIANS. Edited by H. L. Goudge, M.A. *Demy 8vo. 6s.*

THE EPISTLE OF ST. JAMES. Edited with Introduction and Notes by R. J. Knowling, D.D. *Demy 8vo. 6s.*

THE BOOK OF EZEKIEL. Edited H. A. Redpath, M.A., D.Litt. *Demy 8vo. 10s. 6d.*

PART II.—FICTION

Adderley (Hon. and Rev. James), Author of 'Stephen Remarx.' BEHOLD THE DAYS COME. *Second Edition. Cr. 8vo. 3s. 6d.*

Albanesi (E. Maria). SUSANNAH AND ONE OTHER. *Fourth Edition. Cr. 8vo. 6s.*
THE BLUNDER OF AN INNOCENT. *Second Edition. Cr. 8vo. 6s.*
CAPRICIOUS CAROLINE. *Second Edition. Cr. 8vo. 6s.*
LOVE AND LOUISA. *Second Edition. Cr. 8vo. 6s.*
PETER, A PARASITE. *Cr. 8vo. 6s.*
THE BROWN EYES OF MARY. *Third Edition. Cr. 8vo. 6s.*
I KNOW A MAIDEN. *Third Edition. Cr. 8vo. 6s.*

Anstey (F.), Author of 'Vice Versâ.' A BAYARD FROM BENGAL. Illustrated by BERNARD PARTRIDGE. *Third Edition. Cr. 8vo. 3s. 6d.*

Bagot (Richard). A ROMAN MYSTERY. *Third Edition. Cr. 8vo. 6s.*
THE PASSPORT. *Fourth Edition. Cr. 8vo 6s.*
TEMPTATION. *Fifth Edition. Cr. 8vo. 6s.*

CASTING OF NETS. *Twelfth Edition. Cr. 8vo. 6s.*
DONNA DIANA. *A New Edition. Cr. 8vo. 6s.*
LOVE'S PROXY. *A New Edition. Cr. 8vo. 6s.*

Baring-Gould (S.). ARMINELL. *Fifth Edition. Cr. 8vo. 6s.*
URITH. *Fifth Edition. Cr. 8vo. 6s.*
IN THE ROAR OF THE SEA. *Seventh Edition. Cr. 8vo. 6s.*
CHEAP JACK ZITA. *Fourth Edition. Cr. 8vo. 6s.*
MARGERY OF QUETHER. *Third Edition. Cr. 8vo. 6s.*
THE QUEEN OF LOVE. *Fifth Edition. Cr. 8vo. 6s.*
JACQUETTA. *Third Edition. Cr. 8vo. 6s.*
KITTY ALONE. *Fifth Edition. Cr. 8vo. 6s.*
NOÉMI. Illustrated. *Fourth Edition. Cr. 8vo. 6s.*
THE BROOM-SQUIRE. Illustrated. *Fifth Edition. Cr. 8vo. 6s.*
DARTMOOR IDYLLS. *Cr. 8vo. 6s.*
THE PENNYCOMEQUICKS. *Third Edition. Cr. 8vo. 6s.*
GUAVAS THE TINNER. Illustrated. *Second Edition. Cr. 8vo. 6s.*

BLADYS OF THE STEWPONEY. Illustrated. *Second Edition*. *Cr. 8vo. 6s.*
PABO THE PRIEST. *Cr. 8vo. 6s.*
WINEFRED. Illustrated. *Second Edition. Cr. 8vo. 6s.*
ROYAL GEORGIE. Illustrated. *Cr. 8vo. 6s.*
MISS QUILLET. Illustrated. *Cr. 8vo. 6s.*
CHRIS OF ALL SORTS. *Cr. 8vo. 6s.*
IN DEWISLAND. *Second Ed. Cr. 8vo. 6s.*
LITTLE TU'PENNY. *A New Edition. 6d.*
See also Shilling Novels.

Barnett (Edith A.). A WILDERNESS WINNER. *Second Edition. Cr. 8vo. 6s.*

Barr (James). LAUGHING THROUGH A WILDERNESS. *Cr. 8vo. 6s.*

Barr (Robert). IN THE MIDST OF ALARMS. *Third Edition. Cr. 8vo. 6s.*
THE STRONG ARM. *Second Edition. Cr. 8vo. 6s.*
THE MUTABLE MANY. *Third Edition. Cr. 8vo. 6s.*
THE COUNTESS TEKLA. *Fourth Edition. Cr. 8vo. 6s.*
THE LADY ELECTRA. *Second Edition. Cr. 8vo. 6s.*
THE TEMPESTUOUS PETTICOAT. Illustrated. *Third Edition. Cr. 8vo. 6s.*
See also Shilling Novels and S. Crane.

Begbie (Harold). THE ADVENTURES OF SIR JOHN SPARROW. *Cr. 8vo. 6s.*

Belloc(Hilaire). EMMANUEL BURDEN, MERCHANT. With 36 Illustrations by G. K. CHESTERTON. *Second Ed. Cr. 8vo. 6s.*

Benson (E. F.) DODO. *Fifteenth Edition. Cr. 8vo. 6s.*
See also Shilling Novels.
THE CAPSINA. *Second Edit. Cr. 8vo. 6s.*

Benson (Margaret). SUBJECT TO VANITY. *Cr. 8vo. 3s. 6d.*

Bretherton (Ralph). THE MILL. *Cr. 8vo. 6s.*

Burke (Barbara). BARBARA GOES TO OXFORD. *Second Edition.*

Burton (J. Bloundelle). THE FATE OF VALSEC. *Cr. 8vo. 6s.*
See also Shilling Novels.

Capes (Bernard), Author of 'The Lake of Wine.' THE EXTRAORDINARY CONFESSIONS OF DIANA PLEASE. *Third Edition. Cr. 8vo. 6s.*
A JAY OF ITALY. *Fourth Ed. Cr. 8vo. 6s.*
LOAVES AND FISHES. *Second Edition. Cr. 8vo. 6s.*
A ROGUE'S TRAGEDY. *Second Edition. Cr. 8vo. 6s.*
THE GREAT SKENE MYSTERY. *Second Edition. Cr. 8vo. 6s.*

Charlton (Randall). MAVE. *Second Edition. Cr. 8vo. 6s.*

Carey (Wymond). LOVE THE JUDGE. *Second Edition. Cr. 8vo. 6s.*

Chesney (Weatherby). THE TRAGEDY OF THE GREAT EMERALD *Cr. 8vo. 6s.*
THE MYSTERY OF A BUNGALOW. *Second Edition. Cr. 8vo. 6s.*
See also Shilling Novels.

Conrad (Joseph). THE SECRET AGENT. *Second Edition. Cr. 8vo. 6s.*

Corelli (Marie). A ROMANCE OF TWO WORLDS. *Twenty-Eighth Ed. Cr. 8vo. 6s.*
VENDETTA. *Twenty-Fifth Edition. Cr. 8vo. 6s.*
THELMA. *Thirty-Seventh Ed. Cr. 8vo. 6s.*
ARDATH: THE STORY OF A DEAD SELF. *Eighteenth Edition. Cr. 8vo. 6s.*
THE SOUL OF LILITH. *Fifteenth Edition. Cr. 8vo. 6s.*
WORMWOOD. *Fifteenth Ed. Cr. 8vo. 6s.*
BARABBAS: A DREAM OF THE WORLD'S TRAGEDY. *Forty-second Edition. Cr. 8vo. 6s.*
THE SORROWS OF SATAN. *Fifty-second Edition. Cr. 8vo. 6s.*
THE MASTER CHRISTIAN. *Tenth Edition. Cr. 8vo. 6s.*
TEMPORAL POWER: A STUDY IN SUPREMACY. 150th *Thousand. Cr. 8vo. 6s.*
GOD'S GOOD MAN: A SIMPLE LOVE STORY. *Twelfth Edition. Cr. 8vo. 6s.*
THE MIGHTY ATOM. *Twenty-sixth Edition. Cr. 8vo. 6s.*
BOY: a Sketch. *Tenth Edition. Cr. 8vo. 6s.*
CAMEOS *Twelfth Edition. Cr. 8vo. 6s.*

Cotes (Mrs. Everard). See Sara Jeannette Duncan.

Cotterell (Constance). THE VIRGIN AND THE SCALES. Illustrated. *Second Edition. Cr. 8vo. 6s.*

Crane (Stephen) and **Barr (Robert).** THE O'RUDDY. *Cr. 8vo. 6s.*

Crockett (S. R.), Author of 'The Raiders,' etc. LOCHINVAR. Illustrated. *Third Edition. Cr. 8vo. 6s.*
THE STANDARD BEARER. *Cr. 8vo. 6s.*

Croker (B. M.). THE OLD CANTONMENT. *Cr. 8vo. 6s.*
JOHANNA. *Second Edition. Cr. 8vo. 6s.*
THE HAPPY VALLEY. *Third Edition. Cr. 8vo. 6s.*
A NINE DAYS' WONDER. *Third Edition. Cr. 8vo. 6s.*
PEGGY OF THE BARTONS. *Sixth Edition. Cr. 8vo. 6s.*
ANGEL. *Fourth Edition. Cr. 8vo. 6s.*
A STATE SECRET. *Third Edition. Cr. 8vo. 3s. 6d.*

Crosbie (Mary). DISCIPLES. *Second Ed. Cr. 8vo. 6s.*

Dawson (A. J). DANIEL WHYTE. *Cr. 8vo. 3s. 6d.*

Deane (Mary). THE OTHER PAWN. *Cr. 8vo. 6s.*

Doyle (A. Conan), Author of 'Sherlock Holmes,' 'The White Company,' etc. ROUND THE RED LAMP. *Tenth Edition. Cr. 8vo. 6s.*

Duncan (Sara Jeannette) (Mrs. Everard Cotes). THOSE DELIGHTFUL AMERICANS. Illustrated. *Third Edition. Cr. 8vo. 6s.* See also Shilling Novels.

Findlater (J. H.). THE GREEN GRAVES OF BALGOWRIE. *Fifth Edition. Cr. 8vo. 6s.*

THE LADDER TO THE STARS. *Second Edition. Cr. 8vo. 6s.*
See also Shilling Novels.
Findlater (Mary). A NARROW WAY. *Third Edition. Cr. 8vo.. 6s.*
THE ROSE OF JOY. *Third Edition. Cr. 8vo. 6s.*
A BLIND BIRD'S NEST. With 8 Illustrations. *Second Edition. Cr. 8vo. 6s.*
See also Shilling Novels.
Fitzpatrick (K.) THE WEANS AT ROWALLAN. Illustrated. *Second Edition. Cr. 8vo. 6s.*
Francis (M. ⊏.). STEPPING WESTWARD. *Second Edition. Cr. 8vo. 6s.*
MARGERY O' THE MILL. *Second Edition. Cr. 8vo. 6s.*
Fraser (Mrs. Hugh), Author of 'The Stolen Emperor.' THE SLAKING OF THE SWORD. *Cr. 8vo. 6s.*
IN THE SHADOW OF THE LORD. *Third Edition. Crown 8vo. 6s.*
Fry (B. and C.B.). A MOTHER'S SON. *Fourth Edition. Cr. 8vo. 6s.*
Fuller-Maitland (Ella), Author of 'The Day Book of Bethia Hardacre.' BLANCHE ESMEAD. *Second Edition. Cr. 8vo. 6s.*
Gates (Eleanor), Author of 'The Biography of a Prairie Girl.' THE PLOW-WOMAN. *Cr. 8vo. 6s.*
Gerard (Dorothea), Author of 'Lady Baby.' HOLY MATRIMONY. *Second Edition. Cr. 8vo. 6s.*
MADE OF MONEY. *Cr. 8vo. 6s.*
THE BRIDGE OF LIFE. *Cr. 8vo. 6s.*
THE IMPROBABLE IDYL. *Third Edition. Cr. 8vo. 6s.*
See also Shilling Novels.
Gissing (George), Author of 'Demos,' 'In the Year of Jubilee,' etc. THE TOWN TRAVELLER. *Second Ed. Cr. 8vo. 6s.*
THE CROWN OF LIFE. *Cr. 8vo. 6s.*
Gleig (Charles). BUNTER'S CRUISE. Illustrated. *Cr. 8vo. 3s. 6d.*
Hamilton (M.), Author of 'Cut Laurels.' THE FIRST CLAIM. *Second Edition. Cr. 8vo. 6s.*
Harraden (Beatrice). IN VARYING MOODS. *Fourteenth Edition. Cr. 8vo. 6s.*
HILDA STRAFFORD and THE REMITTANCE MAN. *Twelfth Ed. Cr. 8vo. 6s.*
THE SCHOLAR'S DAUGHTER. *Fourth Edition. Cr. 8vo. 6s.*
Harrod (F.) (Frances Forbes Robertson). THE TAMING OF THE BRUTE. *Cr. 8vo. 6s.*
Herbertson (Agnes G.). PATIENCE DEAN. *Cr. 8vo. 6s.*
Hichens (Robert). THE PROPHET OF BERKELEY SQUARE. *Second Edition. Cr. 8vo. 6s.*
TONGUES OF CONSCIENCE. *Third Edition. Cr. 8vo. 6s.*
FELIX. *Fifth Edition. Cr. 8vo. 6s.*
THE WOMAN WITH THE FAN. *Sixth Edition. Cr. 8vo. 6s.*
BYEWAYS. *Cr. 8vo. 6s.*

THE GARDEN OF ALLAH. *Sixteenth Edition. Cr. 8vo. 6s.*
THE BLACK SPANIEL. *Cr. 8vo. 6s.*
THE CALL OF THE BLOOD. *Seventh Edition. Cr. 8vo. 6s.*
Hope (Anthony). THE GOD IN THE CAR. *Tenth Edition. Cr. 8vo. 6s.*
A CHANGE OF AIR. *Sixth Ed. Cr.8vo. 6s.*
A MAN OF MARK. *Fifth Ed. Cr. 8vo. 6s.*
THE CHRONICLES OF COUNT ANTONIO. *Sixth Edition. Cr. 8vo. 6s.*
PHROSO. Illustrated by H. R. MILLAR. *Sixth Edition. Cr. 8vo. 6s.*
SIMON DALE. Illustrated. *Seventh Edition. Cr. 8vo. 6s.*
THE KING'S MIRROR. *Fourth Edition. Cr. 8vo. 6s.*
QUISANTE. *Fourth Edition. Cr. 8vo. 6s.*
THE DOLLY DIALOGUES. *Cr. 8vo. 6s.*
A SERVANT OF THE PUBLIC. Illustrated. *Fourth Edition. Cr. 8vo. 6s.*
TALES OF TWO PEOPLE. *Second Ed. Cr. 8vo. 6s.*
Hope (Graham), Author of 'A Cardinal and his Conscience,' etc., etc. THE LADY OF LYTE. *Second Edition. Cr.8vo. 6s.*
Housman (Clemence). THE LIFE OF SIR AGLOVALE DE GALIS. *Cr. 8vo. 6s.*
Hueffer (Ford Madox). AN ENGLISH GIRL. *Second Edition. Cr. 8vo. 6s.*
Hyne (C. J. Cutcliffe), Author of 'Captain Kettle.' MR. HORROCKS, PURSER. *Fourth Edition. Cr. 8vo. 6s.*
PRINCE RUPERT, THE BUCCANEER. Illustrated. *Third Edition. Cr. 8vo. 6s.*
Jacobs (W. W.). MANY CARGOES. *Twenty-Ninth Edition. Cr. 8vo. 3s. 6d.*
SEA URCHINS. *Fourteenth Edition.. Cr. 8vo. 3s. 6d.*
A MASTER OF CRAFT. Illustrated. *Seventh Edition. Cr. 8vo. 3s. 6d.*
LIGHT FREIGHTS. Illustrated. *Sixth Edition. Cr. 8vo. 3s. 6d.*
THE SKIPPER'S WOOING. *Eighth Edition. Cr. 8vo. 3s. 6d.*
DIALSTONE LANE. Illustrated. *Seventh Edition. Cr. 8vo. 3s. 6d.*
ODD CRAFT. Illustrated. *Seventh Edition. Cr. 8vo. 3s. 6d.*
AT SUNWICH PORT. Illustrated. *Seventh Edition. Cr. 8vo. 3s. 6d.*
James (Henry). THE SOFT SIDE. *Second Edition. Cr. 8vo. 6s.*
THE BETTER SORT. *Cr. 8vo. 6s.*
THE AMBASSADORS. *Second Edition. Cr. 8vo. 6s.*
THE GOLDEN BOWL. *Third Edition. Cr. 8vo. 6s.*
Keays (H. A. Mitchell). HE THAT EATETH BREAD WITH ME. *Cr.8vo.6s.*
Kester (Vaughan). THE FORTUNES OF THE LANDRAYS. *Cr. 8vo. 6s.*
Lawless (Hon. Emily). WITH ESSEX IN IRELAND. *Cr. 8vo. 6s.*
See also Shilling Novels.
Le Queux (W.). THE HUNCHBACK OF WESTMINSTER. *Third Ed. Cr.8vo. 6s.*
THE CLOSED BOOK. *Third Ed. Cr.8vo.6s.*

THE VALLEY OF THE SHADOW. Illustrated. *Third Edition.* *Cr. 8vo.* 6s.

BEHIND THE THRONE. *Third Edition.* *Cr. 8vo.* 6s.

Levett-Yeats (S.). ORRAIN. *Second Edition.* *Cr. 8vo.* 6s.

London (Jack), Author of 'The Call of the Wild,' 'The Sea Wolf,' etc. WHITE FANG. *Fourth Edition.* *Cr. 8vo.* 6s.

Lucas (E. V.). LISTENER'S LURE: An Oblique Narration. *Crown 8vo.* *Fourth Edition.* *Cr. 8vo.* 6s.

Lyall (Edna). DERRICK VAUGHAN, NOVELIST. *42nd Thousand.* *Cr. 8vo.* 3s. 6d.

M'Carthy (Justin H.), Author of 'If I were King.' THE LADY OF LOYALTY HOUSE. Illustrated. *Third Edition.* *Cr. 8vo.* 6s.

THE DRYAD. *Second Edition.* *Cr. 8vo.* 6s.

Macdonald (Ronald). THE SEA MAID. *Second Edition.* *Cr. 8vo.* 6s.

A HUMAN TRINITY. *Second Edition.* *Cr. 8vo.* 6s.

Macnaughtan (S.). THE FORTUNE OF CHRISTINA MACNAB. *Fourth Edition.* *Cr. 8vo.* 6s.

Malet (Lucas). COLONEL ENDERBY'S WIFE. *Fourth Edition.* *Cr. 8vo.* 6s.

A COUNSEL OF PERFECTION. *New Edition.* *Cr. 8vo.* 6s.

THE WAGES OF SIN. *Fifteenth Edition.* *Cr. 8vo.* 6s.

THE CARISSIMA. *Fifth Ed.* *Cr. 8vo.* 6s.

THE GATELESS BARRIER. *Fourth Edition.* *Cr. 8vo.* 6s.

THE HISTORY OF SIR RICHARD CALMADY. *Seventh Edition.* *Cr. 8vo.* 6s. See also Books for Boys and Girls.

Mann (Mrs. M. E.). OLIVIA'S SUMMER. *Second Edition.* *Cr. 8vo.* 6s.

A LOST ESTATE. *A New Ed.* *Cr. 8vo.* 6s.

THE PARISH OF HILBY. *A New Edition.* *Cr. 8vo.* 6s.

THE PARISH NURSE. *Fourth Edition.* *Cr. 8vo.* 6s.

GRAN'MA'S JANE. *Cr. 8vo.* 6s.

MRS. PETER HOWARD. *Cr. 8vo.* 6s.

A WINTER'S TALE. *A New Edition.* *Cr. 8vo.* 6s.

ONE ANOTHER'S BURDENS. *A New Edition.* *Cr. 8vo.* 6s.

ROSE AT HONEYPOT. *Third Ed.* *Cr. 8vo.* 6s. See also Books for Boys and Girls.

THE MEMORIES OF RONALD LOVE. *Cr. 8vo.* 6s.

THE EGLAMORE PORTRAITS. *Third Edition.* *Cr. 8vo.* 6s.

THE SHEEP AND THE GOATS. *Second Edition.* *Cr. 8vo.* 6s.

Marriott (Charles), Author of 'The Column.' GENEVRA. *Second Edition.* *Cr. 8vo.* 6s.

Marsh (Richard). THE TWICKENHAM PEERAGE. *Second Edition.* *Cr. 8vo.* 6s.

THE MARQUIS OF PUTNEY. *Second Edition.* *Cr. 8vo.* 6s.

A DUEL. *Cr 8vo.* 6s.

IN THE SERVICE OF LOVE. *Third Edition.* *Cr. 8vo.* 6s.

THE GIRL AND THE MIRACLE. *Second Edition.* *Cr. 8vo.* 6s. See also Shilling Novels.

Mason (A. E. W.), Author of 'The Four Feathers,' etc. CLEMENTINA. Illustrated. *Second Edition.* *Cr. 8vo.* 6s.

Mathers (Helen), Author of 'Comin' thro' the Rye.' HONEY. *Fourth Ed.* *Cr. 8vo.* 6s.

GRIFF OF GRIFFITHSCOURT. *Cr. 8vo.* 6s.

THE FERRYMAN. *Second Edition.* *Cr. 8vo.* 6s.

TALLY-HO! *Fourth Edition.* *Cr. 8vo.* 6s.

Maxwell (W. B.), Author of 'The Ragged Messenger.' VIVIEN. *Ninth Edition.* *Cr. 8vo.* 6s.

THE RAGGED MESSENGER. *Third Edition.* *Cr. 8vo.* 6s.

FABULOUS FANCIES. *Cr. 8vo.* 6s.

THE GUARDED FLAME. *Seventh Edition.* *Cr. 8vo.* 6s.

THE COUNTESS OF MAYBURY. *Fourth Edition.* *Cr. 8vo.* 6s.

ODD LENGTHS. *Second Ed.* *Cr. 8vo.* 6s.

Meade (L. T.). DRIFT. *Second Edition.* *Cr. 8vo.* 6s.

RESURGAM. *Cr. 8vo.* 6s.

VICTORY. *Cr. 8vo.* 6s. See also Books for Boys and Girls.

Melton (R.). CÆSAR'S WIFE. *Second Edition.* *Cr. 8vo.* 6s.

Meredith (Ellis). HEART OF MY HEART. *Cr. 8vo.* 6s.

Miller (Esther). LIVING LIES. *Third Edition.* *Cr. 8vo.* 6s.

'Miss Molly' (The Author of). THE GREAT RECONCILER. *Cr. 8vo.* 6s.

Mitford (Bertram). THE SIGN OF THE SPIDER. Illustrated. *Sixth Edition.* *Cr. 8vo.* 3s. 6d.

IN THE WHIRL OF THE RISING. *Third Edition.* *Cr. 8vo.* 6s.

THE RED DERELICT. *Second Edition.* *Cr. 8vo.* 6s.

Montresor (F. F.), Author of 'Into the Highways and Hedges.' THE ALIEN. *Third Edition.* *Cr. 8vo.* 6s.

Morrison (Arthur). TALES OF MEAN STREETS. *Seventh Edition.* *Cr. 8vo.* 6s.

A CHILD OF THE JAGO. *Fifth Edition.* *Cr. 8vo.* 6s.

TO LONDON TOWN. *Second Edition.* *Cr. 8vo.* 6s.

CUNNING MURRELL. *Cr. 8vo.* 6s.

THE HOLE IN THE WALL. *Fourth Edition.* *Cr. 8vo.* 6s.

DIVERS VANITIES. *Cr. 8vo.* 6s.

Nesbit (E.). (Mrs. E. Bland). THE RED HOUSE. Illustrated. *Fourth Edition.* *Cr. 8vo.* 6s. See also Shilling Novels.

Norris (W. E.). HARRY AND URSULA. *Second Edition.* *Cr. 8vo.* 6s.

Ollivant (Alfred). OWD BOB, THE GREY DOG OF KENMUIR. *Tenth Edition.* *Cr. 8vo.* 6s.

Oppenheim (E. Phillips). MASTER OF MEN. *Fourth Edition. Cr. 8vo. 6s.*

Oxenham (John), Author of 'Barbe of Grand Bayou.' A WEAVER OF WEBS. *Second Edition. Cr. 8vo. 6s.*

THE GATE OF THE DESERT. *Fifth Edition. Cr. 8vo. 6s.*

PROFIT AND LOSS. With a Frontispiece in photogravure by HAROLD COPPING. *Fourth Edition. Cr. 8vo. 6s.*

THE LONG ROAD. With a Frontispiece by HAROLD COPPING. *Fourth Edition. Cr. 8vo. 6s.*

Pain (Barry). LINDLEY KAYS. *Third Edition. Cr. 8vo. 6s.*

Parker (Gilbert). PIERRE AND HIS PEOPLE. *Sixth Edition. Cr. 8vo. 6s.*

MRS. FALCHION. *Fifth Edition. Cr. 8vo. 6s.*

THE TRANSLATION OF A SAVAGE. *Third Edition. Cr. 8vo. 6s.*

THE TRAIL OF THE SWORD. Illustrated. *Ninth Edition. Cr. 8vo. 6s.*

WHEN VALMOND CAME TO PONTIAC: The Story of a Lost Napoleon. *Sixth Edition. Cr. 8vo. 6s.*

AN ADVENTURER OF THE NORTH. The Last Adventures of 'Pretty Pierre.' *Third Edition. Cr. 8vo. 6s.*

THE SEATS OF THE MIGHTY. Illustrated. *Fifteenth Edition. Cr. 8vo. 6s.*

THE BATTLE OF THE STRONG: a Romance of Two Kingdoms. Illustrated. *Fifth Edition. Cr. 8vo. 6s.*

THE POMP OF THE LAVILETTES. *Second Edition. Cr. 8vo. 3s. 6d.*

Pemberton (Max). THE FOOTSTEPS OF A THRONE. Illustrated. *Third Edition. Cr. 8vo. 6s.*

I CROWN THEE KING. With Illustrations by Frank Dadd and A. Forrestier. *Cr. 8vo. 6s.*

Phillpotts (Eden). LYING PROPHETS. *Third Edition. Cr. 8vo. 6s.*

CHILDREN OF THE MIST. *Fifth Edition. Cr. 8vo. 6s.*

THE HUMAN BOY. With a Frontispiece. *Fourth Edition. Cr. 8vo. 6s.*

SONS OF THE MORNING. *Second Edition. Cr. 8vo. 6s.*

THE RIVER. *Third Edition. Cr. 8vo. 6s.*

THE AMERICAN PRISONER. *Fourth Edition. Cr. 8vo. 6s.*

THE SECRET WOMAN. *Fourth Edition. Cr. 8vo. 6s.*

KNOCK AT A VENTURE. With a Frontispiece. *Third Edition. Cr. 8vo. 6s.*

THE PORTREEVE. *Fourth Ed. Cr. 8vo. 6s.*

THE POACHER'S WIFE. *Second Edition. Cr. 8vo. 6s.*

See also Shilling Novels.

Pickthall (Marmaduke). SAID THE FISHERMAN. *Sixth Ed. Cr. 8vo. 6s.*

BRENDLE. *Second Edition. Cr. 8vo. 6s.*

THE HOUSE OF ISLAM. *Third Edition. Cr. 8vo. 6s.*

'Q,' Author of 'Dead Man's Rock.' THE WHITE WOLF. *Second Ed. Cr. 8vo. 6s,*

THE MAYOR OF TROY. *Fourth Edition. Cr. 8vo. 6s.*

MERRY GARDEN AND OTHER STORIES. *Cr. 8vo. 6s.*

MAJOR VIGOUREUX. *Second Edition. Cr. 8vo. 6s.*

Rawson (Maud Stepney), Author of 'A Lady of the Regency.' 'The Labourer's Comedy,' etc. THE ENCHANTED GARDEN. *Second Edition. Cr. 8vo. 6s.*

Rhys (Grace). THE WOOING OF SHEILA. *Second Edition. Cr. 8vo. 6s.*

Ridge (W. Pett). LOST PROPERTY. *Second Edition. Cr. 8vo. 6s.*

ERB. *Second Edition. Cr. 8vo. 6s.*

A SON OF THE STATE. *Second Edition. Cr. 8vo. 3s. 6d.*

A BREAKER OF LAWS. *A New Edition. Cr. 8vo. 3s. 6d.*

MRS. GALER'S BUSINESS. Illustrated. *Second Edition. Cr. 8vo. 6s.*

SECRETARY TO BAYNE, M.P. *Cr. 8vo. 3s. 6d.*

THE WICKHAMSES. *Fourth Edition. Cr. 8vo. 6s.*

NAME OF GARLAND. *Third Edition. Cr. 8vo. 6s.*

Roberts (C. G. D.). THE HEART OF THE ANCIENT WOOD. *Cr. 8vo. 3s. 6d.*

Russell (W. Clark). MY DANISH SWEETHEART. Illustrated. *Fifth Edition. Cr. 8vo. 6s.*

HIS ISLAND PRINCESS. Illustrated. *Second Edition. Cr. 6vo. 6s.*

ABANDONED. *Second Edition. Cr. 8vo. 6s.*

See also Books for Boys and Girls.

Sergeant (Adeline). BARBARA'S MONEY. *Cr. 8vo. 6s.*

THE PROGRESS OF RACHAEL. *Cr. 8vo. 6s.*

THE MYSTERY OF THE MOAT. *Second Edition. Cr. 8vo. 6s.*

THE COMING OF THE RANDOLPHS. *Cr. 8vo. 6s.*

See also Shilling Novels.

Shannon. (W. F.) THE MESS DECK. *Cr. 8vo. 3s. 6d.*

See also Shilling Novels.

Shelley (Bertha). ENDERBY. *Third Ed. Cr. 8vo. 6s.*

Sidgwick (Mrs. Alfred), Author of 'Cynthia's Way.' THE KINSMAN. With 8 Illustrations by C. E. BROCK. *Third Ed. Cr. 8vo. 6s.*

Sonnichsen (Albert). DEEP-SEA VAGABONDS. *Cr. 8vo. 6s.*

Sunbury (George). THE HA'PENNY MILLIONAIRE. *Cr. 8vo. 3s. 6d.*

Urquhart (M.), A TRAGEDY IN COMMONPLACE. *Second Ed. Cr. 8vo. 6s.*

Waineman (Paul). THE SONG OF THE FOREST. *Cr. 8vo. 6s.*

THE BAY OF LILACS. *Second Edition. Cr. 8vo. 6s.*

See also Shilling Novels.

Waltz (E. C.). THE ANCIENT LAND. MARK: A Kentucky Romance. *Cr. 8vo. 6s.*

Watson (H. B. Marriott). ALARUMS AND EXCURSIONS. *Cr. 8vo. 6s.*
CAPTAIN FORTUNE. *Third Edition. Cr. 8vo. 6s.*
TWISTED EGLANTINE. With 8 Illustrations by FRANK CRAIG. *Third Edition. Cr. 8vo. 6s.*
THE HIGH TOBY. With a Frontispiece. *Third Edition. Cr. 8vo. 6s.*
A MIDSUMMER DAY'S DREAM. *Third Edition. Crown 8vo. 6s.*
See also Shilling Novels.
Wells (H. G.). THE SEA LADY. *Cr. 8vo. 6s.*
Weyman (Stanley), Author of 'A Gentleman of France.' UNDER THE RED ROBE. With Illustrations by R. C. WOODVILLE. *Twenty-first Edition. Cr. 8vo. 6s.*
White (Stewart E.), Author of ' The Blazed Trail.' CONJUROR'S HOUSE. A Romance of the Free Trail. *Second Edition. Cr. 8vo. 6s.*
White (Percy). THE SYSTEM. *Third Edition. Cr. 8vo. 6s.*
THE PATIENT MAN. *Second Edition. Cr. 8vo. 6s.*
Williams (Margery). THE BAR. *Cr. 8vo. 6s.*

Williamson (Mrs. C. N.), Author of ' The Barnstormers.' THE ADVENTURE OF PRINCESS SYLVIA. *Second Edition. Cr. 8vo. 6s.*
THE WOMAN WHO DARED. *Cr. 8vo. 6s.*
THE SEA COULD TELL. *Second Edition. Cr. 8vo. 6s.*
THE CASTLE OF THE SHADOWS. *Third Edition. Cr. 8vo. 6s.*
PAPA. *Cr. 8vo. 6s.*
Williamson (C. N. and A. M.). THE LIGHTNING CONDUCTOR : Being the Romance of a Motor Car. Illustrated. *Sixteenth Edition. Cr. 8vo. 6s.*
THE PRINCESS PASSES. Illustrated. *Eighth Edition. Cr. 8vo. 6s.*
MY FRIEND THE CHAUFFEUR. With 16 Illustrations. *Ninth Ed. Cr. 8vo. 6s.*
THE CAR OF DESTINY AND ITS ERRAND IN SPAIN. *Fourth Edition.* Illustrated.
LADY BETTY ACROSS THE WATER. *Ninth Edition. Cr. 8vo. 6s.*
THE BOTOR CHAPERON. *Fourth Ed. Cr. 8vo. 6s.*
Wyllarde (Dolf), Author of ' Uriah the Hittite.' THE PATHWAY OF THE PIONEER (Nous Autres). *Fourth Edition. Cr. 8vo. 6s.*

Methuen's Shilling Novels

Cr. 8vo. Cloth, 1s. net.

Author of ' Miss Molly.' THE GREAT RECONCILER.
Balfour (Andrew). VENGEANCE IS MINE.
TO ARMS.
Baring-Gould (S.). MRS. CURGENVEN OF CURGENVEN.
DOMITIA.
THE FROBISHERS.
CHRIS OF ALL SORTS.
DARTMOOR IDYLLS.
Barlow (Jane), Author of ' Irish Idylls.' FROM THE EAST UNTO THE WEST.
A CREEL OF IRISH STORIES.
THE FOUNDING OF FORTUNES.
THE LAND OF THE SHAMROCK.
Barr (Robert). THE VICTORS.
Bartram (George). THIRTEEN EVENINGS.
Benson (E. F.), Author of 'Dodo.' THE CAPSINA.
Bowles (G. Stewart). A STRETCH OFF THE LAND.
Brooke (Emma). THE POET'S CHILD.
Bullock (Shan F.). THE BARRYS.
THE CHARMER.
THE SQUIREEN.
THE RED LEAGUERS.
Burton (J. Bloundelle). THE CLASH OF ARMS.
DENOUNCED.
FORTUNE'S MY FOE.
A BRANDED NAME.

Capes (Bernard). AT A WINTER'S FIRE.
Chesney (Weatherby). THE BAPTIST RING.
THE BRANDED PRINCE.
THE FOUNDERED GALLEON.
JOHN TOPP.
THE MYSTERY OF A BUNGALOW.
Clifford (Mrs. W. K.). A FLASH OF SUMMER.
Cobb, Thomas. A CHANGE OF FACE.
Collingwood (Harry). THE DOCTOR OF THE 'JULIET.'
Cornford (L. Cope). SONS OF ADVERSITY.
Cotterell (Constance). THE VIRGIN AND THE SCALES.
Crane (Stephen). WOUNDS IN THE RAIN.
Denny (C. E.). THE ROMANCE OF UPFOLD MANOR.
Dickinson (Evelyn). THE SIN OF ANGELS.
Dickson (Harris). THE BLACK WOLF'S BREED.
Duncan (Sara J.). THE POOL IN THE DESERT.
A VOYAGE OF CONSOLATION. Illustrated.
Embree (C. F.). A HEART OF FLAME. Illustrated.
Fenn (G. Manville). AN ELECTRIC SPARK.
A DOUBLE KNOT.